# Mahāyāna Buddhist Meditation

# Mahāyāna Buddhist Meditation:
## *Theory and Practice*

*Edited by*
MINORU KIYOTA
*Assisted by* ELVIN W. JONES

MOTILAL BANARSIDASS PUBLISHERS
PRIVATE LIMITED • DELHI

*Reprint: Delhi, 1997, 2009*
*First Indian Edition Delhi : 1991*
*Earlier published by the University of Hawaii Press 1978*



ISBN: 978-81-208-0760-0

MOTILAL BANARSIDASS
41 U.A. Bungalow Road, Jawahar Nagar, Delhi 110 007
8 Mahalaxmi Chamber, 22 Bhulabhai Desai Road, Mumbai 400 026
203 Royapettah High Road, Mylapore, Chennai 600 004
236, 9th Main III Block, Jayanagar, Bangalore 560 011
Sanas Plaza, 1302 Baji Rao Road, Pune 411 002
8 Camac Street, Kolkata 700 017
Ashok Rajpath, Patna 800 004
Chowk, Varanasi 221 001

*Printed in India*

BY JAINENDRA PRAKASH JAIN AT SHRI JAINENDRA PRESS,
A-45 NARAINA, PHASE-I, NEW DELHI 110 028
AND PUBLISHED BY NARENDRA PRAKASH JAIN FOR
MOTILAL BANARSIDASS PUBLISHERS PRIVATE LIMITED,
BUNGALOW ROAD, DELHI 110 007

# Contents

# In Memoriam

## Richard Hugh Robinson: 1926–70

Born in Alberta, Canada on June 21, 1926, Richard H. Robinson received his bachelor of arts degree from the University of Alberta in 1947, where he specialized in economics and modern languages. In 1950, he entered the School of Oriental and African Studies of the University of London and received a first-class honors (B.A.) in classical Chinese in 1952. He returned to Canada in 1953. In 1954, he joined the faculty of the University of Toronto and received the degree of doctor of philosophy from the University of London in 1959. He joined the University of Wisconsin-Madison faculty in 1961. While in London, he married Hannah Grenville. Their daughter, Sita, and their son, Neil, were born in Toronto in 1955 and 1957, respectively.

Richard Robinson was constantly interested in expanding his knowledge of languages. Even as a high school student, he sought the instruction of a local Chinese laundryman in Alberta, under whom he began his Chinese studies; while in London, he studied under the eminent Orientalists Professor Edward Conze and Professor David Snellgrove, with whom he worked informally in Sanskrit and Tibetan, respectively. Languages, however, were but tools to probe into the subtlety of Oriental thought, particularly Buddhism, to which he had been drawn since childhood. His attraction to Buddhism took on a new dimension during 1948–49 in Toronto, where he was working at odd jobs in preparation for entering the University of London. He assisted the Reverend Takashi Tsuji of the Toronto Buddhist Church, made friends with Japanese-Canadian Buddhists, began to learn Japanese, and participated in a translation project undertaken by the Aśoka Society of the Toronto Church. His involvement with Japanese-Canadian Buddhists helped greatly in developing a Buddhism amenable to the needs of Japanese-Canadian Buddhists, particularly at a time, at the end of World War II, when the Japanese-Canadian Buddhists were faced with the problem of an ethnic identity. His experience in Toronto contributed much as well in shaping his own professional career.

In 1960, he joined the faculty of the Department of Indian Studies of the University of Wisconsin-Madison, where he taught Indian Philosophy, Indian civilization, and Buddhism, upon which he lectured with great vitality and interest. In the course of his teaching career, he was granted two overseas research grants. On each occasion he went to India, where he carefully observed Indian culture and probed the various facets of Indian philosophical thought. Likewise, he expanded his interest in languages. He discovered new friends among Indians and Tibetans and renewed old friendships. He did not fail, however, to visit other Buddhist countries of Asia—Ceylon, Vietnam, and Japan—on which occasions he gained the regard of many Asian Buddhists and Buddhologists.

In addition to his contributions to many academic journals, he published four significant works: *Chinese Buddhist Verse* (London: John Murray, 1954); *Let's Speak English*, a text for non-English speakers, (coauthored with D. F. Theall and J. W. Wevers, Toronto: W. J. Gage, Ltd., 1960–62); *Early Mādhyamika in India and China* (Madison: University of Wisconsin Press, 1967); and *The Buddhist Religion* (Dickenson: Belmont, California, 1970). He left numerous unpublished manuscripts, among which are an English translation of the *Vimalakīrti-nirdeśasūtra* and the *Awakening of Mahāyāna Faith*, and a *Sanskrit Primer*.

Besides being a teacher and a research scholar, Richard Robinson demonstrated extraordinary administrative and organizational skills. He was chairman of the Department of Indian Studies (now the Department of South Asian Studies) and director of the South Asian Area Center on several occasions. In addition, from 1963 to 1965, he was secretary of the American Institute of Indian Studies. But his greatest contribution came in 1961, when he and his colleagues Professor Robert J. Miller and Professor Murray Fowler established the Wisconsin Ph.D. program in Buddhist studies—the first of its kind ever established in North America.

Richard Robinson was a linguist, a philosopher, and an internationally recognized scholar in Buddhist studies, but above all, he was a friend of the Indians, Tibetans, Vietnamese, and Japanese, a stimulating personality to his colleagues, and an inspiring teacher to his students.

*Namo 'mitābhāya buddhāya*

# Preface

Following the untimely death of Richard H. Robinson, there was a strong wish on the part of many friends, colleagues, and former students to see the birth of a commemorative volume honoring Professor Robinson's contributions to the advancement of Buddhist studies. Actual plans for the making of such a volume began to take definite shape in the spring of 1971 at the meeting of the Association for Asian Studies in Washington, D.C., when a committee was formed for this purpose. The original committee consisted of Minoru Kiyota (then appointed chairman), Mrs. Richard Robinson, Willard Johnson, Arthur Link, and Kathryn Cissell. The committee made a selection of possible contributors and delegated the responsibility of final selection and compilation to Minoru Kiyota, who subsequently chose Mr. Elvin W. Jones as editorial assistant. Funds were forthcoming from the Robinson Memorial Fund, and contributions of papers were solicited. Response was immediate and extremely gratifying; it is unfortunate that, due to the limitations of size, many excellent papers could not be included.

The editors wish to express appreciation and acknowledgment to Mr. Aaron Koseki for preparing the glossary of Chinese characters, to Mr. Leonard Zwilling for proofreading the

Sanskrit terminology used in the articles, to Mr. Otis Smith and Mrs. Georgianna March for proofreading the manuscript, to Mrs. March for assisting with the standardization of the notes, and to Mrs. Mary Jo Smith for typing the manuscript.

# Introduction

These studies and essays are representative of the work of modern Buddhist scholarship. The collection is designed not only for the Buddhologist, but also for the more or less specialist reader in world religion and philosophy for whom, it is hoped, the volume may be of assistance in understanding some of the ramifications of later Buddhist thought. Consequently, the writings here deal primarily with the Mahāyāna, and are developed from Sanskrit, Tibetan, and Chinese sources composed in the third century A.D. and after. The principal method or approach to be found in most of these studies, regardless of the differences in the Buddhological viewpoint of their respective authors, is simply the exposition of classical source material.

Here, as has been the case among Buddhist scholars in general, the viewpoints of the authors are more or less evenly divided between those who tend to view Buddhism as a predominantly rational system and those who view it as pure existentialism. The former will view the core of Buddhist teaching as the outcome and derivative of the process of reasoning, whereas the latter will regard it as a verbal-conceptual formalization of an essentially transrational and yogic-type experience to be judged solely by its being known experientially or existentially. For the former, the core of the formalizations of Buddhism are propositions whose truth or falsity are ascertainable by means of a purely philosophical critique; for the latter, they are merely the signposts pointing the way to a stronger manner of "being here" or *Dasein*.

As serviceable as these approaches may be as emphases or priorities in talking about Buddhism, an actual cleavage between scientific and existentialist thought is, of course, a peculiarly European development and has its genesis in Europe's own intellectual past. Consequently, a hard and fast distinction between the two, at least in the same manner, may not also be altogether applicable to other cultures such as India, for example, where religion, philosophy, and science have developed in other ways. For instance, nothing prevents a philosophy, once taken outside of the European framework, from being existentialism in the prime sense of holding that an individual's potentiality for a given mode of existence cannot be derived from any metaphysics of being, and from being at the same time a philosophy derivable from the process of reasoning, provided that the reasoning process be a critique of thinking, rather than a construction of another system of rationalist dogma or ideology. Buddhism, in fact, appears to be just such a case in point, as long as one considers the primary systems of the Hīnayāna and the Mahāyāna as set forth in the Buddhist sūtras, together with their systematization by the main Buddhist *ācāryas*, Nāgārjuna, Asanga, and others. Subsequently, when Buddhism began to spread over the major portion of Asia, it always did so in association with its philosophies, since Buddhism never presented itself as a new revelation or gnosis, its founder having cautioned his followers about accepting his dharma on the basis of his personal authority rather than scrutinizing it by means of reason. The subsequent developments of Buddhism throughout numerous Asian countries are too multifarious to be generalized.

In this volume devoted to Buddhist meditation, the reader will soon discover that many of the studies and essays deal with the theories of the Mahāyāna, which is as it should be. In both the Mahāyāna systems, the Mādhyamika and the Yogācāra, as well as in the Hīnayāna, the actual nature of the object to be meditated upon is at first purely noetic, and results from a correct analysis of the phenomenal thing. Subsequently, this noetic object is brought into the limits of direct perception through the power of repeated meditative practice; to become an object of meditation at all, a thing must first be established as an object noetically. Consequently, the *āçāryas* of all the Buddhist schools, both Hīnayānist and Mahāyānist, seem to have been unanimous in holding that study and investigation need to precede the practice of meditation, simply in order to establish the number, nature, and so forth of the objects upon which to meditate. In Buddhism, this has always entailed some correct understanding and acceptance of *anātma*, which is the principal object of meditation, for the core of Buddhist teaching is simply the demonstration of *anātma*, and of the paths and final results which arise from meditating upon that view.

# Mahāyāna Buddhist Meditation

# Buddhist Theories of Existents: The Systems of Two Truths

*Elvin W. Jones*

Later (post-fifth century) Indian scholars, when confronted with the enormous mass of divergent canonical and commentarial literature produced by the past, regarded the systems of teachings set forth in the Buddhist scriptures as representative of three distinct enunciations of the doctrine by the Buddha, called "the three turnings of the dharma-wheel."[1] Likewise, they regarded the commentarial traditions which explained the preceding as contained within four major philosophical schools.

The first turning of the dharma-wheel consisted of the teachings of the Hīnayāna; the second was the teaching of the *Prajñāpāramitā* or perfection of wisdom class, a Mahāyāna doctrine; and the third was another kind of Mahāyāna doctrine, as exemplified by the theories of the *Saṅdhinirmocana-sūtra* and others. The theories of the first turning of the dharma-wheel were systematized in the *abhidharmas* of the Vaibhāṣika and Sautrāntika schools; those of the second, by Nāgārjuna around the first century into the Mādhyamika; and those of the third, by Āryāsanga around the fifth century into the school of the Vijñānavāda or Yogācāra. These four systematizations of the three dharma-wheels, the Vaibhāṣika, Sautrāntika, Mādhyamika, and Yogācāra, are the four schools of philosophical tenets produced by Indian Buddhism, the first two belonging to the Hīnayāna, and the latter two to the Mahāyāna. This idea of three turnings of the wheel of the Buddhist doctrine, originally set forth in the *Saṅdhinirmocana-sūtra*, is not, however, an inclusive classification of all the teachings contained in the Buddhist sūtras. Rather, it represents three radically different ontological determinations which served as the basis for three formulations of the entire system of Buddhist theory and praxis. Thus, running the whole range of the ontological spectrum, the first enunciation of the doctrine took as its basis the position that all existents (dharmas) are reals; the second, that all existents are unreals; and the third, that whereas some existents are unreals, others are reals. Thus, after the fifth century, it was a man's determination of the nature of "things," in the direction of a realism or a constructionism,[2] which principally led him to elect to follow the practice of Buddhism according to one of the four schools. The four schools continued to be studied and to serve as the basis of practice until the final disappearance of Buddhism in India in the twelfth century.[3]

Here, however, even Buddhist determinations in favor of a realism differed significantly from those of non-Buddhists. Even in its rise, Buddhism seems to have represented some radical departures from the mode of thinking of the entire ancient world, and so to have laid the ground for later achievements in scientific thought which were indeed to become the jewel ornaments of ancient Indian culture.

The several centuries preceding the appearance of the Buddha were a time of enormous intellectual ferment in North India, when itinerant teachers, of both Brahmanical and non-Brahmanical persuasions, promulgated a wide variety of philosophical doctrines, ranging from Brahmanical orthodoxies rooted in the Upaniṣads to atomism, strict determinism, and skepticism. Often these teachers succeeded in attracting a large following. The multiplicity of available doctrinal options and the obvious bewilderments incidental in determining among them are remarkably paralleled in many ways by the same kind of intellectual foment occurring during the same period in Greece, where the followers of religious fraternities and various philosophical schools, joined shortly by the Sophists, were carrying new theories and scientific information through the cities of Greece. In both these civilizations that were to foster the higher culture that was later to spread throughout a major portion of the world, the early systems of philosophical speculation produced almost at the start the sharp metaphysical cleavages which were subsequently to become one of the hallmarks of philosophy.

The emergence of these early speculative systems with a soteriological import does not appear as something sudden and abrupt, for prior to their appearance the national mythologies apparently had undergone a process of structuring, by means of principles of interpretation derived in part from observation of the regularity and periodicity of meteorological and other natural phenomena, a structuring which made them yield fairly coherent systems of cosmogenesis and soteriology.[4] The early systems of speculation in both Greece and India display a preoccupation with structures already imposed on the national mythologies by the end of the late archaic period, and these structures seemingly provided the early philosophers with sets of presuppositions as they gazed partly at the world and partly at the mythos.

In India, the first system of philosophical speculation was the Sāṃkhya, the earlier formulations of which are to be found in the later Upaniṣads or Vedānta which were developing the theory of identity between an ultimate and monadic basis of the universe called the Brahman and the innermost essence of the living being, the ātman. The Upaniṣads had allegorized and interpreted the hymns and sacrificial formulae of the Vedas in terms of this ātman theory, which was held to have constituted their inner meaning originally. From the matrix of this Upaniṣadic doctrine of the equivalency of the Brahman and the ātman, the Sāṃkhya scheme sought to derive the multiplicity of the phenomenal world from a series of descending permutations or evolutes of a single primary stuff[5] called Nature (prakṛti), which persists as a substratum for its own constantly changing qualities. In the midst of the multiplicity of the things, the prime knower or soul, the primeval Person (puruṣa), creates for itself a labyrinth wherein it is lost and suffers by mistakenly identifying these creations of Nature as somehow related to its own self. Consequently, there exists the possibility of the soul's deliverance from the sufferings involved in the phenomenal world by a gnostic realization of its own original nature as in no way related to Nature's productions. This is to be accomplished, according to the Sāṃkhya scheme, by a course of devolution by means of which the self progressively divests itself of its mistaken identifications with these productions of Nature, beginning with the most gross and concluding with the most subtle, for the soteriological path is an exact reversal of the cosmogenic path through the stages of which the self had become enmeshed and enmired in creation and by the reversal of which it constructs a path of emancipation. Thus, together the two paths constitute a full cycle of a world evolution giving way to a gnostically produced devolution, a cycle of the descent and ascent of the soul.[6]

The same morphology is distinctly discernable in the fragments of the earliest speculative systems produced by the Greeks. Here, too, the whole manifold of the phenomenal world is viewed as the derivative of a single stuff (the *arche* or source) functioning as a substratum which remains identical with itself in the face of its own constant modifications. Similarly discernable almost at the start is the view of the universe as a process of formation by means of a series of descending evolutes of the *arche*—e.g., the Heraclitan downward path *('odos kato)* of permutations from fire to water—and a process of dissolution through a series of ascending devolutes of the *arche*—e.g., the upward path *('odos ano)* of permutations from water back again to fire. That this cyclic process of the universe was seen as serving also as a chariot by which the soul descends and ascends to and from a gross manifestation is also clear. Regarding the cited examples,

Heraclitus states, "It is death for the soul to become water,"[7] "A dry soul is the most excellent and wisest,"[8] and so on, and here the psychic component of the cycle of the universe is too obvious to be overlooked.

In both cultures, this monistic basis or tendency of early philosophy to derive the many from the one appears to have been rooted in the authority of its respective religious traditions, in the Indian instance, in the Upaniṣads as exegesis of the Vedas, and in the Greek instance, in the Hellenic mystery traditions of which the earliest speculators were devotees and initiates.[9] As, however, the articulation of such theological constructs moved from the mythopoetic to the discursive, it quickly came under the sway of correct discourse or logic, and what may have been a cosmos to intuition soon became a chaos to sense. For however transparently self-luminous the unity of the all, or the development of the multiplicity of the phenomenal world from an original unity, may have been to the intuition looking at the mythopoetic, it soon became a web of obfuscation to the reason, when reason was called upon to give strict accounting of it. This is to say nothing of the manifold of phenomena. There soon came to the fore the problems entailed in explaining the genesis of even a single phenomenal thing in terms of the notion of a transformation or modification of one and the same subsistent stuff, since two incompatible demands were being made of the essence of an originating thing, i.e., that it be permanent and that it be impermanent. By virtue of being one and the same subsistent, the substrate substance needed to remain identical with itself, that is to say, to be immutable and permanent, whereas by virtue of its capacity to undergo transformation it needed to be something mutable and hence impermanent. Consequently, the essence of an originating thing, since it was nothing other than the essence of the substrate substance, also had to be a permanent, whereas definitionally, since it was an originate and hence a noneternal, it had to be an impermanent.

Just as in Greece, then, where the earliest systems of the Milesian school that sought to derive all the effects from a single cause soon gave way to other systems of explanation which saw the need for more than a single first principle to account for the genesis of the multiplicity of phenomenal things, so in India, where both the systems of the Jainas and of the Buddhists appear in part as a counterreaction to the monism of the Upaniṣads. The Jainas and the Buddhists, in addition to multiplying the number of real substances, espoused two disparate theories on the problem of the permanence or impermanence of substance and of the essence of an originating entity, so that, with the setting forth of the Buddhist dharma, three radically different determinations had been propounded by the Sāṃkhya, the Jaina, and the Buddhist. As for substance, the Sāṃkhya held one permanent stuff, Nature or prakṛti; the Jaina held five permanent stuffs, life, time, space, virtue, and nonvirtue; and the Buddhist held three permanent stuffs, space and the two kinds of cessation, along with an infinity of impermanent stuffs. As for the essence of the orignating entity, the Sāṃkhya held it to be permanent; the Jain, both permanent and impermanent; and the Buddhist, impermanent.

Here the Jains, by introducing a substantive difference between an originating thing's substance and its attributes, could hold that the essence of an originating thing *qua* substance was something permanent by being the effect of causes which were permanents, whereas by its attributes it was something impermanent. A pot, for instance, was permanent by virtue of its matter, a permanent substance, and impermanent by virtue of its qualities of origination, destruction, and so forth. Both the Sāṃkhya and Buddhism, on the other hand, admitted no substantive difference between a thing's substance and its attributes.[10] Hence, the former came to view empirical change as something only apparent, whereas the latter so viewed empirical perdurability.

For the Sāṃkhya, both the substance and the attributes were modifications of one and the same eternal stuff (Nature or prakṛti), which was without a beginning, a middle, or an end. Consequently, the essence of even an originating thing, being consubstantial with this one eternal cause, needed also to be permanent, as no substantive difference could be admitted between the cause and the effect. Since all existents, including originates, were in essence permanent existents, the result was that causality itself became not a process of a new production, but simply the manifestation or actualization of a potential latent in the cause; for, if the potential did not exist in the cause, the effect could never arise. Here, however, to exist potentially or latently means to be there both essentially and existentially, albeit in an unmanifested manner, and consequently all effects were held to be already in existence even at the time of their producing (i.e., manifesting) causes.

The Buddhist, on the other hand, took the opposite course of determination and held that a cause and effect relation means that the effect depends, not for its actualization, but for its very existence, on the cause. For, if the entity viewed as the effect is already in existence at the time of the cause, what need is there for a cause to produce it? This argument summarizes succinctly the cardinal Buddhist theory of dependent origination *(pratītya-samutpāda)*, wherein whatever comes into existence or originates *depends for its existence* on causes and conditions and cannot for this reason exist as something permanent, all origination being thus a new production and all originates (*saṃskṛta* dharmas) being consequently impermanents.

Although in its simplest formulation—i.e., that of the Vaibhāṣika—the Buddhist theory of the impermanence of all originates permitted a substantive difference between the substance of an originating entity and its attributes of birth, aging, destruction, and so on, it was soon apparent that the quality of destruction was not—as posited by the Vaibhāṣika—a superadded quality appearing simultaneously with the genesis of an originating entity, but rather that annihilation was the very essence of the originating thing itself. Otherwise, it was argued, all things would have to be of the nature of immortality, which is to say, the destruction or annihilation of a thing would be dependent upon its meeting with an external cause, in which case one ought to be able to find at least some examples of things which, having originated, have never met with their causes of destruction and consequently either have never disappeared or are clearly not likely to disappear in the future; and such is not so. In other words, the argument was that, for a thing to be ascertainably impermanent, it must be destroyed in every moment, otherwise it might never be destroyed at all. Consequently, the mainstream of Buddhist thought held that impermanence could mean only momentariness.

Here, the theory of impermanence as momentariness held that a thing's apparent empirical perdurability was a continuum of a seemingly identical object and its gross annihilation, viz., the breaking of a jar by a hammer or the death of a living creature, that it was just the final moment of a constant, uninterrupted series of transformations culminating in a thing's gross annihilation. In every point of time the thing was another thing; origination, duration, and destruction occurred simultaneously in each instant. Consequently, there was no substantive difference between a thing's substance and its attributes, for with every change of attribute—in particular the moment of time of its existence—the thing needed to be viewed as a completely different substance. In sharp contradistinction to the Sāṃkhya, which posited a thing's unity in a first cause, the Buddhists placed unity in an indivisible mathematical unit of a thing's extension, i.e., the impermanent atom,[11] and of a thing's perduration, i.e., an indivisible point of time. These atoms and temporal point units were not only indivisible but also extended, because indivisible units having no extension could never by aggregation produce magnitude, whereas magnitudes, if they were not a composition of indivisible units, became infinitely divisible.

The difficulties connected with depositing extension and indivisibility on the same *locus*, and the unsatisfactoriness of the Buddhist position as well as that of the Sāṃkhya, were to emerge subsequently

Particularly significant here is the predisposition of early philosophical thinking to equate real being with the impartible, and hence the unitary. In other words, it was held, implicitly or explicitly, that for something to be truly existent, it must be of such a nature as to be partless and thus incapable of further division into other parts of the same nature or into other natures more primary and fundamental. Such an impartible will consequently be a genuine unity or "a one," inasmuch as, being simple and uncompounded, it has nothing of multiplicity in it. Viewed in the reverse manner, this means that if sense and conceptual objects can be divided indefinitely, without any limit or measurement to their divisibility, then cognition itself becomes completely indeterminate, because cognition can only cognize the measured and bounded, never the infinite and unbounded. In early Western philosophy, for instance, this consideration seems to have led Plato explicitly to posit unity or "the one" as a necessary basis or ground for being, unity being an *a priori* principle determining that things exist in a measured way. Here, "to be" means "to be one" or "to be by means of participation or dependence on one." Since in Platonism real being is not only unitary but permanent as well, the real world of being exists for Plato as an archetypal or paradigmatic realm utterly outside of time and space, the flow of the sensible world having merely a derived existence and a secondary reality through participating in the former. The phenomenal or sensible world has, in fact, been reduced to an illusion, even though neither Plato nor the later Platonists called it such. This *de facto* reduction of the sensible world to the status of an illusion was detected by St. Augustine, for whom it became a main criticism of the Platonism which he had previously embraced.

Around the first century B.C., this predisposition toward thinking in terms of a real being, along with its concomitant implications, came under a close scrutiny and vigorous attack by Nāgārjuna on purely dialectical grounds. In the Hīnayāna sūtras, many dialectical refinements as well as methods of conducting formal discussion are already evident. Nonetheless, with the spread of Buddhism and the polarization of Indian opinion between the self and the no-self theories, interest in the dialectic as a means for making some satisfactory determination and demonstration was given a special impetus —a situation analogous to the growth of Greek logical interest in the face of the sharp metaphysical cleavage between Heraclitus' "Everything is in flux," and Parmenides' "Nothing moves either by change or in position." Nāgārjuna, easily one of the greatest dialecticians in the history of world philosophy, took all the real existents that both Buddhists and non-Buddhists had posited up to his time and subjected them to a rigorous criticism. Through his analysis, he found all these positions to be unable to explain the nature of things without serious internal contradictions. Hence, he concluded that things are devoid or empty *(śūnya)* of that very mode of being in terms of which they were instinctively grasped, and that things become explicable, in fact, only if they are empty of that mode of being. In other words, according to Nāgārjuna, things exist as phenomena merely, and phenomena are merely names capable of association with a concept; above and beyond the name and the concept, they do not bear any independent, inherent, or intrinsic nature, nor any mode of being behind their existence. Nonetheless, they are not nonexistent either, because they are there as phenomena. The prime target of Nāgārjuna's criticism seems to have been the predisposition, whether of common sense or of philosophical speculation, to view the existing as somehow absolutely existing. If, however, something exists absolutely or really, then it has to be permanent and unchanging, and so *never* nonexistent; otherwise, it cannot have a real nature of being existent. Thus, for instance, that the impermanent atoms of the Buddhists exist is patently self-contradictory for Nāgārjuna, for even though they are called "impermanent," if they have really the nature of existence, then they must be permanent and so cannot appear and disappear. On the other hand, the permanent atoms of the Vaiśeṣika are in the same difficulty, for if they are sometimes in the state of union and at other times in the state of disunion, then their nature changes and, consequently, they are impermanent. And this argument applies for the existence of every other kind of real. In addition to the necessity of real existents to be permanent and unchanging, they must also be either impartible or ultimately based upon the unitary, for the reasons explained previously.

This internal logic of absolutes also appeared in early Greek philosophy in the system of Parmenides, whose conclusions, however, were precisely the opposite of Nāgārjuna's.[12] In an effort to salvage the certainty of knowledge from the skepticism engendered by the Heraclitan position that all phenomenal things are in a state of perpetual flux or pure process, Parmenides sought to discover the existent in the midst of the becoming and took his stand on the dialectical ground that only the existent and never the nonexistent can be an object of cognition. Having dismissed the nonexistent as a possible object of cognition, he proceeded to define the really existent as something necessarily permanent, unchanging, and one, and went on to push his position to its logical conclusion, which posited the "real" universe as one permanent, motionless whole in which any change or movement in place could only be apparent but could not resist analysis—like the Eleatic example of the arrow in flight which cannot move. Such a purely noetic universe, however, seems in the system of Parmenides to have been unable to explain anything about the nature of the changing phenomenal world except its unrealness. Even in its subsequent adaption by Plato and the Neoplatonists, this Eleatic notion of being was not without numerous difficulties. In his famous distinction between "that which is existing always and never becomes" and "that which is becoming always and never is existent,"[13] the former accessible to thought aided by reasoning and the latter the object of opinion aided by sensation, Plato admitted into his system of philosophy both the Parmenidean world of eternal changeless being along with the Heraclitan world of pure process. The subsequent history of Neoplatonist thought is, in part, the story of the problematic of setting up a relationship between the absolutely unchanging and the changing, as more and more of the categories of Greek logic had to be hypostatized to function as links in an intermediary chain relating the two. Finally, during the later days of the Roman Empire, the problem of mediating the absolute and the phenomenal became so acute, psychologically as well as intellectually, that it became an important contributing factor in the final breakdown of Hellenism in the West.

Thus, whereas the internal logic entailed by the notion of real being as something necessarily absolute and static led Parmenides into the construction of a system of extreme monism, it became in the hands of Nāgārjuna in India one of the principal dialectical instruments for revealing the grave self-contradictions involved in applying the notion of real being to explanation of the nature of things, and so for demonstrating indirectly his own system of pure nominalism, which dèlimited the meaning of "to exist" as "to exist as a phenomenon" only and which repudiated all real being altogether.

Nāgārjuna had also thus reduced the whole phenomenal world to an illusion by depriving it of any real being whatsoever, just as Parmenides and many other philosophers have done; unlike other philosophers, however, he did not posit a real being elsewhere, above or beyond the phenomenal world, and he declared the final nature of all things to be just that lack of the kind of real being which things possess for ordinary apprehension, and that it is precisely this false way of apprehending things in which the illusion of the phenomenal world consists.

Consequently, while free perhaps of the problems arising from the stasis necessarily entailed by the notion of real being, the system of Nāgārjuna did not fail to arouse the objections of the schools whose reals he had subjected to criticism and found lacking that very reality. Objections were twofold: first, that his system of pure nominalism was nihilistic, since denying real being to everything must necessarily be denying many Buddhist tenets such as origination, destruction, and the Four Noble Truths, and second, that in such a purely nominalist system, knowledge itself, since it lacks the force of real being, has to become completely indeterminate and undefinable; consequently, knowledge could never affirm or deny with certainty whether things lack real being. Nāgārjuna's response to the former criticism of nihilism was that only someone who denied their real being could *de facto* accept origination, destruction, the cessation of misery and its causes by means of the cultivation of the Path, and so on, since the changes they entail can only occur if they are nonabsolutes, i.e., devoid of a real being.[14] To the objection of the indeterminacy of cognition, his answer was that just as a thing's appearance as a phenomenon is a sufficient certification for its existence, by means of which it may with certainty be delineated from something nonexistent, so cognition, whether perception or inference, knowing just that much existence is a sufficient guarantee for distinguishing a true from a false thesis.[15] It is, he says, just like the instance of the magically created apparition of two elephants which may be seen to struggle and one of which may be seen to defeat the other.[16] In other words, the skepticism which must necessarily be engendered by holding cognition to be indeterminate and incapable of all *a priori* certainty is equally addicted, as a false ideology, to the notion of real being, inasmuch as it assumes that in order to determine the right act of knowing from a wrong act of knowing, right knowing must know absolutely an object which has real being or is predicated upon real being. In this sense, the skeptic is the other side of mistaken ideologue, for the latter finds real being where there is none, whereas the former fails to locate real being and, failing, thinks that he cannot know things with certainty, because for him to be sure that he knows with certainty, he must know some kind of real being. Notwithstanding, knowledge knowing things which are existent merely as phenomena is an adequate basis for exact determination between the true and the false. Consequently, logical proof, rejection, demonstration, and so on are assured even without admitting their real being, for what else is "the existent" except a logical construct?

This answer, while sufficient for some, did not satisfy others, for whom Nāgārjuna's pure nominalism remained too extreme in the direction of nihilism. Consequently, although Nāgārjuna's system was to provide a basis for the practice of the Mahāyāna for the Mādhyamikas, Indian Buddhism was still to evolve another basis for the practice of the Mahāyāna with a new ontology. This last doctrinal synthesis of Indian Buddhism into a system of idealist nondualism was primarily the work of Asanga, who was later joined by his brother, Vasubandhu. It is variously called Yogācāra, Vijñānavāda, and *Citta-mātra* or "mind-only."

Taking its stand on a kind of Indian Cartesianism, a *cogito ergo sum* without the *ego* but simply a "thinking is,"[17] the complex ontology devised by this system of idealist nondualism might be summarized as follows: Even if things are names, names are always associated with concepts, so that the existence of names and concepts cannot be denied. Moreover, every act of conceiving has always an object of conception, since every act of conceiving has always the form of a cognizing-cognitum. This much is given. Among the objects of conception, then, some are purely conceptual in having no existence whatsoever independently of their concept, as for instance: (1) imaginary things, such as a unicorn, or (2) many kinds of abstractions and universals, such as numbers. However, all objects of conception are not purely conceptual like unicorns and numbers, for some conceptual objects are causally efficient and perform work, such as a horse or the effects of virtuous and nonvirtuous actions. The existence of these things, unlike that of the former, is not utterly dependent on their concept, for here no matter how much the concept may be ascribing something false to its object, the basis for that ascription must be something real.

Moreover, although there is guaranteed the existence of a name-concept and the existence of a real basis for a concept the object of which is something causally efficient, it is not also guaranteed that these efficient objects exist just in the manner in which they are apprehended by the concepts we form of them. We may be sure, in fact, that they do not, inasmuch as even a slight analysis reveals that the concept is constantly falsifying the nature of its object, as for instance when it apprehends duration on the momentary, or a self on the non-self. Consequently, the actual problem here, in the instances of these efficient objects, is to make a clear delineation between the true nature or natures which are merely being imputed to it by its concept, for the former nature is existent, whereas the latter is nonexistent. Thus, in the new ontological scheme of the Yogācāra as roughly summarized here, just as in the older system of the Mādhyamika, the phenomenon is something illusory in the sense that it is the *locus* for some kind of false imputation, since it does not exist just as it is grasped by ordinary thought. Consequently, the same phenomenon is likewise the *locus* for a nonillusory cognition, i.e., a cognition shorn of all false ascription. How the Mādhyamika viewed the actual nature of the phenomenal thing has already been briefly discussed. The Yogācāra, on the other hand, held that of the imputations superimposed on the object by its concept, the foremost was the apprehension of a substantive difference between the cognition and its object, for even though in all ordinary instances of the cognition of an external object the form of cognition-cognitum appears as *a something mental* (i.e., the cognition) and *a something nonmental* (i.e., the cognitum), Asanga had decided on grounds similar to those which led Kant to decide in favor of an idealism—i.e., the infinite divisibility of matter—that the external object which appears to its cognition as something substantively different from the cognition itself is in fact substantively the same as the cognition. Rather than representing two different kinds of substantives, the cognition-cognitum are two modalities of the same substantive, and the substantive is a mental. Hence, the actual nature of the object is just its emptiness of this kind of duality. This subject and its ramifications will be discussed later.

Between the time of Nāgārjuna and the time of Asanga, the science of dialectics had become more and more formalized into methods of logic, and a system of a five-membered syllogism was formulated by the Brahmanically orthodox school of the Nyāya. This five-membered syllogism was utilized by Asanga and Vasubandhu. The Nyāya system of logic, however, with its strong affinities to the extreme ontological realism of the Vaiśeṣika and its substantive differences between universal and particular, was ill-suited for use by the Buddhists, whose views were so much further on the side of a nominalism. Subsequently, the Yogācāra school produced a complete logical reform in the person of Vasubandhu's pupil Dignāga, in whose hands logic became a subsidiary, albeit an extremely significant, part of a full-fledged system of epistemology. A complete exposition of Dignāga's investigation of right cognition and its means was accomplished shortly after Dignāga by his disciple, Dharmakīrti. For the Buddhists themselves, this new science of epistemology and logic was an extension of their own *abhidharma*, since it demonstrated with greater force and precision than previously their principal views of impermanence, no-self, and so on, and provided these views with a sound critical basis. For this reason, the teacher Śākyamuni was saluted in the logical school as *pramāṇabhūta*,[18] a being whose knowledge and teaching was exactly in conformity with correct cognition.

Developments of logic after Nāgārjuna had also produced a division of the Mādhyamikas into two positions, for new logical considerations had given rise to questions which had not been decided earlier by Nāgārjuna and Āryadeva. One school of the Mādhyamika, the Svātantrika, insisted on the need for recourse to an independent inference as necessary means for demonstrating truth, whereas the other, the Prāsaṅgika, held that truth was demonstrable without recourse to *independent* inference, which was an inadmissible. The point of controversy here was not the validity of inference or syllogistic reasoning, which was not being questioned by either side; rather, it was a different view of the nature of the basis on which the validity of inference might be acceptably held to depend. The formulator of the Svātantrika position was Bhāvaviveka, and of the Prāsaṅgika position, Buddhapālita and Candrakīrti.

Finally, in addition to the sūtras of the Hīnayāna and the sūtras of the Mahāyāna, which set forth the basic theories which were to be developed into the systems of the Yogācāra and the Mādhyamika, there were a variety of Mahāyāna sūtras dealing with specific subjects such as the Pure Land of Sukhāvati, the tathāgata-garbha or potentiality for Buddhahood existing in all living creatures, etc. These were the common property of the Mahāyānists of both persuasions who in some instances, such as that of the tathāgatagarbha, interpreted them quite differently, and these do not appear to have been representative of any third kind of Mahāyānist school in India.[19]

Still another important class of Buddhist scriptures began to spread widely in India after the fifth century, namely, the tantras. The tantras set forth another method for the practice of the Mahāyāna, a method which was held by its followers to be more effective and rapid than that set forth in the sūtras. Inasmuch as the domain of the tantras was another method of praxis, the tantras did not enunciate any new theory; historically, at least, the Yogācāra and the Mādhyamika provided the theory which the tantric method sought to implement more fully. Thus, the three theories of existents, as briefly set forth in the preceding discussion, appear to represent the three, and only three, ontological determinations on which the theory and practice of Buddhism in India was grounded. These three fundamental positions served as the basis for the formalization of Buddhist teaching into the four schools, the Vaibhāṣika, the Sautrāntika, the Yogācāra, and the Mādhyamika, each of which subsumes a variety of subtypes. The first ontological position, that all existents are reals, is that of the Vaibhāṣika and the Sautrāntika;[20] the second, that no existents are reals, is that of the Mādhyamika;

the third, that some existents are reals whereas some are unreals, is that of the Yogācāra.

Here the meaning of an "existent" is any phenomenon ascertainable as such by means of uncontradicted knowledge. Even in its completely realistic formulations, the theories of the Vaibhāṣika, Buddhism was quite critical and selective in what it was willing to admit into the category of a *bona fide* phenomenon or an existent. In particular, in addition to any kind of originating permanent, it refused to admit any perdurable self or soul or ego functioning as the substratum of the personality or individuality, and this uncompromising denial of any kind of substantive ego enduring from one moment to the next in the personality was one of the principal hallmarks signalizing the Buddhist theory,[21] so that adherence to the no-self doctrine *(anātma-vāda)* was synonymous with Buddhism. On the other hand, the full implications of the no-self doctrine were variously understood and interpreted by the Buddhists themselves in keeping with their determinations of a primarily ontological nature. Consequently, the no-self doctrine was explained differently against varying ontological backgrounds, both realist and nonrealist.

In India as in Greece, philosophy arose and developed fully implicated in the mind's natural bent to see everything in realist or substantialist terms, with little critical examination of its own presuppositions and often faulty lines of questioning. Hence, almost everything belonging to the phenomonology of cognition[22] was first viewed as some kind of substantive existent, these real things including not only specific perceptual data but also the objects of universals, abstractions, relations—every type of conceptual entity, in fact. There was something of a problematic in the area of objects seen in dreams, hallucinations, the illusions of magic, reflections, and so on, which resist somewhat the tendency to be viewed as altogether on a par ontologically with their "real" counterparts. It was only after the development of full-blown substantialist systems of thought that philosophy could consider the possibility of a purely conceptual construction and attempt to delineate it from some kind of self-subsistent nature belonging independently to the object, for this could only be done by a critique of the substantialist theories themselves. Hence, in the course of philosophical criticism, one meets again and again instances in which the inability of a theory to withstand criticism is adduced *a fortiori* as the main support for the proposer's own alternative, and the alternative theory is left standing merely by default rather than by its own power to withstand further critical scrutiny.

The most thorough effort at the construction of a genuine philosophical critique was that of the Mādhyamika. In the later period of Buddhism in India, the arrangement of the Buddhist theories into the four main schools became formalized into a new kind of doctrinal literature of some importance subsequently, especially in Tibet, i.e., the so-called *siddhānta* or texts which delineate the tenets of the Indian philosophical schools, both Buddhist and non-Buddhist. This particular kind of literature was exclusively the product of Mādhyamika scholars, e.g., Bhāvaviveka in the *Madhyamakahṛdaya* and its autocommentary the *Tarkajvālā*, and Śāntarakṣita in the *Mādhyamakālaṁkāra*. Tibetan scholarship subsequently expanded the scheme to treat systematically the varieties of the Mādhyamika.[23] This literature, in no way seeking to view the development of Buddhist philosophy in a historical perspective, represents just the final elaboration of the most ancient Mādhyamika method of demonstrating its own rather difficult viewpoint to others as readily as possible by way of criticism, e.g., Nāgārjuna's criticism of the Abhidharmikas and Āryadeva's criticism of the Sāṃkhyas. Consequently, its scheme of arrangement of the Buddhist schools from lower to higher is purely critical. The chief targets of this criticism are the various entities accepted as ultimate reals by the other schools, along with the concomitant consequences of their admissions. The general movement of its progression from "lower" to "higher" is one from the extreme realism of the non-Buddhist systems to its antithesis, the viewpoint of the Mādhyamika that there is nothing whatsoever which exists as an ultimate or as a real real. The remaining Buddhist schools represent intermediate positions standing nearer to or further from the maximal realism of the non-Buddhists and the no-realism of the Mādhyamika.

Thus, this schematic of the Buddhist schools from lower to higher, beginning with the Vaibhāṣika through the Sautrāntika and the Yogācāra to the Mādhyamika, represents the Mādhyamika's own critical perspective. The higher the school, the fewer the number of reals it admits into its system. The lower schools are systems of the Hīnayāna, and the higher schools are those of the Mahāyāna; "higher" and "lower" is from the Mādhyamika point of view. It appears, moreover, that as a system admits fewer and fewer reals, the more it goes against a natural tendency to see things in realistic terms and, consequently, the harder the system may be to grasp with ease—especially without going from an extremity of hypostatization to another extremity, i.e., negation of the nonhypostatized. Nonetheless, a position equally free of these two extremities, acceptance of the hypostatized or superimposed *(samāropa)* and nihilistic depreciation *(apavāda)* or rejection of the nonhypostatized or the nonsuperimposed, is just the position which each of the Buddhist schools claims for itself, and in the instance of the Mādhyamika is even the meaning of the name, *Mādhyamika* or "middle-ism."

The Tibetan *siddhānta* literature, which this study will now examine, takes two truths as the basis of all the philosophical tenets of the Buddhist systems. Although the idea of two truths is primarily identified with the Mādhyamika, especially by way of Nāgārjuna's famous statement that "the teaching of the Buddha has recourse to two truths," explicit statements distinguishing two truths are to be found in other systems of Buddhist thought, including the scriptures and commentaries of the Hīnayāna, so that a system of two truths, a phenomenal truth and an ultimate truth, is indeed the common property of all the schools of Buddhism. Nonetheless, it is chiefly in the face of the more highly sophisticated ontological considerations that the notion of the two truths becomes particularly significant and revealing, especially where consideration is being given to delineating the self-subsistent character in contradistinction to the purely conceptual or constructed nature of even a *bona fide* phenomenon. In other words, many kinds of phenomena establishable as such by means of uncontradicted knowledge need not also exist as some kind of ultimate real; hence, the efforts of Buddhist philosophy to categorize existents phenomenologically, together with its efforts to determine them ontologically, is the domain of the two truths.

In the Buddhist systems, the distinctions and bases for making the distinctions between the two truths are so varied that it is impossible to generalize them beyond stating that the Buddhist systems always treat the two truths as a genuine dichotomy, which is to say that (1) all things admissable as existent are included in the two truths, and (2) the two truths are reciprocally exclusive. Hence, whatever exists is either phenomenal truth or ultimate truth. If it is phenomenal truth, it is not ultimate; conversely, if it is ultimate truth, it is not phenomenal. Again, by way of example, if the basis for making a distinction between a phenomenal and an ultimate is, as in the Svātantrika Mādhyamika, from the point of view of cognition, and the difference between a phenomenal and an ultimate is one of an object of a dual cognition as opposed to an object of a nondual cognition, any particular object, for instance a table, is a *locus* for both a dual and a nondual cognition. However, the table *qua* table as an object of cognition is not both phenomenal truth and ultimate truth, because the table *qua* table exists as an object of cognition only for a dual cognition, whereas the object of a nondual cognition is just the emptiness *(śūnyatā)* of the table.

Having indicated the dichotomous nature of the two truths, we may proceed to look briefly at the two truths in the various Buddhist systems.

On the two truths in the Vaibhāṣika, the *Abhidharmakośa* says, "When of that—like a pot or water—which is destroyed or reduced by analysis to something else, the cognition does not arise, it exists as a phenomenon *(saṃvṛti sat)*; other things exist as ultimates *(paramārtha sat)*."[24]

What exists as an ultimate for the Vaibhāṣika is a partless atom and an indivisible moment of cognition; every other existent exists as a phenomenon. The ultimate reality set forth here is essentially atomistic, and the stability and perdurability of the phenomenal thing, more apparent than real, is in fact a continuum of the seemingly identical object, the atomistic moments succeeding one another as cause and effect. According to the Vaibhāṣika, the caused thing at the first moment of production is endowed with four qualities—origination, duration, aging, and perishing—which function successively. All other schools of Buddhism as well accept this continuum of successive moments in lieu of any kind of real perdurability. However, the others do not regard the atomistic moments as ultimate truth, and they likewise do not accept a moment of duration other than the moment of origination. Thus, for the other schools, the thing goes instantly from origination to destruction, and the phenomenal thing is annihilated in every instant. This is called by the others "subtle impermanence."

As for the Sautrāntikas who follow reason *(yukti)*, Dharmakīrti says, "Here, whatever is ultimately functional *(paramārthatas artha krīya samārthya)* exists as an ultimate *(paramārtha sat)*."[25]

What exists as an ultimate for this kind of Sautrāntika are caused entities or originates (*saṃskṛta* dharmas). Every other thing, since it is uncaused *(asaṃskṛta)*, such as space, exists as a phenomenon. Because so many of the important distinctions being made here are shared by the Yogācāra and the Svātantrika Mādhyamika (but not by the Prāsaṅgika), this definition needs to be discussed at some length. For all the Buddhist systems, the *definiens* of a dharma or ontological entity is *svarūpagrāhya*, the individuated entity or thing possessed of its own entityness, and it is synonymous with an existent and a cognizable *(jñeya)* and an object knowable through a source of prime right cognition.[26]

Dharmas are variously subdivided, and one of the most important subclassifications is a division into *saṃskṛta* and *asaṃskṛta* dharmas, or caused and uncaused entities. The former originate in dependence on causes and being impermanent; the latter are permanent and never originate. This much applies to all the Buddhist schools, but the following discussion bears mainly on the Vaibhāṣika. The *abhidharma* lists of the Vaibhāṣika enumerate three such uncaused entities (*asaṃskṛta* dharmas), i.e., space *(ākāśa)* and two kinds of cessation *(nirodha)*, whereas the other Buddhist systems find many other uncaused entities (*asaṃskṛta* dharmas) as well. As for "uncaused" *(asaṃskṛta)*, it may be seen that there are two kinds of things which may be called uncaused, i.e., nonentities such as a rabbit's horns which never appear through a source of right cognition and permanent entities such as space, the existence of which may be established through a source of right cognition. The former is altogether nonactual *(abhāva)*, whereas the latter in contradistinction to the former is some kind of actual *(bhāva)*, the *definiens* of an actual *(bhāva)* being the capacity to perform a function or to do work *(artha krīya samārthya)*. Thus, for example, in the Vaibhāṣika system, space is accepted as a permanent nonoriginating entity—an *asaṃskṛta* dharma—and, because movement is regarded as a function of space, space is accepted as a cause of movement. Similarly, the other two *asaṃskṛta* dharmas are accepted as functional *(artha krīya samārthya)*. Thus, in the Vaibhāṣika, all dharmas are functional, and hence all dharmas are actuals *(bhāva)*.

Standing at a higher level of criticism, the Sautrāntika (as well as the other Buddhist systems except the Vaibhāṣika) rejects the notion of a permanent entity's capacity to do work and thus be the cause of anything. Here, for example, the Sautrāntika reasons that, although space never impedes movement, and in that sense motion may be considered a function of space, space itself is never actually a mover or an efficient cause of motion, because objects in space are sometimes in motion, sometimes at rest, whereas space itself is permanent. If space is sometimes a mover and sometimes a nonmover, then inasmuch as the nature of space is changing, space must be impermanent; and this is not so. The same argument was often used by Buddhism against a permanent god *(īśvara)* as the creator of the world: For if there is a time when god does not create the world and a time when he does create it, then because his nature changes, god is not permanent; or, if there is a time of his not creating the world and god is permanent, then he cannot create the world; or, if god, being permanent, is always creating the world, then the world is also permanent and consequently does not depend for its existence on creation by god, a relation of cause and effect being precluded, since the cause and the effect cannot exist at the same time;[27] and so on. Similarly, whatsoever is accepted as permanent cannot be the cause of anything, and therefore permanent uncaused entities (*asaṃskṛta* dharmas) such as space must be accepted as nonfunctional *(artha krīya asamārthaya)* and nonactual *(abhāva)*, the *definiens* of an actual *(bhāva)* being efficient functionality as stated previously. Thus, contrary to the Vaibhāṣika, which accepts all entities (dharmas) to be functional entities, here in the Sautrāntika, only caused entities (i.e., *bhāva*) are functional, whereas uncaused entities (i.e., *abhāva*) are nonfunctional.

Consequently, if something is uncaused *(asaṃskṛta)* and permanent, this is only because it is nonfunctional and hence not existent as anything independent of a concept. This does not mean, however, that these uncaused entities (*asaṃskṛta* dharmas) are completely inexistent, for, as stated, in contradistinction to nonentities (non-dharmas) such as the rabbit's horns, they may be known through a source of uncontradicted knowledge. On the other hand, their existence being totally dependent upon conceptual ascription (i.e., a name and a concept), they are purely noetic entities or *ficta*, in contradistinction to caused entities (*saṃskṛta* dharmas) such as a pot, the existence of which is not dependent on conceptual ascription since caused entities are the direct objects of sense perception and consequently directly cognizable without recourse to naming and conceptualizing. The former, an object of right cognition which exists as a mere *fictum*, is the general character *(sāmanyalakṣaṇa)*. The latter, an object of right cognition which exists by way of its own condition of existing without being a mere *fictum*, is the self-subsistent character *(svalakṣaṇa)* or thing existing independently of conceptual ascription. Thus, uncaused entities such as space exist as phenomena merely, whereas caused entities such as a pot exist as ultimates. Here, the *siddhānta Rin po che'i phreng ba* states:

> Space, which is an uncaused entity *[asaṃskṛta]* is called phenomenal truth because it is real in the face of the phenomenology of cognition, and this "phenomenal" [*saṃvṛti*, lit. "covered up"] means a *fictum* because [thought] obscures the thing which is existent in itself *[svalakṣaṇa]*. . . However, if something is real for the conception belonging to the phenomenology of cognition it is not necessarily included in phenomenal truth, because even an example of ultimate truth, like a pot, is real for the conception belonging to the phenomenology of cognition; likewise [things] such as the self of an individual *[pudgala]* or permanent sound which are real for the conception of a phenomenological cognition do not exist conventionally *[vyavahāra sat]* or as phenomena *[saṃvṛti sat]*.[28]

Thus, the meaning of phenomenal truth *(saṃvṛti satya)* as opposed to the etymological meaning of phenomenal (*saṃvṛti*, lit., "covered up") is an object of cognition which does not exist ultimately (the two truths being dichotomous), but the existence of which is conventionally established through a source of prime right cognition *(pramāṇa)*.

Here, a radical reduction of hypostatized entities has taken place, i.e., the elimination altogether of an independent universal, for if all existents are not substantives, inasmuch as some, such as *asaṃskṛta* dharmas, are determinable not as substantively existent *(dravya siddha)* but as existent through logical construct *(pramāṇa siddha)*, then the object of the general or universal, itself either a substantive or a logical construct, may be determined to exist substantively only when every particular subsumed by the universal is a caused entity (*saṃskṛta* dharma). In such instances—such as "the blue"—the particular and the general, although logically different,[29] are the same entity because neither the particular nor the general has any other referent than the thing which exists independently of conceptual ascription, namely, the *svalakṣaṇa* or self-subsistent character of the thing. Thus, "this blue" (the particular blue) and "the blue" (the general blue) not being two different entities, the object of the universal even though it exists substantively does not exist independently or as other than that of the particular, and vice versa. On the other hand, it often happens that every particular instance subsumed by the universal is not a caused entity—for example, "existence," "object of cognition," "relation," "one," "two," and so on. Taking the example of "existence," space which is uncaused exists; hence, inasmuch as we have a specimen of an existent which is uncaused, an entity which exists without recourse to a cause, "existence" does not need to depend on causes and is permanent. Universals of this type are *asaṃskṛta* dharmas, hence not existent as substantives *(dravya siddha)* but as logical constructs *(pramāṇa siddha)*, and consequently the number of *asaṃskṛta* dharmas, far from being just the three accepted by the Vaibhāṣika, is almost unlimited, for it includes numerous universals and abstractions and all relations.

Here, in the Sautrāntika, everything which exists, whether caused or uncaused *(saṃskṛta* or *asaṃskṛta)*, is nonetheless said to be "determinable as self-subsistent" *(svalakṣaṇa-siddha)*.[30] Since uncaused entities, which are not self-subsistents *(svalakṣaṇa)*, but only generals *(sāmanyalakṣaṇa)*, are being called *svalakṣaṇa-siddha*, determinable as self-subsistent, the term *svalakṣaṇa-siddha* is of a somewhat wider application. It signifies not only the self-subsistent thing which exists independently of the conception (for this is only the caused entity), it also includes general entities which exist as phenomena by way of a final dependence on other things which are of a self-subsistent character—for example, space, the cognition of which depends finally upon objects in space which are self-subsistents. As a definition of *svalakṣaṇa-siddha*, Je tsun pa gives the following in *Dbus ma'i sphyi don:* "At the time of investigating an object which is designated by a name, one finds [something]."[31] Again, if investigation of something designated by a name or expression leads *at the time of investigation* to the discovery of some object as opposed to absolutely nothing at all, as in the instance of "rabbit's horns," that object is some kind of entity and not a nonentity altogether, inasmuch as something is found. Hence, whatever exists is existent by way of a self-subsistent character, either its own or the self-subsistent character of other things.

All these definitions and distinctions stated in connection with the Sautrāntika, which follows reason, are accepted with some modification by both the Yogācāra and the Svātantrika Mādhyamika, and form important elements of the theories of both these systems.

In the Yogācāra, all existents (dharmas) are grouped according to its own cardinal doctrine of *svabhāva-trāya* or three natures as set forth in the *Saṅdhinirmocana-sūtra*. Here, all uncaused entities (*asaṃskṛta* dharmas)—with the exception of śūnyatā—are counted as ascribed entities *(parikalpita)*, and these do not exist self-subsistently *(svalakṣaṇa asiddha)*. All caused entities or originates (*saṃskṛta* dharmas) are counted as dependent entities *(paratantra)*, and these are accepted as self-subsistently existent *(svalakṣaṇa siddha)*. Śūnyatā, which is an *asaṃskṛta* dharma and signifies the two emptinesses of individuals and things (*pudgala* and dharma *nairātmya*), is counted as a final nature *(pariniṣpanna)*. In the Yogācāra system, śūnyatā is the single *asaṃskṛta* dharma exempted from being classified as an ascribed entity *(parikalpita)*, and it alone among *asaṃskṛta* dharmas is accepted as self-subsistently existent.

As for *parikalpita* and *paratantra*, despite a difference of terminology, everything already stated about *saṃskṛta* and *asaṃskṛta* dharmas holds here, with one important modification—the difference with which the Sautrāntika and the Yogācāra employ the terms *svalakṣaṇa* and *svalakṣaṇa-sid-*

*dha.* The Yogācārins define both *svalakṣaṇa* and *svalakṣaṇa-siddha* as "existent without being dependent on conception."[32] Consequently, both *"svalakṣaṇa"* and *"svalakṣaṇa-siddha"* both have exactly the same range of application, and both signify only a thing which is itself self-subsistent and never something the cognition of which depends upon the self-subsistent character of other things, as in the Sautrāntika instances just given. Thus, in the Yogācāra anything existent by its self-subsistent character exists likewise as an ultimate *(paramārtha sat).* In fact, the Yogācārins are saying, just like the Sautrāntika, that (with the Yogācārin exemption of śūnyatā) all *asaṃskṛta* dharmas are conceptual constructs and exist as phenomena merely, whereas *saṃskṛta* dharmas exist as ultimates. Unlike the Sautrāntika, however, *saṃskṛta* dharmas are not the ultimate truth, for ultimate truth is only the final natures (*pariniṣpanna* = the two *nairātmyas*). Thus, as the two truths are dichotomous, all existents, both caused and uncaused, ultimates or nonultimates, are, with the exception of śūnyatā, phenomenal truth.

On the two truths for the Yogācāra, Vasubandhu states in the *Vyākhyāyukti:* "*Parama* [highest] is the gnosis *[jñāna]* which transcends the world, and because it is the object *[ārtha]* of this gnosis, it is *paramārtha* [object of the highest gnosis]."[33]

'Jam dbyangs bzhad pa explains this passage in the following way: "The character of *paramārtha* is its being the final object of understanding of the path of purification, specifically, the two emptinesses, of a thing such as the skandhas, etc. and of an individual [*pudgala* and dharma *nairātmya*]."[34] Thus, except for the final natures *(pariniṣpanna)* which are the two emptinesses *(nairātmya)*, i.e., of individuals and of entities, all things are phenomenal.

Likewise, for the Mādhyamika as for the Yogācāra, all things are phenomenal *(saṃvṛti)* except śūnyatā, i.e., the two *nairātmyas* which are *paramārtha*; however, there is a profound difference between the two systems in what is understood here, and this difference may be seen from the following discussion of *pariniṣpanna.*

Thus far, the two schools of the Hīnayāna, the Vaibhāṣika and Sautrāntika, have been accepting both a substantive matter and a substantive mind and a cause and effect relation between them; in the act of cognizing the pot, for example, the pot existent as a conglomeration of atoms is a cause of its cognition, which is a mental. For this reason, in contradistinction to a concept, the direct object of which is a general image or mental representation, the Sautrāntika hold direct perception always to be nonillusory, because the direct object of perception is the *svalakṣaṇa* or thing which exists independently of conceptual ascription. The Yogācāra, on the other hand, while admitting direct perception to be *nondelusive* in respect to its object of cognition, will not admit it to be *nonillusory.*[35] Yogācāra goes a step farther, holding that not only is there no need to postulate a real substantive matter behind its cognition, but that it is clearly erroneous to do so. Not only is a substantive matter not to be found, but its existence is an impossibility; if a real material substance exists, then one ought to be able to find, at least by way of an intellectual analysis, a final particle of matter or ultimate atom, but such a final material atom is not to be found, on account of infinite divisibility. Hence, the Yogācāra, regarding an independent substantive material stuff as still another hypostatized entity, views the external object *(bāhyārtha)* seen in cognition as another modality of a mental substance rather than a separate material stuff causing the cognition. Hence, although there is a logical difference between cognizer and cognitum, they are both a single substantive entity and that is a mental. Consequently, the cognitum is illusory in the sense that, although it is purely mental, it appears as a nature other than a mental by way of appearing as a real external object, i.e., an independent substantive material stuff. In the same way, the cognizor is illusory inasmuch as its manifest object is illusory. Nonillusory is simply the absence of a substantive difference between the cognizer and cognitum. This is nonduality, and this nonduality is the ultimate truth and the meaning of the emptiness of dharmas for the Yogācāra.

In the Mādhyamika, nonduality and the emptiness of dharmas is something quite different. Of the systems, the Vaibhāṣika, Sautrāntika, and Yogācāra share in common the acceptance that whatever is the ultimate truth *(paramārtha satya)* exists as an ultimate, i.e., is *paramārtha sat.* In the Mādhyamika, on the other hand, existence in ultimate reality *(paramārtha sat)* is the very thing which is negated by *paramārtha satya.* Consequently, in the Mādhyamika, *paramārtha satya* is the mere nonexistence of a thing—the table, for instance, as an ultimate or as a real. Thus, in the Yogācāra, śūnyatā is a final nature *(pariniṣpanna)*, the supreme object of the path of purification, unthinkable, unutterable, and nondual because it is free of a difference between cognizer *(grāhaka)* and cognitum *(grāhya)*; it is empty *(śūnya)* of all things except its own existence in reality, for it exists as an ultimate; it is *paramārtha sat.* On this kind of śūnyatā, Kamalaśīla says in the first *Bhāvanakrama*, "Thus, that understanding of nonduality which is held by the consciousness doctrine [Vijñānavāda] as the highest truth is empty, and by the wisdom of the unmanifest *[nirabhaṣa]* the yogin comes to see this nonduality as ultimately unreal,"[36] for "as things are not really produced from self or other, the cognizer and cognitum are ultimately unreal altogether, and since understanding of nonduality is not of something other than these two and is also upon investigation a nonreal, one must turn away from apprehending this nondual understanding as an ultimate."[37] Thus, emptiness in the Mādhyamika means empty of its own realness, of its own existence as an ultimate *(paramārtha sat)*, as well. Although the Mādhyamika is a nondualist system in the sense that it does not admit an ultimate substantive difference between cognition and its object, duality is not the prime target of the Mādhyamika's criticisms. In the Mādhyamika, nonduality is just the sameness of the cognition *(viṣayin)* and its object *(viṣaya)* by virtue of their inexistence as reals. It is the notion of realistic existence or a real being which is the main target of the Mādhyamika's denials. The nonexistence of all things by way of a real being subsumes the nonduality of cognition and its object, for in such emptiness of real being there is no differentiation *(viśeṣa)*.

The Mādhyamika's reason for this emptiness of a real being is the dependent-arising *(pratītya-samutpāda)* of all existents. That which is a dependent-arising does not exist by virtue of its real being *(svabhāva)*, and this emptiness of real being is a thing's dependent-arising.

Thus, in the Mādhyamika the meaning of dependent-arising is considerably more comprehensive than in the other systems of Buddhism. For the others, "dependent" *(pratītya)* means "dependent upon causes and conditions," and "arising" *(samutpāda)* means "origination"; "dependent-arising" is an origination in dependence on causes and conditions. This means that only caused entities (*saṃskṛta* dharmas) are accepted by the other Buddhist schools as dependent-arisings. However, since the *Kārikās* state, "because there is nothing which is not a dependent-arising, there is nothing which is not empty *(śūnya)*,"[38] the Mādhyamika is accepting all existents (*sarva* dharma) as dependent-arisings. This means not only caused entities (*saṃskṛta* dharmas) but uncaused entities (*asaṃskṛta* dharmas) as well. Consequently, the meaning as well as the application here of "dependent-arising" is more comprehensive than that given previously. "Dependent" means "dependent upon other than self," whereas "arising" means "existing." Here, then, dependent-arising is existence in dependence upon other than self, and this "dependence upon other than self" subsumes "origination in dependence on causes and conditions" while depriving origination itself of the force of a real production. This comprehensive sense of a dependent-arising is stated in the *Kārikās* thus: "As the agent is dependent on the act, and the action on the agent, no producing cause is seen, save only a dependent arising."[39] This passage is commented upon in *Rigs pa'i rgya mtsho* as follows:

> Thus, it is said that the existence of the agent is in dependence on the action, but that there is no [real] production of the action of the agent, and where it is said that one ought to

employ this line of reasoning to other things, it is stated that a prime right cognition *[pramāṇa]* and its object, a *probans* and a *probandum*, exist in dependence upon one another, but that it is not correct that one [really] produces the other. Similarly, the *Ratnāvali* says, "When this exists that arises *[asmin sati idam bhāvati]*" is like when there is a short there is a long. Thus it is said also that it is just as the short is not the producer of the long.[40]

Again, just as a dependent-arising, in the limited sense of an origination in dependence on causes, while negating the permanence of anything caused, establishes conversely the cause and effect of karma, similarly a dependent-arising in the more comprehensive sense of existent in dependence upon other than self, while negating the existence of anything as an ultimate, does establish the existence of things phenomenally. Here again we may quote Nāgārjuna and the comment of *Rigs pa'i rgya mtsho*.

Nāgārjuna says in the *Śūnyatā-saptati:*

> Because all these things are empty of a real being *[svabhāva]*, this is their dependent-arising, *[pratītya-samutpāda]*. The meaning of the emptiness *[śūnyatā]* which is taught by the imcomparable Tathāgata ends with just that. The Buddha, the Blessed Lord, names all the various things by having recourse to the conventional expressions of the world.[41]

and *Rigs pa'i rgya mtsho* comments:

> Thus, it is stated that origination and all the rest are set forth having been named from the point of view of their nominal expressions, because the final meaning of the reality of phenomenal things ends with just this devoidness of a real being, their dependent-arising. The *Kārikās* say, "The doctrine taught by the Buddhas has recourse to two truths." By stating this also, he shows that the emptiness of a real being is the ultimate truth and that origination, and the like, are conventional; but were he not to state as above [i.e., in the *Śūnyatā-saptati]*, someone, not understanding that the meaning of conventional existence is just the phenomenal order of things from the point of view of their nominal predication, may fail to understand

—after so many logical rejections of a real being have been put forward—that the meaning of the statement that all the various things exist by way of their nominal predication is this very establishment of their nonreal being.[42]

Thus, it was the genius of Nāgārjuna which gave a startlingly profound answer to a question which few other philosophers had even seen fit to raise, and he answered negatively by deliberation what others were answering affirmatively by presupposition—that for an appearance of something, there must be some basis or ground which is determinably existent as an ultimate *(paramārtha sat)*. It is just the absence of such a basis which the Mādhyamika has accepted as the highest truth *(paramārtha satya)* and has sought to demonstrate its discoverability through diverse lines of reasoning as well as by criticism of the various entities accepted as ultimates by other schools of thought.

The question arises, if the śūnyatā of the Mādhyamika, unlike that of the Yogācāra, does not exist ultimately *(paramārthatas)* or absolutely by virtue of a real being *(svabhāvatas)*, how does it exist? As stated previously, to exist means here to exist as a phenomenon merely, because it is held that nothing exists as an ultimate. Consequently, śūnyatā is the ultimate truth by virtue of being the supreme object of knowledge of an ārya's gnosis *(āryajñāna)*, but it exists conventionally or phenomenally because its existence conventionally, like any other thing which may be admitted as existent, is determinable by right cognition dependent upon the objects of conventional expressions. Thus, by way of the nonexistence of śūnyatā itself in ultimate reality, an emptiness of emptiness is delineated.

Thus, in the Mādhyamika, ultimate truth is simply śūnyatā itself, i.e., the nonexistence of all things as reals or as ultimates; phenomenal truth is all things admissable as existent, with the exception of śūnyatā, which is the ultimate truth but existent conventionally. However, the full implication of this "nonexistence as a real" is understood differently by the two main systems of the Mādhyamika, the Prāsaṅgika and the Svātantrika. For the Prāsaṅgikas the negation that things exist as ultimates entails the denial that they exist even conventionally by way of any kind of self-subsistent character *(svalakṣaṇa-asiddha)*, whereas for the Svātantrikas such a denial represents an extreme in the direction of nihilism.

Briefly stated, the Prāsaṅgikas hold that things do not exist as ultimates precisely because they do not exist even as phenomena by way of a self-subsistent character *(svalakṣaṇa-siddha)*. The definition of *svalakṣaṇa-siddha* here is as previously stated: "At the time of investigating the object which is designated by an expression [and a concept], one discovers [something]," but *at the time of investigation* the Prāsaṅgika discovers nothing. As stated by the *Satyadvayāvatara*, "When the phenomenon as it appears is investigated by reason, nothing is discovered, and this nothing-to-be-discovered is itself the ultimate truth."[43]

For the Svātantrika, on the other hand, to state the foregoing bluntly without some qualification would be to fall into the problem of the determinancy of cognition. Although not existent as ultimates, things must exist conventionally by way of some sort of self-subsistent character; otherwise, why not perceive a tree or even a cow where one is perceiving a table? Consequently, when a Svātantrika Mādhyamika denies origination, for instance, he always qualifies his negation by an "ultimately" *(paramārthatas)*, because "there is no origination ultimately." By his negation of a real being, he means only that there is no real being as an ultimate. In *Legs bshad snying po*, Tsong kha pa seeks to explain the Svātantrika's position here with a comparison to a magical or hypnotic illusion whereby a piece of wood or a stone is made to appear as a horse or an elephant:

> When a piece of wood or stone [which are] the basis of the illusion appear to the affected vision as a horse or an elephant, it is just an appearance as such to the consciousness, but it cannot be said that the wood, etc. do not appear so. In just the

> same way, when there is the appearance of a sprout from a seed, this is nothing more than merely an appearance, but it cannot be said that this is not produced from that. Should one think, then, that inasmuch as the sprout is produced from a seed [existing] on its own side, it is produced ultimately, there is no criticism, for although there is an appearance likewise of a horse or an elephant from the side of the basis of the illusion [i.e., the wood or stone, etc.], the appearance as such is by virtue of the consciousness belonging to the affected vision, but there is not as there seems a production [of a horse or an elephant] from causes and conditions having an inherent nature. Thus, to hold that there is a production by the power of an inherent nature without admitting [also] by the power of appearing to mind [which is] the ground of the cognition *[viṣayin]* is to hold that there is a production as [a something] ultimate, and in these terms, one should understand the [Svātantrika's] statement "to exist ultimately and in reality," and likewise the statements of the existence-nonexistence of production, etc. of all things [as qualified by the expressions] "in reality," "as an ultimate object," or "in truth."[44]

Consequently, the distinctions of *sva* and *sāmanyalakṣaṇa*, as discussed previously, are accepted by the Svātantrika Mādhyamika, just as by the Sautrāntika and the Yogācāra, with one important difference: whereas for the two latter, whatever is existent by way of a self-subsistent character *(svalakṣaṇa-siddha)* exists as an ultimate *(paramārtha-siddha)*, for the Svātantrika Mādhyamika, both *sva* and *sāmanyalakṣaṇa* are phenomenal truth, for nothing is admitted to exist as an ultimate.

In their discussions of the two truths, little clear and distinct difference actually emerges, at least on the level of meaning, between the Svātantrika and the Prāsaṅgika Mādhyamika. It is principally in their way of explaining the three natures *(svabhāva traya)* set forth in the *Saṇdhinirmocana-sūtra* that their differences come forth most sharply.[45] Consequently, any effort to distinguish between the Svātantrika and the Prāsaṅgika needs to take into account both *satya-dvaya* and *svabhāvatraya* together, and this would entail introducing another complex topic which cannot be explored here.

Investigation of the points of controversy between the two varieties of Mādhyamika is perhaps one of the most rewarding studies in Buddhist philosophy, and the few salient points set forth here are necessarily much too brief. They represent the opinion of Tibetan scholarship, which inherited fairly intact the systems of later Indian Buddhism. Tibetan scholarship in turn is overwhelmingly indebted to Tsong kha pa, whose breadth of rigorous scholarly investigation and depth of philosophical penetration easily entitle him to a place among the foremost *ācāryas* of the Mādhyamika. To attempt to reconstruct the thought of Nāgārjuna set forth in the *Kārikās* and other treatises without the writings of Tsong kha pa would probably be as thankless a task as to attempt to reconstruct the metaphysics of Aristotle without the works of Thomas Aquinas. What particularly distinguishes Tibetan interpretation of the Mādhyamika is its unique way of doing away altogether with substantialist thinking, without falling into either the logical or the ethical relativism characteristic of much contemporary effort to relinquish substantialist thought. Tibetan scholarship does not seem to have found that the denial of every kind of self-subsistence and the relegation of all things to mere words and concepts require the reduction of logical categories to pure operational expedients or the reduction of the objects of all concepts to mere indeterminates; neither does it seem to have had to posit a need to abandon rational thinking, finally, in favor of an aesthetic intuitionalism. These features in particular, the author thinks, commend it to serious study and consideration.

The four schools examined here have each sought to provide the necessary philosophical substructure upon which to view the full import and meaning of the *anātma* doctrine. In the Vaibhāṣika, with its realist notion of nonexistence, the no-self of the individual was viewed as a real, whereas in the Sautrāntika, standing at a higher level of criticism, it was a nonreal. With the development of still more critical theories, whether based on dialectical or epistemological considerations, some kind of no-self of existents, in the sense already indicated, had also to be taken into account. This, in turn, conditioned and deepened the meaning of the no-self of the individual. With the Yogācāra, we have two kinds of no-self, both of which are reals and again, with the Mādhyamika, a still more critical position for which both kinds of no-self are nonreals. In turn, these different ways of understanding the import of the no-self doctrine conditioned the type of meditation which was founded on each, and each has served as a theoretical basis for the development of the Buddhist path.

## NOTES

1. The idea of the Buddha's having taught three distinct positions is set forth in the *Saṅdhinirmocana-sūtra*, which served as the basis for the systematization of the Yogācāra philosophy at the hands of Asanga and Vasubandhu. The division of the Buddhist schools into four is clearly to be found in such (ca. sixth-century) works as Bhāvaviveka's *Madhyamakahṛdaya* and its autocommentary, the *Tarkajvālā*.

The three turnings of the dharma-wheel and their respective ontological positions are set forth in the seventh chapter of the *Saṅdhinirmocana-sūtra*, where the bodhisattva Paramārthasamudgata questions the Buddha about the discrepancy between his statements that origination, destruction, the four truths, the mind-body aggregates, and so on are self-subsistents and his statements that all existents are "without a self-subsistence, without an origination, without a cessation, quiescent from the start, inherently gone beyond ill" (*Saṅdhinirmocana-sūtra*, Peking reprint edition, vol. 29, folio 17b ff.).

2. A realism versus a constructionism, i.e., a view holding things to be truly existent as they appear versus a view holding things to be appearances to cognition merely. As used here, a real denotes an entity which does not depend for its existence on a name and concept, whereas a construct denotes an entity which has no existence of its own independently of naming. From the point of view of the four schools, the Vaibhāṣika is pure realism in holding that all things admissable into the category of existent are existent independently of naming, whereas the Prāsaṅgika has taken a completely opposite course of determination, that all existents are constructs merely. The Sautrāntika-, Yogācāra-, and Svātantrika-Mādhyamika

occupy intermediate positions, determining some existents as reals and some as constructs. The Sautrāntika has determined more existence on the side of realism; the Yogācāra and Svātantrika more existence on the side of constructionism, the Yogācāra allowing more on the realist side than the Svātantrika.

3. Nag tsho lotsaba's *Bstod pa brgyad cu pa*, a eulogy of Atīśa in eighty ślokas, quoted extensively in the *Lam rim chen mo* of Tsong kha pa. Nag tsho draws a picture of the Indian monastery of Vikramaśīla in the eleventh century in which adherents of all four schools were living side by side under one roof (*Lam rim chen mo*, Peking reprint edition, vol. 152, 5b).

4. For mythopoetic cosmological formulations antecendent to Greek speculative efforts, see discussion of Hesiod's *Theogany*, the *Heptamuchos* of Pherecydes of Syros, and so on in the "Forerunners of Philosophical Cosmology," in Kirk and Raven, *The Presocratic Philosophers* (Cambridge: University Press, 1969), pg. 8 ff.

In India, Upanaṣadic speculation is already prefigured allegorically in such later works of the Vedic period as the *Śatapatha-Brāhmaṇa*, where the Upanaṣadic Brahman emerges allegorically under the guise of the Vedic Prajāpati through a series of analogical identifications, i.e., the "Year" = "time" = "space" = "the all" = "the universe" = "the sacrifice" = (most importantly of all) Prajāpati, who in turn is equated with the puruṣa, or primeval Man, who is sacrificed in the creation of the world.

5. Although the Sāṃkhya is a dualistic system in the sense of accepting an ultimate distinction between the knower and the known, puruṣa and prakṛti, only prakṛti is an active creative principle involved in causal production.

6. The cycle of a descent and ascent of the soul is of course symbolical, because in the Sāṃkhya the soul is completely impassive and, consequently, is never actually defiled or purified. This was one of the cardinal Buddhist objections to a soteriology of the Upaniṣadic type, for what, they asked, is defilement and a path of purification to the intrinsically pure?

7. Cited in Porphory's "De Anthro Nympharum," in Thomas Taylor, ed., *Select Works of Porphory* (London: T. Rodd, 1823, pg. 178).

8. Kirk and Raven, *The Presocratic Philosophers*, pg. 205.

9. F. M. Cornford, "Mystery Religions and Pre-Socratic Philosophy," *Cambridge Ancient History*, vol. 4, ch. 15 (Cambridge: University Press, 1939).

10. The generalization that Buddhism did not admit a substantive difference between substance and attribute is made from the point of view of the mainstream of Buddhist thought, as the Vaibhāṣika is the exception which did admit such a difference. This is discussed elsewhere in the study.

11. The Buddhist atom is also a momentary entity constituting a stochastic continuum.

12. The efforts of Stcherbatsky to interpret the Mādhyamika as a monism of the Parmenidean type has by now been fairly discredited by subsequent scholarship, although it is to Stcherbatsky's credit to have seen a similar absolutist use of logic being employed by both Parmenides and Nāgārjuna (*Buddhist Logic*, vol. 1 [New York: Dover Publications, 1962]).

13. The *ti to on aei genesin de ouk echon* and the *ti to gignomenon men aei on de oudepote* of Plato's *Timaeus*, 28 A.

14. Objection (*Mādhyamika kārikās*, Chapter XXIV):

> If all these are empty *(śūnya)*, it follows that you don't have an origination, nor a destruction, nor the four noble truths.

Response (*Mādhyamika kārikās*, Chapter XXIV):

> If these are not empty, it follows that you don't have an origination, nor a destruction, nor the four noble truths. (Tibetan translation, Chapter XXIV, Peking edition, vol. 95, 19a.)

15. The entire *Vigraha-vyavārtini* of Nāgārjuna is devoted to answering this objection of the indeterminacy of cognition, an objection which is stated in the introductory śloka: "If the self-nature of every existent is without being, words, being without self-nature, cannot reject a self-nature."

16. That is, in the *Vigraha-vyavārtini.*

17. A rough paraphrase of the *Madhyāntavibhaga*'s "the unreal imaginings *[abhūtaparikalpita]* exist." This somewhat obscure term is taken by Tsong kha pa in the Vijñānavādin section of *Legs bshad nying po* as signifying every kind of *paratantra-svabhāva*, the *abhutaparikalpita* being one of its principal instances or examples.

18. Most notably, in Dignāga's introductory salutation in his *Pramāṇasamuccaya.*

19. The possible existence of a distinct Tathāgatagarbhavāda in India is likely to be a point of controversy among Buddhologists for some time to come. In his *Study of the Ratnagotravibhaga* (Serie Orientale Roma), for example, Takasaki presumes the existence of a Tathāgatagarbha school as a third Mahāyāna school in India in addition to the Yogācāra and the Mādhyamika, but Takasaki, apparently looking more to the fortunes of the tathāgatagarbha theory in China, has not really posed the question of whether or not such an independent school ever existed in India. There are, to be sure, about ten important Buddhist sūtras expounding the theory of a tathāgatagarbha, but if these teachings were ever formulated to serve as the basis of an independent school, who were its *ācāryas* and why did tathāgatagarbha theory become the common property of both the Yogācāra and the Mādhyamika? And if it were also an independent school, how did it escape being so treated by such Mādhyamika *ācāryas* as

Bhāvaviveka, who were writing shortly after the time of the composition of the *Ratnagotravibhaga* by Maitreyanātha?

20. Although the Sautrāntika ontology displays many features common to the Yogācāra, especially in distinguishing between a self-subsistent and a mentally constructed, its final determination is that all existents are reals, for it holds all existents (dharmas) to exist self-subsistently *(svalakṣaṇa siddha)*, that is to say, either self-subsistent in themselves, like the scholastic *in se sistendo*, or dependent on the self-subsistence of others, like the *in alio inhaerendo*, e.g., space, the notion of which is dependent on objects in space. This way of viewing existence brings the Sautrāntika into conformity with the first turning of the dharma-wheel that all existents are reals, in spite of the scope it gives to the constructed. (See the essay by Geshe Sopa in this volume for some further discussion.) The Yogācāra, on the other hand, excludes from existing self-subsistently *(svalakṣaṇa siddha)* all things which lack their own self-subsistence. These differences in their respective uses of terminology was raised to the surface by Tsong kha pa in *Legs bshad snying po* (Sarnath: Elegant Sayings Press, 1973), p. 56, and subsequently has been further expatiated in the Tibetan *yig-chas* or textbooks used in the monastic colleges.

21. Again, it is the Vaibhāṣika which provides some exception to this uncompromising denial of a substantive ego, for among the eighteen subschools of the Vaibhāṣika, there were some, notably the Vātsīputrīya, which although not denying a self which was an independent, permanent unity such as was accepted by the non-Buddhists, did accept a self which was existent as an independent substantive. It was not, however, denotable as permanent or impermanent, or the same as or different from the mind-body aggregates, the skandhas. This has given rise to discussion and controversy among traditional Buddhist scholars about whether or not this kind of Vaibhāṣika was a holder of a Buddhist theory.

22. In this paper, the term "phenomenology of cognition" is used to signify any act of cognition or anything appearing to cognition. Where this sense is not explicitly indicated by the context, it signifies any act or object of cognition *except* the object apprehended by a wrong conceptual cognition (conceptual in contradistinction to perceptual). Here, the object of conceptual cognition is viewed as twofold, i.e., the *manifest object* and the *apprehended object.* As in the instance of the rabbit's horns, "rabbit's horns" are existent as the object which is manifest to their conception, and both the conception and its object *qua* an object of a conception exist, but they are nonexistent as the object which is apprehended or grasped by thought, the latter object being a nonphenomenon.

23. The final development of the Tibetan *grub mtha'* or *siddhānta* literature occurred within an illustrious circle of encyclopedic scholars associated with Dgong lung monastery in Amdo Province in the latter half

of the eighteenth century, most notably, Lchang-skya, Jig-med dbang-po, and Thu'u bkwan, who in turn look back principally to 'Jam dbang bzhad pa, whose *Grub mtha' chen mo* gave the Tibetan *grub mtha'* its present form. All the foregoing have left large compilations of their literary works, but the fame of each as writers rests mainly on their respective works on *grub mtha'*, or delineation of the positions of the philosophical schools. While taking Indian works such as Bhāvaviveka's *Tarkajvālā* and Śāntarakṣita's *Madhyamakālaṃkāra* as models, *Grub mtha' chen mo* also utilizes the classics of Tibetan Buddhist scholarship, most notably *Legs bshad snying po*. This is Tsong kha pa's single most decisive and significant work of scholarship, dealing with the positions of the schools of the Mahāyāna in India, and one in which he virtually created a kind of metalanguage for reaching the rock-bottom essentials of Indian Buddhist thought. *Grub mtha' chen mo* deals with all the principal schools of Indian philosophy, both Buddhist and non-Buddhist, systematically and in detail. It covers Indian materialism, the philosophy of the Jains, the six schools of Brahmanical orthodoxy (the six *darśanas*), and the four schools of Indian Buddhism, and is justifiably famous for its erudition and the wealth of important information which it brings together into one place. It was followed by other works of the same genre, most notably Lchang-skya's *Thub bstan-lhun po'i mdzes rgyan (Embellishment to Adorn the Four-Sided Mountain of the Muni's Teaching)*, and Jig med dbang po's *Rin po che'i phren ba (Precious Garland)*. Lchang-skya's *Embellishment to Adorn the Four-Sided Mountain of the Muni's Teaching*, a lengthy and substantial work, is distinguished by its style and clarity of presentation, whereas Jig med dbang po's *Precious Garland*, an extremely abbreviated treatment of the same subjects, has provided a most valuable introduction to the study of the Indian philosophical schools. Finally, Thu'u bkomn, a pupil of both Lchang-skya and Jig med byang po, attempted for the first time to deal systematically with the Tibetan schools as well and composed the *Legs bshad shel gyi me long (The Crystal Mirror: An Exposition of the Tenets and Sources of All the Philosophical Schools)*, an extremely learned and polished work in twelve chapters dealing principally with the Tibetan schools. These are treated historically since the Tibetan schools share in common the four positions of Indian Buddhism and cannot be simply delineated by means of doctrinal differences. Jig med dbang po's *Precious Garland* has been translated and published by H. Guenther under the title *Buddhist Philosophy in Theory and Practice* (London: Penguin Books, 1971). However, because this translation is full of obscurantisms and omissions of many important passages of the original text, the text has been retranslated by Geshe Sopa and Jeffrey Hopkins and is included, along with another text, in *Practice and Theory of Tibetan Buddhism*, (London: Rider and Co., 1976).

24. *Rin po che'i phreng ba* (Dharmasala, India: 1967), p. 20.

25. *Grub mtha' chen mo* (Masuri, India: 1962), Ga, 2b.

26. "Prime right cognition" is an attempt at translation, or rather paraphrase, of *pramāṇa* according to its definition in the hands of Dignāga and Dharmakīrti as "new" and "unerroneous" cognition. See F. T. Stcherbatsky, *Buddhist Logic* (The Hague: 1958), pp. 62 ff. and 64 ff.

27. In the logic of Dignāga and Dharmakīrti, only two kinds of logical relation are allowed, tautology and causality. If two objects are related and exist at the same time, the relation is viewed as one of identity, or as tautological. In other words, different names and concepts are being deposited on a single perceptual substratum, i.e., the object is cognized by a cognition which is nonconceptual and which is consequently viewed as a purely perceptual cognition. On the other hand, if two objects existing at different times are related, this relation is viewed as one of cause and effect. This relation is defined as the effect's dependence for its production upon the cause. Consequently, at the time of the effect's existence, since it already exists, there can be no dependence for its existence on a producer. Hence, it is argued that the produced and producer cannot be simultaneous. The reasons for this emerge most clearly in Dharmakīrti's *Sambandhapārikṣā (Examination of Relation)* in which all other relations posited by Indian philosophy are subjected to criticism and found objectionable. The crux of the matter is that they rest on the view of a relation which is substantively different from the *relatum*. Dharmakīrti seeks to argue that such a view is a mere presupposition which has under examination to be discarded. Dharmakīrti's own view that the relation between a logical relation and its *relata* is tautological can only support two possible relations, tautology itself and causality.

28. *Rin po che'i phreng ba*, p. 32.

29. I.e., pramāṇa-siddhi.

30. The discussion follows the Sautrāntika use of the term as as interpreted by *Legs bshad nying po*. See note 20.

31. *Tha snyad btags pa'i btags don btsal ba'i tshe na bsnyed pa rang gi mtshan nyid kyis grub pa'i don no.* (*Dbus ma'i sphyi don*, Tibetan block print)

32. See notes 30 and 20.

33. *Grub mtha' chen mo*. Nga, 43a.

34. *Grub mtha' chen mo*. Nga, 43a.

35. Not nonillusory because, according to Yogācāra, perception which does not go beyond a mental nature represents objects existing externally or as having other than a mental nature.

36. *Tibetan Tripitaka*, vol. 102, f. 35b.

37. *Tibetan Tripitaka*, vol. 102, f. 35b.

38. *Tibetan Tripitaka*, vol. 95, f. 18a.

39. *Tibetan Tripitaka*, vol. 156, f. 154a.
40. *Tibetan Tripitaka*, vol. 156, f. 154b.
41. *Tibetan Tripitaka*, vol. 156, f. 148b.
42. *Tibetan Tripitaka*, vol. 156, f. 148b.
43. *Tibetan Tripitaka*, vol. 101, f. 146a.
44. *Tibetan Tripitaka*, vol. 153, f. 139a.
45. This careful probing of the works of Svātantrika and Mādhyamika authors and their way of accepting the *trisvabhāva* as a means of eliciting their actual thought is again the work of Tsong kha pa and is especially developed in *Legs bshad snying po.*

# *Śamathavipaśyanāyuganaddha:* The Two Leading Principles of Buddhist Meditation

*Geshe Sopa*

Meditation[1] is one of the indispensables for the practice of Buddhism, as it is one of the three disciplines *(trīṇiśikṣāṇi)*—lawful conduct, meditation, and understanding *(śīla, samādhi,* and *prajñā)*—in which the entire practice of Buddhism is contained. The aim of this discussion, then, is to attempt to explicate somewhat the subject of meditation as set forth in the Buddhist sūtras and the commentarial works of major Indian *ācāryas* and of Tibetan scholars, in particular the *Lam rims* of Tsong kha pa.

At the outset, we meet a problem which ought to be noted, namely, the terminology by which the subject of meditation is traditionally explained. Meditation and the procedure of learning how to meditate is a matter at least as technical and as little innate as learning, say to play a piano or to perform surgery. Nonetheless, classical exposition of meditation, although in fact highly technical, makes use of words having a variety of common meanings and connotations which, if taken literally, can easily be misleading and consequently betray the actual subject. For instance, a key term such as *śamathavipaśyanāyuganaddha* might fairly literally be rendered as "tranquility coupled with insight" or "calming joined with insight," and so on, but if such expressions should conjure up in a hearer an image of a man sitting peacefully thinking or intuiting a philosophical concept, the true meaning will have been lost. Such misinterpretation does in fact occur, since *vipaśyanā* has also been characterized by some as "an intense contemplation of philosophical propositions"; similarly, others having a like notion speak therefore of a "dry *vipaśyanā*," in other words, a *vipaśyanā* without *śamatha*, even though the presence of *śamatha* is held to be an indispensable condition for all *vipaśyanā*. The same problem exists for many other key meditative terms such as *layauddhatya*, *karmaṇyatā*, *cittaprasrabdha*, *nābhisaṃskāra*, and so on. In attempting to cope with this problem, we hope that in looking at some of the classical descriptions of the meditative procedure, the actual sense of such terms may become more apparent by way of grasping the psychomental processes entailed in the actual act of meditating, rather than the etymological derivations of the terminology which describes them.

Notwithstanding the great importance of meditation to the practice of Buddhism, there is not, as far as I can determine, a *locus classicus* in the work of any Indian or Tibetan *ācārya* which seeks to set forth a definition of meditation. The reason for this is probably that there is not possible a single definition of meditation that will be all-inclusive of the literally thousands of meditations which Buddhism espoused and practiced. Yet in spite of the obvious complexity of these various details, all of these meditations are reducible to two types, fixative and analytic, and these may be defined and discussed separately.

The division of meditation into fixative and analytic is probably the simplest all-inclusive division of meditation possible, and thus it includes the more familiar division of meditation into *śamatha* and *vipaśyanā*, which will tentatively be rendered as "(mental) stabilization" and "higher vision," respectively. The perfect union of these two, mental stabilization and higher vision *(śamathavipaśyanāyuganaddha)*, is the immediate aim of Buddhist meditative practice, for all the paths of Buddhism—whether Hīnayāna or Mahāyāna including Vajrayāna—depend upon this coupling.

The nature of (mental) stabilization *(śamatha)* is just a one-pointedness of mind *(cittaikāgratā)* on a meditative object *(ālambana)*. Whatever the object may be, and whether it is actually present or imagined merely, concrete or abstract, and so on, if the mind can remain upon its object one-pointedly spontaneously without effort *(nābhisaṃskāra)*, and for as long a period of time as the meditator likes, it is approaching the attainment of mental stabilization. Actual stabilization in addition to the foregoing, however, is a particular state of mental focus *(samādhi)* which is possessed also of a dexterity *(cittaprasrabdha = karmaṇyatā)* elicited by the power of the mind's remaining one-pointedly on its meditative object. Here, the key word is dexterity, for this mental stabilization is a special kind of mental dexterity which can perform a wide variety of functions which the mind would be incapable of doing without it. All such mental stabilization on an object is fixative meditation. However, the term "fixative meditation" is somewhat broader, for prior to and preparatory to the achievement of actual stabilization, there are a variety of states of mental focusing which aim at, but do not completely reach, the dexterity of actual mental stabilization, and these also may be designated as fixative meditations.

These states of mental focusing *(samādhi)* occurring before the actual achievement of mental stabilization which are included within fixative meditation are variously explained. One of the most important methods of explanation is from the point of view of nine mental fixations, beginning with the initial efforts to fix the mind one-pointedly on an object of meditation, up to the attainment of the capacity of the mind to remain effortlessly one-pointed on the meditative object. These are a schematization of nine steps leading up to the attainment of mental stabilization.

The first mental fixation is called "interiorization" and signifies the sporadic concentration which is constantly being interrupted by thoughts and which is achieved at the beginning only by withdrawing the mind again and again from the flow of ideation and fixing it again and again on the object of meditation. The second, called "duration fixation," is an advance in the ability of the mind to remain focused longer on the meditative object. The third, "refixation," means that the mind when it leaves the meditative object is forced back again, as at this stage the mind remains focused on the object more of the time than it is distracted as was the case with the first two mental fixations. The fourth is called "close fixation" because at this point the mind, because of the development of a great power of attention, no longer loses the object of meditation. During this fourth fixation, the mind is held forcibly on the meditative object by a strong power of attention. Consequently, there is a danger of the mental concentration's giving way to a subtle lethargy or torpor *(laya)*. The fifth, called "the disciplined," marks an advance in control over the mind's succumbing to lethargy, for at the time of the fifth fixation, the mind is under a constant surveillance by means of an introspective awareness which watches out for the danger of the mind's becoming lethargic or sinking. When the danger of the mind's becoming lethargic is spotted, the meditator must heighten the mind again by considering the beneficial results of the attainment of mental focus *(samādhi)* or by meditating on a perception of bright light, and so on. As a consequence of too much heightening of the mind, on the other hand, there arises the opposite danger of the mind's becoming overstimulated or excited *(auddhatya)*, and during the sixth fixation, called "the pacified," this is brought under control by watching out with introspective awareness for the danger of arising excitement, and suppressing it by means of reflection on death, the bad results of mental distraction, and so on. At this point, both the power of attentiveness and introspective awareness have been highly developed. Then, during the seventh mental fixation, called "the completely pacified," the meditator especially cultivates the power of effort by means of which he keeps getting rid of even the subtlest lethargy or excitement. When, by the power of such effort, the meditator can extend the duration of the mind's remaining one-pointedly on the meditative object for as long a time as he likes without a trace of even a subtle lethargy or excitement, this becomes the eighth mental fixation, called "the one-pointed." Finally, during the ninth, called "even fixation," the mind remains on the meditative object spontaneously, without effort, and for as long a time as the meditator desires.

With the attainment of the ninth mental fixation, the mind can remain spontaneously and without effort on the meditative object, and at this point the mind has become so completely acclimatized to meditative concentration that all traces of physical sluggishness and mental uneasiness in meditation have been eliminated. As a consequence, there arises a particular sense of felicity of mind and body called "the pleasure of the mind and body tempered for use" *(karmaṇyatā).* At this sense of felicity, which is at first a possible danger to meditative concentration, becomes slighter and slighter, there arises finally a particularly flawless state of concentration in which even a sense of a subtle physical or mental pleasure is no longer noticed, and this is the attainment of actual mental stabilization *(śamatha).*

The process of cultivating mental stabilization through recourse to the foregoing nine mental fixations is sometimes condensed into four placements of the thought, and there are other methods of explanation as well. These steps leading to the attainment of a perfect one-pointedness of mind which is the characteristic of all *śamatha* are all within the category of fixative meditation.

It ought to be fairly apparent that such one-pointedness of mind *per se* is devoid of reflection, or analysis, or discursive thought, and the power to think discursively without losing thereby the clarity of the meditative object which mental stabilization effects is a subsequent development resulting from an additional training of the mind. This power to reflect discursively on the nature of the meditative object *at the time when* the previously mentioned mental stabilization is present is called *vipaśyanā* or "higher vision." Here, by the "nature" of the meditative object is meant, of course, its final or ultimate reality in the sense at least of a limit of cognizibility—but not only that. Objects around us potentially present us with a variety of true qualities which are not at all apparent to simple, naïve observation—for example, impermanence, continuous flux, the Four Noble Truths, and so on. Consequently, a wide variety of true qualities, as well as the ultimate reality, of the meditative object may be said to constitute the nature of the object. More specifically, then, higher vision is a particular understanding *(prajñā)* which is possessed of a dexterity which is elicited by the power of analyzing the meditative object *while mental stabilization is present.* Here again, the key word is dexterity, for superior vision is a quite special kind of mental dexterity, having its own particular properties and uses. All higher vision is analytic meditation, which, as in the instance of fixative meditation, is the somewhat broader term; for here also, prior to the preparatory to the attainment of higher vision, there are a variety of meditations which aim at, but do not reach, the dexterity of actual higher vision, and these, too, are analytic meditations.

Inasmuch as the full attainment of mental stabilization is the condition *sine qua non* for all higher vision, the attainment of higher vision, which is a process quite distinct from stabilization itself, is also called the union of stabilization and higher vision. On the attainment of the union of these two kinds of mental dexterity depend all the paths of purification of the passions *(kleśa).* The word "passions" here ought to be taken in its wider and etymological sense, in which it denotes not just a strong attraction to objects but includes all the affections characterizable as impediments to emancipation, such as hatred, anger, and conceit as well as lust, greed, covetousness, and so on. The word, derived from the Latin *passus,* "to suffer," ought also to carry here its etymological meaning of suffering. For Buddhists, as for many other ancient ethical philosophers, the passions are sufferings, and both the Sanskrit *kleśa* and the Tibetan *nyon mongs*, which we are rendering here as "the passions," carry very strongly this connotation of suffering.

These paths of purifying the passions, in turn, are either mundane *(lāukika)* or transmundane *(lokottara)*, and the elimination of the passions which they effect are, respectively, temporary or lasting. The mundane path brings about a temporary suppression of the passions, whereas the transmundane path causes their complete uprooting or extirpation. In the Buddhist sense, the mundane or world order is a condition which is characterized from top to bottom by impermanence and perpetual flux under the sway of action (karma) and the passions, and the consequent vicissitudes of all its inhabitants as, under the sway of action and the passions, the most superior conditions in the world give way in time to the most inferior. Thus, the highest good cannot be sought in terms of a condition constantly fluctuating under the power of action and the passions, for, as noted often by philosophy, men do not merely wish to possess the good, but to possess it always. Such being the Buddhist view of the instability of the highest good which the mundane condition affords, the specifically Buddhist paths aim therefore at the transmundane where karmic destruction and the like have no foothold.

This path, which we render here as the mundane path for the elimination of the passions, is not a practice peculiar to Buddhism, but has been shared by such non-Buddhist systems of meditation and yoga as Sāṃkhya. It is this system of yoga practice which the Buddha Śākyamuni learned from the Sāṃkhya philosopher and yogin, Udrako Rāmaputra, and the followers of the Hīnayāna cultivate it especially to bring about a fairly rapid alleviation of the passions by means of their temporary suppression. Subsequently, upon the completion of this path they initiate the transmundane path and recapitulate their obliteration of the passions; by this latter path, however, they bring about complete extirpation of true cessation. The followers of the Mahāyāna likewise cultivate the mundane part, less, however, for its value in suppressing the passions as for gaining the kinds of knowledge which its mastery affords, as well as for improving the technical mastery of meditation or yoga, terms which, incidentally, are synonymous.

The mundane path for the elimination of the passions is the yoga practice of the four trances *(catvāri dhyānāni)* and the four formless absorptions *(arūpyasamāpatti)*. Here, the process is fundamentally one of a sublimation of the consciousness by means of the progressive reduction of attachment, "attachment" denoting specifically an attraction to an object which is accompanied by a wrong mental activity, such as being ignorant of the nature and qualities of the object. Thus, the principal method of this practice is the reduction of attachment itself, and since the other passions—jealousy, anger, and the like—depend ultimately upon attachment, this path cuts off their arising as well by the progressive elimination of the arising of attachment. Mastery of each higher trance and absorption has the power of controlling the one immediately below it up to the highest of the absorptions, called variously "the mundane summit" or "neither perception nor nonperception" *(nāivasamjñā-nāsamjñā)*. As this is the climax of the path, there is no position above it which can control the residuum of attachment belonging to the "summit." The elimination of this residuum can only be achieved by recourse to the transmundane path.

As for the actual practice of the four trances and the four formless absorptions, the attainment of mental stabilization is the threshold of the first trance. Actual mastery of the first trance, however, also needs the higher vision which has as its object the superiority of the first trance mentality to the ordinary mentalities of the world of desire. Here, the yogin reviews instead the faults and bad effects arising from attachment to objects of attraction to the five senses and contemplates the comparative superiority and serenity of the qualities of the first trance as they have been learned from study and reflection. Subsequently, he obliterates successively the nonvirtues and the most gross attachments belonging to the world of desire, then the middling, and finally even the smallest. With the eradication of even the smallest attachments, the first trance mentality is fully attained, and the mastery of the first trance is the basis for the development of the five kinds of paranormal cognition *(abhijñā)*, clairvoyance, clairaudience, and so on, each of which has its own particular preparation and mastery. As for the second trance, the yogin now begins to contemplate the comparative superiority and serenity of the qualities of the second trance mentality to that of the first trance, and again he removes successively the most gross, middling, and finest attachments to qualities belonging to the first trance, and the same procedure is repeated for the remaining two trances and the four formless absorptions, each taking the immediately preceding as the basis.

Through each succeeding trance and absorption, the consciousness has become more and more subtle, as fewer and fewer of the sense consciousnesses continue to operate. At the postclimax of the formless absorptions, there is one more absorption not properly belonging to the mundane path, but accessible (to the Āryan individual, that is, one who has attained the "path of vision" *[darśana-mārga]*) only by way of mastery *(maula)* of the highest of the four formless absorptions. In this absorption, called the "cessation trance" *(nirodha-samāpatti)*, the consciousness is so attenuated and subtle as to be tantamount to unconsciousness, since all sense and mental consciousness seem to cease to function. Similarly, at the time of the fourth trance, there is another trance called "no-perception" *(asamjñā-samāpatti)* resembling this one, but on a lower and less profound level. The subject of these two trances would require an essay of its own for a full treatment, for some non-Buddhist yogins have held the "no-perception trance" to be the condition of emancipation; some schools of the Hīnayāna have held that consciouness is in fact suspended during the "no-perception" and "cessation" trances; such Mahāyāna schools as the Yogācāra have used these trance conditions as an argument to support their theory of an *ālaya*-consciouness, to explain the continuity of an individual consciousness before and after these trances; others, such as the Mādhyamikas, have opined that a very subtle form of mental consciousness remains active during these trances; and so on. However one explains the psycho-physical workings of the "no-perception" and "cessation" trances, though, at the point of the absorptions called "the mundane summit," the mundane path of purifying the passions is completed, and the arisen passions which can be removed by a mundane path are completely effaced. Their seeds, however, are not effaced and, for that matter, not even all of the arisen attachments, for, as explained earlier, there is no higher point from which it is possible to establish control over the attachments belonging to the "summit." Hence, the residuum of arisen attachment which cannot be removed remains as a seed or root from which the lower attachments may again ripen. Therefore, it is said in the *First Bhavanākrama* (T.T., Vol. 108, p. 26 [fol. 34b]): "Even though one has developed trance through meditation, this does not destroy the perception of a self. The passions will ripen again for him, for it is like the trance cultivated by Rāmaputra."

Almost everything discussed up to this point does not belong specifically to Buddhist meditation, for the attainment of mental stabilization, higher vision, the union of stabilization and higher vision, the mundane path of the four trances and the four formless absorptions, the five kinds of paranormal cognition, and so on are attainments shared by non-Buddhist systems of yoga. Therefore, in the following discussion, we shall try to set forth briefly the specifically Buddhist paths of meditation not shared by the non-Buddhists.

At the beginning of the previous brief discussion of the mundane path, it was said that the attainment of stabilization is the threshold of the first trance. To speak more precisely, it is the preparation *(sāmantaka)* for the first trance, for each of the four trances and the four formless absorptions has its own particular preparations. This preparation for the first trance, however, is so distinctive that it has been given a special name, "the potential" *(anāgamya)*, for unlike the other preparations it is uncommitted *per se*; like a fork in the road, it can lead in one direction or in another, and it is the necessary point of departure for either direction.

With the attainment of the first trance preparation, "the potential," the yogin may develop first the mundane path and subsequently the transmundane, or he may straightaway begin the development of the transmundane path. It is taught that the Hīnayāna followers of sharp intelligence do generally uproot the passions directly by recourse to the transmundane path alone without prior development of the mundane. Likewise, the followers of the Mahāyāna may elect either course of development, although the purposes for cultivating the mundane path are quite different for Hīnayāna and Mahāyāna. Moreover, the reason why "the potential" is the necessary point of departure for either path is that the development of either path depends upon higher vision, and higher vision is only possible through recourse to some mentality belonging to one of the four trances or the four formless absorptions. Given a choice, the fourth trance mentality would be the most serviceable, because it is free of certain undesirable gross qualities of the first three trance mentalities, and it is not so attenuated as the mentalities belonging to the four formless absorptions. The minimal requirement for the practice of higher vision is the attainment of at least the outer limit of the first trance mentality, that is, the full attainment of mental stabilization coupled with enough attainment of the power of higher vision to be capable of developing the specific preparations for either the mundane or the transmundane path. This is the general preparation called "the potential."

The development of the transmundane path, then, is by means of a higher vision which has as its object some kind of no-self *(nairātmya)*. *Nairātmya* theory, whether in its simplest form of the no-self of the individual or in its more developed form of the two *nairātmya*s, i.e., both the no-self of the individual and the no-self of all existents, is a distinctively Buddhist viewpoint which is not shared by non-Buddhists. According to this viewpoint, self is neither a *bona fide* phenomenon nor any other kind of actual or real, and it is just this false apprehension of a self which is the ultimate basis or ground on which the passions depend. Consequently, the specifically Buddhist paths for elimination of the passions are by way of removing this final ground of apprehension of a self through the direct perception of things as they in fact are, i.e., devoid of selfhood. The production of this kind of direct perception is the immediate aim of Buddhist yoga.

In preparation for the transmundane path, the yogin reviews the truths, the four truths *(catvāryārya-satyāni)* or the two truths *(satya dvaya)*, and in the presence of mental stabilization upon a meditative object begins to analyze the object from the point of view of the truths. The objective of this analysis is a definitive ascertainment of the reality limit of the meditative object. The results of this kind of analytical search for the reality limit of the meditative object in the presence of mental stabilization is a progressive series of penetrations which begin to approach more and more a true perception of the reality of the meditative object. These steps of penetration, which are preparatory to direct perception of the ultimate reality of the object, are known traditionally as "the approximations of the definitive separation" *(nirvedhabhāgīya)*, because they approximate more and more closely separation from the passions and nescience, which are eliminated by seeing the truth. They are schematized as fourfold, beginning with the approximation called "heat" *(ūṣman)* and ending with the approximation called "highest worldly qualities" *(lāukikāgrya-dharma)*. Immediately following the penetration called "highest worldy qualities," there ensues an ascertainment by direct perception *(pratyākṣa)* of the highest reality limit attainable upon a given path, and this moment marks the beginning of the kind of path which we are rendering as the transmundane. For the Hīnayāna, this is a direct, unperverted perception of the four truths; for the Mahāyāna, this is a direct, unperverted perception of emptiness (śūnyatā). Although this perception arises from the course of analytic thinking, it is itself devoid of all discursiveness or reflection, like all other kinds of direct perception.

For Buddhism this attainment of a direct, unperverted perception of the highest truth is the moment dividing the Āryan from the ordinary individual, and subsequently there is nothing further to see by way of seeing the truth. Nonetheless, the final goal of the path is far from attained at this point, for, although with the attainment of the power of direct, unperverted perception of the truth, certain kinds of passions and nescience are easily eliminated, there is still a host of deeply ingrained, inveterate, and difficult-to-erase passions still to be uprooted. The uprooting of these is effected, subsequently, by degrees, beginning with the gross and ending with the fine, through a constant application and recourse to this meditation which directly perceives the truth. When even the smallest of these passions has been uprooted along with its seeds, the final goal of the path is obtained, the condition of emancipation *(vimokṣa)* or freedom from the miseries of the round of existences (saṃsāra), the perfect purification of Arhantship.

The path as we have briefly outlined it is frequently subdivided into five parts or subpaths, the path of accumulation *(saṃbhāra-mārga)*, the path of reaching *(prayoga-mārga)*, the path of vision *(darśana-mārga)*, the path of cultivation *(bhāvanā-mārga)*, and the path of no further training *(asāikṣa-mārga)*. The first two subdivisions, the paths of accumulation and of reaching, belong to the ordinary individuality *(pṛithagjana)*, whereas the last three subdivisions are those of the Āryan individuality. The first moment of the path of vision is, in the Buddhist sense, the point dividing these two kinds of individuality, since the first two paths are stages of practice by means of adhesion through faith whereas the practice of the remaining stages is by means of one's own firsthand perception of the real.

The path of accumulation commences with a devoted attention to the Buddhist teaching and climaxes with the full attainment of mental stabilization. When mental stabilization has been obtained, the yogin commences the practice of the path of reaching, which is primarily the development of higher vision having the truths as its object. The path of reaching is subdivided into four yogic levels which are coextensive with the four "approximations of real separation" already mentioned. At the climax of the highest approximation, called "highest worldly qualities," there ensues the first moment of a direct, unperverted perception of the truths, and this marks the first moment of the path of vision. With the attainment of the path of vision, there begins the actual uprooting of the passions and nesciences, commencing with the most gross and easiest to eliminate. These uprootings are called "riddances by means of seeing" or "seeing riddances," and they are schematized as eightfold, or two seeing riddances for each of the four truths. These two seeing riddances for each of the four truths derive from whether they belong to the mentality of the realm of desire or the mentalities of the four trances and the four formless absorptions. With the extirpation of these eight, there commences the difficult training to remove the subtler and more difficult-to-eradicate passions and nesciences belonging to the mentalities of the desire realm and the realms of the trances and absorptions. This training constitutes the practice of the path of cultivation, and the passions and nesciences eliminated here are called "riddances by cultivation" or "cultivation riddances." These cultivation riddances are schematized as ninefold, from the nine divisions of the foregoing realms, i.e., the mentality of the desire realm, the mentalities of the four trances, and the mentalities of the four formless absorptions. These again are further schematized as eighty-one-fold, i.e., great-great, middle-great, small-great, great-middling, middle-middling, small-middling, great-small, middle-small, small-small, belonging to each of the nine subdivisions of the three realms. With the eradication of the smallest of the small belonging to the "world summit," the path of cultivation is completed, and with the final completion of all the seeing riddances and cultivation riddances, there is obtained the final level and fruition of the path, the path of no further training.

What has been sketched quite briefly is the specifically Buddhist path of purifying the passions by recourse to meditation on *nairātmya*, and is principally delineated negatively by way of the manifold of cessation of the passions and of nescience which is achieved by the cultivation of the path. This manifold of cessation achieved by recourse to meditation on *nairātmya* is shared by both the Hīnayāna and the Mahāyāna. The specifically Mahāyāna path, however, in addition to removing the passion obscurations which are the main obstacles to personal deliverance from the ills of the world, aims also and primarily at the full removal of the knowledge obscurations, which are the chief obstacles to the perfect enlightenment of the Buddha himself, who in addition to accomplishing the path of purification resulting in his own deliverance has acquired a host of noble qualities of great benefit to others as well. Thus, since the goal of the Mahāyāna path is considerably more comprehensive than that of the Hīnayāna, its path is considerably more comprehensive as well, for inasmuch as perfect enlightenment is possessed of these many qualities which benefit others, the path bringing about perfect enlightenment needs also to cultivate the methods of producing these qualities.

Consequently, to bring about the kind of mentality capable of striving for the obtainment of full perfect enlightenment for the sake of others, i.e., the mind to enlightenment or *bodhicitta*, the Mahāyāna path takes as its basis the development of great love and compassion, or the wish to see all living creatures possessed of happiness and free from ills. This attitude of great love and compassion is cultivated at the very start by a variety of methods so that the activity on the path may be properly and efficaciously motivated and thus not fall short of the final goal.

The bare schematization of the Mahāyāna path is like the system of five paths already discussed: development of mental stabilization on the path of accumulation, the steps of higher vision on the path of reaching, the eight seeing riddances on the path of vision, the nine and eighty-one-fold cultivation riddances on the path of cultivation, and so on. However, the actual course of development of the Mahāyāna path cannot easily be generalized in some areas because they have been explained with important variations by the Mahāyāna systems, i.e., the Yogācāra and the two varieties of Mādhyamika, the Svātantrika and the Prāsaṅgika, and each has provided its own specific variation of the details of the Mahāyāna path.

The Yogācāra, for example, distinguishes between the kind of understanding which is produced on the Hīnayāna and the Mahāyāna paths of vision, and holds that the Hīnayāna achieves a direct understanding of the no-self of individuals *(pudgala-nairātmya)*, whereas the Mahāyāna achieves an understanding of the no-self of all existents *(dharma-nairātmya)* as well, *dharma-nairātmya* signifying nonduality for the Yogācāra. The Yogācāra Svātantrika Mādhyamika also makes a distinction between the objects of understanding developed by the paths and holds that one kind of Hīnayāna path, called the Śravaka-vehicle, obtains understanding of *pudgala-nairātyma*; that another kind of Hīnayāna path, called the Pratyekabuddha-vehicle, also reaches an understanding of nonduality like the Yogācāra's idea of śūnyatā; and that the Mahāyāna path alone reaches the full understanding of emptiness (śūnyatā = the two *nairātymas*). According to the Yogācāra Svātantrika Mādhyamika, it is on the basis of a different understanding of no-self that the differences between the paths depend. The Prāsaṅgika Mādhyamika, on the other hand, holds that there is no difference in the understanding of no-self achieved by the Hīnayāna and Mahāyāna paths, and that what differentiates them is the kind of method *(upāya)* which each cultivates, the Hīnayāna lacking mainly the great compassion which is the root of the Mahāyāna. Similarly, there are differences among the Mahāyāna systems in their manner of distributing among the knowledge and passion obscurations the passions and nesciences which constitute the meditation and cultivation riddances, as all nesciences are not reckoned as knowledge obscurations and are frequently put on the side of passion obscurations. Knowledge obscurations denote primarily habit formations which are the depositions of past passions and nesciences and constitute what is sometimes called the "transcendental illusion."

Having indicated roughly that some areas such as these cannot be generalized, it is possible to proceed to the salient features of the Mahāyāna path which are shared by all Mahāyāna systems and by virtue of which they are Mahāyāna.

In addition to the development of the great love and compassion and the mind to enlightenment *(bodhicitta)* which motivate the development of the paths of accumulation and of reaching, at the time of reaching the path of vision the Mahāyāna path joins the cultivation of the full mastery of the perfections *(pāramitā)* to the process of obliteration of the passions. Along with accomplishing the manifold of cessation resulting in one's own individual emancipation, it thereby produces ten levels *(daśa-bhūmi)* approaching progressively closer and closer to full perfect enlightenment.

From the beginning of the first moment of the Mahāyāna's path of vision, the yogin's activity is predicated on two kinds of gnostic knowledge, i.e., at the time of meditation on śūnyatā *(samāhita-jñāna)* and at the time of subsequent understanding *(pṛṣṭha-labdhajñāna)*. At the time of meditation on śūnyatā, he perceives things directly as they are. At the time of subsequent understanding, he sees all things as resembling an illusion of magic, for upon his emerging from such meditation, the "transcendental illusion" again arises even though he understands it to be just like a magical illusion.

On the bases of these two kinds of gnostic understanding, he cultivates the perfections (pāramitā). These perfections are the six: the perfection of giving, of a lawful conduct, of patience, of manly effort, of meditation, and of wisdom. Of these six, the perfection of wisdom alone is on the side of wisdom and the accumulation of gnoses, and the other five are on the side of method and the accumulation of merit. For at the time of full perfect enlightenment, the accumulation of gnoses is the cause of the noncorporeal body (dharmakāya) of the Buddha, whereas the accumulation of merit is the cause of the Buddha's corporeal bodies (saṃbhogakāya and nirmāṇakāya). The actual method of cultivating the perfections is by way of subdistribution, for each perfection entails the others, and there are six hexads, making thirty-six: a giving of giving, a lawful conduct in giving, a patience in giving, an effort in giving, a meditation during giving, a wisdom in giving, a giving of lawful conduct, and so on, up to a wisdom of wisdom. To these six are added another four: the perfections of method, of vowing, of power, and of gnoses, although these do not participate in the method of acquiring the six perfections by means of mastering them one by one through their subdistributions. The cultivation and full attainment of these ten perfections is coextensive with the Mahāyāna paths of vision and of cultivation. On the path of vision the perfection of giving is attained, and this, along with the seeing riddances, constitutes the first of the ten levels *(daśa-bhūmi)*. The remaining nine levels are the stages of the Mahāyāna path of cultivation, and on each of these, one by one respectively, the remaining nine perfections are cultivated and achieved.

During the progress of the ten levels, the yogin has been alternating between two kinds of gnosis, at the time of meditation and subsequent understanding. At the climax of the tenth level, there arises a particular concentration called "the concentration like adamant" *(vajropamasamādhi)*, at the termination of which these two kinds of gnoses *(samāhita* and *pṛṣṭha-labdhajñāna)* arise simultaneously, and there likewise arises the aggregation of physical and mental qualities which constitute full perfect enlightenment or Buddhahood.

The Mahāyāna path as we have discussed it is that taught in the Mahāyāna sūtras, and it is often called "the vehicle of the perfections" *(pāramitāyāna)*. There is yet another kind of Mahāyāna path system, "the adamant vehicle" (Vajrayāna), or the path practice taught in the tantras. According to the tantras themselves, this is a more efficacious system of practice of the Mahāyāna path, because through it Buddhahood can be obtained in a single lifetime, whereas the time required for the development of the *pāramitāyāna* is usually said to be three unmeasured eons or *kalpas*. The differences between the *pāramitāyāna* and the Vajrayāna is mainly in the domain of the method of practice, and both require the development of great love and compassion and the mind to enlightenment, an understanding of śūnyatā, the cultivation of both wisdom (prajñā) and method *(upāya)*, and the practice of the six pāramitās, although the Vajrayāna method of practicing the perfections is not by the *pāramitāyāna* method of subdistribution as we have briefly described it. Likewise, the tantric method of the developing stages *(utpannakrama)* and the perfecting stages *(saṃpannakrama)* are specifically tantric applications of mental stabilization and higher vision. These subjects require a much deeper discussion than can be given here in a general overview of Buddhist meditative practice.

## NOTE

1. The subject of meditation is treated at great length in various Indian Buddhist sūtras and śastras, most notably, the *Saṃdhinirmocara-sūtra*, the *Sūtrālaṁkāra* and *Abhisamayālaṁkāra* of Maitreyanātha, the *Yogacaryābhūmi*, *Abhidharmasamuccaya*, etc., of Asanga, the Three *Bhavanākramas* of Kamalaśīla, and the *Abhidharmakośa* of Vasubandhu, etc. The salient points of our discussion are to be found in these texts. Among Tibetan texts on the subject, *Lam rim chen mo* of Tsong kha pa is by far the most exhaustive. Tsong kha pa's *Lam rim* is in turn a commentary on the *Bodhimārga pradīpa* of Dipamkāraśrījñāna, who is famous in Tibet under the name of Atīśa. In the *Bodhimārga pradīpa*, all the teachings of Buddhism are brought together and presented from the point of view of the objectives of their practices, which Atīśa sees as happiness in this and in future life, final deliverance from the round of transmigrations (saṃsāra), and the attainment of full perfect enlightenment, respectively.

In our paper the discussion of *śamatha* and *vipaśyanā* is to be found mainly in the *Bhavanākramas* of Kamalaśīla. The discussion of the four dhyanas follows chapter VIII of the *Abhidharmakośa* of Vasubandhu. Discussion of the preparation *(samāntaka)* is treated in chapter VIII of the *Abhidharmakośa* and the *Śravakabhūmi* of Asanga. Also, discussion of the transmundane path follows the *Śravakabhūmi* and chapter VI of the *Abhidharmakośa.* The four steps of penetration belonging to the path of reaching, as well as the fivefold path system, are treated at length in chapter VI of the *Abhidharmakośa* and in chapter I of Maitreyanatha's *Abhisamayālaṃkāra.* Schematization of the "riddances" achieved on the paths of seeing and of cultivation are in chapter V of the *Abhidharmakośa* and chapter I of the *Abhisamayālaṃkāra.* Principal discussions of the Mahāyāna path, the six perfections, the ten stages, and so on, are in the *Bodhisattvabhūmi* of Asanga and in the *Abhisamayālaṃkāra.* The general overview of the Hīnayāna and the Mahāyāna, including the Vajrayāna, is that of the *Bodhimārga pradīpa* of Atīśa, and its Tibetan commentaries, Tsong kha pa's *Lam rim chen mo* and others.

# "What Remains" in Śūnyatā: A Yogācāra Interpretation of Emptiness

*Gadjin M. Nagao*

Meditation has occupied a position of cardinal importance in Buddhism throughout its history. From the very beginning, it has been generally accepted that the higher reach of wisdom (prajñā) is attained either through or accompanied by meditation (dhyāna, samādhi, and so on). Examples of this idea can be seen in various formulae such as "the pairing of quietude and insight" *(śamatha-vipaśyanā-yuganaddha)*, and in the last two of the "three disciplines" *(śīla-samādhi-paññā)*, the "five faculties" *(śraddhā-vīrya-smṛti-samādhi-prajñā)*, and the "six perfections" *(dāna-śīla-kṣānti-vīrya-dhyāna-prajñā)*.

Various things were adopted as objects of meditation, such as "impurity," "respiration," the "fourfold truth," and the "three dharma-marks," but later on, in Mahāyāna Buddhism, śūnyatā, or "emptiness," also came to be recognized as an object of this sort. The "three doors to enlightenment" *(trivimokṣamukha)*, which are also called the "three concentrations" *(trisamādhi)*, and which comprehend "the empty," "the signless," and "the wishless" as its members, were widely recommended as objects of practice. Among these three, emptiness may be regarded as the most fundamental, embodying the other two. In this way, although "emptiness" is usually regarded as "nonexistence," it is not merely an ontological or metaphysical concept, but also a decidedly practical one. "Emptiness has far-reading consequences for the religious life," as Richard Robinson has said.[1]

It was Nāgārjuna who established the concept of "emptiness" with a highly philosophical shading, but to him, too, the concept seems to have been significant not only in a philosophical and logical context but also in a religio-practical sense. The Yogācāras, who, as the name suggests, were greatly concerned with yoga-praxis, inherited the Nāgārjunian notion of "emptiness," and, when they elucidated features of yoga-praxis such as the six pāramitās, the ten *bhūmis*, and so on, "emptiness" seems to have been the basis of their theories. The Yogācāra treatises enumerate "ten kinds of mental distractions" *(vikṣepavikalpa)* as obstacles to right meditation; however, many passages of the *Prajñāpāramitā-sūtra* are introduced which act as antidotes to these obstacles and which also convey the full meaning of śūnyatā.[2] Also, the "sixteen kinds of emptiness," which were originally expounded in the *Prajñāpāramitā-sūtras*, are important in the Yogācāra school, where the idea is elaborately expatiated.[3] In their interpretation of "emptiness," however, there are many features peculiar to their own school.

"Emptiness" was not the monopoly of Mahāyāna, for it appears in earlier Buddhism, too; it is not difficult to find the word "empty" in the Nikāyas and Āgamas. Among the Āgamas and Nikāyas, the *Cūḷasuññata-sutta* ("Lesser Discourse on Emptiness")[4] invites our special attention.

In this sutta, the Lord Bhagavān expounds for Ānanda the meditation on emptiness, saying: "I . . . through abiding in [the concept of] emptiness, am now abiding in the fulness thereof," and he goes on to say that, when the monks are gathered in a hall in which there is no elephant, no cow, and so on, the hall "is empty of elephants, cows, etc.," and yet, "there is only this that is not empty, that is to say the one thing [which is not empty but] grounded on the Order of monks." Likewise, when a monk practices meditation in a forest, he perceives no village, no villager, and attends only to one thing that is not empty and grounded in the perception of the forest. His mind being pleased with and freed in the quietness of the forest, he comprehends thus: "The disturbances that might arise from the perception of a village do not exist here . . . " and yet, "there is only this degree of disturbance, that is to say, one thing grounded in the perception of a forest." That is, by practicing "emptiness," he acquires freedom from the disturbances *(daratha)* of villages and villagers, but the loneliness of the forest itself becomes to him a new disturbance, which should be negated through further meditation. By recourse to such meditation and negation, he travels through a number of stages, including the highest stage of trance in the "formless world," to reach, finally, "the concentration of mind that is signless" *(animittaṃ cetosamādhiṃ)*. In this final stage, he is freed from every canker of "outflowing impurities" *(āsava)* and obtains Arhatship; and yet there remains the disturbance *(daratha)* of "the six sensory fields that, conditioned by life, are grounded in this body itself."[5] Thus, his corporeal being, which even the Arhat can never nullify, is his ultimate disturbance. At every stage of the progress just described, the following statement is added:

> It is perceived that when something does not exist there, the latter [the place] is empty with regard to the former. Further it is comprehended that something that remains there does exist as a real existent.[6]

The sutta repeats this sentence eight times in all. It states that "emptiness" is nonbeing on one hand but that there is, on the other, something remaining therein which, being reality, cannot be negated. Emptiness includes both being and nonbeing, both negation and affirmation. This is the true definition of emptiness, as the sutta goes on to say:

> Thus, Ānanda, this comes to be for him a true, not mistaken, utterly purified and incomparably sublime realization of [the concept of] emptiness.[7]

The *Cūḷasuññata-sutta* does not seem to have attracted the attention of the Mādhyamikas, but it is given a special significance in the treatises of the Yogācāra school.

First, the *Madhyānta-vibhāga*[8] expounds the relationship between the "unreal notion" *(abhūtaparikalpa)* and "emptiness" (śūnyatā) in verse I.1. The actualities of daily life are here summed up as "unreal notions," which are a discrimination between, and attachment to, two things—the subject grasping and the object grasped *(grāhaka, grāhya)*. This twoness, though indispensable for discrimination or conceptualization, does not have any reality at all; here, emptiness is found to belong to the "unreal notion" or "imagination." (The adjective "unreal" is used to qualify the notions or imagination which singles out as existents things that are "nonreals," i.e., "empty.") At the same time, however, this "unreal imagination," in spite of emptiness, is constantly operative. Hence, "unreal imagination" again arises in "emptiness."[9]

This rather tortuous argument is repeated in the next verse, I.2, from a slightly different perspective:

> All entities, therefore, are neither exclusively empty nor exclusively nonempty. This is so because of the existence [of the "unreal imagination"], because of the nonexistence [of the duality of the subject and object], and again because of the existence [of the emptiness of the "unreal imagination"], as well as the existence [of the "unreal imagination" as the *locus* of emptiness]. This whole schema is named the Middle Path.[10]

When Vasubandhu comments on verse I.1, he states:

> Thus [in this verse] the characteristic of emptiness has been shown in an unperverted way as stated: "It is perceived as it really is that, when anything does not exist in something, the latter is empty with regard to the former; and further it is understood as it really is that, when, in this place, something remains, it exists here as a real existent."[11]

The words "as stated" suggest that the passage enclosed in quotation marks is a quotation from some scriptural authority; and, if this is the case, the quotation has to be nothing other than the idea of the *Cūḷasuññata-sutta*, the similarity between the sutta and this passage being quite clear.[12] Vasubandhu also observes that, in accordance with this sutta passage, emptiness can be "shown without perversion." And the interpretation of emptiness by the Yogācāras seems actually to be in basic agreement with the point of view of this sutta.[13]

The expression, "something remains" *(avaśiṣṭa)*, however, is enigmatic indeed, for śūnyatá is generally accepted as nonbeing, negative in character, while "something remains" positively asserts the existence of something. Perhaps one should understand this as an ultimate reality which is never denied, not even at the extremity of radical negation; it is, for instance, similar to the situation in which one cannot negate the fact that he is negating. It is affirmation found in the midst of negation, and it is true existence because it is found in negation.

*Madhyānta* I.13, presumably in keeping with the idea stated earlier, expounds a definition of śūnyatā that says:

> Truly, the characteristic of emptiness is the nonexistence of the duality [of subject and object], and the existence of [that] nonexistence.[14]

Emptiness, thus, comprehends not only the "nonexistence" but also the "existence of nonexistence," which turns out to be a special feature of the Yogācāra interpretation. The idea of adding the "existence of nonexistence" was, however, severely attacked by the later Mādhyamikas;[15] according to them, the true meaning of śūnyatā is "nonexistence," i.e., "nonexistence" through and through; to add the "existence of nonexistence" is not only superfluous but also absurd because of the resulting internal contradiction.

In later Chinese Buddhism, however, one encounters the saying: "Truly empty, [hence] unfathomable existence," which is to be understood as the identity of nonbeing and being, negation and affirmation, or as the recovery of existence from nonexistence. Actually, in the *Prajñāpāramitā-*

*sūtra*, too, one reads: "Form is emptiness, the very emptiness is form."[16] The passage "the very emptiness is form" is not redundant and superfluous, nor a repetition of the preceding passage, for it opens up a new horizon of true existence in the wake of negativism of "form is emptiness." Nāgārjuna, too, is said to have established the true significance of worldly phenomena in his *Mūla-madhyamakakārikā*, chapter xxiv.[17] Especially in verse eighteen, he equates śūnyatā, originally identical with *pratītyasamutpāda* ("dependent origination"), with yet another notion, viz. that of "*upādāya prajñaptiḥ*" ("designation having recourse to materials"), and finally with the Middle Path. The whole scheme of this verse looks like a prototype of *Madhyānta* I.1–2, given earlier; the notion of *abhūtaparikalpa* in the latter stands for *upādāya prajñaptiḥ*[18] here, in which all human endeavors, including religio-practical ones, are duly affirmed.

The Yogācāras, on the other hand, in their elucidation of the notions of being and nonbeing, often have recourse to the theory of *trisvabhāva* (the three natures: the imputed, the dependent, and the completely perfected). On certain occasions,[19] śūnyatā is analyzed into three: *abhāva-śūnyatā* ("emptiness as nonbeing"), *tathā-bhāva-*(or *tathā-abhāva-*) *śūnyatā* ("as thus-being" or "as not-thus-being"), and *prakṛti-śūnyatā* ("essential emptiness"), which three are then related to the imputed nature *(parikalpita)*, the dependent *(paratantra)*, and the perfected *(pariniṣpanna)*, respectively. Thus, "emptiness" synthesizes all three natures (which together represent all states of entities without exception), especially those of "nonbeing" and "being" in terms of *parikalpita* and *paratantra*, respectively. "Something remains," mentioned earlier, corresponds exactly to this idea of *paratantra* (thus-being but empty, or not-thus-being, hence empty, as seen before), which was equally a target of attack on the part of the Mādhyamikas.[20]

A statement similar to that of the *Cūḷasuññata-sutta* also appears in other Yogācāra treatises. In the *Bodhisattvabhūmi* of the *Yogācārabhūmi*, for example, "emptiness rightly understood" *(sugṛhītā śūnyatā)* is explained.[21] Here, though there is no evidence of citation, there occurs a passage[22] almost identical with the one quoted in the *Madhyānta-vibhāga*—a passage in which it is emphasized that the unperverted, true view of emptiness is taught. The basic idea is further exemplified by the term *rūpa* ("form"): *rūpa*, which is accepted as real in Abhidharma philosophy, is empty, insofar as it is an entity constructed by thought. But there is still something remaining, which, though itself unfathomable, has reality insofar as it provides a *locus (āśraya)* for the designation *prajñapti-vāda)* of *rūpa*. The interpretation here is different from that of the *Madhyānta*, but there seems to be no essential difference between the ideas of these two treatises.

The passage in question appears also in the *Abhidharmasamuccaya* of Asaṅga, which has been preserved entire in Chinese and Tibetan but only in fragments in the original Sanskrit.[23] It is here closer to the version of the *Bodhisattvabhūmi* than to that of the *Madhyānta*, perhaps indicating that the *Abhidharmasamuccaya* is quoting from the *Bodhisattvabhūmi* (?). This similarity is obvious when the Tibetan (as well as Chinese) versions of these treatises are compared.[24] According to the latter interpretation, what is negated is *ātma-ātmīyatva* ("selfhood and possession"), and what remains as real is *anātmakatva* ("selflessness"). Non-self is cognizable within entities such as skandhas, *dhātus*, and *āyatanas*—the categories maintained by Abhidharma philosophy—but therein does exist "nonself." The process of the argument is identical with that of the "nonexistence and existence of nonexistence" in the *Madhyānta*.

A most interesting exposition of śūnyatā, in this connection, is found in the *Hsien-yang-shêng-chiao-lun* (or *Āryadeśanā-vikhyāpana)* of Asaṅga, which survives only in Chinese, not in Sanskrit or Tibetan. At the beginning of chapter 6, "Establishment of Emptiness," there is a verse that runs as follows:

> When [it is realized that] nothing exists here, and yet something of it remains—then the nonduality of emptiness is explained in accordance with twofold reasoning.[25]

In the prose commentary, the "twofold reasoning" *(yukti)* is explained in this way: (1) the two kinds of selfhood, that of person *(pudgala-ātman)* and that of things *(dharma-ātman)*, do not exist, but (2) the two kinds of nonself *(nairātmya)* do exist. Thus, emptiness is explained as neither eternally existing nor eternally nonexisting. The wording of this reasoning is very close to that of the *Abhidharmasamuccaya*, and the process is again completely identical with the idea of "nonexistence and existence of nonexistence" in the *Madhyānta*.

The verse was most probably composed by Asaṅga himself, and its most interesting feature is that, although in this verse "something remaining" appears in a manner very similar to that of the texts just discussed, it is stated almost as if it were a thought originating with Asaṅga himself. But it is already clear that the idea of "something remains" can be traced, through these Yogācāra treatises, back to the *Cūḷasuññata-sutta*. This may indicate that this particular sutta was very familiar to the Yogācāra school.

When Asaṅga wrote a commentary, the *Kārikāsaptati*,[26] to the *Vajracchedikā Prajñāpāramitā*, he employed the same idea of "nonexistence and existence of nonexistence" in several verses.[27] In the *Prajñāpāramitā-sūtras*, contradictory expressions *(vyatyasta-pada)*[28] are very often seen, such as:

> The Buddha's own and special dharmas . . . just as not the Buddha's own and special dharmas have they been taught by the Tathāgata. Therefore they are called "the Buddha's own and special dharmas."[29]

Or:

> That which is true perception, that is indeed no true perception. Therefore the Tathāgata teaches, "true perception, true perception."[30]

In these statements, what is first negated is next affirmed; the word "therefore" is used even to connect the negation with its succeeding affirmation. The principle of "nonexistence and existence of nonexistence" will be found to be a convenient and wholly suitable basis for interpreting these contradictory expressions.

Indeed, in all the Yogācāra treatises mentioned, the idea of "nonexistence" *cum* "existence of nonexistence" is given as the basic principle for the interpretation of emptiness in this school. And it may be said that the addition of "existence of nonexistence," though an object of controversy, has come from "what remains" as stated in the *Cūḷasuññata*. "What remains," of course, conveys the real meaning of śūnyatā in this school and never implies any "realism" whatever, substantialism being rejected by all Mahāyānists.[31]

A different application of the passage containing the expression "something remains" occurs also in the *Ratnagotravibhāga*. The tenets of the *Ratnagotra* are regarded as rather close to those of the Yogācāras;[32] however, to the extent that the *Ratnagotra* is a treatise expounding the theory of *tathāgatagarbha* ("matrix of the tathāgata"), its understanding of the passage concerned seems to be fairly different from that of the Yogācāras. This point shall now be discussed.

The passage under consideration appears in the prose commentary to verses I.154–155 in which "the emptiness of the tathāgatagarbha" is explained.[33] The tathāgatagarbha, which may also be called *tathāgata-dhātu* ("element of the tathāgata"), *buddhatva* ("Buddhahood"), and so on, is perfectly pure in terms of its primary nature; therefore, there is no contamination to be removed from it, nor any purity to be added to it. As stated in the *Śrīmālādevī-sūtra*, the tathāgatagarbha is empty in respect to contaminations, but by no means empty in respect to the virtues of Buddhahood, which are inconceivable, and far beyond the sands of the River Ganges in number. After these statements, the passage that contains "what remains" is introduced,[34] without any evidence as to whether or not it is a citation.

The differences between the *Ratnagotra*, on the one hand, and the *Madhyānta* and other Yogācāra treatises, on the other, with regard to the understanding of this passage, can be summarized in two points.

1. The theory that the tathāgatagarbha is empty as well as nonempty is established on the authority of the *Śrīmālādevī*; but here the items negated are contaminations only, while the tathāgatagarbha itself is never negated. Contaminations or defilements are always accidental or adventitious *(āgantuka-kleśa)*, not essential to the tathāgatagarbha, and therefore to be counteracted by the practice of meditation, and so on. But the essence of the tathāgatagarbha comprises the immeasurable virtues of Buddhahood, and they are by no means empty.

In this case, the subject of "is not" (negation) and the subject of "is" (affirmation) are different from each other, the former being defilement and the latter virtue. In the *Madhyānta*, however, one and the same entity is the subject of both "is not" and "is," both of nonexistence and of existence. Duality of subject and object, which is essential to the existing *abhūtaparikalpa*, is negated, hence śūnyatā; and the emptiness of what is empty is never negated, never nonexistent, and the *abhūtaparikalpa* takes its shape anew within this sphere of śūnyatā, hence "existence of nonexistence." In such a case, one and the same thing possesses a sort of "double structure" of being and nonbeing. This "double structure" will be seen both in *abhūtaparikalpa* and in śūnyatā; in its aspect of "nonbeing," the *abhūtaparikalpa* necessarily turns out to be śūnyatā, while in that of "being," śūnyatā itself naturally becomes *abhūtaparikalpa*.

But such a "double structure" is not conceivable in the case of the tathāgatagarbha; there is no link between the glorious virtues of Buddhahood and mundane defilements. In the *Ratnagotra* and its authority, the *Śrīmālādevī*, the subject of "is not" is defilement, and that of "is" is Buddhahood. Buddhahood, the essence of the tathāgatagarbha, cannot be simultaneously being and nonbeing—it is "being" through and through, purely, eternally, and absolutely.[35]

2. The understanding of "what remains" in the *Ratnagotra* is also quite opposed to that of the Yogācāra treatises. In the context of the *Ratnagotra*, "what remains" necessarily becomes something remaining after every defilement is

destroyed; that is, what remains is the tathāgatagarbha in terms of the Buddha's virtues, which are never empty. This is just the opposite of the *Cūḷasuññata* and the *Madhyānta* and other treatises, because in the *Cūḷasuññata* "what remains" is ultimately the corporeal being, the strongest hindrance for human spiritual endeavors, and in the *Madhyānta* it is "unreal imagination," which likewise represents the world of delusion. Both of these are mundane entities and disturbances *(daratha)*, far removed from the tathāgatagarbha, which is characterized only by the highest qualities. These latter texts seem to suggest that defilement is very difficult, almost impossible, to erase—it remains even after a sort of enlightenment is obtained. In other words, enlightenment is deepened only to reveal that disturbance cannot be banished even at the final stage. In contrast to this, the *Ratnagotra* seems rather optimistic about the possibility of annihilating defilements.

In the *Ratnagotra*, "what remains" is literally understood simply as an arithmetical remainder; one subtracts defilements from the tathāgatagarbha and the remaining difference is Buddhahood. This arithmetical subtraction[36] involves no error at all. But, given this simple subtraction, the fact that after the annihilation of defilements there always remains a new defilement cannot be adequately explained. In such subtraction, one cannot see the dialectical double character that is fundamentally the character of "emptiness," and whose basic meaning is expressed in the concept of "emptiness."

Or, one might put it in this way: the *Ratnagotra*, although it proposes to discuss "the emptiness of the tathāgatagarbha," does not state explicitly that the tathāgatagarbha is empty, but actually emphasizes, instead, its "nonemptiness"; it tells us that defilement is empty, but that the tathāgatagarbha has no negative qualities. When one is left with this understanding, it is natural to apply the model of arithmetical subtraction to the idea of "emptiness," which was, however, originally dialectical.

Thus, one cannot but have doubts concerning the *Rat-*

*nagotra*'s usage of this expression. Since there is no evidence of quotation, does the passage represent an independent idea original to the author of the *Ratnagotra* commentary? If not, and if its source is the sutta, is the passage not being misapplied? What can have been the purpose of the *Ratnagotra* in introducing this passage into its scheme? If the purpose really was to prove "the emptiness of the tathāgatagarbha," should it not have stated that the tathāgatagarbha is "empty," instead of maintaining its "being" throughout?

Generally speaking, "what remains" is encountered by the practitioner when he is awakened; when consciousness is converted *(āśraya-parāvṛtti)* by training and becomes an entirely pure faith, the truth of tathāgatagarbha will be realized as "what remains." In the tathāgatagarbha doctrine, however, it is generally accepted that the tathāgatagarbha has always existed, so that it is actually not "what remains," but rather "what has existed from the beginning." In the śūnyatā doctrine, on the other hand, the situation is quite the opposite: after śūnyatā is realized through *abhūtaparikalpa*, *abhūtaparikalpa* itself is re-realized as having always existed in "emptiness" and as remaining forever, again in "emptiness." Only when such realization and re-realization of disturbance are combined is Buddhahood manifested, only then is the "perfected" *(pariniṣpanna)*, or the "Middle Path," achieved.

With its double character of being and nonbeing, "emptiness" is the principle that underlies those old Mahāyānic sayings: "Defilement is identical with *bodhi*," "Birth and death are equal to nirvāṇa," "Without destroying defilements one enters into the nirvāṇa," and so on. The double structure found in the relationship between *abhūtaparikalpa* and śūnyatā represents the identity or the nonduality of saṃsāra and nirvāṇa. Unless the double structure of the world, which is characterized as "empty," is apprehended, these Mahāyānic sayings remain meaningless paradoxes.

If, in the doctrine of the tathāgatagarbha, these sayings are still held to be true,[37] it must follow that the tathāgatagarbha, which is often regarded as a supreme *Being*, as stated above, is "empty as well as nonempty," and also that "defilement is the tathāgatagarbha, and the tathāgatagarbha is defilement." In fact, while in the *Ratnagotra* the "mind" is discussed, not in its defiled aspect, but only insofar as it is regarded as "essentially pure" *(citta-viśuddhi, citta-prakṛti)*, and so equated with the tathāgatagarbha, in the later *Awakening of Faith* (Chinese version by Paramartha) the tathāgatagarbha is found within the "ordinary human mind," which exactly corresponds to the "unreal imagination" of the *Madhyānta*. This "unreal imagination" also has the character of "essentially transparent lucidity,"[38] as in the *Ratnagotra* and the *Awakening*. But the "unreal imagination" can be pure and lucid only because it is "empty" through its double character of *abhūtaparikalpa* and śūnyatā —a double character which is not conceivable in the case of the tathāgatagarbha.

## NOTES

1. Richard Robinson, *The Buddhist Religion* (California: Dickenson, 1970), p. 53.

2. Sylvain Lévi, ed., *Mahāyānasutrālaṃkāra* (Paris: H. Champion, 1907), p. 76, XI.77; Étienne Lamotte, ed. and trans., *La somme du grand véhicule d'Asaṅga (Mahāyānasaṃgraha)* (Louvain: Bureaux du Muséon, 1938), vol. II, pp. 115–18; Dignāga, *Prajñāpāramitāpiṇḍārthasaṃgraha*, vv. 19–54, in E. Frauwallner, ed., "Dignāga, sein Werk und seine Entwicklung," *Wiener Zeitschrift für die Kunde Süd-und Ostasiens* III (1959):141–43.

3. Gadjin M. Nagao, ed., *Madhyāntavibhāga-bhāṣya* (Tokyo: Suzuki Research Foundation, 1964), pp. 24-26; Frauwallner, "Dignāga," p. 141, vv. 8–18.

4. *Majjhima Nikāya*, sutta no. 121. See Horner, *Middle Length Sayings*, vol. III, pp. 147 ff. The translation of quotations from this sutta as it appears in this essay is mine.

5. . . . *imam eva kāyaṃ paṭicca saḷāyatanikaṃ jīvitapaccayā.*

6. *Iti yaṃ hi kho tattha na hoti, tena taṃ suññaṃ samanupassati; yaṃ pana tattha avasiṭṭhaṃ hoti, taṃ santaṃ idam atthīti pajānāti.*

7. The *Cūḷasuññata sutta* (*Majjhimanikaya*, sutta no. 121) is discussed by Ruegg in connection with the idea of the tathāgatagarbha. See David Seyfort Ruegg, *La théorie du Tathāgatagarbha et du gotra* (Paris: École

française d'extrême-orient, 1969), pp. 319 ff. Some of the texts to be discussed later are also referred to extensively in this study.

8. Other editions of the *Madhyāntavibhāga* besides my own (note 3) are: Susumu Yamaguchi, *Sthiramati: Madhyāntavibhāgaṭīkā* (Nagoya: Librairie Hajinkaku, 1934; reprinted Tokyo, 1966); V. Bhattacharya and G. Tucci, *Madhyāntavibhāgasūtrabhāṣyaṭīkā of Sthiramati*, Part I (London: Luzac, Calcutta Oriental Series No. 24, 1932); and R. C. Pandeya, *Madhyānta-vibhāga-śāstra* (Delhi: Motilal Banarsidass, 1971). English translations have been published by F. T. Stcherbatsky, "*Madhyāntavibhāgasūtra*," Bibliotheca Buddhica XXX (1936); and by D. L. Friedmann, *Sthiramati*, Madhyāntavibhāgaṭīkā, *Analysis of the Middle Path and the Extremes* (Utrecht: 1937).

9. *Madhyāntavibhāga* I.1: *abhūtaparikalpo 'sti, dvayaṃ tatra na vidyate / śūnyatā vidyate tv atra, tasyām api sa vidyate* / cf. Ruegg, *La théorie*, pp. 323 ff.

10. *Madhyāntavibhāga* I.2: *na śūnyaṃ nāpi cāśūnyaṃ tasmāt sarvam vidhīyate / satvād asatvāt satvāc ca, madhyamā pratipac ca sā /*

11. *evaṃ 'yad yatra nāsti tat tena śūnyam iti yathābhūtaṃ samanupaśyati yat punar atrāvaśiṣṭaṃ bhavati tat sad ihāstīti yathābhūtaṃ prajānātī' ty aviparītaṃ śūnyatālakṣaṇam udbhāvitam bhavati.*

12. The translation from the *Madhyāntavibhāga* is mine. Compare the Sanskrit original with the Pāli text.

13. There must have existed a version of the *Cūḷasuññata-sutta* in Sanskrit, of which the author of the *Laṅkāvatāra-sūtra* had knowledge. The *Laṅkāvatāra-sūtra*, edited by B. Nanjio (Kyoto: Otani University Press, 1923), p. 75, expounds *itaretara-śūnyatā* (mutual emptiness) as follows: *itaretara-śūnyatā punar mahāmate katamā, yad uta 'yad yatra nāsti tat tena śūnyaṃ' ity ucyate . . . aśūnyaṃ ca bhikṣubhir iti bhāṣitaṃ mayā, sa [= prāsāda] ca taiḥ [= hastigavaiḍakādi] śūnya ity ucyate . . .* This passage seems to include some quotations from the *Cūḷasuññata-sutta*; at least the sentence enclosed within single quotation marks is the same as the first part of the passage quoted in the *Madhyāntavibhāga*. The *Laṅkāvatāra-sūtra*, which expounds the doctrines of both the Yogācāra and the tathāgatagarbha, declares the śūnyatā taught in the *Cūḷasuññata-sutta* (or the *itaretara-śūnyatā*, as the *Laṅkāvatāra-sūtra* calls it) to be of inferior character, while the Yogācāras evaluate it as an "unperverted" interpretation. Also cf. Ruegg, *La théorie*, pp. 321, 325.

14. *dvayābhāvo hy abhāvasya bhāvaḥ śūnyasya lakṣaṇaṃ.*

15. For instance, Bhāvaviveka's attack is found in his *Madhyama-kahṛdaya*, chapter V, vv. 10–16 (Peking reprint edition, vol. 96, pp. 11). Cf. Susumu Yamaguchi, *Bukkyō ni okeru Mu to U tono Tairon (Controversy between the Theories of Nonbeing and Being in Buddhism)* (Tokyo-Kyoto: Kōbundō-shobō, 1941), pp. 178–210 and Appendix, pp. 6–8.

16. Edward Conze, *Buddhist Wisdom Books* (London: George Allen and Unwin, 1958), p. 81: *rūpaṃ śūnyatā, śūnyataiva rūpaṃ.*

17. In quoting Candrakīrti's *Prasannapadā*, Tsong-kha-pa argues to this effect in his *Lam-rim chen-mo* (Peking reprint edition, vol. 152, no. 6001), p. 133-2. Cf. my Japanese translation, *Chibetto Bukkyō Kenkyū* (Tokyo: Iwanami, 1954), pp. 124 ff.

18. As for the term *upādāya prajñaptiḥ*, see Jacques May, trans., *Candrakīrti, Prasannapadā Madhyamakavṛtti* (Paris: Adrien Maisonneuve, 1959), p. 161, n. 494; pp. 237–38, n. 840; etc.

19. Lévi, *Mahāyānasūtrālaṃkāra* XIV.34; *Madhyāntavibhāga* III.3, III.7, etc.

20. For instance, Candrakīrti criticizes the notion of paratantra in his *Madhyamakāvatāra*, (VI. 72–83), Louis de La Vallée Poussin, ed., (St. Petersbourg: Biblioteca Buddhica IX, 1912), pp. 166–81.

21. U. Wogihara, ed., *Bodhisattvabhūmi* (Tokyo: Seigo Kenkyukai, 1930–1936), pp. 47–48; N. Dutt, ed., *Bodhisattvabhūmi* (Patna: K. P. Jayaswal Institute, Tibetan Sanscrit Works Series vol. VII, 1966), p. 32. Cf. Ruegg, *La théorie*, pp. 322 ff.

22. *yataś ca 'yad yatra na bhavati. tat tena śūnyam iti samanupaśyati. yat punar atrāvaśiṣṭaṃ bhavati. tat sad ihāstīti yathābhūtaṃ prajānāti.' iyam ucyate śūnyatāvakrāntir yathābhūtā aviparītā.* For the Tibetan translation, see note 24.

23. Chinese versions: Taishō no. 1605, vol. 31, p. 675a;[21] no. 1606, vol. 31, p. 720c.[17] Tibetan versions: Peking reprint edition no. 5550, vol. 112, p. 252–3–1; no. 5555, vol. 113, p. 172–1–6. In Sanskrit, V. V. Gokhale, "Fragments from the *Abhidharmasamuccaya* of Asaṃga," *Journal of the Bombay Branch, Royal Asiatic Society*, NS 23 (1957); Pralhad Pradhan, ed., *Abhidharma Samuccaya of Asanga* (Santiniketan: Visva-Bharati, 1950), p. 40. Cf. Ruegg, *La Théorie*, pp. 321 f.

24. As this portion is lacking in the original Sanskrit published by Gokhale, Pradhan tried in his book to fill in the lacunae by his "retranslation." But because of his misunderstanding of the passage, and also his ignorance about the relationship between the texts mentioned earlier, the passage in question appears here with entirely different features and must be revised thoroughly. The Tibetan versions follow:

*(Bodhisattvabhūmi) gang gi phyir "gang la gang med pa de ni des stong par yang dag par mthong la / 'di la lhag ma gang yin pa de ni 'di na yang dag par yod do zhes yang dag pa ji lta ba bzhin du rab tu shes pa" de ni stong pa nyid la yang dag pa ji lta ba bzhin du phyin ci ma log par zhugs pa zhes bya ste /*

*(Abhidharmasamuccaya) "gang la gang med pa de ni des stong par yang dag par rjes su mthong ba ste / 'di la lhag ma gang yin pa de ni 'dir yod pa'o / / zhes yang dag pa ji lta ba bzhin du rab tu shes so" / /*

*'di ni stong pa nyid la 'jug pa yang dag pa ji lta ba ste / phyin ci ma log pa zhes bya'o /*

25. Taishō no. 1602, vol. 31, p. 553b.

26. G. Tucci, *Minor Buddhist Texts*, Serie Orientale Roma IX, Part I (Rome: Istituto Italiano per il Medio ed Estremo Oriente, 1956), pp. 53 ff.

27. E.g., *sarvābhāvād, abhāvasya sadbhāvān* . . . (v. 11). Also see v. 46 and the commentary on v. 15 (Taishō no. 1513, vol. 25, p. 877a).

28. So called in the *Vimalakīrtinirdeśa*; cf. Étienne Lamotte, *L'Enseignement de Vimalakīrti* (Louvain: Bibliothéque du Muséon, vol. 51, 1962), p. 34.

29. See Edward Conze, ed. and trans., *Vajracchedikā Prajñāpāramitā*, Serie Orientale Roma XIII (Rome: Istituto Italiano per il Medio ed Estremo Oriente, 1957), p. 70 (8).

30. *Ibid.*, p. 76 (14a).

31. The passage which includes "what remains" also appears in the *Madhyamakāvatāra* (la Vallée Poussin, p. 139, ad VI.57), but this is introduced by Candrakīrti to demonstrate the position of the rival Vijñāna school. This passage is close to one found in the *Bodhisattvabhūmi*. Jayānanda comments on this passage as follows (Peking reprint edition, vol. 99, p. 147-5): "*yatra* [in something whatsoever] means 'in the paratantra;' *yan nāsti* [what does not exist] means 'the duality of subject and object does not;' *tat* means 'the paratantra;' *tena śūnyam* means 'is *śūnya* with regard to duality;' *avaśiṣṭaṃ bhavati* [what remains] means 'knowledge which is *śūnya* with regard to duality' *(gzung ba dang 'dsin pas stong pa'i shes pa).*" Jayānanda also comments that the passage is used to introduce the testimony of the *Āgamas* (suttas). We can notice in this commentary that the interpretation is fairly different from that of the treatises mentioned above; that the opponent here attacked by Candrakīrti is the later Vijñānavāda (as distinguished from the earlier Yogācāras), probably the sākāra-vāda, which holds a view of "Idealistic Realism," i.e., the Realism of vijñāna (knowing) or of paratantra.

32. For one thing, the authorship is ascribed to Maitreyanātha, the founder of the Yogācāra school, in the Tibetan tradition.

33. E. H. Johnston, ed., *The Ratnagotravibhāga Mahāyānottaratantraśāstra* (Patna: Bihar Research Society, 1950), p. 76. Jikidō Takasaki, *A Study on the* Ratnagotravibhāga, Serie Orientale Roma XXXIII (Rome: Istituto Italiano per il Medio ed Estremo Oriente, 1966), pp. 300–302. Cf. Ruegg, *La Théorie*, pp. 319 ff.

34. . . . *evaṃ 'yad yatra nāsti tat tena śūnyam iti samanupaśyati / yat punar atrāvaśiṣṭaṃ bhavati tat sad ihāstīti yathābhūtam prajānāti' /*

35. The tathāgatagarbha seems to me to occupy a supreme position—a position akin to that of Brahman or Ātman, or other "Absolute Being," in Brahmanical philosophy. If this is the case, it is difficult for the

tathāgatagarbha to include within itself elements of contamination as entities to be negated, or to possess the "double structure" of *abhūtaparikalpa* = śūnyatā.

36. The "*itaretara-śūnyatā*" of the *Laṅkāvatāra-sūtra* (note 13 above) and the idea of "*gzhan-stong*" in the Jo-nang-pa school have been studied minutely by Ruegg, *La Théorie*, pp. 325 ff., 337. Though I am not quite sure of these ideas, what I have tried to suggest with the phrase "arithmetical subtraction" seems to be applicable to these ideas.

37. Johnston, *Ratnagotravibhāga*, p. 35:[3] . . . *paramārthataḥ saṃsāra eva nirvāṇam ity uktam.*

38. *Madhyāntavibhāga* I.22.

# The Meditational Therapy of the *Madhyāntavibhāgabhāṣya*

*Stefan Anacker*

## INTRODUCTION

The *Madhyāntavibhāgabhāṣya*, or "Commentary on the Separation of the Middle from Extremes," is one of the several commentaries Vasubandhu wrote on basic Yogācāra texts ascribed to Maitreyanātha, and one of the most striking works in Mahāyāna literature. The Maitreyanātha verses are often somewhat enigmatic, and it is impossible to determine to what extent Vasubandhu is innovating in his interpretations. Probably actual innovations are circumspectly few. For instance, in the chapters dealing directly with meditational practice, Vasubandhu follows a program outlined already in the *Abhisamayālaṅkāra*, which in turn draws on Buddhist meditational practices already ancient by its time, though its specific arrangement, and inclusions and exclusions, are its own. It is probably proper to say that the Yogācāra masters in general invented no new meditational practices. Yet they may have used ancient techniques for quite new purposes, and may have rejected a number of meditational possibilities in favor of certain select practices. Both are indicative of new directions. The first point is in fact expressed by Vasubandhu himself, when he says, "The śrāvakas and pratyekabuddhas cultivate the applications of mindfulness for a lack of attachment to their own bodies. Bodhisattvas do it neither for lack of attachment, nor for nonlack of attachment, but for a nirvāṇa without abode."[1] Actually, even the objects of meditation have changed. Vasubandhu says, "The śrāvakas' and pratyekabuddhas' object of meditation is the bodies of their own lifestreams; the Bodhisattvas' is the bodies of both their own and others' lifestreams."[2]

For historical precedent, one might also take note of the parallels to Sāṅkhya methodology in the "metaphysics" of chapter 1, with everything totally turned around, from a Sāṅkhya point of view. As in Sāṅkhya, there is a great masculine and feminine principle, but here the feminine is exalted, includes and can remove the grasping masculine; there is a "psychological cosmology," as in Sāṅkhya, but it is used to totally non-Sāṅkhya ends.

Much of the *Madhyāntavibhāgabhāṣya* may also, as Sthiramati claims, be directed at Mādhyamika. The title itself, as well as echoes of Nāgārjuna's *Mūla-Mādhyamika-kārikās*, seems to support this view. Nāgārjuna's "two-truth system" may in fact not make the *existence* of confusion and suffering real enough. This might help explain the particular emphasis Maitreyanātha puts upon the existence of the construction of that which was not.

There are of course infinite ways to deal with a text as rich as the *Madhyāntavibhāgabhāṣya*. As such, I will let it stand by itself, without much regard for the manner in which it was used in the perhaps more academic circles of Sthiramati and his contemporaries. Too much emphasis on the history of the text might only serve to make us jaded. And this would be a pity, since the revelations it gives are intensely startling, both in themselves and in their implications. In fact, they shatter everything most of us call "reality."

## PREVIEW: "THEORY" AND "PRACTICE"

The very name "Yogācāra" indicates a preoccupation with practice. Practice in a Buddhist context means something that is done for the removal of suffering. In this sense, all theory in the *Madhyāntavibhāgabhāṣya* is also practice, inasmuch as it is a series of expedients directed at different kinds of afflictions human beings are prone to fall into. Actually, such a therapeutic aid is the best thing a theory can be. Given Vasubandhu's relegation of all verbal formulations to the constructed nature, no theory can be ultimately true, and all are finally abandoned. It is thus not surprising that some statements in the *Madhyāntavibhāgabhāṣya* are not always consistent with one another, because they are expedients directed at different problems, at different stages of insight.

In addition, specific meditational practices are described, and are meant to accompany, follow, or precede a reading of the text. The fourth chapter of the *Madhyāntavibhāgabhāṣya* is in fact unintelligible, existentially at least, unless the practices described there have been engaged in. This should not be an insurmountable problem nowadays, when many kinds of Buddhist meditational traditions can be learned even in North America. The applications of mindfulness, which stand as the basis of the meditational course in the *Madhyāntavibhāgabhāṣya* (and have been revived and given a central position in recent Burmese practice) are meditations on the flow of one's body, feelings, consciousness-moments, and all mentally cognizables, and can be practiced by anyone who has any proclivities to meditation. Many of the intermediate meditations can be reconstructed from Vasubandhu's own comments. It may be more difficult to recreate the stages of the bodhisattva, but even these become clearer than usual with Vasubandhu's lucid observations.

## CONSTRUCTIONS POINTING TO CONSTRUCTIONS AND TO A WAY FROM THEM

Vasubandhu takes the bodhisattva ideal very seriously. This means that he will do what he can to help sentient beings in their sufferings. Though he has much to say to persons who are already engaged in a Buddhist path, his antidotes are by no means limited to them.

Suppose Vasubandhu meets an "individual" who is filled with all kinds of anxieties. Whatever they are, you can be sure that they are linked with some sort of a fixed self-view. Western psychiatric practice would perhaps look for origins, and would attempt to categorize the "individual's" reactions symptomatically. "You are doing this, therefore you must have such and such type of problem and this is what you should do"—behind all such expressed or unexpressed notions, the roots of the "individual's" sufferings remain unchallenged. The "individual's" basic premise, that he is in fact an individual (clearly of one or another type) set within a universe in some way in opposition to him, is never questioned. But all Vasubandhu would be willing to admit, when dealing with such a person—and even this he would admit only tentatively—is that here is a case of suffering. And for the suffering to be truly alleviated, the entire outlook must be radically changed. Meditation, to be sure, will help, but not at the outset. "Perversities"—meaning such psychological habits which lead inevitably to suffering, must first be shattered, before the meditational course can be embarked upon with any good result.

Among these "perversities," the notion of "self" or "individuality" is the foremost, and *upāyas* against this view occupy Vasubandhu in large parts of chapter 3. (The dogma of nonself, like all other constructions, is shattered in chapter 5). In the theory which Vasubandhu finds therapeutically most provisionally fruitful, what are called "individuals" are streams of momentary "physiological-psychological" events, and nothing is really fixed and static. The anxieties caused by "self-categorization" rest on a colossal distortion, and it is the commonness of such distortions that makes Vasubandhu say, at least temporarily, that there is a force inherent in the world which accounts for them.

But it is not only the notion of an entity, "self," but also the very distinction between the perceiver and what is perceived, which must be smashed to nothing. And so the *Madhyāntavibhāgabhāṣya* begins with the revelation that all these distinctions are constructed, that none of the dualities which they reveal in fact really exist, that these distinctions are the constructions of that which is not *(abhūta-parikalpa)* and are the ultimate ground of all such suffering. *Abhūta-parikalpa* could also mean "construction of the unreal," but these constructed entities have at least the reality of a dream, or of a magical creation, and Vasubhandhu, later in the book, is quite insistent on the point that these constructions, in fact, do exist in that peculiar sense.[3] That is to say, they *need* not exist: it is possible to eradicate the fundamental duality from consciousness entirely, they can vanish utterly, and once they are no longer perceived as existent, it is as if they had never existed. But as long as they seem to exist, a constructing force is obviously at work. This fundamental source of unnecessary suffering is not explained away: it *exists.* To speak conventionally, people do construct and constrict themselves. So, "There *is* the construction of that which was not."

In our present situation, the suffering-inducing nature of constructions should be apparent: in everything from global policy to personal relationships, ours is a society which has forced itself into unusually constricted molds, all due to the purest of mental constructions.

The shattering of all duality between grasped and grasper —the methods towards the direct realization of this end—are no doubt meditational, but for Vasubandhu, a recognition of the basic problem must precede the meditational program proper. And this recognition is in itself a fundamental conceptual sandblasting of the mental consciousness. For what is it: an absence of a duality between grasped and grasper? How many types of cognitions, concerns, and actions become absolutely impossible with such a realization—when there are literally no more boundaries between "self" and "others," when the consciousness-moment *is* everything it "includes," when categories of all kinds lose their meaning, when there is only a wide-open suffusion in Allness?

From here on, it is already impossible to talk validly. A

mental attention towards talk is always suffused with an implicit dichotomy between grasped and grasper.[4] The emptiness of whatever object of consciousness a bodhisattva might resort to is included in Vasubandhu's "emptiness of ultimate truth." And the attainment of an unafflicted nirvāṇa-saṁsāra is the only excuse for resorting to them.

In accordance with usual Yogācāra *upāya*, the manifold separated objects of sense and understanding are designated as "the constructed nature." What lies behind them becomes termed the "relative" or "interdependent nature," and the absence of any distinctions or boundaries, the eradication of constructions, the realization of Emptiness, becomes designated as the "fulfilled nature."

## OBSTRUCTIONS AND MEDITATIONS

In spite of his thoroughgoing *śūnyavāda*, Vasubandhu, unlike Nāgārjuna in his stricter works, is not reluctant to tell us his intentions. The mere removal of sufferings due to constructions may be enough for the anxiety-ridden "individual" who has visited Vasubandhu earlier. But for Vasubandhu himself, this is concomitant with a great transformation, which affects all aspects of life. Vasubandhu wants to see as close an adherence to the bodhisattva ideal as possible. The second chapter of the *Madhyāntavibhāgabhaṣya*, which deals with obstructions to the realization of this ideal, thus naturally follows upon the first, where "mental constructions, fears, inactivity, and doubts have been brought to complete rest."

From a certain point of view, the new chapter may contain more constructed dichotomies than the first. Nonetheless, it is clear that a progression is intended, in fact, the steps from the Path of Seeing to the Path of Cultivation. Now concepts are brought up not because they are believed in, but because they correspond to practices effective in removing obstructions to that which can be known.

In the fulfilled lifeṣtream, there is neither agitation nor complacency. Agitation does not allow for the necessary calm in face of the disagreeable and hostile, and complacency is clearly an obstacle to compassion and energy. The ancient list of "fetters" makes its appearance as obstructions, but with some changes. Significantly, excitedness, lust for sensuous pleasure, desire for experiences in the realm of images, and desire for experiences in the imageless sphere have been dropped, and a much more explicit breakdown of what was earlier simply called "ill will" *(vyāpāda)* is given, in the form of envy, selfish greed, and basic aversion. The additional obstructions enumerated by Maitreyanātha, verses II.4–8, and further elucidated by Vasubandhu is his comments, show by their contrasts many of the characteristics of the ideal desired. But it is significant that Vasubandhu does not delimit a goal with strings of optatives—this would be too much construction, and too much construction of dubious *upāya* value. Rather he concentrates on a delimitation of obstructions, which are all given as *caitta*-like dharmas. In a Mahāyāna lifestream, there is no lack of activity; there is the full taking up of saṁsāra; sense fields are used to an ultimate extent; there is enormous capacity to evolve; there is confidence, satisfaction with very little, lack of concern with any type of gain, a tremendous compassion, and skill in the Mahāyāna *upāyās* and meditations.

But what is the relation between this ideal and the fulfilled nature? The fulfilled nature has been defined only as the absence of the constructed, and here we have a constructed set of transformations being recommended. But this path is presented only in relation to the removal of obstructions to the fulfilled nature: that is, the path is again a construction tentatively acted upon to effect the removal of constructions.

There is a hint of a further reason for the necessity of the cultivation of such attitudes in chapter 3. The beginning of this chapter looks, at first, like a somewhat scholastic tying together of each of the Four Truths with each of the natures. It should be admitted that Vasubandhu is capable of what seem like scholastic digressions even in a work of such basically serious intent as the *Madhyāntavibhāgabhāṣya.* A case in point is the ten types of factors or causes which exist in the processes of saṁsāra.[5] In Vasubandhu's usual elegant fashion, these are connected with the obstructions, the main topic at hand. But it can be claimed that their initial presence is a somewhat unnecessary intrusion, showing Vasubandhu the Abhidharmika, rather than Vasubandhu the Bodhisattva, at work. But to dismiss the correlation of the Truths with the natures in a similar manner is to miss the point, and in fact it occurs in the *Maitreyanātha* verses themselves. Each of the three natures is connected with the Truth of Suffering. Suffering exists in the constructed nature, because of the clinging that comes through adherence to views of "individuals" and "dharmas." Suffering exists in the relative or interdependent nature, because of the basic characteristics of the world itself. But suffering exists also in the fulfilled nature, "because of connection with suffering." This last phrase would seem to indicate a *voluntary* connection with the sufferings of saṁsāra, even after the natures of the constructed and relative have been realized. This would fit with the usual conception of the bodhisattva as one who remains in suffering states for the alleviation of others' sufferings. Then, even though the fulfilled is freed from any of those sufferings which arise unchecked with adherence to the constructed, it is still involved, and voluntarily so, in the suffering "of others." And in such a context, the necessity of renewing the steps of the path becomes evident, the obstructions to the full taking up of saṁsāra might present themselves over and over and over again, whether or not the "practitioner" has "gone through" the entire meditational program.

As a matter of fact, it is one thing to practice, say, the applications of mindfulness with "one's own" body, feelings, consciousness-moments, and cognizables as the meditational object—this is done by any Hinayāna practitioner—but it is quite another thing to apply them in regard to "others'" bodies, *cittas*, and so on. And this is stated by Vasubandhu to be a salient feature of the practice of the bodhisattvas.[6] So meditation cannot for Vasubandhu be something done exclusively or even mainly in isolation: one is to meditate in the Mahāyāna manner in the marketplace, with everything that confronts one seen for what it is. One is suffused with a one-pointedness of consciousness, "outer-directed" as well as "inner-directed," as one is walking down the street. With the absence of any felt distinction between grasped and grasper, an extraordinary openness of consciousness results. One has first the ability to discern dharmas (a colorless term, *dharma-pravicaya*, but what an amazing kind of perception it involves—the seeing of "matter" as swirling atom-flashes, of all round and within as masses of pulsating moment-events), then the boundaries between all these dharmas vanish, and there is complete one-pointedness of all consciousnesses towards everything "external" and "internal" without any of these distinctions or any other existing.

As for any other, a certain technique is needed for this kind of meditation. And so Vasubandhu speaks of other obstructions which relate directly to the meditational process itself. One-pointedness of consciousness is at first most disturbed by slackness and excitedness. Concentration must be maintained but, on the other hand, any agitation or tenseness must be avoided.[7] When the applications of mindfulness, which stand as the basis of all further meditations here, have been practiced, the four right efforts must be pursued for the arising of beneficial mental events and the removal of non-beneficial ones. Then, for complete mastery in meditational concentration, the four bases of psychic power—desire to act, vigor, consciousness, and exploration—are raised in relation to various flaws in meditation.[8]

The factors conducive to penetration may now be attempted.[9] These are a special series of meditations. One begins, in "coming to heat" with meditation, first upon the impermanence of dharmas, then upon the absence, in reality, of a rise and fall in those dharmas, and finally upon the realization that all the Truths are merely constructs. In the next stage, the "Summit," all mental marks vanish. Because the next state is suffused with equanimity, because all anxiety-causing constructions have been shattered, it is called "equanimities." The "highest mundane dharmas" which follow is a condition where all the personality factors of the "practitioner," and everything "around him" have merged into meditational trance, and one contemplates the nonarising of own-natures in any "inner" or "outer" events. At the end of this process, there is no more false discrimination of any type within the meditational trance.[10]

## COMING OUT OF MEDITATION

Subtle agitations may now present themselves again. Their delimitations, and their antidotes, are given by Vasubandhu with medical precision. Not everyone will have all the agitations he enumerates, as many of them depend upon specific attitudes towards the meditational course itself. Thus, an "agitation due to mental marks" rests on a deliberate intention in one's meditation. (Deliberate intentions in meditation are flaws.) Vasubandhu simply enumerates all possibilities. And constructions to shatter subtler constructions of this kind are immediately built, and successively dismantled.[11]

And what mental territory this covers! We are in fact now ready for another sandblasting of the mental consciousness. For, taken out of its former grooves as it was during the preceding meditations, consciousness is now susceptible again to the "great masculine force," that restless troublemaker, the construction of that which was not. All at once, everything climaxes in the Ten Vajra-Feet, those deep and final thunderbolts. It is one of the most dramatic sequences in philosophical writing.

This is not the sort of arrogant "therapy" that dictates what is to be real and what is not. For finally, everything is equally real, or equally unreal. Objects of sense and understanding are like the magical creation of an elephant in an Indian magican's show: it does not exist as it appears, and yet does not *not* exist, because the apparition itself exists. And the "apparition" exists in the same way that everything else exists—there is then no more gliding of *citta* on terms like "being" and "nonbeing."

The "spiritual man's" pride, so often seen contemporaneously, is thrown into the dungheap. No one is better than anyone else, there is no "one," there is no "other."

## CONCLUSION

There is, finally, no "affliction" and "alleviation" which could be set against each other, either. And there is no detriment in what is termed "affliction," nor excellence in what is termed "alleviation." Afflictions are a mental construction. For by its radiant nature, the *dharma-dhātu*, Emptiness, is unafflicted. All that had disturbed it came from the constructions which have now been melted into it again.

---

# A TRANSLATION OF VASUBANDHU'S MADHYĀNTAVIBHĀGABHĀṢYA

(Chapters 2, 4, and Part of 5)

## Chapter 2. The Obstructions

In reference to the obstructions, the author says:

> The pervading and the limited,
> the excessive and the equal,
> abandoning and taking up,
> are called obstructions of the two. (2.1)

In this passage, "the pervading" is (the obstruction) to the lineage of the bodhisattvas, that is, the obstructions consisting simply of afflictions, and the obstructions to what can be known. To the bodhisattva, both are obstructions. The "limited" is the obstruction to the lineage of the śrāvakas, which is affliction only. (The sole goal of the śrāvakas, the followers of the Hīnayāna, is the eradication of their own afflictions.) The "excessive" is the obstruction in those of violent, impassioned deeds. The "equal" is (the obstruction) in those who make everything alike. An obstruction to the taking up and abandoning of saṁsāra is an obstruction to those of the lineage of the bodhisattvas, because of being an obstruction to a nirvāṇa without abode. In this way, the obstructions of those of the lineage of the bodhisattvas, and of those of the lineage of the śrāvakas, and so on, have been made known. Furthermore,

> The character of the obstructions that are simply affliction is ninefold, being the fetters. (2.1b.)

The nine fetters are obstructions. To what are they obstructions?

> To excitement and to equanimity, and to the seeing of reality. (2.2a)

The fetter of complacency is an obstruction to excitement, and the fetter of aversion is an obstruction to equanimity. Because of the latter, one cannot stay calm in face of the disagreeable and hostile. The rest of the fetters are obstructions to the seeing of reality. How does this occur?

> Leading towards the view of self, obstructing insights regarding this and external objects, the extinction of suffering, the Path, the Gems, others' attainments, and being satisfied with little. (2.2–2.3a)

The fetters become specific obstructions. The fetter of conceit becomes an obstacle leading to the view of self. This is because this view has not been cast off through proper action working against the conceit that those things within and without are "mine." The fetter of ignorance is an obstruction of knowledge about "external objects" and the view of self. This is because it is a lack of knowledge concering the appropriating skandhas. The fetter of adherence to theories is an obstruction to the knowledge of the truth of the extinction of suffering. This is because such adherence goes against the possibility of the extinction of suffering, because of the various anxieties caused by such false views, such as the view of self, or views regarding the permanence or impermanence of the elements of personality. The fetter of adherence to mere rules and rituals is an obstruction to the knowledge of the real truth of the Path, because of adherence (to the view) that highest purity lies elsehwere than it really does. The fetter of constant doubt is an obstruction to the knowledge of the Three Gems (Buddha, dharma, and Buddhist community), because it involves a lack of confidence in the qualities of these three. The fetter of envy is an obstruction to satisfaction in others' attainments, because it wishes to see only others' faults. The fetter of selfish greed leads to a lack of knowledge of satisfaction with little, because of one's obsession with possessions.

> Further obstructions stand in the way of welfare, etc., in ten ways. (2.3)

There are further obstructions that stand in the way of welfare, etc., in ten ways. What are these obstructions,

> The lack of means to rouse oneself from
> inactivity,
> the lack of complete use of one's sense fields,
> careless activity,
> the nonproduction (of the beneficial),
> lack of advertedness, lack of mental attention (to what lies around one),
> the unfulfillment of the necessary preparation to live in the Great Vehicle,
> separation from people of one's spiritual lineage and separation from good friends,
> wearying distress and agitation of mind,
> lack of opportunity to practice the Great Vehicle,
> being forced to live with stupid or frustrated people,
> susceptibility to harm, lack of control, and lack of maturation of insight because of the three,
> depression, sloth, and carelessness in one's nature,
> attachment to rigid becoming, and longing for property,
> muddle-headedness,
> lack of trust, lack of confidence, neverending deliberation,
> lack of reverence for the Good Dharma,
> respect for gain,

lack of compassion,
casting away the scripture,
being ill-read in scripture,
and lack of engagement in meditation. (2.4–8)

These are the obstructions (to welfare, etc.). And what is welfare, etc.?

> Welfare, enlightenment, the full taking up (of saṁsāra) insight, lack of confusion, lack of obstructions, ability to evolve, fearlessness, lack of selfishness, and potency. (2.9)

So that one can know how many obstructions can arise to which of these (beneficial results), welfare, etc., he says:

> By threes, the obstructions to what can be known arise for these. (2.10a)

To each of these beneficial (results), three obstructions can arise. To welfare arises the lack of means to rouse oneself from inactivity, lack of complete use of one's sense fields, and careless activity. To enlightenment arise the nonproduction of beneficial *caittas*, lack of mental attention to what lies around one, and the unfulfillment of the necessary preparation. To the full taking up (of saṁsāra), which is the bodhisattva's vow, arise separation from one's spiritual lineage, separation from good friends, and agitation and distress of mind. To insight arise the lack of opportunity to practice the Great Vehicle and being forced to live with either stupid or frustrated people. Here, stupid people are hopeless fools; frustrated people are harmed persons. To lack of confusion arise three: susceptibility to harm through perversities, a lack of control because of the three kinds of obstructions, afflictions, etc., and lack of maturation in insight which matures confidence. As an obstruction to the abandonment of obstructions arise susceptibility to harm, sloth, and carelessness. To fearlessness arise lack of trust, lack of confidence, and neverending deliberation. To lack of selfishness arise lack of reverence for the dharma, respect for riches and gain, and lack of compassion and lack of rejoicing at the joy of others. To potency arise those [obstructions] because of which one does not attain mastery, that is, casting away the scripture, being ill-read in scripture pertaining to dharma, and lack of engagement in meditation.

Ten factors play in saṁsāra, in affliction, and alleviation. There is the factor of one thing's maintaining another's existence, like the four foods maintaining living beings.[12] There is the factor of one thing's sustaining another, in the sense of providing a support, as the inhabited world does for the world of sentient beings. There is the factor of one thing's manifesting another, as the action of looking does the visible. There is the factor of one thing's transforming another, as fire does that which is being cooked. There is the factor of one thing's disjoining another, such is the relation of a cutting instrument to that which is being cut. There is the factor of one thing's evolving another step by step, such as the action of a goldsmith, who works bracelets out of masses of gold. There is the factor of one thing's giving rise to the idea of another, such as the perception of smoke, etc., giving rise to the idea of fire, etc. There is the factor of one thing's causing the idea of another to be formed, as the justification does the thesis [in an inference schema]. There is the factor of one thing's leading to the attainment of the other, as the Path leads to nirvāṇa, etc. [These kinds of factors exist in relation to the Great Vehicle, as follows:] [An obstruction] in [others'] welfare is an obstruction to its arising, because it can cause it to arise. [An obstruction] in enlightenment is an obstruction to its maintenance, because of its freedom from anger. [An obstruction] is the full taking up [of saṁsāra] is an obstruction to its sustenance, because it is the support of the bodhisattva. [An obstruction] in insight is an obstruction to its manifestation, because it can cause it to be illuminated. [An obstruction] to the absence of confusion is an obstruction to its transformation, because of its being transformed by a turning around of confusion. [An obstruction] to the absence of obstructions is an obstruction to its disjunction, because of its being separated from all obstructions. [An obstruction] to ability to evolve is an obstruction to its evolving, because of its having the character of evolving *citta* in enlightenment.

[An obstruction] to fearlessness is an obstruction to the giving rise of the idea [of the Great Vehicle], because this idea does not arise where there is any fear. [An obstruction] to the absence of selfishness is an obstruction to causing the idea to arise in others, because the lack of selfishness in the dharma causes the idea [of the Great Vehicle] to arise in others. [An obstruction] in potency is an obstruction to its attainment, since it has the character of obtaining various powers.

It is through the desire to obtain enlightenment that the roots of the beneficial are at first caused to arise. Then, through the power of the roots of the beneficial, enlightenment can be obtained. Again, the enlightenment-*citta* is the basis for the arising of the roots of the beneficial. The bodhisattva is the support of the enlightenment-*citta*. Again, with the exercise of the power of the roots of the beneficial obtained through an enlightenment-*citta* which has been caused to arise, perversity will be abandoned by the bodhisattva, and a lack of perversity will be caused to arise. Then, freed from perversity in the Path of Seeing, all the obstructions will be gotten rid of in the Path of Cultivation. Again, the three roots of the beneficial will be evolved to complete supreme enlightenment. Then, through the exercise of the power of this transformation, one will not be afriad of the various kinds of teachings in the deep extensive dharma. Thus, by not being alarmed, seeing the qualities in the dharmas of the teachings, one can explain these dharmas in detail to others. Thereafter, this bodhisattva, having thus obtained the exercise of these powers through these various qualities, obtaining supreme enlightenment, obtains also potency over all dharmas.

> Furthermore, there are other obstructions to the allies, the pāramitās, and the stages. (2.10)

First of all, to the allies of enlightenment:

> The unbeneficiality of the meditational object, sloth, two defects in meditational concentration, nonplanting, views, and susceptibility to harm are states of being flawed. (2.11)

In the applications of mindfulness, the nonbeneficiality of the meditational object is an obstruction. Sloth [is an obstruction] to the right exertions. The two defects in meditational concentration, i.e., a lack of completion [of meditation] due to a deficiency in zeal, vigor, *citta*, or deep reflection, and [a lack of completion of meditation] due to a deficiency in the [secondary] motivational dispositions towards efforts in meditation, are [an obstruction] to the bases of psychic power. To the faculties, nonplanting of the factors conducive to deliverance [is an obstruction]. To the powers, weakness of these same faculties due to interference of adverse factors [is an obstruction]. To the members of Enlightenment, the flaw of views [is an obstruction], due to their working against the Path of Seeing. To the members of the Path, the flaw of susceptibility to harm [is an obstruction], because of its working against the Path of Cultivation.

To the pāramitās, there are these obstructions:

> Obstructions to having wealth, to happy states, to not forsaking sentient beings, to casting off and growth of faults and virtues, to descent, to liberating, to inexhaustibility, to continuance in welfare, to making certain, to enjoyment and maturation of Dharma. (2.12–13)

Here it is explained which result of which among the ten pāramitās is [liable to damage] by which obstructions. In this connection, an obstruction to having some form of wealth is an obstruction to the pāramitā of giving. An obstruction to a happy state is an obstruction for the pāramitā of good conduct towards others. An obstruction to the nonabandoning of sentient beings is [an obstruction] to the pāramitā of tolerance. An obstruction to the casting off of faults and increase of virtues is [an obstruction] to the pāramitā of vigor. An obstruction to descent into what is to be mastered is [an obstruction] to the pāramitā of meditation. An obstruction to the act of liberating oneself and [others] is [an obstruction] to the pāramitā of insight. An obstruction to the inexhaustibility of giving, etc., is [an obstruction] to the pāramitā of skill in means, because of their inexhaustibility through the bodhisattva's resolution. An obstruction to a beneficial uninterrupted continuance in all kinds of rebirths is [an obstruction] to the pāramitā of the vow, because it is through the power of [the bodhisattva's] vow that one takes on rebirths which are favorable to this [continuing in saṁsāra]. An obstruction to making the beneficial unfailing is [an obstruction] to the pāramitā of strength, because it is through the two strengths of thorough knowledge and meditational cultivation that adverse factors are overpowered. An obstruction to enjoyment and maturation of dharma in both oneself and others is [an obstruction] to the pāramitā of knowledge, because of one's not truly understanding the meaning of what one has heard [in the presence of such an obstruction].

An unafflicted lack of knowledge which arises successively in the tenfold *dharma-dhātu* in its all-encompassing, and other, objects, is an obstruction to the stages of Enlightenment. For it is through the first, all-encompassing stage, that one penetrates the all-encompassing stage, that one penetrates the all-encompassing object, by which one understands the sameness of "self" and "others." Through the second stage, [one penetrates] the ultimate object [of the Great Vehicle], by which one decides that one should do practices *[yoga]* for the sake of a complete removal [of afflictions] and cleansing of all aspects in a total removal of afflicting characteristics. Through the third stage, [one penetrates] the ultimate object of that which flows from this, by which one is able, after having realized the ultimate nature of what one has heard flowing from the *dharma-dhātu*, to hurl oneself into the Fire Pit which has the extent of the whole Tri-Chiliocosm. Through the fourth stage, [one penetrates] the objects of nongrasping, for here even the craving for dharma is turned back. Through the fifth stage, [one penetrates] the object of a lack of division in the lifestream, with the ten samenesses of *citta* and intention in purification [i.e., with the sameness of *cittas* and intentions in all ten stages]. Through the sixth stage, [one penetrates] the object where there is neither affliction nor alleviation, because of penetration of the realization that there is no dharma which is being afflicted or purified in dependent origination. Through the seventh stage, [one penetrates] the object of that lack of true diversity, which comes from an absence of mental signs, because of the lack of arising of any diversity of mental signs in the dharmas of the sūtras. Through the eighth stage, [one penetrates] the object that there is neither decrease nor increase, because of the nonseeing of decrease and increase of any dharma in affliction and alleviation. There is a fourfold potency: potency in the absence of discrimination, potency in the purification of the [Buddha-] field, potency in knowledge, and potency in action. One penetrates to the state which is a basis for the first and second potencies in the *dharma-dhātu* on the eighth stage and one completely attains the state which is the basis of potency in knowledge on the ninth stage, and the state which is the basis of potency in action on the tenth stage, which is the state of being able to do actions for the sake of sentient beings through various self-transformations.

In brief,

> Those which are called the obstructions of afflictions, and the obstructions to that which can be known, are all obstructions, and freedom is sought through their destruction. (2.17)[13]

## Chapter 4. The Cultivation of the Antidotes, States Therein, and the Attainment of the Fruit

The cultivation of antidotes is the cultivation of the allies of Enlightenment. This is to be discussed just now. First of all,

> The cultivation of the applications of mindfulness (comes about) through susceptibility to harm, through the cause of craving, through the state of being the essential ingredient, and through lack of confusion, in relation to the Fourth Truths. (4.1)

Susceptibility to harm is increased through the body. Because it has the characteristic of conditioned dharmas, susceptibility to harm, one enters into the Truth of Suffering by an examination of it. Susceptibility to harm is the suffering state of conditioned dharmas, through which those who know see that all is possessed of distress because of suffering. The cause of craving is feelings, and one enters into the Truth of the Origination of Suffering by an examination of them. But the attachment to the idea of "self" is only *citta*, and one enters into the Truth of the Cessation of Suffering by an examination of it, because of the disappearance of any fear of the cessation of self (when one has understood that "self" is only *cittas*). Through an examination of cognizables, one enters into the Truth of the Path, through lack of confusion as regards cognizables which serve to afflict and which serve to alleviate. Hence the cultivation of the applications of mindfulness are determined in relation to entry into the Four Truths.

After this, there is the cultivation of the right efforts.

> The adverse factors and antidotes being known in every way, there proceeds a fourfold vigor, for their removal and approach. (4.2)

From the cultivation of the applications of mindfulness, when adverse factors and antidotes have been completely known in all their aspects, a fourfold vigor for the removal of adverse factors, and for the attainment of antidotes, proceeds. For the forsaking of bad and nonbeneficial dharmas which have arisen, and so forth [i.e., for the arising of beneficial dharmas which have not yet arisen, for the nonarising of unbeneficial dharmas which have not yet arisen, and for the maintenance and further development of beneficial dharmas which have arisen].

> Skill in fixity, for the increase of all alms, directed at the abandonment of the five flaws, following on the eight conditioned factors. (4.3)

In this cultivation of vigor for the removal and acquisition of these factors, a skill in fixity of *citta* is the four bases of psychic power, because they are the cause of increase of all psychic aims. "Fixity" is here to be understood as fixity of *citta*, that is, meditational concentration. Thus, the bases of psychic power occur immediately after the right efforts. Furthermore, they constitute skill in abandoning the five flaws. And, as this skill is directed at the abandoning of the five flaws, it is to be understood as following upon the cultivation of those eight conditioned factors [i.e., the applications of mindfulness and the right efforts]. "What are these five flaws?" one may ask.

> Indolence, falsehood in censure [?], slackness, excitedness, impulse and lack of impulse: These are considered to be the five flaws. (4.4)

Here, slackness and excitedness are made into a single flaw. A lack of impulse is a flaw at the time when slackness and excitedness are being put to rest. Impulse is a flaw when they have been put to rest. The eight conditioned factors which are conducive to abandonment are established as relating to the abandonment and removal of these five. The four which are conducive to the abandonment of indolence are desire to act, effort, faith, and confidence.

These are further to be known as being, respectively,

> The support, that which is supported, its mark, and its result. (4.5a)

The desire to act is the support of exertion. Exertion is what is supported by the desire to act. The mark of this support, desire to act, is faith, because of its longing for truth in firm conviction. The result of exertion, which is thus supported, is confidence, because of the acquisition of special meditational concentrations by one who has undertaken vigor. The remaining four conditioned factors—effort, mindfulness, the state of knowing, volition, and equanimity—are antidotes to the four flaws as they are enumerated. Furthermore, this mindfulness, and so on, can be known as being

> A lack of loss in the meditational object, the recognition of slackness and excitedness, impulse in their removal, and continuance in tranquility in a state of rest. (4.5–6a)

Mindfulness is a lack of loss in the meditational object. The state of knowing is a recognition of slackness and excitedness when a loss of mindfulness has occurred. The impulse toward their removal when they have been recognized is a volition, and equanimity of *citta* is continuance in tranquility once slackness and excitedness have been put to rest.

Immediately upon these bases of psychic power arise the five faculties, faith, etc. And how is their determination?

> When the factors conducive to deliverance have been planted, through sovereignty in applying oneself to the desire to act, from nonloss in the meditational object, nongliding, and discernment. (4.6–7a)

Through sovereignty: When the factors conducive to deliverance, the roots of the beneficial, have been planted in a skilled *citta*, the five faculties, faith, etc., are to be known as being sovereign in practice, by being sovereign in nonloss of the meditational object, by being sovereign in the nongliding about [of *citta*], and by being sovereign in discernment, respectively. When these same [faculties] faith, etc., are powerful, they are called "the powers." And their state of having power follows

> from the adverse factors being diminished

when these are not dissipated by the adverse factors, such as lack of faith, etc.

For what reason is there a successive enumeration of faith, etc., in this way?

> Because the latter are the result of the former (4.7)

Having taken hold of faith, one undertakes vigor, the result of this cause. Having undertaken vigor, mindfulness occurs, and through mindfulness's having occurred, *citta* is concentrated. When *citta* is concentrated, one knows it as it is. [These forces] are called the factors conducive to deliverance, when they have been fully planted.

Now are the factors conducive to penetration to be known

as being in the state of the faculties, or in the state of the powers?

> Two each of the factors conducive to penetration are faculties and powers. (4.8a)

Coming to heat and the summit are faculties; the equanimities and highest mundane dharmas are powers.[14]

Immediately after the powers, the limbs of Enlightment occur. And what is their determination? The limbs of enlightenment are different parts of enlightenment on the Path of Seeing. And among these, the limb which is the support for Enlightenment is mindfulness. The limb which is [Enlightenment] by its nature is the discernment of dharmas. The limb of deliverance is vigor. The limb which persuades others is affection. The limb which causes an absence of affliction is threefold, being confidence, meditational concentration, and equanimity. But to what purpose has the limb which causes an absence of affliction been indicated as threefold?

The initial cause for an absence of affliction is confidence, because confidence is an antidote to that affliction caused by susceptibility to harm. The support for absence of affliction is meditational concentration. And by nature, [absence of affliction] is equanimity.

Immediately upon the limbs of Enlightenment [arise] the limbs of the Path. And how is their determination? On the Path of Cultivation, the limb which serves for its accurate determination is right views, by which one determines one's own realization of what follows upon mundane and supermundane visions. The limb which serves for its acquisition by others is right intention and right speech, because, by its development with speech, it can be caused to be acquired by others. The limb for its cultivation by others is threefold: right speech, action, and livelihood. It is through right speech, i.e., certainty of sermons and discourses, that a cultivation of insight arises [in others]. It is through right action [that one is established] in good conduct, because one no longer does what is not to be done. It is through right livelihood [that one is established] in desiring little, because one seeks garments, etc., only to the extent that they fit with dharma. The limbs which are antidotes to adverse factors are again three: right effort, right mindfulness, and right concentration. Of these there is respectively

> The capacity to serve as antidotes to afflictions, secondary afflictions, and adverse factors to power. (4.11)

For adverse factors are of three kinds: afflictions which are to be abandoned through cultivation; secondary afflictions: slackness and excitedness; and adverse factors to power, hindrances to the bringing about of special qualities.[15] Among these, right effort is an antidote to the first, because of the cultivation of the Path [through right effort]. Right recollection [is an antidote] to the second, because of the absence of slackness and excitedness in mindfulness which is well-established in the objects of tranquility, etc. Right concentration [is an antidote] to the third, because of its bringing about the qualities of supernormal faculties by dwelling in meditation. This cultivation of antidotes may be known in brief as being of three kinds, as favorable to lack of perversity when [*citta*] is perverted; favorable to lack of perversity when unperverted, and unfavorable to perversities when unperverted, in the states of pṛthagjanas, learners, and accomplished ones, respectively (ad 4.12).

For the bodhisattvas, on the other hand,

> there is a distinction as regards objects of meditation, mental attention, and acquisition. (4.13a)

The śrāvakas' and pratyekabuddhas' object of meditation is the bodies, etc., of their own lifestream. The Bodhisattvas' is [the bodies, etc.] of both their own and others' lifestreams. The śrāvakas and pratyekabuddhas are mentally attentive to their bodies, etc., in their aspect of noneternality, etc., but bodhisattvas are mentally attentive with the method of non-apprehension [of bodies and dharmas]. The śrāvakas and pratyekabuddhas cultivate the applications of mindfulness, etc., for a lack of attachment to their bodies, etc. Bodhisattvas do it neither for lack of attachment, nor for nonlack of attachment, but for a nirvāṇa which has no abode.

(IV.13b–18: Delimitation of states in the cultivation of antidotes, and fruits corresponding to them, i.e., the initial state, the state of the learner, the state of the accomplished one, the state of entering into the stages of Enlightenment, the state of going forth [into the next stages], the state of prediction to Buddhahood, in the eighth stage, the state of becoming an effective promulgator, in the ninth stage, and the state of becoming consecrated, in the tenth stage.)

## Chapter 5. The Supremacy of the Vehicle

Now the supremacy of the Vehicle is to be discussed. The author introduces the topic thus:

> Its supremacy is considered to lie in its practice, its support, and its full realization. (5.1)

The threefold supremacy in the Great Vehicle, through which it is a Vehicle having no superior, is the supremacy of its practice, the supremacy of its support, and the supremacy of its full realization.

The supremacy of its practice is to be know as lying in the practice of the ten pāramitās. With these pāramitās

> Practice, moreover, is of six kinds. (5.1) The highest, that lying in mental attention, in conformity to Dharma, in avoidance of the extremes, and distinguished and undistinguished practice. (5.2)

These are the six kinds of practices: practice developed to its highest, practice of mental attention, practice in conformity to dharma, practice of the avoidance of extremes, distinguished practice, and undistinguished practice.

> Its highest form is of twelve kinds. (5.2) Practice is thought to take its highest form with magnanimity, continuity, absence of hardship, power, and encompassing quality, success in its commencement, its possession, its steady flow, and its consummation. (5.3)

Practice is thought to take on its highest form when it is characterized by the following twelve features: magnanimity, persistence, sovereignity in effort, inexhaustibility, continuity, lack of hardship, power, an encompassing quality, and success in its commencement, possession, steady flow, and consummation.

The highest form of practice through magnanimity comes through eminence in lack of desire for all those things that constitute "prosperity" in common parlance. The highest form of practice through persistence comes with the ability to cultivate it even for three uncountable aeons. The highest form of practice through sovereignty in effort comes through exertions to bring about the aims of all sentient beings. The highest form of practice through inexhaustibility comes through the endlessness of one's effortless coursing in the pāramitās, which comes about with a transformation one undergoes with the Great Enlightenment. The highest form through continuity comes through fulfillment of the pāramitās of giving, etc., toward all sentient beings without any interrruption, the ability for which comes about by the trust that one and others are really the same. The highest form through absence of hardship comes when the fulfillment of all the pāramitās, giving to others, etc., is accompanied only by great rejoicing. The highest form of practice through power means the fulfillment of the pāramitās of giving, etc., accompanied by meditational concentration on the treasury of the firmament. The highest form of practice through its encompassing quality means that it is encompassed by knowledge free from constructions. The highest form of practice through success in its undertaking depends on equanimity in its beginning stages; the highest form of practice through success in its possession comes with the first stage; and the highest form of practice through success in its steady flow is characterized by its continuing strong in later stages. The highest form of practice through success in its consummation means that it is climaxed by one's becoming a bodhisattva, or one's becoming a Buddha.

> And the ten pāramitās are considered to exist in an ultimate sense because of them. (5.4)

Because these ten kinds of highest forms [of practice] are found within them, they are called "in their highest form," and it is in this sense that they are pāramitās [lit., "gone to the highest"]. The author at this point reminds us of the ten pāramitās:

> Giving, good conduct, forbearance, vigor, meditation, insight, skill in means, the vow, force, and knowledge: these are the ten pāramitās. (5.5)

What is the action of each of these pāramitās separately?

> Favoring, not harming, forgiveness, the increase of merit, ability, descent and delivery, being unfailing, constantly coursing, sovereign skill and maturation. (5.6)

The bodhisattva favors sentient beings through giving. The pāramitā of good conduct means that he does no harm to others. Because of forbearance, he pardons the harm done him by others. He increases his merits through vigor. Through meditation, he plunges down and sets things going with the supernatural faculties, etc. Through insight, he is able to deliver others by giving them the right advice. Through the pāramitā of skill in means, along with the transformation he undergoes with the great enlightenment, he is able to make his giving, etc., unfailing. Through the pāramitā of the vow, because he is able to embrace all occurrences favorable to the pāramitās, he courses constantly in giving, etc., empassioned for the birth of enlightenment in all sentient beings. Through the pāramitā of force, that is, the twin forces of reflection and cultivation, he is able to course constantly in giving, etc., because they do not allow the antidotes to weaken. Through the pāramitā of knowledge, one experiences again the enjoyment of all the dharmas that are sovereign in giving, etc., because one has rid oneself of confusion as regards these much-praised dharmas, and one brings sentient beings to maturity.

(5.7) What is the practice of mental attention? The practice of mental attention is a mental attention with insight consisting of continually listening, reflecting, and meditating on the dharmas of the Great Vehicle which, according to the manner in which they are prescribed, concern giving, etc.

(5.8) By being attentive with the insight that consists of listening, there arises a nurturing of the basic constituents of existence. With that which consists of reflection, one enters into the meaning of what one has heard. By meditation, finally, one attains ultimate success, by completely purifying one's entrance into the bodhisattva stages.

The practice of mental attention is furthermore to be known as being embraced by ten acts of dharma. And what ten acts of dharma are these?

(5.9) The writing up of the Great Vehicle, worship, giving to others, listening to that which is said by others, and to what one says oneself, taking up [the Great Vehicle], teaching it to others, studying the meanings of the texts for oneself, reflecting, and meditating.

In the sūtras, why is the great fruit of these acts of dharma spoken of to a great degree only in the Great Vehicle, but not in the śrāvaka vehicle?

Because of its distinctiveness and inexhaustibility. (5.10a)

What sort of "distinctiveness" is this? And what sort of inexhaustibility?

due to its favoring others, due to its lack of repose. (5.10b)

It has distinctiveness due to its kindness towards others. And its inexhaustibility should be known as due to its never stopping, because it does not rest even in complete nirvāṇa [but rather remains forever in saṁsāra].

(5.11) What is practice in conformity with dharma? It is of two kinds, being the development of lack of agitation, and of lack of perversity.

Lack of agitation comes about through six kinds of absences of agitation, corresponding to the following six kinds of agitation: agitation in the nature of things, agitation towards the "external," agitation towards the "internal," agitation due to signs, agitation due to susceptibility to harm, and agitation due to mental attention.

At the time of one's emergence from meditation, there is agitation due to the nature of things, because of the collection of five consciousnesses. Gliding towards objects of sense is agitation towards the "external," and the relishing of the meditational state, or excitedness and slackness in regard to it, is agitation towards the "internal." Deliberate intention in one's meditation is agitation because of mental signs, because of attachment to mental signs once signs are made again. Mental attention linked to a sense of "I" is agitation due to susceptibility to harm, because it is through the power of susceptibility to harm that the sense of "I" arises. Agitation due to mental attention is a defective state of *citta*, which arises with mental attention to the Lesser Vehicle.

(5.13–14) A lack of perversity toward mental marks is to be known as seeing that in connection [with a so-called object], one thinks "This is its name," because linguistic habits have not been severed: [such a thought] has meaning only because of past familiarity, basically has no meaning because of perversity.

(5.15) And how is there lack of perversity in regard to the object? A lack of perversity in this connection is that seeing which recognizes, in regard to the object, that it does not exist as it appears, since it appears with duality, i.e., with the division into grasped and grasper, due to the arising of their semblance. This [lack of perversity] is separate from [the idea of] the object's being because of the absence of grasped and grasper; separate from its nonbeing because of the existing presence of the confusion in its appearance.

(5.16) A lack of perversity in regard to mental attention is the cognition that a mental attention towards talk, being suffused with talk of grasped and grasper, is the only support for the discrimination between grasped and grasper. As for mental attention which is the cause for the semblance of grasped and grasper, this mental attention towards talk is itself to be known as the basis for the distinction, because it is suffused with cognitions of verbal specification.

(5.17) Immediately thereafter, the nonbeing and being of objects is discussed [i.e., in what way they can be said to have no being, and in what way they can be said to have being]. They are considered to be like a magical creation, as follows: A magical creation does not exist with the true appearance of an elephant, and so forth [being produced in a magical show], and yet it does not exist! Because of the existence of the illusion itself. In the same way, objects also do not exist as they appear, with the state of having grasped and grasper aspects, but yet they do not exist, because of the existence of the illusion itself. Because of looking at objects like a magical creation, etc. [and by the word "etc.," mirages, dreams, the moon in the water, and other examples are to be understood], mental factors see without gliding, and there is lack of perversity in this lack of gliding, and on this account, also a lack of gliding of *citta* on being and nonbeing.

(5.18) All of this, from visible forms seen by the eye to mentally cognizables seized by *manas*, are only names. This cognition is lack of perversity in regard to the own-characteristic, because of its being an antidote to all discriminations. In regard to which own-characteristic?

the ultimate own-characteristic (5.19)

which, not being just a name, is not comprised by any conventional truth.

(5.19, 20) Not a single dharma exists without the absence of self in dharmas, therefore this *dharma-dhātu*, [emptiness], is the universal characteristic, and the knowledge of this in this way is a lack of perversity in regard to the universal characteristic. The knowledge that the impurity of this *dharma-dhātu* consists only in the nonabandonment of perverse mental attention, and that purity is its abandonment, is nonperversity in regard to impurity and purity.

(5.21) The *dharma-dhātu* being like space, it is pure by

nature, and the duality "pure" and "impure" is only adventitious, arising later. The knowledge of this in this way is lack of perversity as regards the purely adventitious.

(5.22) Because there is neither a person nor dharmas, there can be neither affliction nor alleviation for them.

## NOTES

We are all indebted to Professor Gadjin Nagao for making this text available to the scholarly world; I am additionally grateful to him, as he was my teacher for a year, with the topic of the *Madhyāntavibhāgabhāṣya*.

1. Vasubandhu, *Madhyāntavibhāgabhāṣya*, ad IV.13a.
2. *Ibid.*
3. *Ibid.*, V.17.
4. *Ibid.*, V.16.
5. *Ibid.*, II. 3 ff.
6. *Ibid.*, IV.13a.
7. *Ibid.*, IV.4.
8. *Ibid.*, IV.5b–6a.
9. *Ibid.*, IV.8.
10. Maitreya, *Abhisamayālaṁkāra*, vv. 25 ff.
11. *Madhyāntavibhāgabhāṣya*, V.12–21.
12. The four "foods" are: "morsel food" maintaining the organism itself, contact giving stimuli to sentient beings; *manas* and volition motivating its activity, and consciousness.
13. *Āvaraṇapiṇḍārthaḥ* omitted in my translation.
14. Tibetan: "At the time of coming to heat and the summit, they are faculties; at the time of equanimities and the highest mundane dharmas, they are powers."
15. Thus the Tibetan; the Sanskrit may equally well and punningly read: "hindrances to the removal of the Vaiśeṣika *guṇas*."

# Later Mādhyamikas on Epistemology and Meditation

*Yuichi Kajiyama*

The later Indian Mādhyamika school or the Yogācāra-mādhyamika, represented by Śāntarakṣita and Kamalaśīla, may be characterized in two ways: as a philosophy, it is syncretic; as a religion, it teaches gradual enlightenment. The merit of the school lies in combining these two characteristics.

The major schools of Indian Buddhist philosophy came to completion by the fifth century A.D. Up to that time, the philosophical tradition of Hīnayāna had continued to be maintained in a perfectly systematized form by the Sarvāstivādin. It had, however, been epistemologically more developed by the representation theory of the Sautrāntika. The Mādhyamika, the earliest Mahāyāna school, founded by Nāgārjuna, had continued to flourish in the fifth century, while the subtlest philosophy of radical idealism, developed by the other Mahāyāna school, the Yogācāra, was given its final touch by Vasubandhu in the fifth century. Until its very end in the twelfth century, Indian Buddhism was represented by these four schools.

Soon after Vasubandhu, the Sautrāntika and the Yogācāra philosophies were synthesized by Dignāga (sixth century A.D.)

and Dharmakīrti (seventh century A.D.), who both believed that these two schools shared the same spirit of criticizing Sarvāstivāda realism. Thus, Dharmakīrti carried on the systematizing of a new school, sometimes called Sautrāntika-yogācāra. The other form of syncretism, with which we are now mainly concerned, appeared in the eighth century. Śāntarakṣita and his student, Kamalaśīla, incorporated Yogācāra doctrines and practices into the Mādhyamika system. This new school was called Yogācāra-mādhyamika.

The theory and practice of gradual enlightenment, the other characteristic of the later Mādhyamika Buddhism, may be best illustrated by a historical event which took place in Tibet around 791 A.D. Tibet was then in a period in which it was greatly influenced by Chinese and Indian cultures, among which was early Chinese Zen Buddhism. During the eighth century in Tibet, a Chinese Zen monk called Hva-shan (Mahāyāna) was propounding the theory of sudden enlightenment which maintained that one can attain perfect emancipation instantaneously by means of mystic intuition and without the accumulation of learning, moral merits, and gradual training in meditation. The contemporary Tibetan king, Khri-song sde-tsang, invited Śāntarakṣita, and later Kamalaśīla, to come from India to Tibet. As a result of the Indian acceptance of this imperial invitation, Kamalaśīla, representing the Indian theory of gradual enlightenment, had a public debate with Hva-shan in the monastery of Sam-ye. Kamalaśīla won the debate, causing the waning within Tibet of influences of Chinese Zen in particular, and Chinese culture in general.[1]

In the debate, Kamalaśīla argued that a bodhisattva can attain the highest enlightenment only by combining compassion (*karuṇā*), means of approach (*upāya*), and wisdom (*prajñā*), and that it will not occur all of a sudden without a preceding and prolonged training. Closely interrelated with one another, the three ideas of *karuṇā*, *upāya*, and *prajñā* show the way in which an Indian Buddhist trained himself.[2] Compassion in Buddhist terminology does not mean only sympathy or benevolence, but more importantly stresses the bodhisattva's ideal of saving all sentient beings: he vows to remain in the world of misery until the last living being is emancipated by his teaching, even though he has already attained to enlightenment and is thereby able to pass into nirvāṇa at any time he wishes. Compassion, however, prevents a bodhisattva from being satisfied with lesser types of enlightenment with which he could save only a limited number of people. Instead, compassion urges him on to pursue unstintingly an ever-higher enlightenment. Naturally, this pursuit presupposes the spirit of a discerning attitude, by which he discriminates between the lower and higher doctrines of emancipation. This, in its turn, leads to the idea of the stages of Buddhist training, in which a bodhisattva climbs, criticizing and transcending a lower enlightenment in order to reach a higher one. This process of gradual progress is none other than the development of *upāya*, the means of approach.

Critical examination of all religious and philosophical doctrines, Buddhist and non-Buddhist alike, is referred to also by the term *cintāmayī prajñā*, or wisdom gained by investigation. This is the second of the three kinds of wisdom which have been taught since the time of early Buddhism, the first and the third being *śrutamayī prajñā* (wisdom gained by learning) and *bhāvanāmayī prajñā* (wisdom gained by meditation). The three kinds of wisdom, moreover, form the steps of Buddhist practice. Investigation, as the second step, can accommodate the critical spirit of the Mahāyāna and, therefore, the theory of the threefold wisdom is as much favored by later Mahāyāna as by the Hīnayāna. Investigation is carried on in two ways: according to the authority of scripture *(āgama)*, and according to reasoning *(yukt)*. This idea of investigation came to be modified by Mahāyāna into a more elaborate theory called the "four kinds of reliance" *(catuḥpratisaraṇa)*. A Buddhist student has to rely on the teaching (dharma), but not on a person, i.e., the personality of a teacher; on meaning *(artha)*, but not on letters *(vyañjana)*; on a sūtra teaching explicitly what it aims at *(nītārtha)*, but not on a sūtra the teaching of which implies a hidden intention *(neyārtha)*; and on penetrating knowledge (jñāna), but not on ordinary cognition *(vijñāna)*.[3]

In the days of Śāntarakṣita, when all Indian Buddhist philosophical systems had already appeared, a Buddhist student was usually confronted with the problems of which of the four powerful philosophical schools of Buddhism he should choose to follow and how he could create a system in which the four schools would be arranged in the proper order of merit. An important aspect of this tendency was that lower doctrines were not simply rejected, but admitted as steps leading to understanding of the highest one.

Śāntarakṣita begins his *Madhyamakālaṃkāra* by declaring that entities accepted as real and promulgated by Buddhist and non-Buddhist philosophical schools have in reality no intrinsic nature *(svabhāva)*, and are like a reflection, because they are possessed of neither a unitary nor a plural nature, and because apart from these two kinds of natures there is no other one. What is devoid of an intrinsic nature is nonexistent (cf. v. 1).[4]

Next, he proceeds critically to analyze the following: ātman, which is said to be permanent and unitary; nirvāṇa which the Sarvāstivāda Buddhist regards as an unconditioned *(asaṃskṛta)*, unitary reality; *pudgala*, which the Vātsiputrīya Buddhist maintains to be an undefinable self neither identified with nor different from the five components of individuality *(skandha)*; ether *(ākāśa)* which the Vaiśeṣika and Naiyāyika hold to be a unitary and all-pervading *(vyāpin)* reality; a gross entity called "whole," *(avayavin)* which the same schools consider to be a reality inherent in a gross thing, say a jar, while different from all its parts; atoms *(paramāṇu)* which are not only found in many non-Buddhist schools, but also are accepted by both the Sarvāstivāda and Sautrāntika Buddhists, who maintain them to be the minimum, indivisible units of matter; and so forth. Śāntarakṣita points out that these so-called "real entities" turn out, on examination, to have neither a unitary not plural nature, and that they are therefore nonexistent (cf. vv. 2–13). We shall not be concerned here with details of his arguments against the existence of these entities but will rather refer briefly to some of his criticisms which have direct bearing on our main subject.

Permanent entities such as ātman, *pradhāna* (primordial matter which the Sāṃkhya asserts to be the world-cause), and nirvāṇa as it is maintained by the Sarvāstivādin, can be all repudiated also from the point of view of causal efficiency *(arthakriyā)*, besides which they are pursued by the logic of the dichotomy of unity and plurality. Since Dharmakīrti, it has been an established truth that the criterion of existence is causal efficiency. What is permanent and unchangeable is incapable of action (i.e., has no causal efficiency) and, therefore, it is not existent (cf. v. 8).

The Sarvāstivādin regards *pratisaṃkhyānirodha* (cessation obtained by thorough knowledge) or nirvāṇa as an unconditioned, unitary reality which permanently exists independently of cognition grasping it, but which, however, can be intuited by the true wisdom a yogin acquires through meditation practice. Śāntarakṣita, however, contends that nirvāṇa cannot be single, insofar as it is related to the flux of successively arising momentary cognitions. If the nature of nirvāṇa, which has been known by an intuitive cognition, continues to exist even when another intuitive cognition occurs following the former, then these two cognitions, having the same object, would not be distinguishable from each other. On the contrary, if one and the same nature of nirvāṇa is not known by these two successive cognitions, nirvāṇa would be as much momentary as ordinary cognition. How then could it be called an unconditioned entity, which is to say, a permanent, unchangeable entity? (cf. vv. 3–5).

As for the view regarding atoms as unitary, minimum units of matter, there are various theories about the way in which atoms are united together to form a gross body. Some say that they are in contact with one another; some say that they are gathered together with intervals remaining between them; others say that they are in close contiguity, there being neither contact nor intervals between them. Irrespective of the way in which atoms are gathered together, Śāntarakṣita argues, the existence of atoms cannot be established. When an atom is surrounded by other atoms in the ten directions, is the atom in the center of a unitary nature or of a plural nature? If it faces the atom in the front by the single nature, at the same time facing the other nine atoms by the same nature, then all the ten atoms would occupy one and the same spot (i.e., the front spot). Resulting from this view, a gross thing such as a mountain would be reduced to the size of one atom, which is ridiculous. If the opponent wishes to avoid this absurdity, saying that the atom in the center faces the ten surrounding atoms by its ten natures (i.e., its ten segments), then the atom would have a plural nature (or many segments). Thus, the unity of the nature of an atom as well as its indivisibility would not stand careful scrutiny. This view goes against the idea of the atom which considers it as the minimum unit of matter (cf. vv. 11–13).[5]

All substances and ultimate factors which opponent schools claim to be unitary, noncomposite realities are, by critical scrutiny, seen to be plural in nature. Since unity forms the very essence of the idea of ultimate realities, the opponents are not in a position to admit their plurality or compositeness. As a result, ultimate realities prove to be neither unitary nor plural in nature, which means that they are not existent at all. Many of Śāntarakṣita's arguments are based upon those made by preceding Yogācāra philosophers, especially Vasubandhu and Dharmakīrti.

The Sarvāstivādin maintains the eighteen cognitive categories *(aṣṭādaśadhātu*, or six organs of cognition, six kinds of objects, and six kinds of consciousness) as rigorously comprehending all phenomena. Śāntarakṣita criticizes the Sarvāstivādin position, saying that if atoms do not exist, ten out of the eighteen categories are condemned to be nonexistent, because the five sense organs and the five kinds of external objects are said by the Sarvāstivādin to consist of atoms. If they are nonexistent, the other eight (mental faculty, its objects or ideas, and six kinds of consciousness) are also unreal, since their reality is recognized only in relation to the foregoing ten categories. Thus, all their preferred realities do not withstand the scrutiny of the Mādhyamika (cf. vv. 14–15).

Now, Śāntarakṣita classifies philosophical systems under two groups: one is dualism *(dvaya-naya)* in which the grasping (*grāhaka*, cognition) and the grasped (*grāhya*, cognitum) or mind and matter, respectively, are both admitted to be real. This categorization includes the Sarvāstivāda and Sautrāntika philosophies. The other group is nondualism *(advaya-naya)* represented by the Yogācāra philosophy which maintains the existence of mind only. Śāntarakṣita further subdivides dualism into the theory of cognition without images *(anākārajñānavāda)* as is maintained by the Sarvāstivāda, and that of cognition with images as is represented by the Sautrāntika.[6]

The principle of the Sarvāstivāda philosophy is an analysis of a whole into its constituents. It maintains that only elemental factors are real, whereas a whole composed of those factors is unreal. For example, individual trees which constitute a forest are alone real, while the forest is not. In the same way, the world as it is cognized by us is dissected into three factors, viz., consciousness, cognitive faculty, and object of cognition. An ultimate reality is an elemental factor which possesses one particular nature and function. It never has two or more natures and functions; if so, it could be further divided. Thus, consciousness only illumines; the cognitive organ merely perceives; and the object, having its form, is merely cognized. The Sarvāstivādin is led to the conclusion that consciousness is pure illumination and that, like a clean crystal, it does not undergo any morphological transformation, that is to say, it does not contain an image or representation when it cognizes an external object.[7] The form of a cognition belongs not to consciousness, but to an external object. If we cognize a book, for example, the book is seen as having the form of a book, our visual faculty sees it, and our consciousness illuminates or understands. In the terminology of Indian philosophy, this kind of theory is called *anākārajñānavāda*, or a theory that knowledge is not endowed with an image.

What is contrary to this is the Sautrāntika theory that knowledge is endowed with the image of its object. This is called *sākārajñānavāda*. The Sautrāntika admits the existence of the external world, but, he says, it is not perceptible. Its existence is postulated or inferred since, when a cognition takes place, there must be something external that causes or stimulates the cognition. An external object, as a cause, throws its form into our consciousness or knowledge, which is the effect. What knowledge knows is the image of the object, or a representation in our mind itself. When we see a book, what we are actually seeing as the book is in reality the representation in our own mind, since the book external to us is never seen, remaining always as "something." The reason the Sautrāntika believes in the existence of an imperceptible external world is that unless something is externally existent, we cannot explain why a particular cognition occurs only at a particular place and time, and not always and everywhere. To the Sautrāntika, what determines a cognition in nature, space, and time is an external reality.

When examining the Sarvāstivāda's *anākārajñānavāda*, Śāntarakṣita points out the essential difference between knowledge and matter. Matter, being insentient and unconscious, requires something else—a sentient being having consciousness—in order to be known. On the other hand, knowledge is a quality of consciousness and does not depend on other things for its manifestation, but is illuminated by its own self, being likened unto a lamp. Moreover, the self-illuminating function of knowledge is not construed as a relation of the agent and its action, since there are in reality no parts such as cognizer, cognitum, and cognition in knowledge. Thus, cognition is not that which occurs from the interaction of two or three different things, but rather is of itself self-cognition *(svasaṃvedana)*. If, as the Sarvāstivādin says, consciousness has no image of its object, how can a material object be known? Since matter is totally different in nature from consciousness, the Sarvāstivādin can establish no relation whatsoever between the two. Besides, if consciousness always remains the selfsame amorphous state when it cognizes various objects, how can we distinguish between the cognition of a blue object and that of a yellow one? (cf. vv. 16–17).[8]

To give a decisive blow to the *anākārajñānavāda*, Śāntarakṣita refers to the *sākārajñānavāda*, which, he thinks, surpasses the former in merit. According to the latter theory, the cognition of an external object, as a cause, throws its image into knowing. This image, as an effect, is part and parcel of knowing. The image, which belongs to knowing, is cognized by the same knowledge. Thus, what is figuratively called the cognition of an external object is none other than the self-cognition of knowledge (cf. vv. 20–21).[9]

With regard to the Sautrāntika theory of *sākārajñāna*, however, Śāntarakṣita sets forth a question. Whereas it is an established fact that knowledge is a unitary, incomposite modality, and the image thrown into it by an external reality is always manifold like a varicolored picture, how can the Sautrāntika claim an identical relationship between the unitary knowledge and the plural image? (cf. vv. 22–23).[10] Without proving the case for making such an identity, he cannot assert that the image is cognized by knowledge. Śāntarakṣita insists that since knowledge is unitary, an image in it cannot be plural in nature, which contradicts our experience, and that if an image is variegated, knowledge cannot be unitary, which is again not the case.

Regarding this difficult problem, opponents of Śāntarakṣita, including the Sarvāstivādin and Sautrāntika, try to solve the contradiction by resorting to similes. Their arguments can be outlined as follows. When a needle rapidly penetrates many petals of a lotus flower, it seems to have done so at once, although in actuality it has pierced one petal after another in succession. A torch that is whirled quickly gives rise to the untrue conception *(bhrānti)* of a circle of fire (cf. v. 24).[11] In the same way, no matter how variegated an image may be, we nonetheless come to have the wrong conception of a single image because its parts are seen in quick succession. Śāntarakṣita, however, makes his opponent silent by citing contrary examples. Even if the words *latā* and *tālaḥ* or *saraḥ* and *rasaḥ* are pronounced in quick succession, they are heard separately and distinctly without being heard simultaneously and understood confusedly in meaning (cf. v. 25).[12] Purely conceptual cognitions not accompanied by perceptions occur in rapid succession, each lasting only for a moment. Why do they not form one unitary cognition if a rapid succession gives the wrong concept of simultaneity? The same thing can be said of all cognitions (cf. v. 26).[13] The examples of a whirled torch and needled lotus petals are not warrantable either. The erroneous cognition of a circle of fire is not a creation of memory joining together the past perceptions, because the circle is seen very clearly, whereas the object of memory cannot be seen clearly. Therefore, the error is made not by conceptual cognition or memory but by the sense organ which has been confused by the quick succession of objects. In the case of needled lotus petals, the wise will easily determine that they are pierced not simultaneously but successively, just as many copper plates can only be pierced one after another. Thus, the opponents should not say that a quick succession of perceptions gives birth to the wrong conception *(vikalpa)* of a single perception (cf. vv. 27–30).[14]

Some of the Sautrāntikas contend that just as different kinds of perceptions—visual, auditory, and so forth—occur at the same time, even many of the same kind of perceptions can occur simultaneously. That is to say, while we see a picture, as many visual perceptions as there are colors in the picture (e.g., blue, white, red) arise at once. Each perception, having a part of the varicolored picture as its object, manifests a single image, and many perceptions occurring simultaneously form the whole of the varicolored picture. Thus, there is no incompatibility between the plurality of the image and the unity of the cognition (cf. v. 31).[15]

Śāntarakṣita argues against them as follows. If you once begin to divide an image into components of white, blue, and so forth, then you have to continue to divide even the part of white into many sections until you reach the minimum units, which are nothing less than atoms. But atoms are perceived by none of us (cf. vv. 32–33).[16] The Sautrāntika cannot elude this difficulty, because he himself has an established theory that the five kinds of sense cognition have aggregates (of atoms) as their object.[17] The sixth, or mental cognition *(manovijñāna)* cognizes feeling *(vedanā)*, ideation *(saṃjñā)*, or volition *(saṃskāra)* always together with consciousness *(citta)*; as the result, a mental cognition is also plural in nature (cf. v. 34). After all, the Sautrāntika cannot solve the problem of the incompatibility between the singleness of cognition and the plurality of its image.

The Yogācārin, a radical idealist, asserts that the Sautrāntika postulation of an external reality is an unnecessary complication. We can explain cognition without supposing the existence of matter. Just as some cognitions appear to us in a dream without there being any external things causing those cognitions, so latent impressions *(vāsanā)* accumulated in our mind since the beginningless past, when they ripen, can give rise to representations in our knowledge. What we usually consider as an external object is in reality none other than an image in knowledge. Mind perceives its own image, which is caused not by an external reality, as the Sautrāntika holds, but by the preceding moments of mind. However, the Yogācārin's epistemology is not very different from the Sautrāntika doctrine of *sākārajñāna*, except that the former does not postulate the imperceptible external reality, preferring instead the doctrine of the preceding moments of mind.

Śāntarakṣita greatly appreciates the Yogācāra doctrine as based both on scripture and reasoning.[18] Candidly, he admits that he himself owes many of his arguments to the Yogācārins. This opinion seems to be one of the reasons he is called a Yogācāra-mādhyamika. So long as he argues against both non-Buddhist and Buddhist dualists, Śāntarakṣita freely employs Yogācāra theories. However, he is not completely satisfied with the Yogācāra standpoint of philosophy. Śāntarakṣita asks: Is an image or representation in mind real or not? If this image is real and true, the Yogācārin cannot escape the same dilemma into which the Sautrāntika has fallen, which is to say, he is confronted by the problem of how unitary knowledge can have a variegated image which is plural in nature as its perceptual object (cf. v. 46).

Whether an image in mind is real or not is a decisive problem which caused a schism in the Yogācāra school. One group, named Satyākāravādin ("one who asserts images to be true"; also called Sākāravādin), claimed that an image is as real and true as the essence of knowledge or the two are inseparable on the grounds that an absolutely unreal image cannot come into existence. The other group, named Alīkākāravādin ("one who asserts images to be false"; also called Anākāravādin), dividing cognition into essential and subordinate parts, held that what is absolutely real is only the illuminating function *(prakāśamātra)* that is the essence of cognition; moreover, an image illuminated by it is a false fiction which disappears when one is enlightened. For example, we need only but consider the case in which a cognition is erroneously produced when we look at a shell on the beach and mistake it for silver, and then our mistake is sublated a moment later by a correct image of the shell coming to mind. An image in a dream is cancelled when one awakes. If an image can be negated by another, we must reason that the image must be in general untrue. The illuminating function of cognition, on the other hand, is never contradicted by any other thing, because it always remains the same illumination whether images illuminated by it are cancelled or not. Ratnākaraśānti (eleventh century A.D.), who is a later exponent of this theory, further argues that if all images are essential to cognition and are as true as the pure illumination, all people cognizing real images become, as a result, Buddhas, and that no distinction between enlightened and deluded persons would be possible.[19] The Satyākāravādin, like Jñānaśrīmitra (eleventh century A.D.), contends that a deluded person always interprets an image by conceptual thinking *(adhyavasāya = vikalpa)*, whereas an enlightened one is bereft of concepts which are the cause of erroneous cognition; and that, therefore, a discrimination can be made between a Buddha and an ordinary man despite the fact that both have images in common.[20]

To return to Śāntarakṣita's criticism of the Satyākāravāda-yogācārin, he questions whether images caused by the ripening of latent impressions in mind are as much real as the essence of cognition. The Yogācārin is also driven to a dilemma in which he has to admit either the plurality of cognition or the unity of the image. Suppose that cognition and an image are inseparable; if the image is not manifold, movement in one part of the world of cognition would cause the whole world to move, and yellow in one part would dye all the rest yellow (cf. v. 47). If the Yogācārin tries to escape this absurdity, he has to contradict the unity of cognition by confessing the manifoldness of its image, which is inseparable from the essence of cognition. Since either case involves incompatibility, we should conclude that cognition and its image are separate and distinct things (cf. v. 46).

Some of the Satyākāravādins contend, as the Sautrāntikas have done, that many of the same kind of perceptions, which are images, can occur at one and the same time, just as different kinds of cognitions arise simultaneously. And since many cognitions, each of which has one image, occur at once, the manifoldness of the image is explained without contradicting the singleness of cognition.[21]

Śāntarakṣita, however, points out that their theory is contrary to canonical traditions. One sūtra says that it is impossible for two minds to occur simultaneously;[22] another sūtra, that every sentient being is but one stream of cognition. The opponent may contend that these passages refer to the *ālayavijñāna* (basic consciousness) which exists singly in each sentient being, but not to ordinary cognitions *(pravṛttivijñāna)*, two or more of which can arise simultaneously. Śāntarakṣita says that the Yogācārin cannot refer to the *ālayavijñāna* as a single entity because, according to his own tradition, it manifests itself as a body with cognitive organs, their objects, and environments.[23] Moreover, Dharmakīrti, the most revered master of Yogācāra philosophy, says that cognitions of the same kind, such as two visual perceptions or two concepts, never arise together, although different kinds of cognitions may occur simultaneously.[24] And, finally, the opponent should not have recourse to a random argumentation disregarding his own tradition.[25]

Regarding the sūtra passage, however, the Yogācārin proposes another interpretation. The word "one" in the passage can be synonymous with "mere" or "only" without meaning a numeral. Hence, what the passage intends to say is that every sentient being consists of mind only, being bereft of a soul *(ātman)* and those things which belong to it *(ātmīya)*, or being bereft of the dichotomy of the grasping and the grasped *(grāhaka, grāhya)*. With the passage being so understood, there is no incompatibility in the *ālayavijñāna* manifesting itself as various forms, since no idea of "one-mind" which may contradict variety is found there.[26]

Against this improved interpretation, Śāntarakṣita demonstrates a unique critique which has added much to his credit. If knowledge were admitted by the Satyākāravādin to consist of parts as many as the number of its variegated forms, then it would be difficult for him to avert the same kind of criticism which is made regarding the reality of atoms (cf. v. 49). A dilemma ensues from the idea of atoms: an atom, if it is combined with other atoms situated around it by its many natures (or segments), presupposes its being many-natured (or many-sided), which contradicts the idea of atom as a unitary entity. On the contrary, if an atom has only one nature (or does not have many segments), a number of atoms collected together would occupy one and the same spot, which would reduce a gross thing to the size of an atom (cf. note 5). In the Yogācārin's argument, many images in knowledge must be further divided until they finally become cognitive atoms, the idea of which necessarily faces exactly the same dilemma as material atoms. The Yogācārin, who maintains the reality of images, cannot contend that cognition is bodiless *(amūrta)* and that, therefore, a criticism directed to material bodies should not be applied to cognition. Since the Yogācārin recognizes the reality of cognition alone, a cognition which appears having extended images is not different from a bodily thing.[27]

Having refuted the Satyākāravāda-yogācārin, Śāntarakṣita deals next with the Alīkākāravāda-yogācārin's theory. According to the latter, in the highest truth *(paramārtha)* cognition is, like a clean crystal, not stained by images;[28] images are manifested erroneously by the force of the ripening of perverted latent impressions accumulated in the mind, just as visions of a horse and an elephant are conjured up from a lump of clay by uttering a magical formula (cf. v. 52). Since an image is an unreal or false manifestation, this school seems to succeed in freeing itself from the incompatibility between a unitary cognition and a plural image.

Śāntarakṣita, however, puts forward a question. If images are unreal, how can they be perceived so clearly as experienced by us? In other words, how does one explain the fact that aside from images, we do not perceive illuminating cognition alone (cf. v. 53)? Where there is no object, we do not obtain its cognition. An unreal image neither has the nature of knowledge nor the efficiency to cause knowledge endowed with its image, and is like a flower in the sky and the horns of a horse (cf. vv. 55–56). Thus, the Alīkākāravādin's assertion that unreal images are manifested is simply untenable. Furthermore, we do not find any relation which connects the real but unmanifested illumination of cognition and the unreal but manifested images. If the relation of identity *(svabhāva)* is admitted, it would follow that the image is as real as the illumination of cognition, or that the illumination is unreal as much as the image. Nor is a causal relation *(tadutpatti)* possible between the two, because this relation presupposes difference in time of a cause and its effect, whereas the illumination and the image occur simultaneously (cf. v. 57). If an image has no cause, it is difficult to explain why it is only manifested from time to time, and not continuously. But if it has a cause, then it is as real as the *ālayavijñāna* which also has the nature depending on its cause or its preceding moments *(paratantrasvabhāva)*. The image appearing because of latent impressions is not entirely unreal, just as a white shell will appear as yellow to one who suffers from jaundice, in which case the perceived shell is not totally unreal (cf. v. 60).

Neither the Satyākāravāda- nor the Alīkākāravāda-yogācārin has been able to explain the reason a unitary cognition appears with a plural image. Having scrutinized the so-called realities proposed by the Sarvāstivādin, Sautrāntika, and Yogācārin by means of the dichotomy of unity and plurality, Śāntarakṣita declares that everything, mental as well as material, turns out on examination to have neither a unitary nor a plural nature, and that no entity is real in the sense of the highest truth, though its existence may be admitted in the sense of conventional truth *(saṃvṛti)* (cf. vv. 62–63).

An opponent raises a question. If everything is empty of an intrinsic nature, would not even unwise people understand the truth, as they easily know the absence of a jar from a particular place? Śāntarakṣita answers: Because they are deluded by their wrong habit of imagining things as real, they cannot understand the truth by perception, just as they do not perceive that everything is in actuality perishing at every moment *(kṣaṇikatva)*. The truth of emptiness, therefore, is to be understood through inference based on sound probans by those who have shaken off false imagination, unless they are yogins who, being endowed with supernormal insight, can grasp the truth by perception (cf. vv. 73–75).

The opponent further contends that if everything is empty of an intrinsic nature, a syllogism, its component members, and its verbal expression are not established. Unless Śāntarakṣita states a proof for his thesis of emptiness, the thesis remains unproved; but if such a proof is stated, then his assertion that everything is nonexistent fails, since the proof least must be existent.

To this objection, Śāntarakṣita replies as follows: Insofar as logic is concerned, he does not have recourse to a particular doctrine of his own school, but he uses terms as they are generally understood by the wise and the unwise equally. An inference must be manipulated in the domain of ordinary verbal usage *(vyavahāra)*, otherwise two parties engaged in discussion would not have a common ground of discourse. Logic is demonstrated and has its effect in the world of practical knowledge, and the Mādhyamika does not deny the practical function of logic if he knows that probans and probandum are not existent in the sense of the highest truth (cf. vv. 76–77).

The question of the incompatibility between universal emptiness and its demonstration by logic and words is an old one which all Mādhyamikas since Nāgārjuna have met with.[29] Another traditional criticism of the philosophy of emptiness is that the Mādhyamika, in denying everything, is identical with a nihilist *(nāstika)* who denies causality, both moral and physical.

Śāntarakṣita briefly but persuasively argues against the criticism. Although everything is in reality free from the manifold fiction of human ideas *(prapañca)*, unwise people are attached to both imagined existence and nonexistence. This fact itself makes us infer that in the minds of people there are seeds or latent impressions accumulated by the succession of deeds and rebirths occurring since the beginningless past, and that it is those seeds, and not external things, which cause ideas and images of both an existent and a nonexistent to appear. As is known to us all, ideas arise not at once, but in succession. This fact is contrary to the nihilist opinion that things occur without cause as much as it is against the metaphysical opinion that there is a permanent cause of the world such as *īśvara* (god) or *pradhāna* (the world-cause of the Sāṃkhya), because things arising gradually cannot be produced accidentally without causes, nor have they a permanent, self-identical cause. The existence of such seeds postulates our past and future lives. Therefore, the Mādhyamika, unlike nihilists and those who maintain the existence of an ultimate cause, can establish causal relation by logic in the domain of conventional truth. The possibility of emancipation by means of insight into emptiness is proved by the Mādhyamika (cf. vv. 79–83).

With regard to moral and physical entities established in the sense of conventional truth by the Mādhyamika, it is asked if they are to be considered as ideas or as external realities. Śāntarakṣita on this occasion introduces the interpretative positions of two divisions of the Mādhyamika. The one group, whom Kamalaśīla, the commentator on the *Madhyamakālaṃkāravṛtti*, explains as followers of Bhāvaviveka, maintains that the Buddhas have taught the theory of mind-only to repudiate the existence of a soul which is conjured up by non-Buddhist philosophers as the subject of actions *(kartṛ)* and the enjoyer of their fruits *(bhoktṛ)*. This opinion of the one group of Mādhyamikas is tantamount to saying that external things can be as real as mind insofar as conventional truth is concerned, although the soul must be denied. Therefore, this group of Mādhyamikas is closer to a Buddhist dualist, in this case, to the Sautrāntika, in admitting the existence of an external reality in the sense of conventional truth.

The other group is in favor of Yogācāra doctrine, arguing that an object of cognition is not an external reality, and that the Sautrāntika postulation of the external world as the cause which bestows an image into mind is untenable. They follow the Yogācārin who has replaced such an external reality by the immediately preceding moment of mind containing an impression or seed as the cause of the image of the present moment of mind; furthermore, they think that sūtras such as the *Saṃdhinirmocana*, the fundamental scripture of Yogācāra philosophy, must be relied on by the Mādhyamika, too. This group of Mādhyamikas wishes to interpret the world of conventional truth according to the Yogācāra idealism (cf. vv. 91–93).[30]

Even the standpoint of Yogācāra philosophy, however,

must be transcended by people with deeper insight when the highest truth is in question. It is necessary for them to examine the doctrine of mind-only by the logic of unity and plurality in order to know the unreality of mind from the view of the highest truth.

Śāntarakṣita summarizes the process of his investigation of Buddhist philosophies in verse:

> Based on [the standpoint of] mind-only, one must know the nonexistence of external entities; based on this [standpoint of emptiness], one must know that an intrinsic nature *(svabhāva)* is really lacking even in mind. (v. 92)

The three stages of epistemological investigation counted in this verse can be increased to five when the whole process of the foregoing discussions is taken into account: (1) the Sarvāstivāda stage, in which external realities are recognized as much as mental ones; (2) the Sautrāntika stage, in which mental images are regarded as objects of cognition and the external world is reduced to the imperceptible cause of cognition; (3) the Satyākāravāda-yogācāra philosophy, which, replacing the external world by impressions in mind, asserts that the image in mind is as real as the illumination of mind; (4) the Alīkākāravāda-yogācāra epistemology, which admits the reality of the illumination of mind alone, rejecting images as false; (5) the Mādhyamika theory of emptiness, which denies even the existence of the illumination of mind.

Śāntarakṣita traces his own theory back to the following two verses of Nāgārjuna:

> Here nothing is produced, nothing is annihilated either; appearance and disappearance take place only in our knowledge. The four material elements *(mahābhūta)* taught [by philosophers] are in fact reduced to cognition. If seen from [a standpoint in which] cognition is shaken off, is it not true that it [or cognition] is human imagination too?[31]

A talented disciple of Śāntarakṣita, Kamalaśīla, who spent the latter half of his life in Tibet, wrote three *Bhāvanā-*

*kramas*, in which he gave a succinct summarization of the philosophy and meditation practice of his teacher. The following is a translation of some important portions of the first *Bhāvanākrama*, together with interpretations.

> . . . Or one should examine [various theories] by reasoning *(yukti)* in the following way. All existent things are either material or mental. Of these, material things, such as a jar, have no single nature since they are characterized as being [composed of] different [particles when examined] in view of atoms. But it is neither possible that they, being a collection of many atoms, are of a plural nature, for atoms surrounding [an atom in the center] in the front, in the back, and so forth, must be necessarily divided into many sides like the front, the back, and so on, and cease to be atoms [since they lose indivisibility as the essential nature of an atom]. Apart from a single and plural nature, there is no other which can be called the intrinsic nature of a thing. Therefore, seen from the standpoint of the highest truth, these material things are empty of any intrinsic nature just like things seen in a dream and other [illusory cognitions] [p. 202, 1.12, to p. 203, 1.2] . . .
>
> Mental things also, when examined in the same way, prove to be empty of any intrinsic nature. For the fact that external things such as blue are nonexistent leads us necessarily to admit that the mental groups, beginning with cognition, are manifested in the forms of a blue thing, etc. [p. 203, 1.6–10] . . .
>
> Then, these [mentals] cannot be of a single nature because they appear with various images such as blue, etc., or with the dichotomized images of subject and object. Since unity and plurality are incompatible, [a mental] which is single cannot have a plural image. And when a nature of unity is not established, a nature of plurality cannot possibly be [ascribed to the mental], for plurality means the collection of single entities.
>
> Or one may suppose that all these images of color-form, and so on, appear in it [i.e., in mind], although they are actually unreal *(alīka)*. If so, however, cognition itself would be judged as unreal, because cognition is not separated from the nature of these [images]. Aside from the nature of the [images] manifested from [cognition] itself, no other nature of cognition is to

be found. And color-form, and so on, are not manifested by themselves [since they do not exist as separate things from cognition]. When these things which by nature belong to cognition are unreal, we must admit that all cognitions are unreal as well. This is the reason why the Blessed One taught that cognition is like illusion.

Thus it is concluded that everything in the world is unreal as seen from the standpoint of the highest truth, because everything is empty of an intrinsic nature, either unitary or plural. [p. 203, 1.12, to p. 204, 1.3]

It is obvious that Kamalaśīla, following Śāntarakṣita, criticizes Bahirarthavādins (those who admit the existence of external things) or the Sarvāstivādin and the Sautrāntika on the one hand, and the Yogācārin on the other. It is also clear that the Yogācārin is classified into Satyākāravādin and Alīkākāravādin. While arguing in this way, Kamalaśīla cites many verses from the *Laṅkāvatāra-sūtra* as an authority, a reliance on which he shares with Śāntarakṣita and Ratnākaraśānti. It seems that this sūtra, which was compiled after the establishing of basic Yogācāra doctrines and which was written with an intention to synthesize Mādhyamika and Yogācāra doctrines, suggested to later Mādhyamika philosophers a method whereby to accord a proper rank to each of the Buddhist philosophical systems.

Śāntarakṣita, in writing the *Madhyamakālaṃkāravṛtti*, did not say much about meditation practice, because the work was primarily concerned with philosophical viewpoints. Kamalaśīla, on the other hand, wrote his *Bhāvanākramas* with intentions to initiate Tibetan Buddhists into the stages of meditation practice whereby to climb up gradually one stage after another in order, finally, to attain perfect enlightenment. Besides, the *Bhāvanākramas* were written just after Kamalaśīla had won the famous controversy at Sam-ye mentioned earlier. Thus, the books mainly consist of descriptions of the meanings and methods of meditation practice.

In brief, the process of the practice of Mahāyāna Buddhists is as follows: A yogin is exhorted to acquire three kinds of wisdom: *śrutamayī* (wisdom by learning), *cintāmayī* (wisdom by investigation), and *bhāvanāmayī prajñā* (wisdom by meditation). The second kind of wisdom *(cintāmayī)* consists of investigation by reasoning *(yukti)* and by reference to authority of scripture *(āgama)*, and discrimination between the implicit *(neyārtha)* and explicit meaning *(nītārtha)* of the teachings in the sūtras, and so on. Meditation, the basis of the third kind of wisdom, is practiced in the following way: (1) by mastering *śamatha* or the tranquilization of mind through the observation of moral and yogic rules, nine stages of *śamatha*, four dhyānas, and so on; then (2) by *vipaśyanā* (analysis of the object of meditation from the point of view of what has been studied by investigation). The importance of *vipaśyanā* has been stressed especially by Mahāyānists. In the practice of tranquilization, they say, there is not much difference between non-Buddhists, Hīnayānists, and Mahāyānists alike, but what makes Mahāyāna meditation different from others is the doctrine that is investigated and the analysis of the meditative object. Furthermore, Mahāyāna Buddhists believe that obstructions to emancipation consisting of moral defilements and false knowledge cannot be annihilated merely by tranquilization, and that analysis is also necessary. When a yogin succeeds in mastering both tranquilization and analysis, he proceeds to practice both simultaneously. This is called (3) *śamathavipaśyanāyuganaddha*. When he succeeds in this last meditation, he is placed in the preliminary stage called *adhimukticaryābhūmi* for the ten stages of bodhisattva. In each of the following ten stages, he repeats *śamatha*, *vipaśyanā*, and *yuganaddha* to annihilate his defilements more completely and to attain to wisdom regarding various doctrines and supernatural powers. After completing these ten stages of a bodhisattva, he finally attains Buddhahood.

The investigations of various philosophical systems, Buddhist as well as non-Buddhist, are made chiefly in two places of the foregoing process. The yogin does it when he strives for acquiring *cintāmayī prajñā* before entering into meditative practice itself. In this stage, he, as a philosopher, uses his knowledge of epistemology and logic to criticize different doctrines of non-Buddhist and Hīnayāna systems of philosophy and, in so doing, becomes sure of the supremacy of Mahāyāna, especially Mādhyamika philosophy. Secondly, when he practices *vipaśyanā*, he meditates on each of the doctrines of the four Buddhist schools, according to a method taught in the *Laṅkāvatāra-sūtra*[32] and other sūtras. He visualizes the whole world as consisting of the eighteen categories of factors, (i.e., six objects, six cognitive organs, and six cognitions) according to the Sarvāstivāda and Sautrāntika systems which recognize the existence of external realities. Then, transcending this theory, he enters into that of the Yogācāra school and sees the world as the representations of his own mind alone. Lastly he goes beyond this theory, seeing that even the mind is empty of an intrinsic nature and realizing that the world is nonexistent in the sense of the highest truth, as the Mādhyamika teaches.

Besides this lucid description of the combination of philosophy and meditation, we owe another matter to Kamalaśīla that is very important to our present study. His interpretation throws much light on the just-mentioned three verses from the *Laṅkāvatāra-sūtra*, no matter how different it may be from the original meaning of the verses. As cited by Kamalaśīla, the verses read:

> *cittamātram samāruhya bāhyam arthaṃ na kalpayet;*
> *tathatālambane* (1) *sthitvā cittamātram atikramet.* (v. 256)
>
> *cittamātram atikramya nirābhāsam* (2) *atikramet;*
> *nirābhāse* (3) *sthito yogī mahāyānaṃ sa paśyati.* (v. 257)
>
> *anābhogagatiḥ śāntā praṇidhānair viśodhitā;*
> *jñānaṃ nirātmakaṃ śreṣṭhaṃ nirābhāsena* (4)
> *paśyati.* (v. 258)

In the *Laṅkāvatāra-sūtra* and the *Madhyamakālaṃkāravṛtti*—if the Tibetan translation is correct in the latter—v. 258d reads: *nirābhāse na paśyati.* And when it is cited by Ratnākaraśānti in his *Prajñāpāramitopadeśa*, it reads: *theg pa chen pos [po?] mthoṅ bar ḥgyur = mahāyanaṃ sa paśyati.*[33]

As will be seen from the following translation of Kamalaśīla's interpretation, he reads particular meanings at least in four words in these verses. According to him, *tathatālambane* in v. 256c means *advayalakṣaṇe tathatālambane* (1); *nirābhāsam* in v. 257b, *dvayanirābhāsam* (2); *nirābhāse* in v. 257c, *advayajñānanirābhāse jñāne* (3); and *nirābhāsena* in v. 258d, *advayanirābhāsena jñānena* (4). Here (1) *tathatālambana* and (2) *dvayanirābhāsa* refer to the illumination bereft of images *(prakāśamātra)* maintained by the Alīkākāravāda-yogācāra school, while *advaya(-jñāna-)nirābhāsa-jñāna* that appears in (3) and (4) refers to the absolute emptiness asserted by the later Mādhyamika as meaning that which exceeds the *prakāśamātra* of the Alīkākāravādin, in spite of the same *nirābhāsa* that recurs in the sūtra itself.

If we understand the progress in epistemological stages according to Kamalaśīla's interpretation, it becomes clear that *cittamātra* at the very beginning of v. 256 must mean not Yogācāravāda in general, but rather the standpoint of the Satyākāravāda. The original verses could be interpreted in this way; but we cannot ascribe such an intention to the author of the *Laṅkāvatāra-sūtra*, the compilation of which occurs centuries before the controversy between the Satyākāravādin and Alīkākāravādin.

Interpreting in this way, Kamalaśīla succeeds in making these three verses correspond to the theory of gradual transcendence of Buddhist epistemologies, which he as well as his teacher maintains. This will be clear from the following translation.

> Concerning this, the stages of meditation on wisdom are taught in brief in the *Laṅkāvatāra-sūtra:*
>
> Having ascended [the truth of] mind-[with-images] only, the yogin should not imagine external objects [to be existent]; abiding in the meditation having as its object suchness [or il-

lumination marked by the absence of cognizer- and cognitum-parts], he ought to go beyond mind-[with-images] only. (v. 256)

Having thus gone beyond even mind-[with-images] only, he should go also beyond [the illumination] without the manifestation [of the two parts]; abiding thus in the nonmanifestation [of the illumination without the two parts], the yogin intuits [the truth of] the Great Vehicle. (v. 257)

He attains an effortless state [of mind], quiescent and purified by his vows; by means of the nonmanifestation [of the illumination without the two parts] he regards what was [formerly considered] the highest knowledge as devoid of its nature. (v. 258)

The meaning of these lines is as follows: In the first stage, the yogin should examine those material things which other people imagine to be external objects. Are they different from cognition or are they mere manifestations of cognition itself, as it is the case with [images seen] in the state of a dream? If they are external to cognition, examine them in view of atoms. When the yogin investigates, analyzing atoms into their segments, he does not find [the existence of] those objects. It occurs to him who is not seeing [the reality of atoms] that all things [in the world] are mind-only, external objects being totally nonexistent. This is the reason why it is said: Having ascended to [the truth of] mind-only, the yogin should not imagine external objects [to be existent]. It advises him to abandon [the habit of] imagining the existence of material things, because all conditions of their perception being satisfied, they are not seen because of his [careful] examination.[34]

Having revealed [the unreality of] material things, he then should consider immaterial things. As for what is called "mind-only," he should think that when there is no object, the subject which is in relation to the object cannot exist either; and, therefore, that the mind is devoid of subject and object, that is to say, the mind is without duality [*advaya*]. Abiding thus in the [meditation] having "suchness" as its object and being characterized by nonduality, he should go beyond that "mind-only" too. It means that he should, surpassing the image of subject, abide in the knowledge of nonduality in which the two [subject and object-parts] are not manifested.

Having thus surpassed "mind-only," he would go beyond

even the knowledge without manifestations of the two [images]. For this he should think that things arise neither from their own selves nor from other things and that when subject and object are unreal *[alīka]*, the mind, being not different [from the two], cannot be true, either. Here, too, he must abandon attachment to ascribing reality to the cognition of nonduality *[advayajñāna]*, and he must abide in the knowledge of nonmanifestation of even nondual knowledge *[advayajñānanirābhāsa-jñāna]*.

In this way he becomes established in the understanding of the lack of intrinsic nature of everything. Abiding in it, he enters into the nonconceptual concentration *[nirvikalpa-samādhi]* because he enters into the highest truth. When the yogin abides in the knowledge of nonmanifestation of nondual knowledge, he, being established in the highest truth, sees [the truth of] the Great Vehicle. (p. 210, 1.7–p. 211, 1.20)

. . . Concentration *[samādhi]* is not of the nature of complete darkness, but marked [only] by one-pointedness of mind. Since it is said that one in the state of concentration intuits things as they really are, concentration is surely in accordance with insight *[prajñā]*, but it is not contrary [to insight, i.e., it is not of the nature of ignorance]. Therefore, when one in the state of concentration examines with insight, he intuits the nonmanifestation of all things; this is the highest nonmanifestation *[paramo'nupalambhaḥ]*. The yogin's stage so characterized is called an effortless state *[anābhogagati]*, because in it he has nothing more to see beyond it. It is called quiescent, because there manifold discourse *[prapañca]*, marked by concepts such as existence and nonexistence, totally cease. (p. 214, 11.3–10)

. . . Again, how is this stage of the yogin purified? Reply: It is purified by his vow. The bodhisattva, because of his great compassion, has made a vow that he will do everything for the benefit of all sentient beings; because of the force of this vow he strives for doing always more and more good deeds, such as benevolence. By this habit, his stage is so purified by the [vow] that although he knows the nonexistence of an intrinsic nature in all things, his consideration for all sentient beings does not subside and he stays in this world of transmigration so long as it lasts, and without his being stained by the faults of the world.

Again, how is [his state] effortless and quiescent? The reason for it is given [in the answer]: By means of [insight into] nonmanifestness, he regards even what has been [formerly considered] the highest knowledge as devoid of an intrinsic nature. For by means of the knowledge of nonmanifestation of even nondual knowledge, the yogin sees as devoid of a kernel or devoid of an intrinsic nature even that knowledge marked by nonduality as the highest or the supreme truth. Thus, [his state is] effortless, because nothing more to be seen is existent; quiescent, since it is free from all concepts. (p. 217, 1.14, to p. 218, 1.6)

In the foregoing sections taken from Kamalaśīla's *Bhāvanākrama* I, four stages are plainly distinguishable: (1) the preliminary stage in which external realities admitted in the systems of the Sarvāstivāda and Sautrāntika are presented as the object of criticism; (2) the stage in which only the mind with manifested images is admitted—the system of the Satyākāravāda-yogācāra school forms the object of meditation; (3) the meditation stage in which the images of cognition as well as the duality of subject and object are condemned to be unreal and in which the knowledge without duality is proclaimed to be real—this being the standpoint of the Alīkākāravāda-yogācārin; (4) the stage in which even the nondual knowledge *(advayajñāna)* or the pure illumination of cognition *(prakāśamātra)* is declared to be empty of an intrinsic nature. This latter stage is the highest one proclaimed by the Mādhyamika. Kamalaśīla's description of the method of gradual transcendence of Buddhist philosophies for the attainment of the final truth of emptiness perfectly corresponds to that of his master, Śāntarakṣita.

## NOTES

I thank Professor Masamici Ichigo, my academic colleague, to whom I owe many of the identifications of verses in the *Madhyamakālaṃkāra*. I also express my heartfelt gratitude to Professor Louis O. Gómez who, having read a portion of this paper, gave me useful suggestions, and to Messrs. Leslie Kawamura and Kenneth O'Neill for their correction of the English text. Since the present paper was written in 1972, much work regarding the

*Madhyamakālaṃkāra* and related texts has been done by my colleagues, especially Professors Ichigo, Kazufumi Oki, Shōryū Katsura, and others. I regret that I cannot incorporate the results of their studies in this paper, due to limitations of space and time.

1. The controversy of Sam-ye and its historical and philosophical background have been studied by many modern scholars, such as P. Demiéville, G. Tucci, H. Sato, D. Ueyama, and others. See especially Paul Demiéville, *Le concile de Lhasa* (Paris: Bibliothèque de l'Institut des Hautes Études Chinoises, vol. VII, 1952); and G. Tucci, *Minor Buddhist Texts*, "Introduction."

2. Kamalaśīla's argument in the debate in Sam-ye is reflected in his three *Bhāvanākramas*, Peking reprint edition vol. 102, mos. 5304, 5310, and 5311; and *Bhāvanākrama I* in G. Tucci, *Minor Buddhist Texts*, Part II (Rome: Instituto Italiano per il Medio ed Estremo Oriente, 1958).

3. Cf., for example, Ratnākaraśānti, *Prajñāpāramitopadeśa*, Peking reprint edition vol. 114, no. 5579, 237.3.6–8 (f.153,a).

4. Śāntarakṣita, *Madhyamakālaṃkāra*, Peking reprint edition vol. 101, no. 5284. In the following, main arguments in *Madhyamakālaṃkāra* are introduced in the form of free exposition. At the end of an argument I add in parentheses the number(s) of the kārikā(s) of *Madhyamakālaṃkāra* which contain the argument. In so doing, I use freely Śāntarakṣita's own commentary, as well as Kamalaśīla's commentary, without giving pages and lines, except in important cases. See Śāntarakṣita, *Madhyamakālaṃkāravṛtti*, Peking reprint edition vol. 101, no. 5285; and Kamalaśīla, *Madhyamakālaṃkārapañjikā*, Peking reprint edition vol. 101, no. 5286.

5. In his *Viṃśatikā* Sylvain Lévi, ed. (Paris: H. Champion, 1925), Vasubandhu analyzes atoms quantitatively: if an atom is combined with another six atoms situated around it, it must be six-sided (i.e., have six segments), which contradicts the idea of an atom as an indivisible minimum unit of matter; if, on the contrary, an atom does not have segments, a number of atoms collected together would occupy one and the same spot, which would reduce a gross thing into the size of an atom—this being ridiculous. Śāntarakṣita, on the other hand, criticizes atoms qualitatively rather than quantitatively, changing the idea of the segments of an atom into that of intrinsic natures. This distinction, however, is not strictly observed by him when, for example, he says that a mountain would be reduced to the size of an atom.

. . . *alaṃkāra* vv. 11–13 are almost identical with vv. 1989–90 of Śāntarakṣita, *Tattvasaṃgraha, with the commentary* Pañjikā *of Kamalaśīla*, edited by Swami Dwarikadas Shastri (Varansai: Buddha Bharati, 1968). In the following notes, the sign = means that the verses are identical or almost identical.

6. Cf. . . . *alaṃkāravṛtti* 4.2.2–4 (f. 56, bl–4); . . . *alaṃkārapañjikā* 20.2.8 (f. 96, b8) ff.

7. Cf. . . . *alaṃkāravṛtti* 4.2.3 (f. 56, b3): *rnam par zhes pa ni zhel gong dag pa lta bu yul gyi rnam pa mi 'dsin par brjod pa ste.*

8. . . . *alaṃkāra* vv. 16–17 = *Tattvasaṃgraha* vv. 1999–8000.

9. . . . *alaṃkāra* vv. 20–21 = *Tattvasaṃgraha* vv. 2004–5. For *sākāra-jñānavāda* and *anākārajñānavāda*, see Yuichi Kajiyama, *An Introduction to Buddhist Philosophy: An Annotated Translation of the Tarkabhāṣā of Mokṣākaragupta* (Kyoto: Memoirs of the Faculty of Letters, Kyoto University, no. 10, 1966), paragraph 8.1 and note 148.

10. . . . *alaṃkāra* vv. 22–23 = *Tattvasaṃgraha* vv. 2036–37.

11. . . . *alaṃkāra* v. 24 = *Tattvasaṃgraha* v. 1246.

12. . . . *alaṃkāra* v. 25 = *Tattvasaṃgraha* v. 1250.

13. . . . *alaṃkāra* v. 26 = *Tattvasaṃgraha* v. 1251.

14. . . . *alaṃkāra* vv. 27–30 = *Tattvasaṃgraha* vv. 1252–55.

15. See Kamalaśīla's *Pañjikā* on the *Tattvasaṃgraha*, p. 696, 1.17–697, 1.2.

16. *Ibid.*, p. 697, 11.2–6.

17. Cf Manorathanadin's commentary of Dharmakīrti's *Pramāṇavārttika, edited by Rāhula Sāṅkṛtyāyana, Appendix to the Journal of the Bihar and Orissa Research Society* XXIV, XXV, XXVI (Patna, 1938–40), II, v. 194: "*saṃcitālambanāḥ pañcavijñānakāyāḥ.*"

18. Cf. . . . *alaṃkāravṛtti* on v. 45.

19. Cf. the *Prajñāpāramitopadeśa* 243.3.6–7 (f. 168, a6–7): *de dag gi ltar na gsal ba thmas cad phyin ci ma log pa'i rang gi ngo bo myong ba'i phyir, thams cad 'khrul pa med par 'gyur ro. des na sems can thmas cad rtag tu grol bar 'grul la, rtag tu yang dag par rdsogs pa'i sangs rygas nyid du 'gyur ro.* See also Y. Kajiyama, *An Introduction to Buddhist Philosophy* (Kyoto: Memoirs of the Faculty of Kyoto University, 1966).

20. For a more detailed description of the Sākāravāda-yogācārins and Anākāravāda-yogācārins, see Kajiyama, *Buddhist Philosophy*, paragraph 32.1 and note 418 = Appendix II. I prefer the terms "Satyākāravādin" and "Alīkākāravādin" to "Sākāravādin" and "Anākāravādin," respectively, since in so terming them we can easily distinguish these two schools of the Yogācāra from the Sautrāntika as a Sākārajñānavādin and the Sarvāstivādin as an Anākārajñānavādin. Śāntarakṣita himself, however, uses the terms "Sākāravādin" and "Anākāravādin" more frequently.

21. Cf. . . . *alaṃkāravṛtti* 6.3.8–6.4.1 = f. 62, a8–b1.

22. Manorathanandin, commenting on the *Pramāṇavārttika* II, v. 502, cites the passage: *asthānam etad yad dve citte yugapat saṃpratipadyeyātām.*

23. Cf Nagao, *Madhyāntavibhāgabhāṣya*, p. 48, 11.7.8: *nimittaṃ pratiṣṭhādehabhogasaṃgṛhītam*; and A. Thakur, ed., *Ratnakīrtinibandhāvalī*, Tibetan Sanskrit Works Series vol. III (Patna: K. P. Jayaswal Research Institute, 1957), p. 122, 11.7–8: . . . *pratisantānaṃ ca svapnavad abādhitadehabhogapratiṣṭhādyākāraprakāśamātrātmake jagati vyavasthite . . .*

24. Cf. *Pramāṇavārttika* II, v. 502, with Manorathanandin's commentary.

25. Cf. . . . *alaṃkāravrtti* 6.4.1–5 = f. 62, b1–5.

26. Cf. *ibid.*, 6.4.5 ff. = f. 62, b5 ff.

27. Śāntarakṣita's argument here is cited in Mokṣākaragupta's *Tarkabhāṣā*; see Kajiyama, *Buddhist Philosophy*, pp. 150–51. The argument is lacking in the Sanskrit text, but is found in its Tibetan translation.

28. See also Kamalaśīla's *Pañjika* on the *Tattvasaṃgraha*, in which Śubhagupta cites Vasubandhu's *Madhyāntavibhāga* I, v. 16cd: *abdhātukanakākāśaśuddhivac chuddhir iṣyate (buddhiḥ)* as a doctrine of the Anākāravāda-yogācārin's.

29. See, for example, Nāgārjuna, *Vigrahavyāvartanī*. Buddhist Sanskrit Texts no. 10 (Darbhaga: The Mithila Institute, 1963), vv. 1–2 (the opponent's questions) and 21–24 (Nāgārjuna's answer).

30. Tibetan Buddhists classify the Mādhyamikas first under Prāsaṅgika and Svātantrika; and they divide the latter into Yogācāra-mādhyamika-svātantrika, represented by Śāntarakṣita, and Sautrāntika-mādhyamika-svātantrika, represented by Bhāvaviveka. Śāntarakṣita is a follower of Bhāvaviveka, the founder of the Svātantrika school, in that he, unlike the Prāsaṅgika, gives importance to logic and manipulates categorical syllogisms. But he is closer to the Yogācāra than to the Sautrāntika, in that he does not admit the reality of the external world even in the sense of conventional truth. The Prāsaṅgika, represented by Candrakīrti, follows the Sarvāstivāda dualism in interpreting conventional truth. The foregoing classification made by Tibetans is based on Śāntarakṣita's argument in this part of the *Madhyamakālaṃkāra*.

31. Nāgārjuna, *Yuktiṣaṣṭikā*, Peking reprint edition vol. 95, no. 5225, vv. 21 and 34. As cited by Śāntarakṣita, v. 21 reads: *'di la skye ba ci yang med, 'gag par 'gyur ba ci yang med; skye ba dang ni 'gag pa dag, shes pa 'ba 'zhig kho na'o.* The Sanskrit texts of these two verses are found in Jñānaśrīmitranibandhāvali, A. Thakur, ed., Tibetan Sanskrit Works Series vol. 5 (Patna: K. P. Jayaswal Institute, 1959), p. 545, v. 25 and v. 27. Śāntarakṣita changes the original reading so that the verses may be interpreted according to his own theory. I believe that my translation of v. 34 is supported by Kamalaśīla, who says, "it or cognition does not appear in true wisdom," in . . . *alaṃkārapañjikā* 37.1 (f. 138.b).

32. See D. T. Suzuki, trans., *Laṅkāvatārasūtra* (London: Routledge and Kegan Paul, 1956), ch. 10, vv. 256–58.

33. P. L. Vaidya, ed., *Saddharmalaṅkāvatārasūtra*, Buddhist Sanskrit Texts no. 3 (Darbhaga: The Mithila Institute, 1963), p. 124; . . . *alaṃkāravṛtti* 13.3.3–4 (f. 79, b3–4); and Ratnākaraśānti, *Prajñāpāramitopadeśa* 249.4.2 (f. 183, b2).

34. *Vicārayed*, p. 211, 1.3, should be corrected in such a form as *vicārayataḥ*.

# Yogic Direct Awareness as Means of Valid Cognition in Dharmakīrti and Rgyal-tshab

*Charlene McDermott*

## INTRODUCTION

> For what is water but human thought always running downward to low places unless it be held back by the firm control of an obstacle. Water gathered together in a vessel is thought, intent on meditation and arrested by its intentness. The gathering of the waters is the meditation of the heart.[1]

A single species of ingathering and the insight to which it leads comprise the topic of the present study; the direct awareness of yogic meditation[2] as discussed by Dharmakīrti from an epistemological point of view in the first chapter of his *Nyāyabindu* (with *ṭīkā* by Dharmottara) and as commented on by the Tibetan Buddhist philosopher Rgyal-tshab.[3] Material from the *pratyakṣa* chapter of Dharmakīrti's *Pramāṇavārttika*, and Rgyal-tshab's commentary thereupon, is also utilized where needed for clarification and support.[4]

I confine myself to these texts and their predominantly analytic approach to yogic direct awareness,[5] thereby not attempting to treat the subject exhaustively. Such an enterprise would require, among other things, considering the systematic explorations of *yogipratyakṣa* in the Indian tradition (notably Jñānaśrīmitra's *Yoginirṇayaprakaraṇa* and the related treatise *Sarvajñasiddhi*, written by Jñānaśrīmitra's pupil Ratnakīrti),[6] not to mention the glosses of the other Tibetan logicians. Too, the *prajñāpāramitā* (Tibetan *phar-phyin*) as well as the *pramāṇa* (Tibetan *tshad ma*) side of the ledger would have to be taken into detailed account,[7] the better to apprehend this hybrid experience. In addition, it would be useful to place in historical perspective the evolution, peculiar to the logical school of Buddhism, of the notion of *yogipratyakṣa* as a special sort of yogic prowess,[8] warranting a highly technical explication.

Despite their unquestionable importance, however, the foregoing matters cannot be taken up (except incidentally) within the compass of a study whose purpose is to air the intriguing and topical epistemological issues raised by Rgyal-tshab in the course of composing his *Nyāyabindu* commentary.[9] The epigrammatic signposts which introduce each section and subsection of my investigation point to ramifications of these issues germane to the interests of the comparative philosopher. This goes likewise for allusions in passing, in footnotes throughout the paper, to Western philosophical and psychological parallels; they comprise an assemblage of many crosscultural "reminders" (in Wittgenstein's sense of the term). Subsequent studies will be devoted to pursuing each of these leads further.

Now let us turn to Rgyal-tshab's remark concerning "the difficult sphere [or section], the establishment of omniscience *[thams cad mkhyen pa]* in regard to yogic direct awareness, as the object *[don]* of the chapter on direct awareness."[10] Two comments can be made here. First, the word *don* [Sanskrit *artha*] means "object" in the sense of "aim," *telos*, or "goal." Hence Dharmakīrti (and Rgyal-tshab follows him in this) first gives a careful and detailed analysis of each of the three *ordinary* varieties of direct awareness and the perceptual acts to which they lead. He then *climaxes* his discussion with an attempt to treat yogic direct awareness or *yogipratyakṣa* with equal rigor. (There are strong indications, however, in both root text and Tibetan commentary, that a purely *speculative* approach to this subject is inadequate.)

Second, *re* the foregoing *thams cad mkhyen pa* (Sanskrit *sarvajñatā*), note that the Dharmakīrtian school of Buddhist epistemology distinguishes (and concentrates upon) *sarvajñatā*, or omniscience *vis à vis* the direct intuition of the truths necessary for salvation, from *sarvasarvajñatā*, or omniscience without restriction.[11]

Note, too, Rgyal-tshab's need later in the *Rig-thigs-'grel* (hereafter referred to as *RTG*) to brush aside some skeptical misgivings concerning a yogin's unlimited knowledge. In A-13-4 he flatly "rejects the erroneous notion of those who do not accept the transcendental [meditational] knowledge which accrues to a yogin, etc."[12]

At least two steps would seem to precede this rejection on the part of Rgyal-tshab: (1) Lest the remainder of the discussion reduce to an eristic exercise on the level of that concerning the properties of the Son-of-a-barren-woman, the bare logical *possibility* (i.e., the self-consistency) of the notion of an omniscient person must be established; and (2) following this, the questions of the authenticity and proper interpretation of such a being's cognitive experiences can and will be taken up in order."[13]

Now it is true that the term "omniscient being" often figures in Dharmakīrti's logical writings as a mere substitution instance in certain specimens of modes of valid reasoning. However, this is precisely because "omniscient being" is representative of a particular class of terms which refer to concepts of entities whose existence is problematic, in the sense that existence admits of neither confirmation nor disconfirmation via ordinary experience. Hence, no apodictic conclusions can be drawn concerning such entities. But this is precisely the sort of *nihil obstat* we need. Logic leaves open the possibility that an omniscient being *can* exist in reality.[14] Moreover, not only is the notion of a yogin's transcendental direct awareness self-consistent; as Rgyal-tshab notes in A-11-4 to A-11-5 *(RTG)*,[15] what is apprehended thereby is not to be regarded as standing in contradiction to the objects apprehended by means of ordinary valid cognitive processes. That is, if *yogipratyakṣa* is *trans*rational, it is not therefore *anti*rational.[16] Thus, even the skeptical adversary who lacks faith in Buddhist doctrines and teachers must perforce be more receptive to the words of those who, presumably in possession of the proof of the pudding, attest to the genuineness of *yogipratyakṣa*.

Pressing still further, supposing the skeptic were to concede, tentatively, the facticity of the reports of such experiences. Still the question remains, in what sense is *yogipratyakṣa* correctly classifiable as a means of valid cognition or *pramāṇa*? And even provided it proves to be a *pramāṇa*, what is the value in so characterizing it and what is the scope of such a means of cognition? The sections that follow will explore these matters.

## DEFINITION AND ELABORATION OF SIGNIFICANT EPISTEMIC ATTRIBUTES

Even now one perceives something of the innermost reality as if through a mist—*St. Gregory the Great*[17]

### DEFINITION

*Yogipratyakṣa* is indeed classifiable as a means of valid cognition by logicians of Dharmakīrtian persuasion. Moreover, as its name plainly indicates, it is regarded as a means of attaining *direct* rather than indirect knowledge (or knowledge mediated through concepts).[18] That is, it is placed under the rubric of perception, *pratyākṣa* (Tibetan *mngon sum*), rather than that of inference, *anumāna* (Tibetan *rjes su dpag pa*);[19] and all *pratyākṣas* or direct awarenesses must, as a matter of definition (Sanskrit *lakṣaṇa*; Tibetan *mtshan nyid*), be: (1) free from conceptual construction (Sanskrit *kalpanāpoḍha*; Tibetan *rtog pa dang bral ba*) and (2) nonillusory (Sanskrit *abhrānta*; Tibetan *ma ḥkhrul ba*).[20]

In the Buddhist logical tradition, a list comprising the following four *pratyākṣas* is standard: (1) ordinary sensory (Sanskrit *indriya*; Tibetan *dbang po*) awareness; (2) and (3) the two species of inner awareness—viz., awareness of one's sensory awarenesses and awareness of one's emotive states; (4) yogic "intuition" or yogic direct awareness.[21] Of these, the first three are said to be found also in ordinary men, whereas the last occurs only in Āryans. Concerning this customary listing of four *pratyākṣas* or *mngon sums*, Rgyal-tshab says on A-13-4 *(RTG)* that "the number is certain relative to a purpose."[22] Here the immediate purpose is epistemological analysis, itself relative to the long-range soterial purpose which is the bringing about of adherence to the Buddhist path. But the point is that there is no finality in this or any other taxonomic catalog. The door is left open for other varieties of direct insight, e.g., for cognition of the minds of others (Sanskrit *paracittajñāna*; ṣas or *mngon sums*, Rgyal-tshab says on A-13-4 *(RTG)* that "the number is certain relative to a purpose."[22] Here the immediate purpose is epistemological analysis, itself relative to the long-range soterial purpose which is the bringing about of adherence to the Buddhist path. But the point is that there is no finality in this or any other taxonomic catalog. The door is left open for other varieties of direct insight, e.g., for cognition of the minds of others (Sanskrit *paracittajñāna*; Tibetan *gzhan sems shes pa*), and so on,[23] and for the ultimate dissolution of all philosophical distinctions. There, utility extends only to explaining the phenomenal world in the sense of explaining it away, in the face of ever deeper penetrations into reality.

Characteristic (1), or being devoid of conceptual construction, signals the crucial distinction between cognitions which are direct or immediate, on the one hand, and cognitions mediated through concepts on the other.[24] By stipulating (2), or nonillusoriness in the previous *definiens*, the Buddhists intend to demarcate veridical from pseudocognitions, or those cognitions whose intended objects are in some way divergent from or totally ungrounded in empirical reality.[25]

While fulfilling the requirements of the generic definition stated earlier,[26] *yogipratyakṣa* is set apart from its congeners (and from other varieties of superknowledge) because it alone affords a full penetration into the nature of the Four Noble Truths of Buddhism and their sixteen aspects. A-15-3 *(RTG)* refers to remarks concerning the fourth variety of seeing *(bzhi pa ni)*: "through wisdom arising from contemplation [Sanskrit *bhāvanāmayīprajña*; Tibetan *sgom pa las byung ba'i shes rab*] on an object [first] subjected to a systematic logical analysis, whose real nature [or quintessential force] is the sixteen aspects of the Four [Aryan] Truths."[27]

First note the propadeuctic function of logic in this remark of Rgyal-tshab.[28] As for the Truths mentioned, they are, of course:

1. the Truth of the ill or suffering of mundane existence (Sanskrit *duḥkhasatyam*; Tibetan *sdug bsngal bden pa*), with special attention being given to the aspect of the impermance of phenomena (Sanskrit *anityataḥ*; Tibetan *mi rtag pa*);
2. the Truth of the motive force behind or origin of the suffering of mundane existence (Sanskrit *samudaya-satya*; Tibetan *kun ḥbyung baḥi bden pa*);
3. the Truth of the cessation of the above existence along with its causes (Sanskrit *nirodhasatya*; Tibetan *ḥgog paḥi bden pa*);
4. the Truth of the path that leads to that cessation (Sanskrit *mārgasatya*; Tibetan *lam gyi bden pa*).[29]

Next, in A-15-5 *(RTG)* Rgyal-tshab describes the penultimate stage of the progress, in which the yogin's experience is not yet complete (Tibetan *ma rdzogs pa*), "from which there emerges a clear manifestation comprising completion of the yogin's cognition . . . and this cognition, nonerroneous and free from conceptualization with respect to an ultimately real object, depends on a principal cause which is calming [or tranquillization; Sanskrit *śamatha*; Tibetan *zhi (bar) gnas pa*] intimately conjoined with higher [or superior] vision [Sanskrit *vipaśyanā*; Tibetan *lhag (par) mthong (ba)*]."[30] Thus, the provenance of the climactic experience from the preceding subculminational meditational moment, the appropriate preliminary logical moves being indispensable to the whole process; and this experience marks the first moment of the pellucidity of Āryanhood, the inception of the Path of Vision.[31]

It cannot be overemphasized that in the course of intensive meditation thereupon, the Four Truths are no longer merely grasped in an abstract intellectual sense, as they are in the initial stages of their comprehension by logical means alone. Rather, in *yogipratyakṣa* the *satyas* or Truths become so deeply engrained on the seer's being by each repeated endeavor of his, that the intrinsic nature of his mind, which supports the act of apprehending those Truths, itself receives nutritive support and "firming" through his very process of meditative apprehension.[32] The Truths have become, as it were, the Buddhist saint's inner "Archimedean point," ultimately enabling him to lever away the whole mass of delusion and ill.

In sum, the Āryan's "gnosis" proceeds from a tripartite basis consisting of (1) what accrues to preliminary study and learning *(śrutamayī)*, followed by (2) the outcome of logical investigation *(cintāmayī)*, and crowned by (3) the fruit of concentrated contemplation *(bhāvanāmayī)*.[33] One is tempted to say, paraphrasing Kant: "*Bhāvanāmayī* without *cintāmayī* is empty; *cintāmayī* without *bhāvanāmayī* is blind." Put still more simply, only when *bhāvanāmayī* crowns *cintāmayī* does one "see" with the utmost clarity and vividness.

Apropos, since Dharmakīrti has given careful attention in both the *Nyāyabindu* and the *Pramāṇavārttika* to clarity (Sanskrit *sphuṭatva*; Tibetan *gsal ba*) as a feature of all *pratyākṣas*—his definitional requirement that a *pratyākṣa* be free from conceptual construction, amounting in the long run to his positing clarity (in the sense of vividness or vivacity) as the hallmark of all *direct* cognition[34]—a separate subsection next takes up the matter of *sphuṭatva* with special emphasis on its connection with *yogipratyakṣa*. Following that, the third subsection comprises a similarly detailed consideration of the not unrelated[35] requirement that each *pratyākṣa* be nonillusory.

## ON *SPHUṬATVA*

> All the perceptions of the human mind resolve themselves into two distinct kinds, which I shall call *Impressions* and *Ideas.* The difference betwixt these consists in the degree of force and liveliness with which they strike upon the mind, and make their way into our thought or consciousness. Those perceptions which enter with most force and violence we may name *impressions*; and under this name I comprehend all our sensations, passions and emotions, as they make their first appearance in the Soul. By ideas I mean the faint images of these in thinking and reasoning. . . . Impressions and ideas differ only in their strength and vivacity.—*David Hume*[36]

Possession of *sphuṭatva* or clarity (i.e., vividness, liveliness, vivacity) is a *necessary (though not a sufficient)* condition to which all putative *pratyākṣas* must conform.[37] But the clarity characteristic of *yogipratyakṣa* is functionally independent of the five senses.[38] By a paramount act of self-control, the Buddhist yogin deliberately inhibits the incursion of sensory stimuli (while simultaneously "disconnecting" the mechanism of conceptualization). Furthermore, the vividness with which the Āryan "sees" the Four Truths is *not* even conditioned by *immediately preceding* sensory awareness; hence, *yogipratyakṣa* can be distinguished from *mānasa-pratyākṣa*, with which it has sometimes been confused.[39]

Finally, as the third subsection will argue, there is a crucial epistemic difference between a yogin's act of direct awareness and the specious but clear-seeming visions of "those afflicted by thievish dreams, insanity, fear, pain and desire, who see irrelia as if present in front of them."[40]

So much by way of contrast and denial concerning the *sphuṭatva* of *yogipratyakṣa.* The most perspicuous graduated *positive* description of the yogin's success in "brushing away the cobwebs of conceptualization" *(vidhūtakalpanājālam)*[41] is probably the well-known account in *Nyāyabinduṭīkā*, page 12-1 to 12-3,[42] wherein three successive grades or degrees of clarity are enumerated: (1) a prelibationary experience followed by (2) a deeper (though still beclouded) contemplative awareness, this on the very threshold of Āryanhood and leading to (3) a climactic seeing "as clear [or vivid] as if one were gazing at an *āmalaka* [i.e., a small fruit] on the palm of one's hand." (Stage 3 is a terminus which is, at the same time, a first step on the Path of Vision, where the "vision" alluded to differs from those that preceded it, not merely in the degree of its intensity, but in its very essence.)

Here Rgyal-tshab rests content with a mere abbreviated version of his predecessor's gloss:

> According to what is said by the teacher Dharmottara, [at first it is] as if [one's view] were obstructed by [a cloud] of mica; in the state [or condition] approaching the extreme limits, one envisions the object of concentrated contemplation as if it were an *āmalaka* situated in the palm of one's hand.[43]

Note that while *yogipratyakṣa* is free from the macaronic clutter of signals from the "external" world, the Buddhists' abundant use of similes and metaphors unabashedly borrowed from statements descriptive of ordinary visual awareness is apt to obscure this fact.[44] It is easy enough, however, to adduce cases of similar figurative usage in the Western mystical tradition. St. Bonaventure, for instance, in his *Breviloquium* 11 and 12, speaks of the eye of the body, the eye of reason, and the eye of contemplation, and this from a tradition dating back at least to Denis the Areopagite; and Denis himself depicts a darkness wherein ordinary sensations cease and one's spiritual eyes are opened. Such examples could be multiplied indefinitely, which would seem to point to a feature endemic in the very endeavor to verbalize such experiences, and not to something which uniquely flaws the Buddhist attempts.

## ON *ABHRĀNTI*

> Within Western culture we have strong negative attitudes towards Altered States of Consciousness: there is the normal (good) state of consciousness and there are pathological changes in consciousness. Most people make no further distinc-

> tions. . . . In a broader perspective it is clear that man has functioned in a multitude of states of consciousness and that different cultures have varied enormously in recognition and utilization of, and attitudes towards, ASCs. . . . It could be expected that within psychology and psychiatry there would be far more exact terms for describing various ASCs and their components, but except for a rich (but often not precise) vocabulary dealing with psychopathological states, this is not true.—*C. Tart*[45]

Referring back to *abhrānta*, the second of the two essential characteristics stipulated in the definition of *pratyākṣa*, how, precisely, are the genuine instances of *pratyākṣa* as *pramāṇa* to be distinguished from those nonveridical awarenesses which closely resemble them? In particular, how is one to differentiate the insights of a Buddhist saint from those of the thaumaturge, the psychopath, the blundering dreamer, or the "freaked-out" tripster?

Here again, *propter brevitatem*, we consider only the words of Dharmakīrti and of Rgyal-tshab. Recall, first, that one of the conclusions of the foregoing section is that knowledge mediated by a concept does *not* manifest itself clearly. Rgyal-tshab enlarges on this as follows: "Since there is pervasion by the nonpossession of a clear mental manifestation as object, in case there is constructive mental synthesis in connection with a concept."[46] That is, the presence of a conceptual construction entails the absence of a clear *prima facie* mental manifestation or reflex (Sanskrit *pratibhāsa*; Tibetan *snang ba*). The contrapositive, of course, also holds: viz., the occurrences of a clear *snang ba* in a given case signals that there is no conceptual intermediary operative. Rgyal-tshab is quick to point out that, while it *is* the hallmark of nonconceptuality, a clear or vivid mental panorama *is not*, in itself, a guarantee of the existence of a veridical object of cognition. For, towards the end of 282-B in *Tshad-ma-rnam-'grel* (hereafter to be referred to as *TMNG*), Rgyal-tshab considers (and finally answers in the *affirmative*) the question of whether dreams, fear, and so on (recall the *Pramāṇavārttika* passage quoted previously), and meditational exercises are capable of engendering clear *snang bas*, in the absence of any real objective correlates. Here he counters the opinion that there can be no clear direct "seeing" of a spurious object, by explicitly asserting the possibility of "the emergence through repeated yogic practice of a clear mental manifestation in regard to an erroneous object. As in the case of the [pseudoperception engendered] in the course of [meditating on] impurity."[47] Here, according to Rgyal-tshab, we have an instance of a concept-free and therefore *gsal bar snang ba* which is *'khrul ba* or erroneous—this in direct contrast to the case of the yogin's comprehension of not-self (Sanskrit *anātman*; Tibetan *bdag med)* which, although *lacking in clarity* (because indirectly apprehended), is nonetheless nonerroneous *(ma 'khrul ba)* as will be argued subsequently.

Now the Buddhist yogin who contemplates the Four Āryan Truths, in the course of his intensive and prolonged meditations, also evokes his object, and this with ever greater luminosity. In this case, however, there is no question of his having given rise to a mere subjective creation, as if via a principle of sufficient wishing. Rather, the yogin, as the *Pramāṇavārttika* tells us, employs a genuine means of valid cognition or *pramāṇa*, which puts him in touch with what has aleady been ascertained to be real.[48] Moreover, his meditative activity is also efficacious in leading him to still higher levels of spirituality and transcendent insight.

Here, and this is consonant with Dharmakīrti's theories about perception in general, efficacy in directing human purposive activity (and not some *intrinsic* attribute of the *snang ba* itself) is the touchstone of the authenticity of (in this case) the yogin's perception. But, given the limited information supplied by Dharmakīrti and his commentators,[49] it is difficult to see how one not well along the way to full enlightenment is to derive any comfort or utility from the discriminative criterion which stems from the philosopher's words.

It would seem, then, that the logical writings of Dharmakīrti contain a surprising amount of residual untidiness concerning the difficulties connected with distinguishing a veridical perception from one that has misfired. But there is, I think, a moral to be drawn from the fact that neither has any other Eastern or Western philosopher yet come up with an entirely satisfactory solution to this fundamental epistemological problem; and the moral is simply that the relationship between cognitive phenomena (both ordinary and extraordinary) and other sub-, supra-, and defective conscious states is far more complex than has heretofore been supposed. The demand for a hard and fast distinction between genuine and counterfeit perceptual acts is just one symptom of an *a priori* commitment to an untenably simplistic dogma about the structures and workings of the human psyche, which dogma the findings of modern experimental psychology are only beginning to dislodge.[50] Hence the relevance of the plea, implicit in the quotation from Tart at the beginning of this subsection, for the recognition, unprejudiced understanding and utilization of a much broader spectrum of "Altered States of Consciousness."

## PRACTICAL ASPECTS

> [The psyche] fashions itself a ladder for itself—*St. Gregory the Great*[51]

Not withstanding the avowedly speculative orientation of our study, to set things in proper balance we now turn very briefly to a consideration of the practical (viz., ascetico-contemplative[52] *cum* moral-spiritual) aspects of this many-runged ascent. It has aleady been remarked that the trans-phenomenal gaze of *yogipratyakṣa* is regarded as being reserved exclusively for Āryans[53] (and that in point of fact, very few ever succeed at the prerequisite self-transformation, in regard to both wisdom and compassion, a transformation so radical that it is perhaps more accurately described as an act of "transpeciation"). But to categorize the Buddhist yogin's seeing as *extraordinary*—the portion of the happy few—is not to imply that it is *unnatural*. On the contrary, it is supremely natural, evincing the maturation of one's inherent Buddha potential.

In a being sufficiently purified and becalmed by appropriate exercises, a spiritual progress through well-delineated stages can be charted, in which theoretical and practical elements stand in a close symbiotic relationship to one another. Typically, a Path of Accumulating Merit (Sanskrit *sambhāramārga*; Tibetan *tshogs lam*), in the course of which one assimilates percepts and instructions for an incalculable eon, is thought to lead to a Path of Training (Sanskrit *prayoga-mārga*; Tibetan *sbyor lam*) wherein rigorous purgation, self-tranquilization, and a high degree of philosophical attainment become ancillary to entrance upon the Path of Vision (Sanskrit *darśana-mārga*; Tibetan *mthong lam*). Thereafter, the Path of Concentrated Contemplation (Sanskrit *bhāvanā-mārga*;[54] Tibetan *sgom lam*) leads to the Path of Fulfillment (literally, the Path beyond Studentship: Sanskrit *aśaikṣa-mārga*; Tibetan *mi slob pa'i lam*). Here yogic techniques are instrumental in enhancing the yogin's breadth and depth of comprehension of the Four Truths, and this fuller comprehension, in turn, effects further purification and control, and so on.[55]

## CONCLUSION

Words cannot describe the passing beyond the limits human significance—*Dante*[56]

Implicit in the foregoing investigation into the sources, intrinsic nature and consequences of *yogipratyakṣa* is a delimitation of the proper spheres of the phenomenal and the transphenomenal. Frustratingly enough, much of what is most important about our subject lies beyond the limits of the former; whence any attempt to comprehend (and to explicate) the yogin's insight via the unaided machinery of reason—discursive language and conceptual constructs—would appear to be foredoomed to court paradox or come to the full stop of ineffability.

With more than a little irony, one notes the spate of words emanating from the supposed barrier constituted by the supralinguistic and supraconceptual. For example, from Dharmakīrti himself we have: "A yogin's knowledge surpasses what can be conceived";[57] for which assertion neither Jñānaśrīmitra nor Ratnakīrti can be adjudged remiss in the task of providing an extensive commentary.[58]

But the yogin's vision, born out of his condition of pristine spontaneity, has, so it seems, relegated all predicates (even "real" and "unreal") to the realm of fictitious constructs. In fact, the very notion of the Buddhist saint's intellectual and spiritual "ascent" (at least so his course tends to be regarded from a worldly point of view) is itself exposed as no more than part and parcel of a mock show. As we are told in section 19 of Kamalaśīla's *First Bhāvanākrama:* "So also in consequence of that illusion which consists in the accumulation of virtue and knowledge, the illusion of yogic knowledge arises in the yogin. . . . [But] the yogin like the magician recognizes the illusion for what it is and therefore he has no attachment to it, because he knows that it is not real."[59]

It is much the same, *at least superficially*, in the Western mystical tradition. Figures of speech such as "learned ignorance" or "cloud of unknowing" come to mind. Perhaps an even more familiar illustration is St. Thomas Aquinas' famous dictum: "We know God as unknown" *(Deum tamquam ignotium cognoscimus).* And not unlike the bodhisattva's posttransic efforts to partially reconstruct "the all-pervading nature of the Absolute"[60] is St. Augustine's "return to the vocal utterances of the human mouth, where discourse has [both] a beginning and an end,"[61] in the aftermath of Augustine's having mentally transcended the very bounds of heaven itself.

Without wishing to deny the refractoriness of our subject matter, it is well to pause not and note that at least some of the difficulties which crop up in attempting to formulate an adequate epistemological theory of *yogipratyakṣa* are not peculiar to its elusive nature as such. One especially interesting illustration of this point is the case of the yogin's alleged cognitions of not-self or unsubstantiality (Sanskrit *anātman*; Tibetan *bdag med*). Obviously a denial in the absolute sense is central to the construction of this concept,[62] which would seem, *prima facie*, to deprive the would-be cognizer of any possible cognitive content. Hence Rgyal-tshab, in his *Nyāyabindu* commentary, finds it necessary to lay to rest the Sautrāntika doubts concerning the yogin's ability to cognize *bdag med*.[63]

Now, since both Rgyal-tshab and Dharmakīrti concur in the opinion that such a cognition is nonillusory (i.e., *abhrānta*), the Buddhist saint's comprehension of *bdag med* or *anātman* cannot simply be written off as the mere grasping of a phantasmagoric object, spawned by his own psyche in the course of his meditational exercises, and having no existence outside of that meditational context.

The veridicality of the yogin's cognition of *anātman* can be established by tracing that cognition to its source in his experiencing of impermanence (Sanskrit *anityatā*; Tibetan *mi rtag pa nyid*). And while this experience also hinges on a type of denial or negation, nonetheless the negation operative in the *mi rtag pa* case is of the *min dgag* and not the *med dgag* variety (cf. note 62). Hence a residual positive element, the direct yogic insight into momentariness,[64] is available to the experiencer to appropriate as the content of his cognition. The upshot of this discussion is that *bdag med* is properly knowable by the yogin; however, since Rgyal-tshab here concludes that it is *not directly* knowable, it is not, strictly speaking, an object of *yogipratyakṣa* (or *rnal 'byor mngon sum)*.[65] But anyone acquainted with Buddhist logic will recognize the case of *bdag med* to be assimilable *(mutatis mutandis)* to those cases of analyses of terms legitimately referring to "nonexistent" entities in the ordinary man's discourse (e.g., to the well-known example of the horn whose existence on the head of a rabbit is denied).[66] The former account of matters stands or falls with the latter. The fact that the one case devolves on paranormal perceptual activity, does not, in itself, suffice either to vitiate or to vindicate our explanation. In a larger sense, both cases serve ultimately to direct each man to the point where, by means of *prajñā*, he, as a perfect yogin, no longer perceives any essence of things, whence "no representation of a thing arises in him; and so not even the representation of a no-thing arises in him."[67]

## NOTES

My thanks to the National Endowment for the Humanities, who made possible the research on which this study is based.

1. Richard of St. Victor, *Benjamin Major*, Book V, ch. 11, cited in C. Kirchberger, trans., *Richard of St. Victor: Selected Writings on Contemplation* (London: Faber and Faber, 1957), p. 198. Richard actually borrows this metaphor from Hugh, also a "Victorine" or member of the school of St. Victor.
2. Sanskrit *yogipratyakṣa*; Tibetan *rnal 'byor mngon sum.*
3. Dharmakīrti, *Nyāyabindu*; Dharmottara, *Nyāyabinduṭīkā*, F. Stcherbatsky, ed., in *Bibliotheca Buddhica* VII (1918); and Rgyal-tshab, *Rig-thigs-'grel* (Tibetan block print). My current involvement with the Tibetan commentarial tradition dates from a series of conversations with the late Richard Robinson, who, to encourage my emerging awareness of "Tibet's rich contribution to world cultural ecology" (as he put it), arranged for me to work under his colleague Geshe Sopa, of the University of Wisconsin-Madison. I cannot adequately express my debt to Geshe Sopa for his help in reading Rgyal-tshab's commentaries.
4. Dharmakīrti, *Pramāṇavārttika* (Varanasi: Baudhha Bharati, 1968); and Rgyal-tshab, *Tshad-ma-rnam-'grel* (Tibetan block print).
5. Viz., an approach whose primary concern is the *cognitive import* of *yogipratyakṣa.* To what extent is such an experience assessable as a means of valid cognition (Sanskrit *pramāṇa*; Tibetan *tshad ma*)?
6. See, respectively, A. Thakur, ed., *Jñānaśrīmitranibandhāvalī*, Tibetan Sanskrit Works Series vol. V (Patna: K. P. Jayaswal Research Institute, 1959), pp. 323–42; and Thakur, *Ratnakīrtinibandhāvalī*, pp. 1–28.
7. Standard texts for this in the Tibetan school with which we are here concerned include the *Abhisamayālaṃkāra*, via Haribhadra's *Sphuṭārthā* or *'grel pa don gsal*, in *Analysis of the Abhisamayālaṃkāra*, E. Obermiller (London: Luzac and Co., 1933), and Rgyal-tshab's *Rnam-bshad-snying-po'i-rgyan* (Tibetan block print).
8. To be distinguished, at least provisionally, from the *abhijñās* (superknowledges) which also accrue to the Buddhist Āryan and from the attainments of the sufficiently advanced non-Buddhist yogin, who is said to be capable of acquiring five of the *abhijñās*, the sixth or ultimate insight into the truth of cessation being reserved exclusively for the Buddhist saint.

On the *abhijñās* see, for example, M. Eliade, *Yoga: Immortality and Freedom*, W. Trask, trans. (Princeton: Princeton University Press, 2nd ed., 1969), pp. 178–85. Vācaspatimīśra's *Nyāyakaṇika*, (Pandit, New Series vol. XXVI, 1907), includes an account of the alleged omnisciences of both the Brahmanical and the Buddhist yogin. See esp. 110.16, 147.4 ff., and 205.16 ff. See also J. Shah, *Akalaṅka's Criticism of Dharmakīrti's Philosophy* (Ahmedabad: L.D. Institute of Indology, 1967), p. 232, for a discussion of the Jaina conception of *kevala-jñāna* or omniscience.

9. Rgyal-tshab's commentary to the "*pratyākṣa*" chapter, it will be noticed, is more or less Sautrāntika in its orientation.

10. *RMG* B-2-1: *Mngon sum lehu'i don rnal 'byor mngon sum thams cad mkhyen pa bsgrub pa dka' ba'i gnas dang.*

11. For more on this, see, e.g., Kajiyama, *Buddhist Philosophy*, pp. 136–37.

12. *Spyod pa po sogs rnal 'byor pa'i shes pa khas mi len pa dag gi log par rtog pa bsal ba'i phyir.*

13. Duns Scotus, it will be recalled, has a well-known "coloration" of the Anselmian ontological proof for the existence of God, which amounts to Scotus's appending to that proof a demonstration of the *noncontradictoriness* of the notion of God *qua* infinite being. See E. Bettoni, ed. and trans., *Duns Scotus* (Washington: Catholic University of America Press, 1961), pp. 135–36. Despite the undeniable Scotistic tenor of (1) and (2), I do not wish to impute the self-conscious procedural explicitness of Duns Scotus to the Buddhists. But other remarks made by Rgyal-tshab, plus the passages cited in the note which follows, indicate that Dharmakīrti and his followers were not insensitive to the need to counter charges of inconsistency in regard to the epistemic claims they made on behalf of *yogipratyakṣa*.

14. See F. T. Stcherbatsky, *Buddhist Logic*, vol. 2 (New York: Dover Publications, 1962), pp. 56, 185–87. See also Kajiyama, *Buddhist Philosophy*, pp. 134–36, for Mokṣākaragupta's citation of Ratnakīrti's proof of the possibility of *sarvajñatā*, the type of omniscience with which Dharmakīrti and his followers are primarily concerned. And as a matter of fact, even *sarvasarvajñatā*, or unrestricted omniscience is dealt with in Mokṣākaragupta's demonstration on pp. 136–37.

15. *RTG: tha snyad pa'i tshad ma'i gzhal bya don dam pa'i tshad mas sun 'byin pa bden pa gnyis tsha grang ltar khas len dgos pa'i rigs pa'i rnam gzhag zhib tu khong du ma chud pa'i mu cor smra ba 'bah zhig tu shes par bya'o.*

16. At least in this respect, there is no parallel with the previously mentioned Victorines (see note 1), who bifurcate the insights of higher contemplation into: (1) a species *above* ordinary human reason *but not contrary* to it; and (2) a species both *above and contrary* to reason. See Kirchberger, *Richard of St. Victor*, p. 142.

17. *Iamque de intimis aliquid quasi per caliginen conspicit.* (St. Gregory the Great, *Moralia* viii, 50; J. P. Migne, *Patrologia Cursus Completus*, vol. 57.)

18. For the Buddhists there are two and only two means of valid cognition or *pramāṇas:* (1) the direct *(pratyākṣa)*, and (2) the indirect or inferential *(anumāna)*.

19. In fact, it was no doubt the need to accommodate this supernal species of direct awareness alongside of its three mundane siblings (see later), that was a factor motivating the Buddhist logicians to frame their definition of direct awareness as broadly as possible. In contradistinction to some of the definitions proffered by their non-Buddhist adversaries, the Buddhist definition omits restrictive references to the usual sensory modalities as the exclusive, or even the primary, channels of direct awareness. See M. Hattori, *Dignāga on Perception* (Cambridge: Harvard University Press, 1968), pp. 36–70.

20. See *RTG* B-11-4; also A-12-1. In addition, a minimal presupposition, implicit in the very ability to frame this definition, is that all *pratyākṣas qua pramāṇas* (or means of valid cognition) yield self-consistent (Sanskrit *avisaṃvādin*; Tibetan *mi slu ba*) knowledge. See note 18 of my "Direct Sensory Awareness," *Philosophy East and West* 23 (July 1973): pp. 343–60.

21. Sanskrit (2) *mānasa-*, (3) *svasaṃvedana-*, and (4) *yogipratyakṣa*; Tibetan (2) *yid kyi*, (3) *rang rig*, and (4) *rnal 'byor mngon sum*, respectively.

22. *RTG: dgos pa la bltos pa'i grangs nges so.*

23. See note 7.

24. Cf. B. K. Matilal, *Epistemology, Logic, and Grammar in Indian Philosophical Analysis* (The Hague: Mouton, 1971), pp. 37–38. Note that although *pratyākṣas* are devoid of *conceptual* determination, they are not therefore to be construed as vague or hazy; quite the contrary, as will be seen in the section on *sphuṭatva.*

25. See, e.g., *Nyāyabindu* 4.2–4.7 and 9.5–9.19 for instances and etiological explanations of certain aberrant psychological phenomena, including both illusions of perception and the more controversial "illusions of sensation." More about the problem of recognizing defective *pratyākṣa ni* for what they are is found in the section on *abhrānti.* Regarding the larger issue raised by the Yogācārins—the fact that in a sense even "veridical" ordinary cognitions are trained by a transcendental illusion, see note 20 of my "Direct Sensory Awareness."

26. See, e.g., *RTG* A-15-6, which begins by describing *yogipratyakṣa* or *rnal 'byor mngon sum* as "cognition nonerroneous and free from conceptualization with respect to an ultimately real nature or object [Sanskrit *bhūtārtha*] arising from . . . " Note 30 following quotes this passage in its entirety and translates it.

27. *RTG* A-15-4: *bden pa bzhi'i rnam pa bcu drug dngos stobs kyi rigs*

*pas gtan la phebs pa'i don sgom pa las byung ba'i shes rab kyis.* Cf. also *TMNG* 282 A-6: *sngar le'u gnyis par bshad pa'i rnal 'byor pa'i rgyud kyi bden bz'i'i gnas lugs mngon sum du rtogs pa'i shes pa de dag chos can.*

28. Although the ultimate insight is surely beyond the power of logic to attain, a thoroughgoing logical investigation of our subject matter is a necessary prerequisite for entrance upon the "Path of Vision." The demand for antecedent purification of the "gold" of the Buddha word by the application of stringent logico-epistemological criteria is a well-known motif in late Buddhist logic. See, e.g., Hattori, *Dignāga on Perception*, p. 73.

29. See, for example, Y. Y. Obermiller's more detailed discussion of the subject in his *Analysis of the* Abhisamayālaṃkāra (London: E. J. Brill, 1932–33), pp. 35–38.

30. *RTG* A-15-5 to A-15-6: *de las byung ba'i gsal snang rdzogs pa'i rnal 'byor pa'i shes pa chos can. . . . lhag mthong dang zung du 'brel bai'i zhi gnas kyi bdag rkyen la brten nas yang dag pa'i don la rtog bral ma 'khrul pa'i shes pa yin pa'i phyir ro.*

31. Cf. *TMNG* 281-5: *yang dag pa'i don la dmigs pa'i z'i lhag zung 'brel gyi ting nge 'dzin bsgom pas chos mchog gi skabs su thob pa'i ting nge 'dzin de'i bdag po las mthong lam skad cig dang po'i yang dag pa'i don mngon sum du rtogs pa'i lhag mthong gi ye shes skye ba lta bu'o.* It goes without saying that, in this context, talk of moments is only a matter of pragmatics. Strictly speaking, a yogin's experience surpasses all methods of temporal (and spatial) mensuration. Nonetheless, it may be instructional to single out or isolate for emphasis aspects or "moments" both preceding and within the peak experience itself; whence the traditional emphasis on each, in turn, of sixteen aspects of the transcendent vision of *yogipratyakṣa* will extirpate. See E. Conze, *The Large* Sūtra *on Perfect Wisdom* (London: Luzac, for the Oriental Studies Foundation, 1961), p. 201.

32. See, for example, the description in *TMNG* 282 A-3: *rten brten goms pa'i rtsol ba re res . . .*

33. This is discussed by G. Tucci in his summary of the contents of Kamalaśīla's *Bhāvanākrama* I; see esp. pp. 160–64 of Tucci, *Minor Buddhist Texts*, Part II. Kamalaśīla's writings are representative of one very influential line of development stemming from Dharmakīrti, the Yogācāra-mādhyamika-svātantrika school. The basic tenets of this school are very lucidly summarized in Geshe Sopa and Elvin Jones, "A Light to Yogācāra Svātantrika: The Steps of Meditation—The Three *Bhāvanākramas* of Kamalaśīla" (unpublished manuscript, 1968), Part I.

34. All *pratyākṣas* or direct awareness can be seen to possess a characteristic *sphuṭatva*; its absence is symptomatic of an indirect act of cognition or one mediated through conceptual constructions and thereby obscured, commensurately less vivid. See, e.g., Dharmakīrti, *Pramāṇavārttika*, p. 184, v. 283: *na vikalpānubaddhasyāsti sphuṭārthāvabhāsitā.* See also Stcherbatsky, *Buddhist Logic*, vol. 2, p. 398, note 5.

35. See again Stcherbatsky, *Buddhist Logic*, vol. 2, p. 17.

36. David Hume, *A Treatise on Human Nature* (London: T. H. Green and T. H. Grose, 1886, repr. 1964), Book I, part I, section 1, except for the last sentence, which is from Book I, part 1, section 7 of the same work. T. Govier, "Variations on Force and Vivacity in Hume," *Philosophical Quarterly* 22 (1972):44–52, points out that Hume uses several "I-V" terms (or terms referring to an idea's clarity or amount of detail) interchangeably—viz., "vivacious," "lively," "intense." All of these also seem to be intersubstitutable *salve veritate* in contexts translating the Buddhist technical term *sphuta* here under analysis. Accordingly, we shall employ the I-V terms as virtual synonyms in the discussion that follows.

37. The clarity or vividness under discussion here is decidedly *not* to be equated with *conceptual determinancy.* In fact, any *sphuṭatva* which accrues to our conceptual constructions is merely derivative from some antecedent direct awareness, is a mere "faint image" of some "livelier impressions," to put it in Hume's language.

38. Ratnakīrti, "Sarvajñasiddih," pp. 1–28 of *Ratnakirtīnibandhavālī*, A. Thakur, ed. (Patna: K. P. Jayaswal Research Institute, 1957), p. 14-33, considers the question: *kinca tadyogi jñānamindriyajñānā-dbhinnanabhinnam va.* Compare his *na cendriyajñānasya bhāvanā* (*ibid.*, p. 15-4) with the same assertion in Jñānaśrīmitra, *Yogiṇirnayaprakaraṇa* ed., A. Thakur (Patna: K. P. Jayaswal Research Institute, 1959), p. 328-12. Only in the yogin's state of radical introversion can the mind function in its pristine autonomy.

39. See, for example, Kajiyama, *Buddhist Philosophy*, p. 46.

40. *Pramāṇavārttika*, p. 184, v. 282: *kāmaśokabhayonmādacaurasvapnādyupaplutāh abhūtānapi paśyanti purato "vasthitāniva."*

41. *Ibid.*, p. 184, v. 281.

42. Stcherbatsky, "Dharmottara's *Nyāyabinduṭīkā*," p. 12.1 to 12.3: *tadiha sphuṭābhatvārambhāvasthā bhāvanāprakarṣah abhrakavyavahitamiva yadā bhāvyamānam vastu paśyati sā prakarṣaparyantāvasthā karatalāmalakavadbhāvyamānusyārthasya yaddarśanaṃ tadyoginaḥ pratyakṣam.* In this regard, the Buddhist pilgrim fares more happily than does his Christian counterpart. Gregory the Great, for example, resignedly admits in his *Moralia* that regardless of the degree of its moral progress, the human mind is still obliged to look on the ultimate truth under the shroud of some sort of imagery: "Yet this unsubstantial and hasty vision, which results from contemplation or rather, so to speak, this semblance of a vision, is called the face of god." (*Moralia*, XXIV, II, translation from Oxford Library of Fathers, 1851)

43. *RTG* A-15-6 to B-15-1: *slob dpon chos mchog gi gsung nas. lhang tsher gyis bar du chod pa bzhin du. sgom bya'i don mthong ba de ni rab kyi mtha'i gnas skabs yin la. lag mthil du she sgong bzhag pa bzhin du mthong ba ni mngon sum yin no zhes gsung ngo.*

44. The *prajñā* eye or eye of analytic vision *(zhes rab kyi span)* comes to mind immediately.Too, the description of a momentary particular (Sanskrit *svalakṣaṇa*; Tibetan *rang gi mtshan nyid*) as producing a mental reflex whose clarity is inversely proportional to its distance from the beholder (*Nyāyabindu* 13-14—here, one's expectations of an analysis at least as sophisticated as that of Berkeley's *New Theory of Vision* are, alas, unfulfilled) further manifests Dharmakīrti's tendency to draw on ordinary optical phenomena as paradigms. In all fairness, it must be added that Dharmakīrti is stipulating here a sufficient (and not a necessary) condition for the presence of a *svalakṣaṇa*, so that he is by no means to be interpreted as imputing spatial attributes to all *svalakṣaṇas*, for those which figure in a yogin's experiential realm are surely aspatial.

45. C. Tart, *Altered States of Consciousness* (New York: John Wiley & Sons, 1969), pp. 2 and 3. On page 2, Tart defines an "altered state of consciousness" for a given individual as "one in which he clearly feels a *qualitative* shift in his pattern of mental functioning, that is, he feels not just a quantitative shift . . . but also that some quality or qualities of his mental processes are *different*." Tart also includes an alternative definition of an altered state of consciousness more palatable to those with behaviorist commitments.

46. *TMNG* 282-B-6: *Rnam par rtog pa dang rjes su 'brel zhing rtog pa'i blo yin na don gsal bar snang ba can ma yin pas khyab pa'i phyir.*

47. *TMNG* 282-A-3: *Phyin ci log gi don goms pas gsal snang 'byung ste mi gtsang ba dang*. For more on the generative powers of protracted and uninterrupted contemplation, see Manorathanandin's commentary to verse 285 of Dharmakīrti's *Pramāṇavārttika*, p. 185. Note the germaneness of Rgyal-tshab's and Manorathanandiṇ's remarks to the discussion of the "Perky effect" in note 50 following.

48. Cf. the *Pramāṇavārttika*, p. 185, v. 286: *tatra pramāṇam saṃvādi yat prān nirṇitavastuvat tad bhāvanājam pratyakṣamiṣṭam, śeṣa upaplavāh*, and a segment of Manorathanandin's commentary thereto, which reads as follows: *prāk prathamaparicchede nirḥitaṃ vastu satya catuṣṭayaṃ tasminniva yathā aryasatyaviṣayam bhāvanābalajaṃ samvāditvat partyakṣaṃ pramāṇam, evamanyadapīdṛśam.*

49. And Rgyal-tshab's glosses do not constitute a significant improvement on Dharmakīrti's treatises in this regard.

50. To cite just two from a vast number of pertinent examples of the fruits of recent research, first, the experiments of Perky (1910) point to, among other things, a difference in degree and not in kind, between genuine sensations and those which are the mere confections of our imagination. In a concluding paragraph of his "Imagery and Reality: Can They Be Distinguished?" in W. Keup, ed., *Origins and Mechanisms of Hallucinations* (New York: Plenum Press, 1970), pp. 103–11, S. J. Segal, whose own

research is an extrapolation from the findings of Perky, finds reasons for saying: "Perhaps the basic psychological assumption that distinction between the 'real' and the 'illusory' is an 'innate given' is wrong: perhaps the percept and the image do not really differ at all." And, to take the second example from the same anthology in which Segal's paper appears, I. Feinberg ("Hallucinations, Dreaming and REM Sleep," *loc. cit.*, pp. 125–32) presents a critical survey of experimental studies relating to the testing of Aristotle's hypothesis "that the hallucinations of madness result from aberrant functioning of those mechanisms which normally produce hallucinations during sleep, i.e., the mechanisms of dreaming."

51. *Sibi de seipse gradus ascensionis facit.* St. Gregory the Great, *Homiliarum in Ezechielem* II, vol. 8, J. P. Migne, *Patrologia Cursus Completus*, vol. LXXVI, Paris, 1857–86, to which the Buddhist logician might well add, "a ladder giving access to the insight into its own voidness and the voidness of that voidness."

52. M. Eliade's term. Cf. his *Yoga: Immortality and Freedom*, p. 108.

53. *TMNG* 282-A-1: *nyan thos dang rang sangs rgyas dang theg pa chen po pa dang.* In this connection, the commentarial tradition from which Rgyal-tshab descends never tires of stressing the points of superiority of the bodhisattva's adherence to the Paths listed following over the corresponding courses pursued by each of the other two sub-varieties of Āryan: the śrāvaka and pratyekabuddha.

54. Note that the Path of Vision (or Path of Illumination) and the Path of Concentrated Contemplation cannot really be regarded as separate entities "inasmuch as there is no difference regarding the object of these Paths, viz., the [Absolute] reality which is first intuited on the Path of Illumination" (Obermiller, *Analysis*, p. 47). There is, however, therapeutic value in meditating on these (from an empirical point of view) as if different from one another.

55. One of the fruits of entering upon the Path of Vision (and this by no means an incidental or "fringe" benefit) is the extirpation of one hundred twelve varieties of defiling elements (Sanskrit *kleśa*; Tibetan *nyon mongs*): viz., those due to perverse views. See Obermiller, *Analysis*, pp. 146–48. Interestingly enough, however, so-called "innate" defilements do not yield to this method of expurgation, requiring instead concentrated contemplation. Indeed, just as a washerman employs a stronger solvent at the last stages of laundering a soiled garment, so, the higher the *bhūmi* or stage of spiritual progress, the stronger the measures which must be taken to expunge the ever subtler residual *kleśas*.

56. *Trasumanar significar per verba no si poria.* Dante, *Paradiso*, Canto I, line 20, C. H. Grandgent, ed. (Cambridge: Harvard University Press, 1972).

57. *Acintyā yogināṃ gatiḥ. Pramāṇavārttika*, p. 253, end of v. 532.

58. *Yoginirṇayaprakarṇa*, p. 329, 1.4 ff.; "Sarvajñasiddhi," pp. 20–21.

59. Translated by Tucci, *Minor Buddhist Texts*, p. 174.

60. Obermiller, *Analysis*, pp. 144–45.

61. Remeavimus ad strepitum oris nostri ubi verbum et incipitur et finitur, St. Augustine, *Confessions*, William Watts, trans. (Cambridge: Harvard University Press, 1968), IX–24.

62. More precisely, this case involves a *prasajya-pratiṣedha* (Tibetan *med par dgag pa*), a negation or denial wherein the negative element predominates, as contrasted with a *paryudāsa* (Tibetan *min par dgag pa*) or denial in which the negative element is subordinated to a positive commitment (as it is, for example, in the case of asserting that a given pot is not white, where the import of the assertion is that the pot is some color *other than* white and not that the pot is wholly devoid of all color). For a fuller explanation, see J. F. Staal, "Negation and the Law of Contradiction in Indian Thought: A Comparative Study," *Bulletin of the School of Oriental and African Studies* XXV (1962):52–71.

63. See *RTG* B-15-3, where Rgyal-tshab explicitly entertains the objection that "there is no object of that" *(de'i don min te)*.

64. Which insight is available to ordinary men only imperfectly and indirectly via the devices logic provides. See, e.g., my *An Eleventh Century Buddhist Logic of "Exists"* (Dordrecht, Holland: D. Reidel Publishing Co., 1969).

65. "This means that one has true knowledge of the essenceless [or insubstantiality] of personality [Tibetan *gang zag gi bdag med*; Sanskrit *pudgala nairātmya*] only by implication [Tibetan *shugs la*; Sanskrit *sāmarthyat*] in a *prasajyapratiṣedha*." *RTG* B-15-4: *med par dgag pa gang zag gi bdag med ni shugs la rtogs par 'dod do.*

66. Just as, on the basis of directly experienced rabbit sensations, the ordinary man warrantably denies the occurrence of a horn on a rabbit's head, so, having directly experienced ephemeral or momentary point instants of reality, the yogin is ultimately justified in formulating the absolute denial of any real factual basis (Sanskrit *vastu*; Tibetan *ngo bo*). In this regard, perhaps the most crucial difference between the man on the street and the yogin is that the full panoply of *svalakṣaṇas* (or momentary point instants), which comprise the foundation of *both* normal and paranormal perceptual experiences, is directly intuited only by the latter. But neither the *phrase* "hornless rabbit" nor the expression "ātman-less point instant" is in a privileged position as regards *contact* with extralinguistic reality. Both designations are mere universals (Tibetan *spyi mtshan*), linguistic fictions.

67. Tucci, *Minor Buddhist Texts*, p. 171. That is, the yogin is beyond the thralldom of the "ineluctable modality of the visible."

# Fa-tsang's Brief Commentary on the *Prajñāpāramitā-hṛdaya-sūtra*

*Francis H. Cook*

## INTRODUCTION

The introduction to this study is in three parts: (1) an analysis of Fa-tsang's understanding of the Indian Buddhist doctrine of emptiness, as revealed in his commentary on the *Prajñāpāramitā-hṛdaya-sūtra (Heart Sūtra)*, (2) a discussion of some of the implications of this sūtra to meditation, and (3) some brief comments on the text and translation.

### FA-TSANG'S UNDERSTANDING OF EMPTINESS

Fa-tsang (643–712 A.D.), the author of this commentary, was the third patriarch of the Chinese school of Buddhism called Hua-yen, and its real founder. He inherited the partial work of his two predecessors, Tu-shun and Chih-yen, and, with an impressive gift for seeing relationships and for syncretistic thinking, welded many diverse strands of Buddhist thought into the architectonic grandeur of Hua-yen philosophy. This philosophy, often referred to as "totalism," has seemed to many students of Buddhism to be a distinctly Chinese creation, with no close parallel in Indian Buddhism, despite the fact that its roots are to be found in a sūtra of Indian origin (the *Avataṁsaka-sūtra*). Some Japanese scholars have seen this philosophy as a prime example of Chinese Taoist influence on imported Indian Buddhist ideas.[1]

Hua-yen totalism is difficult to summarize briefly. The concrete world "out there" is a perfect fusion of the phenomenal *shih* and absolute *li*, of form *se* and emptiness *k'ung*.[2] To say that something is empty is to say that it lacks any kind of self-existence *(svabhāva)*, and while the external world appears to be divided into many separate entities, each with a distinct form and function, all are alike empty of any substance or essence which would make them truly distinct and independent. Thus, to speak of the static relationship between things, things can be said to be essentially *identical*; i.e., empty of self-existence. However, this emptiness is never found apart from concrete reality, or apart from "form," to use the sūtra terminology; emptiness is expressed in forms, and these forms are seen as exerting causal influences on each other. Thus, to speak of their dynamic relationship, things can be said to be *interdependent*. Now, while it may seem strange to speak of a cosmos in which all things are identical and interdependent, these two relationships are nothing but other ways of saying that everything is empty, *sarvaṃ śūnyam*.

The result of this sort of analysis of the mode of being of the *dharma-dhātu* is a deemphasis of the differences between things and an emphasis on seeing being in its totality. Distinctions are submerged, hierarchies disappear, past, present, and future merge, and in this vast organism of interdependent parts, any part acts simultaneously as cause and effect. There is, then, a very intimate relationship between any one individual and all other individuals (or the totality). Because each and all individuals are lacking in self-existence and have their being purely through intercausality, the whole is dependent on the part, because without the part, there can be no whole. (It must be remembered that *each* part has this relationship to the whole simultaneously.) At the same time, however, the part has no existence and no meaning outside the context of the totality, because it is a part of a whole. Thus, the part creates the whole and the whole creates the part, in a view of existence which Hua-yen calls *fa-chieh yüan-ch'i* or the interdependent origination of the cosmos (Sanskrit *dharma-dhātu pratītya-samutpāda*).[3] Along with this interdependence, there is a relationship of essential identity among the parts of the whole.

The final consequence of this view of being is a doctrine of the completely free interfusion, or interpenetration, of the parts in the whole, and this is the distinctively Hua-yen doctrine of *shih shih wu-ai*, the nonimpediment of a thing with any other thing. For instance, though the present is the present, because of the principle of interdependence (emptiness), the present includes past and future, which remain past and future. Or, to give another example, the practices of the bodhisattva can rightly be seen as the cause of Buddhahood-effect, but because of emptiness, they can be seen as result, because they too, in their emptiness, are merely manifestations of the Buddha. If, as Hua-yen claims, the *dharma-dhātu* is the body of Vairocana, where can I not find the Buddha?[4] Everything, in fact, in the Hua-yen cosmos is worthy of respect and honor, because everything manifests the totality of being and reality.

This resumé of Hua-yen philosophy is important to remember when reading Fa-tsang's commentary on the *Heart Sūtra*, because he was the architect of this philosophy and because Hua-yen philosophy is heavily indebted in some way to the *prajñāpāramitā* doctrine of śūnyatā as expounded in that sūtra. If we study this philosophy of totalism as it is elaborately presented in some of Fa-tsang's writings, such as the *Hua-yen i ch'eng chiao i fen-ch'i chang*[5] it becomes clear that his system is constructed out of a number of important Buddhist concepts, foremost of which are the doctrines of śūnyatā, the three natures *(trisvabhāva)*, and the seed of Buddhahood (tathāgatagarbha). It is especially evident from the number of supporting quotations from *śūnyavāda* sūtras and śāstras, as well as the key terms of the whole discussion—"existence and emptiness"—that the Hua-yen system is heavily, even predominantly, indebted to the Indian Buddhist concept of emptiness for its structure. And yet, in view of the peculiar nature of the Hua-yen world view, one may ask whether Fa-tsang really understood the Indian doctrine. His commentary on a sūtra which presents the very heart of this doctrine should be a good test of his understanding.

Probably the two most revealing passages in the commentary are those devoted to the lines of the sūtra which begin, "O Śāriputra, form is not different from emptiness, emptiness is not different from form," and so on, and the following lines which begin, "They are not produced, not destroyed." I have numbered the paragraphs of the commentary with arabic numerals for easier reference in the following discussion.

The commentary on the passage beginning "O Śāriputra" (15) shows how the sūtra attempts to educate the Hīnayānists, represented by Śāriputra, in the true meaning of emptiness. Fa-tsang first denies that emptiness refers merely to the absence of a unifying self or substance in the skandhas and then positively asserts that emptiness refers also to the absence of a self in each of the skandhas itself. Emptiness is not only *ātma-śūnyatā*, but also *dharma-śūnyatā.* In a previous passage (12), commenting on the sūtra passage "He [Avalokiteśvara] contemplated the five groups, and all were empty," Fa-tsang remarks that what Avalokiteśvara contemplated was the twofold emptiness. Next (16), Fa-tsang denies that *dharma-śūnyatā* is an emptiness which results from the absence, or destruction, of form and the other dharmas. "Form," he says, "is identical with emptiness; it is not emptiness (which is the result) of the destruction of form."

In paragraph 17, Fa-tsang shows how the sūtra simultaneously corrects the mistaken apprehension of emptiness by immature bodhisattvas, who may believe that (1) form is something apart from emptiness, (2) emptiness annihilates form, and (3) emptiness is an entity *wu.* Fa-tsang clears up each error with a quote from the sūtra: (1) the sūtra says that form is not different from emptiness, so form is not something apart from emptiness; (2) the sūtra says that form is identical with emptiness, and so emptiness is not the result of the annihilation of form; (3) the sūtra says that emptiness is identical with form, and so emptiness is never a separate entity independent of form. That is, one should not, attempt to seize emptiness with the word "emptiness," and thus hypostatize it. "Emptiness" is a purely operational term meant to expose the fictional nature of entities conceived as absolutely existing, and it will not do to make emptiness into one of these fictional entities. Fa-tsang evidently knew that even "emptiness" is empty, and this is reflected in his comments on the Four Holy Truths ("There is no suffering, origination, cessation, or path") in 27, when he concludes that even these most holy things, including nirvāṇa, "are empty and nonexistent."

Having said what emptiness is not, Fa-tsang proceeds in 18 to show "the true meaning of emptiness." Basically, the discussion shows that when form and emptiness are seen in mutual relationship, they can be seen in three different ways: (1) They are mutually opposing. To say that form is empty is to negate form in some sense. Conversely, to say that emptiness is form is to affirm form and negate emptiness. (2) They do not oppose each other. Form can not *really* annul emptiness because it is not an absolutely existing form; in fact, it is an empty form. Emptiness can not *really* harm form because it is not an emptiness of annihilation; in fact, it is an emptiness which coexists always with form. Finally, (3) emptiness and form are mutually creative; *hsiang-tso* each makes the other possible. Were there no emptiness, there would be no form, and, conversely, were there no form, there would be nothing of which it could be said that it is empty. Fa-tsang, in this latter passage, gives an expanded version of the statement in the introductory paragraph of the essay (1) in which he says, "Existence is the existence of the empty, and therefore does not [absolutely] exist. Emptiness is the emptiness of the existent, and therefore is not [absolutely] empty [in the sense of nonexistence]." Shih-hui comments on this by saying that the former is like the existence of an empty house, while the latter is like the emptiness of the existent house.[6] He further remarks that true emptiness is not the nullity of the horns of a hare or the hairs of a tortoise.[7] In a word, emptiness and form are mutually dependent.

I do not see how these statements can be seen as anything but orthodox *śūnyavāda*, despite the tendency of some students of Hua-yen to see them as being somehow especially "Hua-yen."[8] The first statement simply asserts the proposition that if form is empty, then in *some* sense, form is negated. But the sūtra itself says that form is empty, so this is not an invention by Fa-tsang. To say that form, or any dharma, is empty is to negate its ultimacy and reduce it to the status of an illusion. The second statement seems to contradict the first, saying that even though form is empty, emptiness does not, and can not, *really* annihilate form. Emptiness is not synonymous with absence or annihilation, and we may recall Shih-hui's analogy of the empty house, as well as Fa-tsang's instructions to the śrāvakas. Emptiness is identical with form, not with the utter nonbeing of form. Here, we need only refer to statements by Nāgārjuna, Candrakīrti, and others, who have refuted the erroneous notion that emptiness is synonymous with nonbeing. Candrakīrti says that a synonym for emptiness is "the Middle Way," meaning the middle position between annihilation, or nonbeing, and absolute being, meaning having an eternal, immutable self-existence.[9] The third statement affirms the mutual creativity of form and emptiness—in other words, their mutual dependence. This is really a synthesis of the first two assertions and attempts to show that the two states of emptiness and form coexist; that is, form is empty but is not annihilated. Form is empty, and just because of this absence of a *svabhāva*, form is possible. This seems in its own way to be a reflecton of Nāgārjuna's denial of the notion of *svabhāva* for the reason that if dharmas *did* possess an unvarying, permanent substance, no modification would ever be possible, resulting in a situation in which everything would always be just as it is. Therefore, no self-improvement could occur, since the *kleśa*s would stay as they are, and wholesome dharmas such as prajñā could never increase.[10] Fa-tsang's knowledge of this argument is, I believe, shown in his quotation from the *Mādhyamika-kārikā* which says that "Since there is the principle of śūnyatā, all dharmas can be perfected," and the quotation from the *Pañca* to the effect that "If dharmas were not empty, there would be no path, no result," and so on. Thus, form is possible only because of emptiness. Conversely, emptiness does not annihilate form, because emptiness does not mean nullity. "True emptiness" as Fa-tsang calls it, is merely a quality which a dharma has, and were there no dharmas, there would be no emptiness. Thus, emptiness is possible only because there are dharmas, and the two form each other reciprocally. This seems to me to be a clear recognition of the Indian Mahāyāna teaching that emptiness is interdependent origination *(pratītya-samutpāda)*; i.e., it is the mode of existence of concrete entities.

In summary, then, what did Fa-tsang know about emptiness? (1) He knew that emptiness is not restricted to a personal self but applied equally to all dharmas, and he was thus aware of the Mahāyāna doctrine of the twofold emptiness. (2) He knew that emptiness is not itself merely a more spiritualized entity among lesser entities. (3) He knew that emptiness is not the annihilation of concrete reality, but is something said of dharmas. (4) He knew that to say that something is empty in the Buddhist sense means that it has no independent being *(svabhāva)* and comes into existence and passes back out of existence because of the confluence of conditions (23). In other words, he knew Nāgārjuna's dictum to the effect that emptiness is interdependent origination. (5) Finally, there are indications that he understood that emptiness is also empty; i.e., that emptiness is only a device aimed at cleansing the mind of error. In commenting on the sūtra passage which says that the Four Holy Truths are empty, he seems to have realized that even the holiest teachings of Buddhism, nirvāṇa and emptiness not excluded, are as empty as anything else.

Fa-tsang appears to have had a sound understanding of the doctrine of emptiness, for his comments on the sūtra do not have anything of a particularly "Hua-yen" nature in them. Then, it may be asked, how does this faithful reproduction of classical Indian Buddhist doctrine become translated into Hua-yen philosophy? Professor Conze once remarked that to him, Zen was merely *prajñāpāramitā* with jokes. I would like to say here that Hua-yen is *prajñāpāramitā* without the Indian distrust of the natural. For Hua-yen is a Chinese restatement of the *prajñāpāramitā* doctrine of śūnyatā assimilated with such doctrines as tathāgatagabha and *trisvabhāva*, but it is the doctrine of emptiness seen from a different perspective, or perhaps with a different emphasis.

Whatever we may say about the doctrine as it was propounded in India, it certainly had the function of being a corrective to a basically self-centered, discriminative approach to experience. Functionally, therefore, it was negative, in that its aim was the destruction of erroneous views and the devaluation of common-sense experience. The Chinese were well aware of this function, and it plays a crucial role in all Chinese schools of Buddhism. Fa-tsang's appropriation of the doctrines of the three natures *(trisvabhāva)* for his system, for instance, shows that he knew that the task of the Buddhist was to remove conceptual superimpositions from the concrete world of tathatā (or *parinișpanna*, in the three-natures doctrine).

What is meager or lacking in Indian Buddhist literature, however, is a positive appreciation of the concrete world seen in the light of emptiness. There is, for instance, nothing in Indian art like the lyrical landscape paintings of Chinese Sung art. What is specially remarkable about the Hua-yen system is its strong emphasis on the phenomenal *shih*. While acknowledging the emptiness of phenomena, it nevertheless does not consider the phenomenal to be negligible or mean when rightly seen as empty, which is to say, interdependent. In exploiting the teaching that emptiness is exactly identical with form, and thus seeing the two as exactly coterminous, Hua-yen has come to bestow an absolute value not only on the concrete world in its totality, but on each individual which participates in this whole. The cosmos is not an emanation or outward appearance of some shadowy substance named Vairocana lurking behind it; it is Vairocana itself. What can be despicable if everything is the body of the Buddha?

The Hua-yen view of the cosmos as the realm of dharmas which exists through interdependence *(fa-chieh yüan-ch'i)* sees existence as an organism of infinite size, composed of an infinity of phenomena which are infinitely interrelated through identity and intercausality. These phenomena are each distinct in appearance and function—a mouse and the Son of Heaven have nothing at all in common. But their marks or characteristics are superficial, and ultimately they are completely identical in their emptiness. But being empty, as Fa-tsang well knew, means that their concrete existence and their functions are absolutely determined by other conditions, and Hua-yen says in fact that the conditions are also infinite, for all of creation conspires to make a mouse a mouse. At any rate, a thing is what it is only by virtue of conditions; it has a *pārabhāva* mode of existence. Hua-yen claims that individual A is A because of conditions B, C, D, and so on *ad infinitum*. However, simultaneously, B is B only because of conditions A, C, D, and so on. This interdependence simultaneously pertains among all individuals which comprise the *dharma-dhātu*, which means everything. Since the totality is only the sum of all individuals, the individual is the cause for the whole; on the other hand, the part has no meaning and no existence outside the context of being, and so the whole is the cause of the part. The upshot of this is a strong insistence upon dissolving the individual into the whole, upon seeing Being instead of beings, and this eradication of the congenital habit of splitting the fabric of being up into little morsels, each with its own independent being, is presumably the goal of all Buddhism. Past, future, and present merge into each other, spatial boundaries vanish, everything no matter how "humble" or "mean" is the whole of reality, and there is no place where I cannot find enlightenment. Everything is necessary to everything else in this great "cosmic ecology," and worthy of veneration and gratitude, when seen in the light of emptiness.

The Hua-yen appropriation of the emptiness doctrine, then, was not a distortion of the doctrine itself, whereby emptiness was conceived in a substantialist manner, or some other similar error. The Hua-yen cosmos as identity and interdependence is the Buddhist world of emptiness. What is peculiarly Chinese in this use of the doctrine is the positive appreciation of the relationship between thing and thing *shih*; that is, an appreciation for the harmony, or organic unity, pertaining in what is essentially a "family" relationship among the infinity of individuals which comprise the universe. It is a mark of Fa-tsang's genius that he could use the emptiness doctrine in this manner while not at all disturbing its original Indian intent, which was to destroy attachment to the world as conceived by the unenlightened.

## MEDITATION AND THE *HEART SŪTRA*

Buddhist philosophy, whether in its Indian form of the emptiness doctrine, or in its Chinese garb as Hua-yen, is never divorced from the primary Buddhist task of meditation. Fa-tsang shows in his commentary that he was well aware of the relationship of the message of the *Heart Sūtra* to meditation.

Buddhist philosophy has its source in the meditative experience, and in its assurance that it presents truth and reality to the Buddhist, urges him in the direction of meditation again. *Ehi passika*, come and see. The Buddha's injunction to the inquirer to discover the truth himself still holds after 2,500 years, for it is not enough to give a merely intellectual acquiescence to the truths of Buddhism, one must *see* them himself, and live them in his life. No better example can be given of this fact, that Buddhist philosophy begins in the meditative experience, than that of Hua-yen Buddhism itself. It appears certain from the writings of the first three Hua-yen patriarchs that what is now a rather complex and difficult philosophy began as a simple meditative exercise by Tu-shun, the first Hua-yen master. Tu-shun sat and saw in his mind's eye the

Hua-yen universe of identity and interdependence, and his writings, now extant only as fragments imbedded in the works of his successors, do not show any "philosophical" activity on his part at all. It remained for the second patriarch, Chih-yen, to begin to work out this view of existence in a more philosophical manner, and it was the task of the third master, Fa-tsang, to create the final system.[11] Though the Hua-yen system is extremely eclectic and is the result of syncretism, the basic insights probably go back to meditative experiences. Thus, as mentioned earlier, Hua-yen is held out as a *reasonably accurate* representation of the way in which things really exist, but at the same time it is a lure for the Buddhist to perform the task of meditation himself and *see* that, in fact, this is the true state of reality. The world of Hua-yen is the world as seen by the Buddhas, not by ordinary folk. A person might have a very fine understanding of Hua-yen philosophy in a scholarly manner, but unless he has seen existence as empty he will not be empty himself, which means that he is still as bound by delusion, hatred, and attachment as anyone else. This is, of course, equally true of the teachings of the *Heart Sūtra*; they must be lived experiences for their medicinal properties to work.

The teachings of the sūtra are in the nature of a report by Avalokiteśvara who, when engaged in the practice of meditation (or "contemplation," as I have translated it), *saw* that the five skandhas are all empty. And, as the sūtra says, he crossed over beyond all suffering, to the other shore which is nirvāṇa. This is, as Fa-tsang remarks in his commentary (13), the benefit of *experiencing* and *seeing* true emptiness. Avalokiteśvara was not an armchair philosopher who wished that things were empty, or who arrived at such a conclusion on the basis of a chain of logical thought; he experienced and saw phenomenal existence as empty. And only by experiencing and seeing it was he able to end all moral and intellectual faults within himself and cut off all future rebirth in the realm of saṃsāra. Avalokiteśvara is a great bodhisattva, far advanced in wisdom, and close to Buddhahood, but, nevertheless, he is a paradigmatic figure, for he shows all men the way by which they can put an end to the anguish and turmoil of life which Buddhists call *duḥkha*. We, like Avalokiteśvara, must *experience* and *see* the emptiness of things, and the assertions of the sūtra are only a report and a promise.

But how does one "see" what Avalokiteśvara saw? Certainly not with our physical eyes, for emptiness is, as we have seen, no thing which can be seen in this manner. Seeing emptiness requires a special kind of vision, one which might be called "inner vision," and which is often referred to as "meditation" or "contemplation." The word which Chinese usually use for ordinary seeing is *chien*, but the Chinese translation of the Sanskrit text of the sūtra by Hsuan-tsang uses the word *kuan*, which carries the connotation of close inspection, examination, and observation. In the commentary, when relating meditation to the central message of the sūtra (20), Fa-tsang uses *kuan* to translate the Sanskrit *vipaśyanā* in a discussion of the two types of mind training, *śamatha* and *vipaśyanā*. Now, in Indian Buddhism, *vipaśyanā* is an exercise in the close scrutiny of the characteristics of the skandhas, dharmas, and other compounded elements, and it is supposed to be done in conjunction with exercises in tranquility *(śamatha)*, or stilling the externally directed activities of the mind.[12] Once the mind has reached a state of alert calmness, the meditator begins the proper business of meditation, which is carefully, minutely to analyze the characters or marks of dharmas, which is *vipaśyanā* or Chinese *kuan*.

Fa-tsang uses the two terms, *śamatha* and *vipaśyanā*, *chih* and *kuan*, in his discussion of the relationship of meditation to the message of the sūtra, but he does not, of course, define the terms themselves, since the commentary is very brief. However, the three commentators on Fa-tsang's commentary do devote some space to elucidating the terms, and it would appear that the Indian tradition of meditation as embodied in the simultaneous practice of *śamatha* and *vipaśyanā* was preserved into the Sung period, when most of these commentaries were composed. Shih-hui says that *śamatha* means "stopping," *chih*, which consists of the stopping, or stilling, of the "marks" of all external things, which seems to be identical with the interiorization process of *śamatha* in Indian texts. *Vipaśyanā*, he says, means "close scrutiny" *(kuan)* and consists of the analysis of the marks of rising and ceasing of interdependent origination *(pratītya-samutpāda)*, which is similar to Indian Buddhist definitions of this practice.[13] At any rate, Fa-tsang seems to have inherited the traditional scheme of *śamatha* and *vipaśyanā*, at least as it was codified by the T'ien-t'ai master Chih-i (20), suggesting that peculiarly Hua-yen meditations such as *hai-yin san-mei* (Sanskrit *sāgara-mudrā samādhi*), and those alluded to in such treatises as *Hua-yen wu chiao shih kuan*,[14] were performed basically on Indian models.

More interesting than the form of meditation as understood by Fa-tsang is his understanding of the function of *vipaśyanā* as applied to the central theme of the sūtra: form is empty, and emptiness is form. It is here that he not only shows just how much he was in the tradition of Mahāyāna Buddhism, but more important, he illuminates some of the deeper significance of the remarkable assertions of the *Heart Sūtra*. In commenting on the sūtra passage, "O Śāriputra, form is not different from emptiness, emptiness is not different from form" (20), he first says that when one sees form as identical with emptiness, one perfects the practice of *śamatha*, and when emptiness is contemplated as identical with form, one perfects the practice of *vipaśyanā*, and he concludes that when the two are practiced together, they are ideal. Continuing this line of commentary, he then says that when one sees that form is empty (which he has designated as *śamatha*, or tranquility), one acquires great wisdom and no longer dwells in saṃsāra. On the other hand, when one contemplates emptiness as form, one acquires great compassion *(mahā-karuṇā)* and does not abide in nirvāṇa, and because he is attached neither to the world nor to nirvāṇa, the bodhisattva is able to engage in the practice which is without abiding place *(wu-chu-ch'u-hsing)*. One is reminded of the bodhisattva in the

*Vajracchedikā Sūtra* who leads countless beings into nirvāṇa and yet has no thought of beings or nirvāṇa. Shih-hui remarks on this passage from Fa-tsang's commentary that contemplating form as identical with emptiness means that one sees dharmas as birthless in their own-being, being free of false views, and acquiring the knowledge which stops abiding in saṃsāra. Contemplating emptiness as form means seeing the coming together of all dharmas through causes and conditions, seeing that karma and the fruit of karma *(karmaphala)* are never lost, raising a great compassion for all beings, and not abiding in nirvāṇa.[15]

According to this description of the practice of contemplation, *śamatha* and *vipaśyanā* both have very important functions with respect to the fundamental teachings of the *Heart Sūtra.* At least, as Fa-tsang understood it, *śamatha*-tranquility has the basic function of destroying the illusory notion of separate, distinct entities; by seeing that dharmas are completely lacking in a *svabhāva*, or, as Shih-hui says, by seeing that the "marks" of dharmas are illusory and therefore that distinctions are false, one ceases to engage in false views, and one acquires emancipation. In a manner of speaking, this is the whole point to Buddhist meditation and other practices, for the perception of emptiness is the door to the liberated life. The irreducible demand on the Buddhist who wishes to achieve the highest goal of the religious life is that he make actual in his own life the teaching of the sūtra which says that *form is identical with emptiness.*

It is the irreducible demand, but not the final one. For self-enlightenment in Buddhism is, in fact, not the goal but only the door to the real goal. The true goal of Mahāyāna Buddhism is the bodhisattva's life of compassionate activity, which might be said to be the dynamic expression in life of the perception of emptiness. Thus, while self-liberation is only possible through the perception of the emptiness of all things, the bodhisattva becomes frozen to his new perception if he can not move beyond it. He must therefore come to see that even though things are empty, this emptiness is expressed always in form and is in fact merely the true mode of form. In contemplating the process of interdependent origination, the meditator comes to see that *emptiness is form*, and in so doing he relinquishes his attachment to emptiness and nirvāṇa and once more becomes involved in the concrete world. His perception of emptiness is not really lost, but becomes expressed in compassion.

According to Fa-tsang, then, the *Heart Sūtra* expresses what may be the highest religious perception of Mahāyāna Buddhism, which is, paradoxically, that the true nirvāṇa is acquired by the bodhisattva who rejects nirvāṇa and devotes his life to the selfless practice of compassion.[16] For Mahāyāna Buddhism had discovered the fallacy of trying to eradicate the idea of a self and selfish action while striving for one's own private emancipation. Paradoxically enough, however, when one strives unceasingly to benefit all other beings, one acquires the self-benefit of emancipation at the same time. Shih-hui says, in fact, that there is only a slight difference between the self-benefit of great prajñā and the benefiting of others which is great karuṇā and that, indeed, the two aid each other.[17] The great Japanese philosopher, Nishida Kitarō, says that the two are really one and the same, for compassion is nothing more than knowing things as they really are, thus suggesting again that compassion is simply the dynamic side of Buddhist wisdom.[18] It is, I believe, for this reason that Fa-tsang says that when *śamatha* and *vipaśyanā* are practiced together, they are ideal. The perception of things in their emptiness frees the bodhisattva from attachment to the world; the perception of emptiness as things frees the bodhisattva from attachment to nirvāṇa and allows him to become engaged in the world of form. His meditation is a ceaseless oscillation between *śamatha* and *vipaśyanā*, his career a perpetual movement between prajñā and karuṇā. This is the true Buddhist life, according to Mahāyāna.

The *Heart Sūtra* touches in more than one way on the deepest truths of Buddhism, and in so doing is truly the "heart" of the teachings of Mahāyāna. These truths arose out of the dedicated meditation of many devoted Buddhists, and the appearance of these truths in Buddhist canonical literature is, as Fa-tsang says, "a lofty torch which illuminates the dark path of life." They inspire us, and they guide us, to meditate and find the same truth within ourselves.

## THE TEXT

Fa-tsang's *Brief Commentary on the* Sūtra on the Heart of the Perfection of Wisdom *(Pan-jo po-lo-mi-to hsin ching lüeh shu)*, is item number 1712 in the *Taishō Shinshū Daizōkyō*, occupying about three and a half pages. It was written as a leisure exercise when Fa-tsang was not occupied assisting Śikṣānanda on his translations, according to a postface to the commentary. It was done in the second year of Ch'ang-an (702 A.D.), when Fa-tsang was close to sixty years of age, after he had written the immense commentary on the *Avataṁsaka-sūtra* (the *T'an hsüan chi*), his *Hua-yen i ch'eng chiao i fen-ch'i chang*, and several other basic Hua-yen treatises. The commentary uses as its basic text the Chinese translation of the *Heart Sūtra* by Hsüan-tsang (*Taishō* no. 251). Fa-tsang very likely chose this translation over that of Kumārajīva because he was most familiar with it, having served in his younger days on the translation bureau of Hsüng-tsang, and perhaps had even helped in the Chinese translation of the sūtra. There are, I believe, no really important deviations from the Sanskrit version published by Edward Conze, and interested readers are referred to Professor Conze's remarks in his article on the sūtra in *Thirty Years of Buddhist Studies* for variations in the several Chinese translations of the sūtra and deviations from extant Sanskrit versions.[19]

The *Taishō* text of the commentary is very good and presents no difficulties outside several mispunctuations. The commentary is, as I have remarked before, straightforward in style and content, completely lacking in the endless divisions and subdivisions (and often sub-subdivisions) which students of Fa-tsang have become accustomed to in the longer treatises. The commentary has the virtue of brevity, and more than this, very clearly shows the implications and ramifications of the sūtra passages in its phrase-by-phrase, and often word-by-word, commentary. I have been unable, in the short space of my own introduction, to discuss all the points which Fa-tsang makes in his commentary, and I leave it to the reader to draw his own conclusions about the aptness of some of Fa-tsang's remarks. My own understanding of the commentary, as reflected in the introduction, notes, and translation itself, has been greatly aided by three other commentaries on Fa-tsang's commentary:

1. *Pan-jo hsin-ching lüeh-shu-lien-chu-chi*, by Shih-hui. A Sung commentary. Number 1713 in the *Taishō Shinshū Daizōkyō*, pages 555–568.
2. *Pan-jo hsin-ching lüeh-shu-hsien-cheng-chi*, by Chung-hsi. A Sung commentary. *Zokuzōkyō* I.41. pp. 340–356.
3. *Pan-jo hsin-ching lüeh-shu-hsiao-ch'ao*, compiled by Ch'ien Ch'ien-i. A Ming commentary. *Zokuzōkyō*. I.41. pp. 357–390.

In my translation of the commentary, I have tried to keep the interested reader in close contact with the *Taishō* text by giving page and register inside parentheses, thus (553b). I have numbered the five main sections of the commentary, according to Fa-tsang's divisions, with roman numerals. The arabic number to the left of a paragraph is my own numbering for reference purposes. The sūtra text is given in capitals.

---

# A BRIEF COMMENTARY ON THE *PRAJÑĀPĀRAMITĀ-HṚDAYA-SŪTRA*

*by Fa-tsang*

1. (552a) The True Source and Pure Model[20] is serene, and is isolated from skillful devices.[21] The abstruse principle of

wonderful enlightenment is mysterious and profound, and transcends words and forms. Even though true and false are both destroyed *[min]*, the two truths continually exist. Emptiness and existence[22] are both done away with *[wang]* and [yet] eternally manifest as the same. For that reason, true emptiness always exists. That is, emptiness is spoken of by means of [the concept of] existence. Illusory existence is always empty. That is, existence is shown by means of [the concept of] emptiness. Existence is the existence of the empty and therefore does not [absolutely] exist. Emptiness is the emptiness of the existent, and therefore is not [absolutely] empty. Because of nonexistent existence, existence is not eternal. Because of nonempty emptiness, emptiness is not annihilation. The four attachments are done away with already,[23] and the hundred negations are then dispelled.[24]

2. The abstruse significance of the *Prajñāpāramitā-sūtra*, how can we speak of it? If one were to calculate all the things [in it] and deal with them in detail, they are said to exceed 200,000 verses. If you bring together the essentials, the essence is exhausted in 14 lines. Even though one affirms that he understands the true teaching and comments on it, the extensiveness or minuteness of this depends on circumstances. The principle which transcends words [in all its forms] is perfectly interfused and all are revealed [regardless of the form].

3. The *Sūtra on the Heart of Wisdom* truly is a lofty torch which illuminates the dark path of life. It is a swift vessel which aids [those drowning] in the ocean of suffering. It is the best for aiding beings and guiding them out of the darkness of delusion. Thus, with regard to wisdom *[prajñā]*, subtle discernment is the essence. As for perfection *[pāramitā]*, reaching the other shore is the function. "Heart" *[hṛdaya]* refers to the essential and abstruse. *Sūtra* is a "thread" and means "teaching." The scripture and its essence form the title in accordance with a figure of speech. Therefore, it is called *Sūtra on the Heart of the Perfection of Wisdom.*

4. I shall explain this sūtra by dividing it into five topics. (1) The reason why the sūtra was preached. (2) The collection

[of sūtras] in which it is included. (3) The intention of the tenet. (4) An explanation of the title. (5) An explanation of the text.

## I

5. The reason why the *sūtra* was preached. The *Ta-chih-tu lun* says [552b], "Just as Sumeru, king of mountains, is made to shake and move neither without a cause nor with merely a few causes, so also the teaching of wisdom *[prajñā]* arises from many causes and conditions. [It was taught] (1) to block the false views of non-Buddhists, (2) to convert the [adherents of] the two vehicles [śrāvakas and pratyekabuddhas] to the Mahāyāna, (3) to prevent the immature [*hsiao*; lit., "small"] bodhisattva from being confused about emptiness, (4) to cause enlightenment with regard to the two truths and the middle way, and the arising of correct views, (5) to illuminate the Buddha's superior merits and beget pure faith, (6) to cause the arousing of the thought of great awakening *[mahābodhi]*, (7) to cause the cultivation of the bodhisattva's deep and extensive practices, (8) to cause the smashing of obstacles of all kinds, (9) to cause the acquisition of enlightenment and nirvāṇa, (10) to benefit beings in later times." In summarily discussing these ten, the idea of the reason for the teaching is comprehended.

## II

6. The collection [of sūtras] in which it is included. In the three collections, it is included in the collection of sūtras. In the two collections, it is included in the collection of the bodhisattva. In the teachings which are true or provisional, it is included in the true teaching.

## III

7. The intention of the tenet. The tenet consists of what the words express. The intention is the point of the tenet. Now, first the general [discussion], then the particular. In general, the tenet consists of the three kinds of prajñā: (1)

Real-mark *[shih-hsiang]*;[25] i.e., the true nature which is contemplated. (2) Contemplation; i.e., the wonderful wisdom *[hui]* which contemplates. (3) Literature; i.e., the teaching as words. These are the tenet because there are no more than these three. There are three parts to the particular discussion. (1) One pair of teaching and essence; i.e., the teaching as literature is the tenet, and the remaining two points [given previously] are the intention. (2) The pair consisting of wisdom and what is seen [*ching*; lit., "realm"]; what is seen, consisting of true emptiness, is the tenet, and the wisdom of contemplation is the intention. (3) The pair consisting of cause and effect; the causal practice which is *bodhi* is the tenet, and the resultant merit which is *bodhi* is the intention.

## IV

8. *Prajñāpāramitā-hṛdaya-sūtra (Sūtra on the Heart of the Perfection of Wisdom)*. Four, the explanation of the title. There are three divisions. (1) The teaching and its essence are divided into two. "Heart of prajñā" is the essence which is explained. The one word *sūtra* is the teaching which does the explaining. The name of the teaching, which can explain, *prajñā*, is made in accordance with its essence. (2) The dharma and the figure of speech within the essence which is explained are divided into two parts. That is to say, *prajñā (-pāramitā)* is the essence which is explained. The word "heart" *[hsin]* is a figure of speech for what is withdrawn [from the larger forms of the sūtra]. The wonderful essence of the [larger versions of the *Prajñāpāramitā (-sūtra)*] is compared with the human heart as the chief part, or essential, and draws together the very basic. (3) With regard to the just-mentioned dharma, there are essence and function, again divided into two parts. That is, prajñā is the essence. It means "wisdom" *[chih-hui]*; i.e., the true source of the abstruse, wonderful experience of enlightenment. *Pāramitā* is the function. This means [literally] "reaching the other shore." That is, through this wonderful wisdom, one overturns saṃsāra, transgressions are terminated, and one reaches

the limit of true emptiness. One avoids not reaching the wisdom of the other shore, and it gets its name from this. Its name is derived, that is, from the fact that essence and function are identical, because of the figure of speech, and because of the teaching of the essence [heart].

V

9. (552c) "Avalokiteśvara, the Bodhisattva." From here on, in part five, the text is explained. Since this is the *Heart Sūtra* [consisting of the heart or essence of the teaching on wisdom], the usual introduction [i.e., "Thus I have heard, The Lord was dwelling in Rājagriha," etc.] is lacking, as well as a conclusion concerning the dissemination *liu-t'ung* [of the sūtra]. There are two parts to the text: [A] it thoroughly explains prajñā, and then, [B] it shows, from the words "utter the mantra" on, the esoteric prajñā, *mi-mi-pan-jo*. The reason for discussing these two is that it thoroughly illuminates and clearly discusses, and thereby causes one to produce prajñā-understanding and eliminate the obstacle consisting of defilements *[kleśa]*. With the esoteric words of the mantra, one is caused to intone and [thereby] to produce merit and destroy the obstacle consisting of bad karma. In order to destroy the two obstacles and perfect the two majesties, it discusses these two parts. In the former [part A], there are also two parts. First, there is an abbreviated advertisement [giving the situation of the *sūtra*], and then there follows the gist [of the teaching of *prajñā*]. From "O Śāriputra, form is not different from emptiness," on, is the part which clarifies and extensively explains the true meaning. Because the heart [of the teaching] is not revealed suddenly, there is first a brief statement of the situation. Since it does not abbreviate what it is able to present, there follows an extended explanation. Also, the former is the brief advertisement of the practice which is relied on, and the latter refers to the expanded exposition. There are also four parts to the first [i.e., the advertisement]: (1) the person who does the contemplating, (2) the practice engaged in, (3) the realm [i.e., object] of the contemplating and practicing, and (4) the benefit of contemplation.

10. A1. The person who contemplates. Avalokiteśvara *[Kuan tzu-tsai]*[26] is the person who contemplates; i.e., he gets his name from the fact that he contemplates freely *[kuan-tzu-tsai]* the realm of the nonobstruction between the noumenal and phenomenal *[li-shih]*. He also gets his name from contemplating beings and going to aid them freely, without impediment. The former [explanation] is made with regard to wisdom; the latter is made with regard to compassion. *P'u* is *bodhi*, and this means "enlightenment." *Sa* is *sattva*,[27] and this means "being." This means that this person seeks *bodhi* above by means of knowledge and aids *beings* below by means of compassion, because his name is derived from the realm [of his activity].

11. "When Practicing the Profound Perfection of Wisdom." A2. The practice which is engaged in. The wonderful practice of prajñā is of two types: (a) Shallow; this means prajñā [relative to] the emptiness of the person. (b) Deep; this is prajñā [relative to] the emptiness of dharmas. Now, it distinguishes the shallow from the deep and therefore speaks of "practicing the *profound* prajñā." In saying "when," [or, "on the occasion of"] it means that at one time, this bodhisattva, like (the adherents to) the two vehicles [i.e., śrāvakas and pratyekabuddhas], engaged in the meditation on the emptiness of the person. Therefore, says the *Lotus Sūtra*, "He who obtains deliverance with the body of a śrāvaka shall manifest a śrāvaka's body." Now, since it is not that occasion, it says, "when practicing the profound prajñā."

12. "He Contemplated *[chao-chien]* the Five Groups [skandhas] and All Were Empty." A3. The realm [object] of the contemplating and practicing; i.e., he saw the five groups as all empty in their own-being *[svabhāva]*. That is to say, what he saw was the principle of the profound wisdom consisting of the twofold emptiness.

13. "He Crossed over All Suffering." A4. The benefit. In experiencing and seeing true emptiness, all defilements were terminated, and he was able to divorce himself from the two forms of saṃsāra, that which comes from allotment *[fen-tuan*;

i.e., the result of past karma],[28] and that which results from voluntary self-transformation *[pien-yi]*, and to experience the absolute, joyous fruit of *bodhi* and nirvāṇa. Therefore, it says, "he crossed over all suffering." This concludes the brief advertisement.

14. (553a) 2. "OŚĀRIPUTRA, FORM IS NOT DIFFERENT FROM EMPTINESS, EMPTINESS IS NOT DIFFERENT FROM FORM. FORM IS IDENTICAL WITH EMPTINESS, AND EMPTINESS IS IDENTICAL WITH FORM. THE SAME IS TRUE OF FEELINGS, CONCEPTUALIZATION, KARMIC VOLITION, AND CONSCIOUSNESS." From here on, the second part deals with the expanded explanation of the true meaning. There are five parts. (1) Dispelling the skepticism of nonbelievers. (2) Illuminating the essence of the dharma. (3) Showing what is to be abandoned. (4) Discussing what is acquired. (5) Concluding with praise for the superior power [of the sūtra]. In the first, there are four parts: (a) correctly removing the skepticism of the small vehicle; (b) simultaneously removing the skepticism of bodhisattvas; (c) showing the correct concept; (d) explaining contemplation and practice.

15. 1a. First, it says, "O Śāriputra," and this shows who the skeptical person is. "Śāri" is the name of a bird, and is interpreted as being an egret. Because this person's mother was as quick in intelligence as the eyes of that bird, she was called "Śāri." Now, this is her son, and he takes his name from his mother. He got his name from his mother, who was named after that bird, and so he is called "Son of Śāri." He was foremost [among the Buddha's disciples] in quickness and wisdom. The sutra gives him the place of honor [among the śrāvakas], and explains his skepticism. This skepticism is as follows: "Our small vehicle sees that the groups [skandhas] during the state of existing with basis *(sopadhiśeṣa)* are without a self.[29] What is the difference between this and your doctrine of the emptiness of dharmas?" Now, this is explained in this manner. Your tenet is that the absence of a self in the groups is called "emptiness of the groups"; but it is not that

[each of] the skandhas itself is empty. In this case, the groups [themselves] are different from emptiness. Now it is shown that the groups are intrinsically empty of self-existence, which is different [from what you hold].

16. There is also this skepticism: "In our small vehicle, when one enters the state of being without a basis [i.e., at the extinction of the psychophysical being *[nirupadhiśeṣa]*, body and mind are both terminated. What is the difference between this and 'emptiness is without form,' etc?" This is the explanation. In your doctrine, form is not [intrinsically] empty, but when form is destroyed, then there is emptiness. This is not so. Form is identical with emptiness; it is not the emptiness [which is the result] of the destruction of form. Therefore, what we maintain is not the same [as what you teach]. Inasmuch as these two are the extent of the small-vehicle skepticism, we have explained them.

17. 1b. Second, simultaneously removing the skepticism of bodhisattvas. The *Ratnagotra-vibhāga-śāstra [Uttaratantra]* says that the bodhisattva has three doubts when emptiness confuses him. The first is that emptiness is different from form, as he grasps on form as being external to emptiness. Now, [the sūtra] shows that form is not different from emptiness, and this removes that doubt. Second, he believes that emptiness annihilates form, and he seizes on the emptiness of annihilation. Now, [the sūtra] shows that form is identical with emptiness. It is not the emptiness [resulting from] the cessation of form. Thus, that doubt is removed. The third doubt is that emptiness is a thing *[wu]*, and he seizes on emptiness as being an entity. Now [the sūtra] shows that emptiness is identical with form. One should not seize emptiness with emptiness.[30] Thus, that doubt is removed. These three doubts are consequently terminated, and true emptiness is revealed.

18. 1c. Third, revealing the correct concept. Form and emptiness in relation to each other have three meanings. First, there is the meaning of mutual opposition. A passage a little further on says, "In emptiness, there is no form," etc.,

because emptiness injures *[hai]* form. In accordance with this, it should be said that "in form, there is no emptiness," because form opposes emptiness. The reason for this is that if they exist together *[hu-ts'un]*, they necessarily destroy *[hu-wang]* each other. Second, there is the meaning of not being mutually opposing. This means that since form is illusory *[huan]*, form necessarily does not obstruct emptiness. (553b) Because emptiness is true emptiness, it does not necessarily obstruct illusory form. If emptiness did obstruct form, then it would be a destructive emptiness, and would not be true emptiness. If [form] were to obstruct emptiness, then it would be real form and not illusory form. The third shows the meaning of mutual creativity *[hsiang-tso]*. That is, if this illusory form were to have an essence, then it would not be empty, and therefore it would not be illusory form. The *Pañca-viṁśatisāhasrikā-prajñāpāramitā-sūtra* says, "If all dharmas are not empty, then there is no path, no result," etc. The *Madhyamika-kārikās* say, "Since there is the principle of emptiness, therefore all dharmas are able to be perfected." True emptiness is also like this. You should understand it according to the foregoing [quotations]. Therefore, true emptiness has four meanings altogether: (1) The meaning of [emptiness] abrogating itself and forming the other [form], because emptiness is identical with form; i.e., form is manifested and emptiness is obscured. (2) The meaning of obscuring the other and revealing itself, because form is identical with emptiness; i.e., form is terminated and emptiness is revealed. (3) The meaning of existing together, because obscurity and revelation are nondual, which is the true emptiness. This means that form not being different from emptiness is illusory form, and thus form exists. Emptiness not being different from form is called true emptiness, and thus, emptiness is revealed. Through this reciprocal nonimpediment, the two exist together. (4) The meaning of both alike being submerged *[min]*, because essence and characteristics altogether are completely taken away, both are done away with, and the two extremes [of existence and emptiness] are cut off.

19. Form seen from the standpoint of emptiness also has four meanings. (1) Itself [form] being obscured while the other [emptiness] is revealed. (2) Itself being revealed while the other is obscured. (3) Both existing together. (4) Both being submerged. Consider these on the model of the foregoing. In this case, illusory form exists and is done away with without obstruction. True emptiness is obscured and revealed freely. They are united in uniformity, and universally pervade [each other] freely. This is the dharma.

20. 1d. Fourth, the explanation with regard to contemplation *[kuan]* and practice. There are three parts. First, one contemplates form as identical with emptiness and in this way achieves the practice of tranquility *[chih]*.[31] When one contemplates emptiness as being identical with form, one achieves the practice of contemplation *[kuan]*.[32] Emptiness and form are not two different things, and they are manifested all at once in a single thought-instant. That is, when tranquility and insight are practiced together, then they are ideal. Second, when one sees that form is empty, one achieves great wisdom and no longer dwells in saṃsāra. When one sees that emptiness is form, one achieves great compassion and does not dwell in nirvāṇa. Because form and emptiness are not two different things, the thoughts of wisdom and compassion are neither exterminated nor achieved, and this is the practice without an abiding place *[wu-chu-ch'u-hsing]*.[33] Third, chih-che Ta-shih [i.e., T'ien-t'ai Chih-i], on the basis of the *Keyura-sūtra*, establishes the concept of the one mind and three contemplations. The first is the contemplation consisting of entering emptiness from the false; i.e., because [form] is identical with emptiness. Second is the contemplation of entering the false from emptiness; i.e., because emptiness is identical with form. The third is the contemplation of the sameness *[p'ing-teng]* of the empty and false, because form and emptiness are not different.

21. "O ŚĀRIPUTRA, ALL DHARMAS HAVE THE MARK OF EMPTINESS." 2. Illuminating dharma-essence *[fa-t'ai]*. There are two parts to this, the general and the spe-

cific. Now [with regard to the general explanation], it says, "all dharmas have the mark of emptiness." The groups [skandhas] and so forth are not just one, and so it [speaks in the plural and] says "all dharmas." It illuminates the form of this emptiness, and so it speaks of the "mark of emptiness." The *Madhyānta-vibhāga-śāstra* says, "The nonexistence of duality and the existence of this nonexistence are called the mark [or characteristic] of emptiness."[34] When it says "nonexistence of duality" *[wu-erh]*, it means that there is no one who grasps and nothing to be grasped. When it speaks of the "existence of this nonexistence" *[yu-tz'u-wu]* it means that there are grasper and grasped. It being neither two nor not two is the mark of emptiness.

22. (553c) "THEY ARE NOT PRODUCED, NOT DESTROYED, NOT IMPURE, NOT PURE, DO NOT INCREASE, DO NOT DECREASE." (b) In the specific explanation there are six "nots" in three pairs.[35] There are also three explanations [*vis-à-vis* each pair]. (1) With regard to states. (2) With reference to dharmas. (3) With reference to contemplation and practice. Now, first with regard to states: "They are not produced, not destroyed" refers to the state of the ordinary person prior to dwelling in the Way. It means that ordinary persons die here and are reborn there, turning over [on the wheel of rebirth] for long eons of time. This is the state of saṃsāra. Since true emptiness is divorced from this [state], it says "not produced, not destroyed." Second, "Not impure, not pure" refers to the bodhisattva abiding in the Way. It means that all bodhisattvas' obstacles, the impurities, are not yet exterminated, and pure conduct has already been started. This is called the state of impure and pure [mixed]. Since true emptiness is apart from this [state], it says "not impure, not pure." Third, "Do not increase, do not decrease" refers to the state of Buddhahood, after dwelling in the Way. The obstacle of delusion in saṃsāra has, since ancient times, not been terminated, and now this decrease is finished. Cultivating and producing the multitude of merits has, since ancient times, not been perfected, and now this increase has

been perfected. True emptiness is divorced from this [state], and so it says "do not increase, do not decrease." Also, the *Treatise on Buddha Nature*[36] establishes three kinds of Buddha nature. That existing before one undertakes practice is called "abiding-of-self-nature Buddha nature" *[tzu-hsing-chu-fo-hsing]*. That which exists while one is undergoing training is called "drawing-out Buddha nature" *[yin-ch'u-fo-hsing]*. That which exists after one's training is completed is called "arriving-at- the-result-and-acquiring-it Buddha nature" *[chih-te-kuo-fo- hsing]*. However, Buddha nature is only one, and it is divided into three parts apropos these states. Now, true emptiness is not different, and is divided apropos these states. Also, in the *Treatise on the Nondifferentiation of the Realm of Dharmas*,[37] it first speaks of an impure state, then of a state of both impurity and purity [mixed], and last of the state of unmixed purity. They are all the same as this [discussion of states].

23. (2) With reference to dharmas. This means that even though this true emptiness is the same as form, etc., still, form arises from conditions, but emptiness is not produced. In obedience to conditions, [form] also ceases to be, but true emptiness is not extinguished. Also, in following the current [of rebirth], it is not soiled, and in escaping obstacles, it is not purified. Also, the termination of obstacles is not a decrease, nor is the fulfillment of merits an increase. Birth and extinction, etc., are the mark of made dharmas [i.e., *saṃskṛta* dharmas]. In explaining this in order to show the mark of true emptiness, it says "mark of emptiness."

24. (3) Last, with reference to contemplation and practice. The contemplation of the threefold naturelessness (of dharmas) is set forth from the standpoint of the three natures *[trisvabhāva]*. The contemplation of marklessness is done with reference to the discriminated nature *[parikalpita-svabhāva]*; i.e., it is empty, lacking the ability to come into existence or cease to be. The contemplation of birthlessness is made with reference to the nature which consists of dependence on the other *[paratantra-svabhāva]*; i.e., dependent on the other [for

their existence], impure and pure are conditioned, and are without any nature [of their own]. The contemplation of naturelessness is made with reference to the perfected nature *[pariniṣpanna-svabhāva]*; i.e., the former two [natures] do not exist, nor are they extinguished. The wisdom of contemplation shines and manifests, yet does not increase. Also, the nature which is bondage or escape from obstacles neither increases nor decreases. Also, false dharmas neither are produced nor cease. Interdependent origination is neither pure nor impure. True emptiness neither increases nor decreases. By means of these three kinds of naturelessness, the mark of true emptiness is illuminated.

25. "THEREFORE, IN EMPTINESS THERE IS NO FORM, NO FEELING, NO CONCEPTUALIZATION, NO KARMIC VOLITION, NO CONSCIOUSNESS. THERE IS NO EYE, EAR, NOSE, TONGUE, SKIN, OR MIND. (554a) THERE ARE NO FORMS, SOUNDS, SMELLS, TOUCHABLE THINGS, OR MENTAL OBJECTS. THERE IS NO VISUAL ELEMENT, AND FINALLY, THERE IS NO ELEMENT OF MENTAL CONSCIOUSNESS." (3) Showing what is abandoned. Now, there are many categories in the detailed list of dharmas to be abandoned in true emptiness. In summary, there are four. (1) Analysis and synthesis of the characteristics of the dharmas. (2) Interdependent origination in forward and reverse orders. (3) Cause and result of impurity and purity. (4) Knowledge and object; that which knows and that which is known *[neng-so]*. Now, first, "Therefore, in emptiness" refers to the previous "not produced, not destroyed," because they are in true emptiness. "No form," etc., means that in true emptiness there are no dharmas such as the five skandhas. This refers back to the discussion of mutual antagonism [between emptiness and form], and therefore it says "no." Reality and Noumenon, none of these annihilate form and the like, because being empty of self-existence, these things do not require annihilation. With regard to the five skandhas, form [in all its varieties] is combined to make one [skandha], and mind is divided into four.[38] Second, "no eye,"

etc., means that in emptiness there are no twelve sense bases.[39] The twelve sense bases combine mind [in all manifestations] to make a half. That is to say, the mind-base *[mana-āyatana]* all together, and the dharma-base *[dharma-āyatana]* are one [whole] part. If you divide form [into its different manifestations], it makes ten halves; i.e., the five [material] faculties and five [objective] realms make ten bases, and along with the dharma-base makes one part. Third, "no visual element," etc., means that emptiness is lacking in the eighteen elements *[dhātus]*.[40] In the eighteen elements, both form and mind are divided. You can understand this in correspondence with the above. The explanation of these lists is in accordance with treatises on *abhidharma* and other works.

26. "THERE IS NO IGNORANCE AND NO TERMINATION OF IGNORANCE, AND SO ON UP TO NO BIRTH AND DEATH AND NO TERMINATION OF BIRTH AND DEATH." (2) This is the topic of interdependent origination *[pratītya-samutpāda]* in regular and reverse orders. "No ignorance" is the topic of contemplating in regular order the onward flow of ignorance. Because in its nature it is empty, [the sūtra] says, "no ignorance." "No termination of ignorance" is the topic of contemplating in reverse order the extermination of ignorance. Because of true emptiness, there is nothing to be terminated. This represents the first link [of the twelve links of interdependent origination]. There are ten more links, and each is to be understood in the same way as the above, so it says, "and so on up to," meaning up to the last link. That is to say, birth and death is also completely empty in flowing onward and becoming extinct.[41]

27. "THERE IS NO SUFFERING, ORIGINATION, CESSATION, OR PATH." (3) The topic of cause and result with regard to impurity and purity. Suffering and origination [the first two parts of the Four Holy Truths] are mundane cause and effect. That is, suffering is the recompense [effect] consisting of birth and death. When it starts, it causes disgust. Origination [*chi*; lit., "accumulation"] is its cause. That is [origination] is action [karma] which is defilement *[kleśa]*.

When one becomes disgusted with suffering and exterminates its cause, at first [suffering] is a result [of former karma] and later it is a cause [of exterminating the cause of suffering]. Cessation and the path are supramundane cause and effect. Cessation is the result consisting of nirvāṇa. When it rises, it is the cause for joy. The path is its cause; that is, the Eightfold Holy Path. One cultivates it last. All are empty and nonexistent.

28. "NO KNOWLEDGE AND NO ACQUISITION." (4) The topic of realm and wisdom, that which knows and that which is known *[neng-so]*.[42] Not only are there no dharmas in the previously mentioned emptiness, but the wisdom which knows emptiness is also unobtainable. Therefore, it says, "no knowledge." Also, emptiness, that which is known, is also unobtainable. Therefore, it says, "no acquisition." Question: Formerly you said that [554b] "emptiness is identical with form," etc., showing that form and so on are not annihilated. Then why does this passage say that they are all nonexistent? Would not this emptiness be [merely] extinguished form? Answer: Even though the former [passage] did not obstruct existence, still, by no means did it not terminate it *[wei-ch'ang-pu-chin]*. Now [here] all these [dharmas] are done away with, and yet, by no means does it not posit them *[wei-ch'ang-pu-li]*. Therefore, the *Pañcaviṁśati-sāhasrikā-prajñā-pāramitā-sūtra* says, "Dharmas do not exist, and in such a way exists this nonexistence." This [present argument] refers to "not anything that exists," while the former [argument of earlier passages] referred to existence [of dharmas] in this way. Also, the former refers to their mutual destruction. There is only one dharma, with two interpretations, and they do not conflict in accordance with the discussion.

29. "BECAUSE THERE IS NOTHING TO BE ACQUIRED." (4) Showing what is acquired. There are two parts. First, the following [passage of the sūtra; i.e., "because there is nothing to be acquired"] is established on the basis of what went before [i.e., "no knowledge and no acquisition"], and then what is acquired is correctly shown. Now, first, it

says, "because there is nothing to be acquired." This establishes the present passage on the basis of what was said before. *Yi* is the same as *yu* [i.e., "as a result of"]. *Ku* is the same as *yin* [i.e., "cause"]. This means that as a result of a cause consisting of nothing to be acquired, there is a subsequent acquisition of something.[43] The *Pañcaviṁśati-sāhasrikā-prajñāpāramitā-sūtra* says, "There is nothing to be acquired, and therefore it is acquired."

30. "BECAUSE THE BODHISATTVA RELIES ON THE PERFECTION OF WISDOM." Next, showing what is acquired. There are two parts. First, the bodhisattva is shown acquiring nirvāṇa, which is the result of cutting off the obstacles, and then all Buddhas are shown acquiring *bodhi*, which is the result. The first part also has two parts. First it presents the individual [under discussion] who relies on this dharma, and then, after, he cuts off the obstacles and acquires the result. Now, first, it says "the bodhisattva," and this shows who the person is. The meaning [of "bodhisattva"] was discussed earlier. "Relies on the perfection of wisdom" shows that his practice is based on the dharma. "Because" connects the passage with the next one.

31. "HIS MIND IS WITHOUT OBSTACLES." Second, cutting off obstacles and acquiring the result. There are three parts. First, he perfects his practices; second, he cuts off obstacles; and third, he acquires the result. Now, first, it says "his mind is without obstacles"; this is the perfection of practice, because delusions do not obstruct his mind, and the realm [of the knowable] does not obstruct wisdom.

32. "BECAUSE THERE ARE NO OBSTACLES, HE HAS NOTHING TO FEAR. HE IS UTTERLY DIVORCED FROM ERRORS AND DREAMLIKE NOTIONS." Next is the cutting off of obstacles. It says, "because there are no obstacles." This ["because"] leads to the next part of the sentence. "He has nothing to fear" means he has no fear of demons outside.[44] That is to say, evil *conditions* are stopped. "He is utterly divorced from errors and dreamlike notions" means errors in the form of internal obstacles are gone; that is to say, evil *cause* is eliminated.[45]

33. "THERE IS ABSOLUTE NIRVĀṆA." Finally, he acquires the result. Nirvāṇa in our [Chinese] language is "perfect cessation." This means that no merits that are not completely possessed is styled "perfection." No obstacles that are not eliminated is styled "cessation." There is an allusion to a different [type of nirvāṇa], which is the small-vehicle apparitional city [in the *Lotus Sūtra*] which is established as a provisional device, but here one single acquisition is eternal, and so it says "absolute."[46] "Absolute" can also be explained as meaning that wisdom can absolutely exhaust the limit of nirvāṇa.

34. (559c) "BECAUSE ALL THE BUDDHAS OF THE THREE PERIODS HAVE RELIED ON THE PERFECTION OF WISDOM." Second, the acquisition of the result, which is *bodhi.* There are two parts. First, the individuals who relied on the dharma are presented, and then the acquisition of the result is shown. The first means that none of the Buddhas of the three periods [of past, future, and present] had different ways. There is only this one door, and so it says "relied on the perfection of wisdom."

35. "THEY ACQUIRED *ANUTTARA-SAMYAK-SAṂBODHI.*" [i.e., "the highest, right, uniform enlightenment"]. Next, correctly showing the acquisition of the result. *Anuttara* means "without a superior" *[wu-shang]. Samyak* means "right" [*cheng*, i.e., correct]. The next *sam* [in *sambodhi*] means "uniform" *[teng].*[47] *Bodhi* means "enlightenment." That is to say, "the highest, right, uniform enlightenment." Enlightenment has two meanings. One is "right enlightenment." I.e., it is knowledge which accords with the absolute *[li].* One correctly contemplates the real truth. The other meaning is "uniform enlightenment." I.e., it is knowledge which accords with the phenomenal *[liang].* One universally contemplates the conventional truth. All attain the extreme limitless, and so it is called "highest." The foregoing is the realm of that which is acquired.

36. "THEREFORE KNOW THAT THE PERFECTION OF WISDOM IS A GREAT MYSTERIOUS MANTRA, A MANTRA OF GREAT KNOWLEDGE, THE HIGHEST

MANTRA, THE MANTRA WITHOUT COMPARISON." (5) The summary, which praises its superior power. There are two parts. The first is specific praise, and the second is the general conclusion. Now, first, it says, "therefore know"; what comes after is established according to what was said before [in the foregoing lines, and so there is a consequential "therefore"]. As a result of relying on prajñā, the bodhisattva acquires the result, *bodhi* and nirvāṇa. "Therefore know that [the perfection of] wisdom is a great mantra," etc., praises its superior power. In summary, it praises four merits in three ways each. (1) With reference to the dharma: (a) it gets rid of obstacles and does not falsify, so it is called a great mysterious mantra; (b) wisdom mirrors without obscurity, and so it is called a mantra of great knowledge; (c) nothing can surpass it, so it is called the highest mantra; (d) it is unique, absolute, and beyond comparison, so it is called the mantra without comparison. (2) With regard to the power of its merits: (a) it can block defilements [of a moral nature]; (b) it can block ignorance; (c) it causes the perfection of causal practices; (d) it causes the perfection of resultant merits. (3) With regard to states: (a) it bypasses the [state of] ordinary persons; (b) it goes beyond the [state of] small [vehicle]; (c) it transcends [the state of] cause [i.e., causal practices]; (d) it is equal with result. This means that it merges with equality with the incomparable state [of enlightenment]. Therefore, it says, "without comparison." The *Treatise on the [Sūtra on the] Ten States* says, " 'Incomparable' means that if you compare the Buddha with ordinary beings, there is no comparison." With regard to repeating the word "comparable" [*teng*, i.e., *wu-teng-teng*], since this [mantra] and the *dharma-kāya* are comparable, why does it not simply say "without comparison" *[wu-teng]*? The reason is that it shows that [the mantra] is comparable to perfect enlightenment [i.e., *wu-teng-teng* = the mantra is comparable to *(teng)* the incomparable *(wu-teng)*].

37. "IT CAN GET RID OF ALL SUFFERING, FOR IT IS TRUE, NOT FALSE." Second, the general conclusion, praising its superior merit. That is, ["all suffering"] means the

three kinds of suffering, the eight kinds of suffering, all suffering.[48] Also, [rebirth consisting of] allotment and transformation are also suffering. It gets rid of suffering definitively, so it says, "it is true, not false." The foregoing is not the same in the expanded and abbreviated [versions]. This is the conclusion of the general discussion and revelation of prajñā.

38. (555a) "THEREFORE, UTTER THE MANTRA OF THE PERFECTION OF WISDOM; UTTER THE MANTRA, SAYING." (B.) From here on, the second [major] division [of this commentary] shows the esoteric prajñā. There are two parts. First, what follows is based on what was mentioned above [and hence the consequential "therefore" in this clause]. Second, the words of the mantra are disclosed. Earlier, it said, "it is a great mantra," but it has not yet shown what the words of the mantra are, so now it shows them.

39. *"GATE, GATE, PĀRAGATE, PĀRASAMGATE, BODHI, SVĀHĀ."* Second, correctly showing the words of the mantra. This has two meanings. First, [the mantra] is not to be explained, because the esoteric words *[mi-yü]* of the Buddhas ought not to be explained [to beings] in the causal state [prior to enlightenment]. One should simply chant [the mantra], support it, remove obstacles, and accrue merit, and not necessarily demand an explanation. Second, if an explanation is required, *gate* means "gone" and "passed beyond"; i.e., it is the power of the merits of profound wisdom. When it repeats *gate*, it means that oneself shall pass beyond and others shall pass beyond. With regard to *pāragate*, *pāra* means "the other shore" [i.e., "beyond"], that is, "gone to the other shore to be reached." With regard to *pārasamgate*, the *sam* means "wholly"*[tsung]* and "universally" *[p'u]* This means that oneself and all others shall universally pass beyond, and will wholly reach the other shore. With regard to the word *bodhi*, one might ask, "Reached the other shore which is what?" It is the place which is great *[bodhi]*. As for the word *svāhā*, it means "quickly";[49] that is, it causes what was done before to be quickly perfected.

40. This brief commentary is finished, and I lay down my brush. I will recollect what I have written in these verses:

The deep abstruseness of prajñā
Is hard to become acquainted with in many eons.
I have praised and explained it according to my ability,
And I hope I have understood the true tenet.

The *Brief Commentary on the Sūtra on the Heart of the Perfection of Wisdom.* Done at the capitol by Fa-tsang, in the second year of Ch'ang-an [A.D. 702]in leisure time when not translating sūtras [with Śikṣānanda].[50]

NOTES

1. See, for instance, Shigeo Kamata, *Chūgoku Kegon Shisō Shi no Kenkyū* (Tokyo: Zaidan Hōjin Tōkyō Daigaku Shuppankai, 1965); and Kamata, *Chūgoku Bukkyō Shisō Kenkyū* (Tokyo: Shunjūsha, 1968).

2. Fa-tsang, like many Chinese Buddhists, commonly uses "existence" and "form" interchangeably, so that in discussing the *śūnyavāda* relationship between emptiness and form, he tends to oppose emptiness with existence, a uniquely Chinese custom. It will be less confusing if it is kept in mind that when Fa-tsang uses the term "existence," he means "form and other dharmas."

3. See Fa-tsang's analogy of the barn and barn rafter in the tenth chapter of *Hua-yen i ch'eng chiao i fen-ch'i chang*, Taisho vol. 45, no. 1866, p. 507c.

4. See my article, "The Meaning of Vairocana in Hua-yen Buddhism," *Philosophy East and West* 22 (October 1972), pp. 403–415.

5. Cited in note 3. See particularly ch. 10, pp. 499a–509a.

6. Shih-hui, *Pan-jo hsin-ching lüeh-shu-lien-chu-chi*, Taisho vol. 34, no. 1713, p. 557c. See also Ch'ien, *Zokuzōkyō*, Eun Maeda, Tatsue Nakano *et al.*, comp. and ed. (Kyōto: Kyoto Zōkuzō-shoin, 1905–12), I.41.363c.

7. Shih-hui, *Pan-jo hsin-ching*, p. 558c.

8. This is the opinion of Garma C. C. Chang, in his recent book on Hua-yen, *The Buddhist Teaching of Totality* (University Park: Pennsylvania State University Press, 1971), pp. 203–204.

9. See, for instance, Candrakīrti, *Prasannapadā*, Jacques May, trans. (Paris: Adrien Maisonneuve, 1959), esp. ch. 24, pp. 222, 237.

10. *Ibid.*, ch. 24, v. 24.

11. *Hua-yen wu chiao shih-kuan*, Taisho vol. 45, no. 1867, is attributed to Tu-shun, but it is considered to be a work of Fa-tsang, who used Tu-

shun's material. It is fundamentally an analysis of *śamatha* and *vipaśyanā* as practiced by Hīnayāna, early Mahāyāna, developed Mahāyāna, "suddenists," and Hua-yen.

12. There is a discussion of this in Paravahera Vajirañāṇa Mahāthera's *Buddhist Meditation* (Columbo: M. D. Gunasena, 1962), chs. 2, 3, 4, and 25 ff. See also Edward Conze's remarks on *vyavalokayati* in his commentary on the *Heart Sūtra* in *Buddhist Wisdom Books*, pp. 78–79.

13. Shih-hui, *Pan-jo hsin-ching*, p. 564b. Compare with Vajirañāṇa's comments in *Buddhist Meditation*, p. 22 *(vipassanā)* and chs. 25, 26.

14. Cited in note 11. Hai-yin san-mei is discussed in almost all works on Hua-yen. Some representative works are Ryōei Yusugi, *Kegongaku Gairon* (Kyoto: Ryūkoku University Press, 1941), pp. 53 ff.; and Kyōshin Kamekawa, *Kegongaku* (Kyoto: Hyakkaen, 1949), pp. 6, 17, 18.

15. Shih-hui, *Pan-jo hsin-ching*, p. 564c.

16. *Laṅkāvatāra-sūtra*, Suzuki, trans., ch. 4.

17. Shih-hui, *Pan-jo hsin-ching*, p. 564c.

18. Kitarō Nishida, *A Study of Good*, V. H. Viglielmo, trans. (Tokyo: Printing Bureau, Japanese Government, 1960), ch. 5, "Intelligence and Love," pp. 185 ff.

19. Edward Conze, *Thirty Years of Buddhist Studies* (Columbia: University of South Carolina Press, 1968).

20. This sounds very Chinese, perhaps Taoist, but it does not, I believe, conflict with my own interpretation of Hua-yen as a positive application of the doctrine of *pratītya-samutpāda*. Shih-hui, *Pan-jo hsin-ching*, p. 555c, says that "source" refers to prajñā and tathatā; i.e., they are the source of dharmas. But if emptiness is *pratītya-samutpāda*, as Nāgārjuna says, then emptiness, and so on, are the source of dharmas. I don't believe we need to read anything of a substantialist or emanationalist nature into the word "source." Fa-tsang says that form, and so on, are the result of interdependent origination (23).

21. Literally, "rabbit snares and fish traps" *(ch'üan-t'i)*. Shih-hui says they are figures of speech for "words," "words" meaning the verbal skillful devices which try to express truth. *Pan-jo hsin-ching*, pp. 555c–556a. See also Morohashi, *Dai Kanwa Jiten*.

22. In his introduction, Fa-tsang uses the word "existence" instead of "form," which is the sūtra usage. It is evident here, in this rather Chinese manner of expressing the terms of the sūtra, that "existence" was understood in the sense of "form"; i.e., phenomena.

23. The "four attachments" *(ssu-chih)*, are listed in several alternative groups. Chung-hsi, *Zokuzōkyō* I.41, p. 341c, lists as possible: (1) same, (2) different, (3) existent, (4) nonexistent. These may be the more traditional list of the four attachments—seeing things as permanent, pleasant, having an atman, and lovely. There are also other possibilities.

24. The hundred negations, according to Chung-hsi, *Zokuzōkyō* I.41, p. 341c, is just a variation of the above four attachments, the number being arrived at by a process of multiplying these four by four forms of negation, the three time periods, and so on.

25. Ch'ien's comment on *shih-hsiang* (*Zokuzōkyō* I.41, p. 266a) has led me to translate this as "real-mark": "Real-mark is the mark [or characteristic] of emptiness which all dharmas have."

26. "Avalokiteśvara" is commonly translated as "The Lord Who Beholds [All Beings]," "Lord of the Beheld [World]," and so on, but the name is problematic. Hsüan-tsang's translation, *Kuan-tzu-tsai*, is similar to these meanings. As the commentary shows, he beholds freely, in a lordly fashion. The other translation of his name into Chinese, *Kuan-yin*, perhaps results from an incorrect division of his name into *Avalokita* (Beholds) *svara* (Sounds) (of the weeping of mankind), instead of *Avalokita* (Beholds) *īśvara* (Lord, or Freely).

27. *P'u-sa* is the Chinese transliteration of "bodhisattva."

28. The two types of saṃsāra are: (1) that resulting from past karma (i.e., one's allotment), and (2) that which is voluntarily undertaken by bodhisattvas in a spirit of compassion, in order to aid beings in the six gatis. The latter consists of existence in a "mind-made body," as mentioned in the *Laṅkāvatāra-sūtra*, p. 118. An extended discussion of the two types of saṁsāra can be found in *Vijñaptimātratā-siddhi*, Louis de la Vallée Poussin, trans. (Paris: Geuthner, 1928–48), pp. 501–13.

29. *Sopadhiśeṣa* is existence in bodily form. It usually refers to the nirvāṇa of the Buddha while he was still living. *Nirupadhiśeṣa* is the state of the Buddha in nirvāṇa after physical death. They mean "with *upadhi* remaining" and "without *upadhi* remaining," *upadhi* apparently being the psychophysical basis of embodied existence.

30. That is, one should not reify emptiness. In his *Early Mādhyamika in India and China* (Madison: University of Wisconsin Press, 1968), p. 49, Richard Robinson says: "Emptiness is not a term outside the expressional system, but is simply the key term within it. Those who would hypostatize emptiness are confusing the symbol system with the fact system." Fa-tsang is rejecting this hypostatization, showing, I believe, that he knew how emptiness was to be understood.

31. Sanskrit *śamatha*.

32. Sanskrit *vipaśyanā*.

33. That is, without abiding in, or being attached to, saṃsāra or nirvāṇa. Ch'ien, *Zokuzōkyō* I.41, p. 375b.

34. This quote is identical with Paramārtha's translation of the *Madhyāntavibhāga*, Taisho vol. 31, no. 1599, p. 452b: *wu erh yu t'zu wu shih erh ming k'ung hsiang / ku fei yu fei pu yi yi pu yi*. The Sanskrit original is: *Dvayābhāvo hy abhāvasya bhāvaḥ śūnyasya lakṣanaṁ / na bhāvo nāpi cābhāvaḥ na pṛthaktvaika lakṣanaṁ*, according to the edition of the *Madhyāntavibhāga-bhaṣya* edited by Nagao, pp. 22–23.

35. The "six nots" are a variant list of the "eight nots" in Nāgārjuna's *Mādhyamika-kārikās*.

36. *Fo-hsing lun*, Taisho vol. 31, no. 1610.

37. *Ta-ch'eng fa-chieh wu ch'a-pieh lun*, Taisho vol. 31, nos. 1626 and 1627.

38. The five skandhas, form *(rūpa)*, feeling *(vedanā)*, conceptualization *(saṁjñā)*, volition *(saṃskāra)*, and consciousness *(vijñāna)*, are abstract groupings of psychophysical factors. There are several varieties of form, but in the list of the *skandhas* they are all subsumed under the category of "form." "Mind" is divided in four forms to make up the rest of the skandhas.

39. The twelve *āyatanas* are the six sense bases with their corresponding objects:

| | |
|---|---|
| eye | physical forms |
| ear | sounds |
| nose | smells |
| tongue | tastes |
| body | touchables |
| mind | mental objects (dharmas) |

Here, all the mental factors (the last four skandhas) are called "mind," and make up one-half of the last category above. Combined with its object, it makes one whole part.

40. The eighteen *dhātus* (elements) are:

| | | |
|---|---|---|
| eye | visual consciousness | forms |
| ear | auditory consciousness | sounds |
| nose | olfactory consciousness | smells |
| tongue | gustatory consciousness | tastes |
| body | tactile consciousness | tangibles |
| mind | mind consciousness | dharmas |

41. This refers to the twelve-limbed cycle of dependent origination. Read from the twelfth item back in reverse order, the list shows the ultimate cause of suffering to be ignorance. Read in regular order, from ignorance to the twelfth item, old age and death, the list shows how the twelfth item can be removed. The sūtra mentions only the first and twelfth items as an abbreviated way of saying that the whole twelve-limbed cycle of dependent origination is empty.

42. The characters *neng* and *so* in any context mean literally "what can," or what performs an action or is the agent, and "what is acted upon," or the passive recipient of the action. One is passive, the other active. It is difficult to translate them smoothly out of a grammatical context.

43. The grammatical lesson by Fa-tsang is interesting, because the whole

grammatical sequence *yi . . . ku*, which is usually translated simply as "because . . . " or "as a result of. . . . " is explained here as meaning that the initial *yi* means "because," and the final *ku* means "cause" in the sense that "because there is nothing to be acquired" is the cause for the subsequent acquisition of something. This is supported by the quotation from *Large Sūtra*.

44. "External demons" are any objective condition for man's existential plight.

45. "Internal obstacles" are subjective causes such as ignorance, hatred, and desire. These, in conjunction with external conditions, result in rebirth in saṃsāra.

46. This is a reference to a simile in the *Lotus Sūtra*, in which the nirvāṇa of the small vehicle is likened to an illusory city created by a guide who wishes to encourage tired travelers on further to the real city. Once the travelers reach the illusory city (= nirvāṇa in the small vehicle), the guide (= Buddha) tells them that it is not the final destination, for the real city (= true nirvāṇa) is still further on. See the chapter called "Ancient Devotion" in H. Kern, trans., *Saddharmapuṇḍarīka Sūtra* (New York: Dover Publications, 1963), p. 181.

47. The *saṃ* of *saṃbodhi* is usually translated as "perfect." Fa-tsang translates it as "equal" or "uniform" *(teng)*. Fa-tsang wishes to say that Buddhahood comprises two kinds of enlightenment, "right" *(cheng)*, and "uniform" *(teng)*. Ch'ien, *Zokuzōkyō* I.41, p. 338b–c, says that right enlightenment transcends falsity, while uniform enlightenment (or "universal enlightenment," as Ch'ien has it) transcends not only the enlightenment of the small vehicle, but the ten stages of the bodhisattva's career as well, and therefore the enlightenment of the Buddha illuminates both the phenomenal and the absolute.

48. The three kinds of *duḥkha* are (1) *duḥkha-duḥkha*, suffering resulting from heat, cold, disease, and the like; (2) *vipariṇāma-duḥkha*, suffering resulting from change, as when happiness vanishes; and (3) *saṃskāra-duḥkha*, suffering which is inherent in the five skandhas. The eight kinds of suffering are those mentioned at the conclusion of the stereotyped form of the twelve-limbed interdependent origination formula—birth, old age, sickness, death, and so forth. Chung-hsi, *Zokuzōkyō* I.41, p. 355d.

49. I do not know how *svāhā* comes to be translated "quickly" *(su chi)*, nor do the commentaries explain it. The conventional translation is discussed in Edward Conze's translation of the *Heart Sūtra* in *Buddhist Wisdom Books*, p. 106.

50. The commentary proper ends with the short poem. These last lines are the beginning of a postface which I have not translated, because of limitations of space and because it adds nothing to the understanding of the sūtra, nor does it illuminate any more of Fa-tsang's grasp of the sūtra.

# Fa-sheng's Observations on the Four Stations of Mindfulness

*Leon Hurvitz*

This study is planned as part of a larger examination of the impact made on receptive Chinese by the Buddhist notion of salvation. It looks at the question, of course, from two points of view, that of the Indians (as presented to the Chinese in translation, for they read no language but their own) and that of the Chinese reaction. In connection with the Indian point of view, this writer has published a previous study on Vasubhadra;[1] the text which this study will examine is similar to Vasubhadra's. The procedure will be to single out the portion of that text dealing with the Four Stations of Mindfulness *(catvāri smṛtyupasthānāni)*, to translate them or, as the case may be, to paraphrase them, and then to deal with the larger, principally canonical, issues. It should be pointed out that the same issue is treated in detail in chapter 36 of the *Ta chih tu lun.*[2]

The work in question, bearing the Chinese title *A-p'i-t'an hsin lun*, is ascribed to a certain "Fa-sheng." The original title may have been *Abhidharmahṛdaya* or *Abhidharmasāra*; as to the author's name, one thinks of such possibilities as Dharmajit, Dharmottara, Dharmodgata, Dharmaśreṣṭha, and others, but there can be no certainty. The work survives in three versions. (1) The earliest, consisting of aphorisms in verse, interspersed with prose comments, was translated in 376 A.D. by Saṃghadeva (one of the translators of the Vasubhadra work mentioned previously) with the aid of the great Hui-yüan of Lu-shan (314–386 A.D.). (2) The second is a similar translation, except that here the verses alone are ascribed to Fa-sheng, the prose to a certain Upaśānta. The translation was made in an unspecified year under the Northern Ch'i (550–577 A.D.) by Narendrayaśas. (3) The third, finally, is the same thing with a somewhat extended commentary, the latter ascribed to "Fa-chiu" (Dharmatrāta?). This translation was done under the Liu-Sung (420–479 A.D.), also in an unspecified year, by Saṃghavarman, an Indian missionary who arrived in China in 433. Hui-yüan and his master Tao-an, the focal figures in this series of studies, would have had access only to the earliest translation. On the advice of a friend, however,[3] I am making use of all three to arrive at my findings.

The issue is the same as that treated in the piece on Vasubhadra: the path to salvation, as specified in those abhidharma works to which Tao-an and Hui-yüan would have had access. In (1) the problem will be found treated in T28.818a–820b. In (2) it is in T28.848b–852a. In (3) it is in T28.907c–916c. In all three it consists of a chapter entitled *hsien sheng p'in* ("chapter on the worthy saints"), where *hsien sheng* presumably represents *ārya*. In the present study, the core text will be (1), since that is the only one that Tao-an and Hui-yüan would have seen. The core text will, however, be eked out by the other two, particularly by (3), which contains a type of preface missing from the first and second both. Within that framework this study will focus exclusively on the theme of the Four Stations of Mindfulness.

The chapter under consideration deals with the cultivation (*hsiu*, representing *bhāvanā?*) of religious practice. This is considered to be on three levels, as stated in the following verse:

The first is named "initiator of deeds";
The next is the one of "already repeated practice";
While he who has "already transcended attention"
Is to be known as the third sort.

Happily, the *Abhidharmakośa* has the same categories.[4] "Initiator of deeds" translates *shih yeh*, which, in turn, stands for *ādikarmika* (cf. Gokhale vi.10), rendered in French by M. Louis de La Vallée-Poussin (vi.150), hereafter known as LVP, as "le commençant."[5] "Already repeated practice" stands for *yi hsi hsing*, whose original, as we now have it (Gokhale, *ibid.*), is *kṛtajaya*, rendered LVP vi.151 as "le maître." *Yi hsi hsing*, on the other hand, as well as Paramārtha's *yi shuo hsi ch'eng hsing* (T29.270a), would seem to suggest *kṛtacaya* instead. Lastly, "already transcended attention" stands for *ssu wei yi tu*, whose original (Gokhale vi.11) was *atikrāntamanaskāra*, rendered LVP vi.151 as "un maître absolu dans l'acte d'attention."

The prose commentary repeats the three categories, then proceeds to define them. (a) The "initiator of deeds" is the practitioner on the stage extending from the awareness of uncleanness *(pu ching, aśubhā)* up to, but not including, the power to direct his attention to any and all objects, even imaginary ones *(ching chieh yi chieh ssu wei fen, viṣayādhimukti-manasikārabhāga?)*. (b) The one of "already repeated practice" is the person on the stage that begins with the four stages of mindfulness, as seen in terms of the character peculiar to each *(tzu hsiang nien ch'u, svalakṣaṇasmṛtyupasthānāni?)*, and ends "ere yet he has got wholesome roots of a definite and certain portion" *(wei ts'eng te chüeh ting fen shan ken*, of which the last five syllables may represent *niyatabhāgakuśalamūlāni)*. (c) Everything beyond that point appertains to him who has "already transcended attention," because "it is the Path of the Single Vehicle."[6]

The second *ardhaśloka* of *Kośa* vi.15, as given by Gokhale, is *kāyaviccittadharmāṇāṃ dvilakṣaṇaparīkṣaṇāt//*, rendered by LVP vi.14c–d as "Par la considération des caractères, doubles, du corps, de la sensation, de la pensée et des *dhar-*

*mas.*" To that, he comments (vi.158 f.) as follows: "Le caractère propre, c'est-à-dire la nature propre *(svabhāva)*. Les caractères communs, à savoir: 'Tous les *saṃskṛtas* sont impermanents; tous les *dharmas* impurs *(sāsrava)* sont douloureux; tous les *dharmas* sont vides *(śūnya)* et non-soi *(anātmaka)*.' " *Vyākhya* 529 (ad vi.15) reads as follows:

> By the expression "for the achievement of speculative cognition" is meant "in order to achieve wisdom." For, this side of wisdom, the defilements are not utterly cast off, not even by one of perfect concentration. "The defilements are the killers of gnosis," as the Scriptures say. Whence does one know that speculative cognition is achieved by this realization of the four stations of mindfulness? From Scripture. "A Path of but one approach, O mendicant monks, is this one, to wit, the Four Stations of Mindfulness. A unique accumulation of the wholesome is this one, to wit, the Four Stations of Mindfulness." Such is the Word. By the *vid* of *kāyavid* is meant *vedanā* [sensation]. "By 'own character' is meant 'own being.' " Which own being? In the case of the body, the reference is to the latter's being composed of elements and their derivatives. In the case of sensation, it refers to experience. In the case of thought, it refers to the fact of becoming aware. The own-being of those other than these three is the respective one appropriate to each of them . . . . The expression "the dharmas other than the three" is used by naming them collectively, without distinguishing the latter one from another. In case a distinction were made, they would be specified as "body, etc." Then all dharmas, constituted and unconstituted, are to be [so?] viewed.

LVP v.158, n. 1, says, " . . . La practique des *smṛtyupasthānas* produit la connaissance parfaite, car Bhagavat a dit: . . . ." LVP refers the reader to *Saṃyutta* vv. 167, 146. Both are contained in the *Mahāvagga*, specifically in the forty-seventh section of the *Saṃyuttanikāya* as a whole, the section devoted to the Stations of Mindfulness, as its title *(satipaṭṭhānasaṃyutta)* indicates. In view of the emphasis of the present study, however, we shall first give the particular sūtra from the respective *Āgama*,then the corresponding text from the *Saṃyuttanikāya*, where one exists. The Chinese sources in question are (1) Guṇabhadra's translation of the *Saṃyuktāgama*, entitled *Tsa a-han ching*,[7] (2) another translation of the same, entitled *Pieh yi tsa a-han ching*,[8] translated by a person unknown, and (3) a third translation of the same, also going by the title *Tsa a-han ching*, likewise by an unknown translator.[9]

---

### *Tsa a-han Ching* 24.605 (2.170C–171A), Entry 1

Thus have I heard. Once the Buddha was dwelling in Śrāvasti land, among the Jeta trees *[Jetavana]*, in the park of the Benefactor of the Lonely *[Anāthapiṇḍada]*. At that time the World-Honored One declared to the *bhikṣus*: "There are four stations of mindfulness. Which four? They are called 'the station of mindfulness that observes the body as a body' *[shen shen kuan nien ch'u, kāye kāyānupaśyanāsmṛtyupasthānam?]*, so for sensations and thought, and the station of mindfulness that observes the dharmas as dharmas." When the Buddha had preached this sermon, the *bhikṣus*, having heard what the Buddha preached, with joy carried it out respectfully.

### 24.606 (2.171A), Entry 2

Thus have I heard. Once the Buddha was dwelling in Śrāvasti land, among the Jeta trees, in the park of the Benefactor of the Lonely. At that time the World-Honored One declared to the *bhikṣus*: "There are four stations of mindfulness. Which four? They are called 'the station of mindfulness that observes the body as a body,' so for sensations and thought, and the station of mindfulness that observes the dharmas as dharmas. It is in this way that a *bhikṣu*, when his practice with respect to the Four Stations of Mindfulness is complete, with subtle striving and by resort to expedient devices, with right mindfulness and right knowledge, must learn." When the Buddha had preached this sermon, the *bhikṣus*, having heard what the Buddha preached, with joy carried it out respectfully.

*Saṃyuttanikāya* **47.24 (p. 173 f.),** *Suddhasuttaṃ*

The scene was Sāvatthi. "Four, O mendicant monks, are these stations of mindfulness. Which four? Here, O mendicant monks, the mendicant monk courses in the body, mindful of the body, ascetically disciplined, fully conscious and mindful, putting off envy and ill disposition toward the world. These, O mendicant monks, are the Four Stations of Mindfulness."

**24.607 (2.171A), Entry 3**

Thus have I heard. Once the Buddha was dwelling in Śrāvasti land, among the Jeta trees, in the park of the Benefactor of the Lonely. At that time the World-Honored One declared to the *bhikṣus*: "There is one vehicle-path for purifying the beings, enabling them to outpass grief and sorrow, to annihilate woe and agony, to gain dharmas in accord with Reality: to wit, the Four Stations of Mindfulness. Which four? The station of mindfulness that views the body as a body, so for sensations and thought, and the station of mindfulness that views the dharmas as dharmas." When the Buddha had preached this sermon, the *bhikṣus*, having heard what the Buddha preached, with joy carried it out respectfully.

**47.18 (p. 167 f.)** *Brahmasuttaṃ*

One time the Blessed One was disporting Himself at Uruvelā [Uruvilvā], on the bank of the river Nerañjarī [Nairañjanī], by the goatherd's banyan tree, having just had His enlightened intuition. Then indeed to the Blessed One, withdrawn and concealed as He was, occurred this thought: "Of a single course is the way to the purification of the beings, to the overcoming of pain and woe, to the assuagement of suffering and ill disposition, to the comprehension of rational truth, to the bearing of direct witness to nibbāna [nirvāṇa], to wit, the Four Stations of Mindfulness. Which four? Let the mendicant monk course in the body, observing the body, ascetically disciplined, fully conscious, mindful, ridding himself of envy and ill disposition toward the world. Or let the mendicant monk course in sensations, or in thought, or in the dharmas, observing the dharmas, ascetically disciplined, fully conscious, mindful, putting off envy and ill disposition toward the world. Of a single course is the way to the purification of the beings, to the overcoming of pain and woe, to the assuagement of suffering and ill disposition, to the comprehension of rational truth, to the bearing of direct witness to nibbāna, to wit, the Four Stations of Mindfulness."

Then indeed Brahmán, the Lord of Sahā, being fully aware in his own thought of the thought of the Blessed One, as a strong man might stretch out his bent arm or bend his outstretched arm, just so made his appearance before the Blessed One, concealed as He was in the Brahmán world. Then indeed Brahmán, the Lord of Sahā, baring one shoulder and joining palms in the direction of where Blessed One was, said this to the Blessed One: "Just so, O Blessed One! Just so, O Well Gone One! Of a single course, Lord, is the way to the purification of the beings, to the overcoming of pain and woe, to the assuagement of suffering and ill disposition, to the comprehension of rational truth, to the bearing of direct witness to nibbāna, to wit, the Four Stations of Mindfulness. Which four? Let the mendicant monk, Lord, course in the body, observing the body, ascetically disciplined, fully conscious, mindful, putting off envy and ill disposition toward the world. Or let the mendicant monk course in sensations, Lord, or in the dharmas, Lord, observing the dharmas, ascetically disciplined, fully conscious, mindful, ridding himself of envy and ill disposition toward the world. Of a single course, Lord, is the way to the purification of the beings, to the overcoming of pain and woe, to the assuagement of suffering and ill disposition, to the comprehension of rational truth, to the bearing of direct witness to nibbāna, to wit, the Four Stations of Mindfulness."

Thus spoke Brahmán, the lord of Sahā. Having thus spoken, he then spoke again as follows:

Of a single course is the way that He Who sees the
cessation of birth, Who is solicitious of
welfare, understands,
The very way by which men have crossed the stream
in the past, and shall cross it, and are
crossing it.

### 24.608 (2.171A), Entry 4

Thus have I heard. Once the Buddha was dwelling in Śrāvasti land, among the Jeta trees, in the park of the Benefactor of the Lonely. At that time the World-Honored One declared to the *bhikṣus*: "If a *bhikṣu* separates himself from the Four Stations of Mindfulness, then he separates himself from the holy Dharma which is in accord with Reality. If he separates himself from the holy Dharma which is in accord with Reality, then he separates himself from the holy Path. One who separates himself from the holy Path separates himself from the Dharma of sweet dew. One who separates himself from the Dharma of sweet dew cannot escape from birth, old age, sickness, and death, from care and grief, agony and woe. I declare that he cannot gain release from woe. If a *bhikṣu* does not separate himself from the Four Stations of Mindfulness, then he does not separate himself from the holy Dharma which is in accord with Reality. One who does not separate himself from the Dharma which is in accord with Reality does not separate himself from the holy Path. One who does not separate himself from the holy Path does not separate himself from birth, old age, sickness, and death, from care and grief, agony and woe. I declare that that man is released from a multitude of woes." When the Buddha had preached this sermon, the *bhikṣus*, hearing what the Buddha preached, with joy carried it out respectfully.

### 47.33 (p. 179 f.), *Viraddhasuttaṃ*[10]

By whomsoever, O mendicant monks, the Four Stations of Mindfulness have been missed, by them has been missed the noble path to the proper annihilation of woe. By whomsoever, O mendicant monks, the Four Stations of Mindfulness have been gained, by them has been gained the noble path to the proper annihilation of woe. Which four? Here, O mendicant monks, the mendicant monk courses in the body observant of the body, ascetically disciplined, fully conscious and mindful, putting off envy and ill disposition toward the world; and so for sensations and thought. He courses in the dharmas observant of the dharmas, ascetically disciplined, fully conscious and mindful, putting off envy and ill disposition toward the world. By whomsoever, O mendicant monks, the Four Stations of Mindfulness have been missed, by them has been missed the noble path to the proper annihilation of woe. By whomsoever, O mendicant monks, the Four Stations of Mindfulness have been gained, by them has been gained the noble path to the proper annihilation of woe.

**24.609 (2.171AB), Entry 5**

Thus have I heard. Once the Buddha was dwelling in Śrāvasti land, among the Jeta trees, in the park of the Benefactor of the Lonely. At that time the World-Honored One declared to the *bhikṣus*: "I will now tell of the origin of the Four Stations of Mindfulness and of the submersion of the Four Stations of Mindfulness. Listen with discernment and think well thereon! What is meant by 'the origin of the Four Stations of Mindfulness' and 'the submersion of the Four Stations of Mindfulness'? When food collects, the body aggregates. When food is annihilated, then the body disappears. If in this way one dwells in observation in keeping with the origination of the body, dwells in observation in keeping with the annihilation of the body, and dwells in observation in keeping with the origination and annihilation of the body, then one dwells with no point of reliance and never takes anything from the various worlds. In this way, when contact originates, then sensation aggregates; when contact is annihilated, then sensation disappears. If in this way one dwells in the observation of sensation in keeping with the dharma of origination, dwells in the observation of sensation in keeping with the dharma of submersion, and dwells in the observation of sensation in keeping with the dharmas of origination and submersion, the one dwells with no point of reliance and never takes anything from the various worlds. When name-and-form is annihilated, then thought disappears. If one dwells in the observation of thought in keeping with the dharma of origination, dwells in the observation of thought in keeping with the dharma of submersion, and dwells in the observation of thought in keeping with the dharmas of origination and submersion, then one dwells with no point of reliance and never takes anything from the various worlds. When attention originates, then dharmas collect; when attention is annihilated, then dharmas disappear. If one dwells in the observation of dharmas in keeping with the dharmas of origination and submersion, then one dwells with no point of reliance and never takes anything from the various worlds. This is called 'the origination of the Four Stations of Mindfulness' and 'the submersion of the Four Stations of Mindfulness.' "

When the Buddha had preached this sermon, the *bhikṣus*, having heard what the Buddha preached, with joy carried it out respectfully.

**47.42 (p. 184)**, *Samudayasuttaṃ*

45. *catunnaṃ bhikkhave satipaṭṭhānānaṃ samudayaṃ ca atthaṅgamaṃ ca desessāmi / taṃ suṇātha / ko ca bhikkhave kāyassa samudayo āhārasamudayā kāyassa samudayo āhāranirodhā kāyassa atthaṅgamo / phassasamudayā vedanānaṃ samudayo phassanirodhā vedanānaṃ atthaṅgamo / nāmarūpasamudayā cittassa samudayo nāmarūpanirodhā cittassa atthaṅgamo / manasikārasamudayā dhammānaṃ samudayo manasikāranirodhā dhammānaṃ atthaṅgamo ti /*

Of the Four Stations of Mindfulness, O mendicant monks, will I now tell you the origin and the disappearance. Listen thereto! What now, O mendicant monks, is the origin of the body? With the origin of food originates the body, and with the destruction of food is the disappearance of the body. With the origin of contact originate the sensations, and with the destruction of contact is the disappearance of sensations. With the origin of name-and-form originates thought, and with the destruction of name-and-form is the disappearance of thought. With the origin of attention originate the dharmas, and with the destruction of attention is the disappearance of the dharmas.

**24.610 (2.171B), Entry 6**

Thus have I heard. Once the Buddha was dwelling in Śrāvasti land, among the Jeta trees, in the park of the Benefactor of the Lonely. At that time the World-Honored One declared to the *bhikṣus*: "I will tell of the cultivation of the Four Stations of Mindfulness. Listen with discernment and think on it well! How does one cultivate the Four Stations of Mindfulness? As follows: With respect to the inner body, one dwells in observation and mindfulness of the body, with refined striving and by resort to devices, with right knowledge and in right mindfulness, taming the cares and woes of the world. So it is with sensations, thought, and dharmas. With respect to internal dharmas, to external dharmas, to dharmas both internal and external, one dwells in observation and mindfulness, with refined striving and by resort to devices, in right mindfulness and right knowledge, taming the cares and woes of the world. This is called the cultivation by a *bhikṣu* of the Four Stations of Mindfulness." When the Buddha had preached this sermon, the *bhikṣus*, hearing what the Buddha preached, with joy carried it out respectfully.

The cultivation of the Four Stations of Mindfulness in past and future He also preached in this way.

**47.2 (p. 142),** ***Satisuttaṃ***

One time the Blessed One was disporting Himself at Vesālī [Vaiśālī], in the forest of the rows of mango trees. There indeed the Blessed One addressed the mendicant monks: "O mendicant monks!" "Lord!" the mendicant monks responded to the Blessed One. The Blessed One said this: "Mindful, O mendicant monks, let the mendicant monk behave himself, mindful and fully conscious. This, look you, is our teaching. How then, O mendicant monks, is the mendicant monk to be mindful? Here, O mendicant monks, a mendicant monk courses in the body observant of the body, ascetically disciplined, conscious and fully mindful, putting off envy and ill disposition toward the world. It is in this way, O mendicant monks, that the mendicant monk is mindful. How then, O mendicant monks, is the mendicant monk to be fully conscious? Here, O mendicant monks, the mendicant monk acts with full attention to his comings and goings; with full attention to his forward looks and his backward looks; with full attention to his bends and stretches; with full attention to the way in which he carries his inner robe, his alms-bowl, and his outer robe; with full attention to eating, drinking, chewing, and tasting; with full attention to his defecation and urination; with full attention to his going, standing, sitting, sleeping, waking, talking, and keeping silent. It is thus indeed, O mendicant monks, that a mendicant monk is fully attentive. Mindful, O mendicant monks, let the mendicant monk behave himself, mindful and fully conscious. This, look you, is our teaching."

**24.611 (2.171BC), Entry 7**

Thus have I heard. Once the Buddha was dwelling in Śrāvasti land, in the midst of the Jeta trees, in the park of the Benefactor of the Lonely. At that time the World-Honored One declared to the *bhikṣus*: "There is a collection of wholesome dharmas and a collection of unwholesome dharmas. What is meant by 'collection of wholesome dharmas'? By that are meant the Four Stations of Mindfulness. This is rightly said. What is the reason? By the 'unique, homogeneous, full, and pure collection' is meant the Four Stations of Mindfulness. Which four? By that is meant the state of mindfulness that observes the body in the body, so for sensations and thought, and the state of mindfulness that observes dharma in dharma. What is meant by 'collection of unwholesome dharmas'? By 'collection of unwholesome dharmas' is meant the Five Obstacles. This is rightly said. What is the reason? By the 'unique, homogeneous, indifferent and full[?] collection of the unwholesome' is meant the Five Obstacles. Which five? By this is meant the obstacle of greed, the obstacle of anger, the obstacle of torpor, the obstacle of indifference and regret[?], and the obstacle of doubt." When the Buddha had preached this sermon, the *bhikṣus*, hearing what the Buddha preached, with joy carried it out respectfully.

### 47.5 (p. 145 f.), *Akusalarasisuttaṃ*

The scene was Sāvatthi [Śrāvasti]. There indeed the Blessed One said this: "When I speak, O mendicant monks, of the 'accumulation of the unwholesome,' I wish to be understood as referring precisely to the Five Obstacles. This, O mendicant monks, is nothing but an accumulation of unwholesomeness, to wit, the Five Obstacles. Which five? The obstacle of lust, the obstacle of malice, the obstacle of sloth and torpor, the obstacle of pride and indifference, and the obstacle of doubt. When I speak, O mendicant monks, of the 'accumulation of the unwholesome,' I wish to be understood as referring precisely to these Five Obstacles. This, O mendicant monks, is nothing but an accumulation of unwholesomeness, to wit, these Five Obstacles. When I speak, O mendicant monks, of the 'accumulation of the wholesome,' I wish to be understood as referring precisely to the Four Stations of Mindfulness. This, O mendicant monks, is nothing but an accumulation of wholesomeness, to wit, the Four Stations of Mindfulness. Which four? Here, O mendicant monks, a mendicant monk courses in the body observant of the body, ascetically disciplined, fully conscious and mindful, putting off envy and ill disposition toward the world. He does the same for sensations, thought, and dharmas, coursing in the dharmas observant of the dharmas, ascetically disciplined, conscious and fully mindful, putting off envy and ill disposition toward the world. When I speak, O mendicant monks, of the 'accumulation of the wholesome,' I wish to be understood as referring precisely to these Four Stations of Mindfulness.

This, O mendicant monks, is nothing but an accumulation of wholesomeness, to wit, these Four Stations of Mindfulness."

**24.612 (2.171C), Entry 8**

Thus have I heard. Once the Buddha was dwelling in Śrāvasti land, among the Jeta trees, in the park of the Benefactor of the Lonely. At that time the World-Honored One declared to the *bhikṣus*: "As a man might take in hand four kinds of strong bow and, by means of his great strength, shoot at the shade of many *tāla* trees, [his arrow] swiftly passing through unobstructed, in that way the voice-hearers of the Thus Come One in their four varieties, by resort to their superior devices, their sharp faculties, and their wisdom, fulfill a hundred years in the presence of the Thus Come One, preaching Dharma and dispensing instruction for a hundred years. Except when eating, resting, defecating, urinating,[11] and sleeping, they are ever preaching and ever listening, their wisdom being bright and sharp, scouring the bottom of what the Thus Come One preaches, receiving and keeping it without hindrance or obstacle, never asking the same question twice in the presence of the Thus Come One. The preaching of Dharma by the Thus Come One has neither end nor limit. If one should listen to Dharma for fully a hundred years, then come to the end of one's life, the preaching of Dharma by the Thus Come One could still not be exhausted. Be it known that what the Thus Come One preaches is incalculable and endless, the meaning and substance of the words and phrases [? *ming chü wei shen*] being also incalculable, having neither end nor limit, by which are meant the Four Stations of Mindfulness. Which four? By this is meant the station of mindfulness of the body, so for sensations and thought, and the station of mindfulness of the dharmas." When the Buddha had preached this sermon, the *bhikṣus*, hearing what the Buddha preached, with joy carried it out respectfully.

All Scriptures concerning the Four Stations of Mindfulness are to end with the following phrase, to wit, "For this reason a *bhikṣu*, cultivating himself in the Four Stations of Mindfulness and giving rise to superior desires, is to learn with subtle striving and by resort to expedient devices, with right mindfulness and right knowledge.

**24.613 (2.171C–172A), Entry 9**

Thus have I heard. Once the Buddha was dwelling in Śrāvasti land, in the midst of the Jeta trees, in the park of the Benefactor of the Lonely. At that time the World-Honored One declared to the *bhikṣus*: "There is an accumulation of the unwholesome and an accumulation of the wholesome. What is the accumulation of the unwholesome? By that are meant the three unwholesome faculties *[ken*, lit. "roots," but clearly representing *indriyāṇi]*. This may be called a right statement. What is the reason? By 'accumulation of the purely unwholesome' are meant the three unwholesome faculties. Which three? By this are meant the unwholesome faculty of lust, the unwholesome faculty of anger [*yi*, but representing *dveṣa*, 'hatred'], and the unwholesome faculty of delusion. What is the accumulation of the wholesome? By this are meant the Four Stations of Mindfulness. What is the reason? That wherein the purely good is full and perfect is called the Four Stations of Mindfulness. This may be called a right statement. Which four are meant? By this are meant the station of mindfulness of the body and the stations of mindfulness of sensations, thought and dharmas." When the Buddha had preached this sermon, the *bhikṣus*, having heard what the Buddha preached, with joy carried it out respectfully.[12]

"As with the three unwholesome faculties,

"So with the three kinds of evil deeds, to wit, evil deeds of body, evil deeds of mouth, and evil deeds of mind;

"So with the three notions, to wit, notions of desire, notions of anger, and notions of harm;

"So with the three spheres, to wit, the sphere of desire, the sphere of anger, and the sphere of harm." When the Buddha had preached this sermon, the *bhikṣus*, having heard what the Buddha preached, with joy carried it out respectfully.

### 47.47 (p. 188), *Duccaritasuttaṃ*

Then indeed yet another mendicant monk approached to where the Blessed One was, etc.: "Very well, Lord! Let the Blessed One teach me the Dharma in digested form, by the hearing of which Dharma I, alone and secluded, undisturbed and ascetically disciplined, may course with resolute will." "In that case, O mendicant monk, purify the very beginning in wholesome dharmas. What, now, is the beginning of wholesome dharmas? Here, O mendicant monk, you shall abandon evil deeds of body and realize good deeds of body. You shall abandon evil deeds of speech and realize good deeds of speech. You shall abandon evil deeds of mind and realize good deeds of mind. For as you, O mendicant monk, shall abandon evil deeds of body and realize good deeds of body, as you shall abandon evil deeds of mind and realize good deeds of mind, so, O mendicant monk, shall you, leaning upon moral conduct and taking a firm stand in moral conduct, realize the Four Stations of Mindfulness. Which four? Do you here, O mendicant monk, course in the body observant of the body, ascetically disciplined, fully conscious and mindful, putting off envy and ill disposition toward the world; and so for sensations and thought. For as you, O mendicant monk, shall in this way, leaning on moral conduct and taking a firm stand in moral conduct, realize the Four Stations of Mindfulness, so, O mendicant monk, whatever shall befall you, whether by night or by day, only growth in the wholesome dharmas is to be expected therefrom, not decline, etc., etc." And that other mendicant was one of the worthies. [?]

### 24.614 (2.172A), Entry 10

Thus have I heard. Once the Buddha was dwelling in Śrāvasti land, amid the Jeta trees, in the park of the Benefactor of the Lonely. At the time there was an alien *bhikṣu* who had come into the Buddha's presence, where, bowing his head to the Buddha's feet and withdrawing and sitting to one side, he humbly addressed the Buddha, saying, "O World-Honored

One! When You speak of 'a man of great stature,' to whom are you referring, saying, 'He is a man of great stature,' or 'He is not a man of great stature'?" The Buddha declared to the *bhikṣu:* "Good, good! O *bhikṣu*, you are an able questioner! What the Thus Come One means by 'man of great stature' now hear with discernment and think on it well, for I will now tell it to you. If a *bhikṣu* dwells in mindfulness of the body, observing the body, and if, after he has dwelt in mindfulness of the body, observing the body, his thought does not take leave of desire, if it neither gains release nor puts an end to the outflows of existence, I say that he is no man of great stature. What is the reason? That his thought is not liberated. If a *bhikṣu* dwells in mindfulness, observing sensations, thought, and dharmas, and if this thought does not take leave of desire, if it neither gains release nor puts an end to the outflows of existence, then I do not call him a man of great stature. What is the reason? That his thought is not liberated. If a *bhikṣu* dwells in mindfulness of the body., and if his thought does contrive to take leave of desire, if his thought does gain release and puts an end to the outflows of existence, then I say that he is a man of great stature. What is the reason? That his thought is liberated. If a *bhikṣu* dwells in mindfulness, observing sensations, thought, and dharmas, and if, after he has dwelt in mindfulness, observing sensations, thought, and dharmas, his thought takes leave of lust, if his thought gains release and puts an end to the outflows of existence, then I say that he is a man of great stature. What is the reason? That his thought is liberated. These are called, respectively, 'the man of great stature' and 'he who is not a man of great stature' among the *bhikṣus*." When the Buddha had preached this sermon, the *bhikṣu*, having heard what the Buddha preached, with joy carried it out respectfully, then, bowing to His feet, departed.

### **47.11 (p. 158),** *Mahāpurisasuttaṃ*

The scene was Sāvatthi. Then indeed long-lived Sāriputta [Śāriputra] approached to where the Blessed One was and, having approached and greeted the Blessed One, sat to one side. Having sat to one side, the long-lived Sāriputta then said this to the Blessed One: " 'Great man, great man,' says the Lord. In what sense, Lord, is he a great man?" "It is by virtue of the liberation of his thought, Sāriputta, that I call him a 'great man.' Or it is by virtue of the unliberated state of his thought that I say that he is 'not a great man.' How then, Sāriputta, does he become liberated in thought? Here, Sāriputta, the mendicant monk courses in the body observant of the body, ascetically disciplined, fully conscious and mindful, putting off envy and ill disposition toward the world. As he courses in the body, observant of the body, his thought becomes disenchanted with, liberated from, the outflows by not clinging to them. So for sensations and thought. He courses in the dharmas observant of the dharmas, ascetically disciplined, fully conscious and mindful, putting off envy and ill disposition toward the world. As he courses in the dharmas, observant of the dharmas, his thought becomes disenchanted with, liberated from, the outflows by not clinging to them. It is in this way, Sāriputta, that he becomes liberated in thought. It is by virtue of the liberation of his thought, Sāriputta, that I call him a 'great man.' Or it is by virtue of the unliberated state of his thought that I say that he is 'not a great man.' "

**24.615 (2.172AB), Entry 11**

Thus have I heard. Once the Buddha was dwelling in Śrāvasti land, amid the Jeta trees, in the park of the Benefactor of the Lonely. At that time the venerable Ānanda, wearing his robes and carrying his *pātra*, entered Śrāvasti city, begging for food. On the way he thought, "Just now I have been to a *bhikṣuṇī*-convent." As soon as he had arrived at the nunnery, the *bhikṣuṇīs*, seeing the venerable Ānanda coming from afar, speedily prepared a seat for him and begged him to take it. At the time the *bhikṣuṇīs*, bowing down to the feet of the venerable Ānanda, withdrawing and sitting to one side, humbly addressed the venerable Ānanda, "We *bhikṣuṇīs* cultivate the Four Stations of Mindfulness, dwelling with thought bound. Of ourselves we know the prior and the posterior, the superior and the inferior." The venerable Ānanda declared to the *bhikṣuṇīs*: "Good, good! Sisters, one should learn in the manner in which you have spoken. For anyone who in cultivating the Four Stations of Mindfulness has the skill to dwell with thought bound should be able in this way to know the prior and the posterior, the superior and the inferior." At that time the venerable Ānanda for the *bhikṣuṇīs'* sakes preached various dharmas. When he had preached various dharmas, he rose from his seat and left. At the time the venerable Ānanda begged for his food in Śrāvasti city. He then returned to his quarters and, when he had taken up his robe and *pātra* and washed his feet, he went into the presence of the Thus Come One, where he bowed his head to the Buddha's feet, then, withdrawing and sitting to one side, reported in detail what the *bhikṣuṇīs* had said to him. The Buddha declared to Ānanda: "Good, good! It is in this way that one must learn the Four Stations of Mindfulness, dwelling with thought bound. For, when one does so, one knows the prior and the posterior, the superior and the inferior. What is the reason? When one seeks thought outside, then one is compelled to look for thought, and thought distracted is never liberated. Know all this as it really is! If the *bhikṣu*, with respect to the body, dwells in mindfulness observant of the body, and if, when with respect to the body, he has dwelt in mindfulness observant of the body, his body becomes addicted to sleep and his mind-dharma becomes lazy, then that *bhikṣu* is to give rise to pure faith and take hold of pure marks. For, once he has given rise to thought of pure faith and paid close attention to pure marks, his thought shall then be delighted. When it has been delighted, he shall give rise to joy. Once his thought has rejoiced, then his body shall be at rest. Once his body is at rest, then he shall experience bodily pleasure. Once he has experienced bodily pleasure, then his thought shall be collected. He whose thought is collected is a disciple of the Saints. He is to study in this way: 'With respect to this doctrine, I will collect my externally disturbed thought and cause it to rest, giving rise to notions neither of perception nor of observation.' Having neither perception nor observation, he dwells in the pleasant station of having cast off mindfulness [?]. Once having taken this pleasant stand, he knows things as they really are. The mindfulness of sensation, of thought, and of the dharmas is also like this." When the Buddha had spoken this sermon, the venerable Ānanda, hearing what the Buddha said, with joy carried it out respectfully.

**47.10 (pp. 154–158),** ***Bhikkhunupassayasuttaṃ***

Then indeed the long-lived Ānanda, dressing himself in the forenoon and taking his alms-bowl and his robe, approached to where there was a certain abode of mendicant nuns; having approached, he sat on a seat designated for him. Then indeed right many mendicant nuns approached to where the long-lived Ānanda was; having approached, and having greeted the long-lived Ānanda, they sat to one side. Having sat to one side, the mendicant nuns then said this to the long-lived Ānanda: "Here, my lord Ānanda, right many mendicant nuns, coursing in the Four Stations of Mindfulness with thought well established, are aware of the excellent gradual distinction. [?]"

"Just so, my ladies! Just so, my ladies! For whosoever it be, my ladies, whether mendicant monk or mendicant nun, who courses in the Four Stations of Mindfulness with thought well established, has this to expect, to wit, that he or she shall be aware of the excellent gradual distinction. [?]" Then indeed the long-lived Ānanda, having taught, endowed, sharpened, and delighted them with talk of Dharma, rose from his seat and went off.

Then indeed the long-lived Ānanda approached to where the Blessed One was; having approached, and having greeted the Blessed One, he sat to one side. Having sat to one side, the long-lived Ānanda said this to the Blessed One: "Now I, Lord, dressing myself in the forenoon, and taking my alms-bowl and my robe, approached to where there was a certain abode of mendicant nuns; having approached, I sat on a seat designated for me. Then indeed, Lord, right many mendicant nuns approached to where I was; having approached, and having greeted me, they sat to one side. Having sat to one side, Lord, the mendicant nuns then said this to me: 'Here, my lord Ānanda, right many mendicant nuns, coursing in the Four Stations of Mindfulness with thought well established, are aware of the excellent gradual distinction. [?]' Having been thus addressed, Lord, I said this to the mendicant nuns: 'Just so, my ladies! Just so, my ladies! For whosoever it be, my ladies, whether mendicant monk or mendicant nun, who courses in the Four Stations of Mindfulness with thought well established, has this to expect, to wit, that he or she shall be aware of the excellent gradual distinction. [?]' "

"Just so, Ānanda! Just so, Ānanda! For whosoever it be, Ānanda, whether mendicant monk or mendicant nun, who courses in the Four Stations of Mindfulness with thought well established, has this to expect, to wit, that he or she shall be aware of the excellent gradual distinction. [?] Which four? Here, Ānanda, the mendicant monk courses in the body, observant of the body, ascetically disciplined, fully conscious and mindful, putting off envy and ill disposition toward the world. For him, coursing in the body observant of the body, there arises the body as an object, a burning fever in the body, or sluggishness of thought, or his thought is distracted outward. That mendicant monk, Ānanda, is to apply his thought to any symbolic object that inspires confidence. For one who applies his thought to any symbolic object that inspires confidence, delight is born. For one delighted, joy is born. For one in a joyful state of mind, the body becomes allayed. One whose body is allayed experiences happiness. For a happy person, thought becomes concentrated. He reflects thus: 'For what purpose I concentrated my thought, that purpose has been achieved by me. Now, then, I withdraw!' Not only does he withdraw; he also neither thinks nor deliberates. 'I am without thought or deliberation, inwardly and happily mindful.' Such is the object of his intuition. Yet again, Ānanda, the mendicant monk courses in the sensation, or in thought, or in the dharmas observant of the dharmas, ascetically disciplined, fully conscious and mindful, putting off envy and ill disposition toward the world. For him, coursing in the dharmas, observant of the dharmas, there arise the dharmas as an object, a burning fever in the body, or sluggishness of thought, or his thought is distracted outward. That mendicant monk, Ānanda, is to apply his thought to any symbolic object that inspires confidence. For one who applies his thought to any symbolic object that inspires confidence, delight is born. For one delighted, joy is born. For one in a joyful state of mind, the body becomes allayed. One whose body is allayed experiences happiness. For a happy person, thought becomes concentrated. He reflects thus: 'For what purpose I concentrated my thought, that purpose has been achieved by me. Now, then, I withdraw!' Not only does he withdraw; he also neither thinks nor deliberates. 'I am without thought or deliberation, inwardly and happily mindful.' Such is the object of his intuition. Such indeed, Ānanda, is realization through application.

"How, then, Ānanda, is realization through nonapplication? Not applying his thought outward, Ānanda, the mendicant monk has this intuition: 'Unapplied outward is my thought.' Then he has this intuition: 'Both fore and aft it is unconcentrated, liberated, unapplied.' Then he has this intuition: 'I am coursing in the body observant of the body, ascetically disciplined, fully conscious and happily mindful.' Not applying his thought outward, Ānanda, he has this intuition: 'Unapplied outward is my thought.' Then he has this intuition: 'Both fore and aft it is unconcentrated, liberated, unapplied.' Then he has this intuition: 'I am coursing in sensations observant of sensations, ascetically disciplined, fully conscious and happily mindful.' Not applying his thought outward, Ānanda, he has this intuition: 'Unapplied outward is my thought.' Then he has this intuition: 'Both fore and aft it is unconcentrated, liberated, unapplied.' Then he has this intuition: 'I am coursing in thought observant of thought, ascetically disciplined, fully conscious and happily mindful.' Not applying his thought outward, Ānanda, he has this intuition: 'Both fore and aft it is unconcentrated, liberated, unapplied.' Then he has this intuition: 'I am coursing in the dharmas observant of the dharmas, ascetically disciplined, fully conscious and happily mindful.' Such indeed, Ānanda, is realization through nonapplication. It is in this way, Ānanda, that I have taught realization through application and realization through nonapplication. What is to be done by a teacher who seeks the welfare of his listeners and who is compassionate, that have I done for you, acting out of compassion. These, Ānanda, are the foot of trees, these the solitary spots. Meditate, Ānanda, be not negligent, nor later remorseful. This, look you, is our teaching!"

Thus spoke the Blessed One. Pleased at heart, the long-lived Ānanda rejoiced at what the Blessed One had said.

---

In the versions translated by Saṃghadeva and Narendrayaśas, the chapter begins at this point. After an introductory remark, stating that, the exposition of the *kleśas* having been given, that of the *āryas* is now to begin, there is an opening verse. In Saṃghadeva's version, it reads as follows:

> In this way the Sage severs His labors
> And his multitudinous fears. The basis [of the severance]
> And the like, the right knowledge *[cheng chih,* representing *samyagjñāna?]*
> [which is] the expedient means [thereto],
> I will now tell. Listen well!

(Certain syntactic liberties had to be taken in order to preserve the order the verses.) By deducing the overall meaning from the two versions just mentioned and that of Saṃghavarman, one concludes the meaning to be as follows: The means *[upāya]* on the exercise *[yoga]* whereby the *ārya* puts an end to both defilement *[kleśa]* and fear *[bhaya]* is the acquisition of right knowledge [presumably *samyagjñāna*], which I will now describe.

Since there is no commentary to this particular śloka in Saṃghadeva's version, one cannot be certain how Tao-an may have understood it. Since it is not unlikely that he discussed these matters with his missionary-translators, we shall now give some description of their doctrinal implications. There is commentary on this śloka in the versions of both Saṃghavarman and Narendrayaśas. While the two are far from identical, there is still enough overlap to derive a certain common meaning. One might phrase that in the following terms:

> To review the question of the *kleśas*, the word *fan nao* is used because the *kleśas* continually belabor (*hsiang hsü fan lao* in Narendrayaśas's [N] version, coinciding with Samghadeva's *lao*, while Saṃghavarman [S] has *je nao*, 'afflicts,' thus coming closer to the meaning of the original) the beings. By 'fears' is meant the basis of all afflictions (N), the source of all *karman* and rebirth (S). The 'right knowledge' mentioned in the verse is the gnosis produced by *śamatha* (a word given by N in transcription). The approach thereto consists of a series of acts, notably a morally disciplined way of life (N; *chieh*, representing *śīla*, while S singles out *shih*, i.e., *dāna* or, possibly, *tyāga*?), conducing to deliverance.

It is not irrelevant to mention that, according to the *Kośa*, eradication of fear is tantamount to the attainment of Buddhahood, since it is the Buddha, and He alone, who is free of fear. Kārikā iv.58 (cf. Gokhale, p. 87) reads as follows:

> *cittakṣepo manaścitte sa ca karmavipākajaḥ /*
> *bhayopagatavaiṣamyaśokaiś cākurukāminām //58//*

This is rendered as follows in Vallee-Poussin iv.125 f.:

> . . . 58a. Le trouble-mental se produit dans la connaissance-mentale . . . 58b. Il naît de la rétribution de l'acte . . . [126]

> 58c–d. Par la frayeur, l'attaque des démons, l'irritation des éléments, le chagrin.

As much of the *bhāṣya* as bears on this he renders as follows in iv.127 f.:

> A l'exception du Bouddha (20b), les Āryas ne sont pas exempts du trouble de la pensée: leur pensée peut être troublée à la suite du déséquilibre *(vaiṣamya)* des éléments. Mais le déséquilibre des éléments n'est jamais, dans leur cas, rétribution: . . . (128) Ni la frayeur, ni l'attaque des êtres démoniaques, ni le chagrin ne peuvent troubler la pensée des Āryas, car ils sont au dessus des cinq craintes, ils n'accomplissent aucun acte désobligeant *(aprasādika)* qui excite la fureur des êtres démoniaques, ils connaissent à fond la nature des choses.

The *Vyākhyā* reads as follows:[13]

> By "elsewhere than in a Buddha" is meant that this does not apply to a Buddha by reason of His great accumulation of merit. That is to say that thought may also be distracted by the disequilibrium of the elements, not [merely] by one's deeds. How? "The thought of the Exalted Ones is [not] distracted" otherwise "than by the disequilibrium of the elements." Why? —one might ask. "Because of the retribution previously," in the status of an ordinary person, "of determined acts and of the nonretribution of undetermined ones" in the status of an Exalted One. ["Ni la frayeur, ni l'attaque des êtres démoniaques, ni le chagrin ne peuvent troubler la pensée des Āryas,] because They have transcended the five fears." The five fears are fear for one's livelihood, *aślokabhaya*, *pariṣacchāradya-bhaya*, the fear of death, and the fear of an evil destiny. Now *aślokabhaya* is fear of ill-repute. *Par[i]ṣacchāradyabhaya* is embarrassment in an assembly. The phrase "of unobliging deeds" refers to deeds in which no pleasure is to be taken. "Because of Their intuitive knowledge of dharmahood" means by virtue of Their intuitive understanding that everything having outflows is woeful, that all constituents are impermanent, that all dharmas are without a self.

Saṃghadeva goes on to say that one who does not arrest

his thought cannot launch right views.[14] The statement is followed by a pair of ślokas:

> First, to one's own body *[svakāye? svakāyasthāne?]*
> One attaches one's thought, thus causing it to be firm.
> One wishes also to bind the sense-feet
> And to put an end to the *kleśa*-enemies.
>
> These devices, with respect to the body,
> Are firmly fixed as a matter of reality.
> The sensations and this thought
> And the dharmas are also to be viewed like this.

Again we are dealing with the Four Stations of Mindfulness, which have been treated just above. The "sense-feet" renders *shih tsu*, which is common to all three versions. It presumably renders an original *vijñānapādān*. Neither the *Kośa* nor the *Visuddhimagga* has this term, but they do have *viññāṇa-kāya/vijñānakāya*, which presumably stands for the same thing, viz., the six senses. The fifth and sixth verses of this translation, ignoring prosodic considerations entirely, probably represent something like *imāv upāyau kāye tattvato niyatau.* "This thought" (tz'u hsin) is represented in the other two versions by "one's own thought" *(tzu hsin*, i.e., *svacittam).* The commentary in Saṃghadeva's version is brief enough to give in full:

> This body has the mark of uncleanness *[aśuci]*, the mark of impermanence *[anitya]*, the mark of woe *[duḥkha]*, and the mark of selflessness *[anātmaka]*. These marks being a fixed reality, to that body of one's own as the single object one fixes one's thought, separating oneself from distraction of thought. First, from the point of view of reality *[tattvataḥ?]*, one views the marks of the body. Next one views sensations, then finally one views thought. With them as companions, with them as a base, one extends the view to that of the dharmas to be numbered with thought and corresponding to it. Also, the constituents not corresponding to thought, in keeping with their natures *[bhāvataḥ?]* and their marks *[lakṣaṇa-taḥ?]*, are to be treated thus. The meanings of the said body, sensations, thought, and dharma shall now be brought forth in due order.

In other words, the Four Stations of Mindfulness consist of applying to each of four objects, viz., body, sensations, thought, and dharmas, the views that they are unclean, impermanent, woeful, and devoid of a self. This is in perfect accord with the tradition of the *Kośa*, where we read (LVP vi.162): "Les *smṛtyupasthānas* sont enseignés dans l'ordre comme contrecarrants de la quadruple méprise *[viparyāsa]*, croire à la pureté, au bonheur, à la permanence, au soi. . . . Ils sont donc quartre, ni plus ni moins."[15] The *Vyākhyā* comments:

śuci*viparyāsasya* pratipakṣeṇa *kāyasmṛtyupasthānaṃ* / sukha*viparyāsasya* pratipakṣeṇa *vedanāsmṛtyupasthānaṃ* / *yat kiṃ cid veditam idam atra duḥkhasyeti* / nitya*viparyāsasya* pratipakṣeṇa *cittasmṛtyupasthānaṃ* / *cittasya laghuparivartitvāt* / ātma*viparyāsasya* pratipakṣeṇa *dharmasmṛtyupasthānaṃ* / *piṇḍavibhāgato dharmāṇām anātmakāritvād dharmamātraṃ rahitam ātmaneti* [532] *dharmanirvacanataḥ* / *dharmā ime pṛthakpṛthag avasthitāḥ* / *na ca kaś cit svataṃtra ātmeti* /

As a counteragent to the false contruction of purity there is the station of mindfulness of the body. As a counteragent to the false construction of joy there is the station of mindfulness of sensation. Whatever sensation is experienced is one of woe. As a counteragent to the false construction of permanence there is the station of mindfulness of thought, because of the ease with which thought moves about. As a counteragent to the false construction of the self there is the station of mindfulness of the dharmas. For the enunciated doctrine of the dharmas says that there are only dharmas, devoid of self, since there is no ātman to fashion them, and this because of their respective independence as separate pieces. There is no self whatever that is its own master.[16]

The versions of Narendrayaśas and Saṃghavarman both divide the verse passage into two ślokas, each followed by a prose commentary. The content of the commentary will now be summarized:

## NARENDRAYAŚAS ON THE FIRST ŚLOKA.

One may concentrate one's thought on any single point, such as the tip of the nose, or the space between the brows, thinking of the impurity of the body *(pu ching, aśubhā)*, of inhalation and exhalation *(ānāpāna)*, or of the elements *(dhātu)*. One concentrates one's thought on something within one's own body, not outside of it. One attaches one's thought to it because thought, as exemplified in the *kleśas*, can no more stay still than can a frightened monkey. One rivets one's attention to the *kleśas* because it is only in that way that one can sever them.

## SAṂGHAVARMAN ON THE FIRST ŚLOKA.

*To the foregoing he adds the following:*

One may, for example, fix one's attention on a toe. One must concentrate on one's own body because looking at any other body is like looking at a corpse. The threefold contemplation (of *aśubhā*, *ānāpāna*, and *dhātu*), furthermore, is possible only when one considers one's own body, no more than the first being possible in the case of any other. Lust *(t'an yu, rāga)* is counteracted by the view of uncleanness, discursive reasoning[17] by breath control, while he who is driven about by (false) views is saved by means of contemplation of the elements.[18] Each takes pleasure in doing what the Master has taught. The first two being explained elsewhere, the view of the elements shall be explained here and now.

The stupid fellow takes a wrong view of things. In his inability to understand *pratītya-samutpāda*, he accumulates bad karman, which in turn accumulates *kleśas*. In what is in fact the workings of *pratītya-samutpāda* he fancies a self to be at work, then becomes the prisoner of this view and others like it. On the other hand, he may do good deeds, as a reward for which he will get a good friend *(shan chih shih, kalyāṇamitra)*, through whose good offices, in turn, he will see things for what they are: He will understand the true nature of the body, the role of karman, and the marks of the body, i.e., the six elements of which the body is made up. He will understand, for instance, that the earth element does not crumble when moistened by the water element; that the water element cannot flow when restrained by the earth element; that the body does not rot when kept ripe by the fire element; that it can grow when kept in motion by the wind element; that food can enter and leave the body by passing through the element of empty space; that the body can do things when united with the element of consciousness.[19]

Further, he sees the body to be a collection of filth, subject to change as easily as a heap of sand can be blown about by a wind. This leads him to the gateway of deliverance called the Empty *(k'ung, śūnya)*. He takes no pleasure in the round of births and deaths, which leads him to the gateway of deliverance called the Wishless *(wu yüan, apraṇihita)*. Taking no pleasure in saṃsāra, he faces toward nirvāṇa, which leads him to the gateway of deliverance called the Signless *(wu hsiang, animitta)*. If he can free himself of notions *(hsiang, saṃjñā)*, seeing that everything constituted is doomed to destruction, then for him the elements have served their purpose.

## NARENDRAYAŚAS ON THE SECOND ŚLOKA.

With thought fixed to one object, one may observe the real marks of the body, that is, an unperverted understanding of those marks in keeping with their real meaning *(shen shih hsiang che wei pu tien tao hsiang ju yi yeh, kāyasya bhūtalakṣaṇānīty anena yathārthāviparītalakṣaṇānīty ucyate?)*. By "real marks" are meant two things, viz., peculiar marks *(tzu hsiang, svalakṣaṇāni)* and common marks *(kung hsiang, sāmānyalakṣaṇāni)*. By the former are meant part of the ten *rūpāyatanas* (i.e., the five material sense organs and their respective objects of cognition) and the *dharmāyatana*. By the latter are meant the four characteristics of impermanence *(wu ch'ang, anitya)*, woe *(k'u duḥkha)*, emptiness *(k'ung, śūnya)*, and selflessness *(wu wo, anātmaka)*.

The order of sequence of this observation is as follows: Once the practitioner sees that bodily matter, consisting as it does of atoms, is subject to disintegration every moment, his sojourn at the station of mindfulness of the body is complete. From then, he proceeds to that of sensation as easily as water flows through a track between two cultivated fields. Sensation follows the body since it is of all nonmaterial things the least subtle, and it too is viewed in terms of marks both peculiar and common. Since sensation depends on the mind,[20] that is the next object of mindfulness. When the mind is definitively released,[21] the sojourn at the station of mindfulness of thought is complete. Thence one proceeds to the station of mindfulness of the dharmas in order to observe all other dharmas, by which are meant the two remaining skandhas (saṃskāra and *vijñāna?*) and the *asaṃskṛta-dharmas*. These too are to be viewed in terms of peculiar marks and common ones.

## SAṂGHAVARMAN ON THE SECOND ŚLOKA

The practitioner cultivates the view of uncleanness, *ānāpānasmṛti*, and the view of the approach to the elements (?*chieh fang pien kuan*, representing a possible *dhātūpāyaparīkṣaṇā?*). After pausing on each of them, he then views body, sensations, thought, and dharmas each in terms of reality *(chen shih hsiang*, standing for *tattvalakṣaṇataḥ?)*. "Reality" refers to that which is "not upside down" *(pu tien tao, aviparyasta?)*, while "terms" *(hsiang, lakṣaṇa)* refers to the particular *(tzu hsiang, svalakṣaṇa)* and the general *(kung hsiang, sāmānyalakṣaṇa)*. The five skandhas are then matched against the Four Stations of Mindfulness as follows:

| *skandha* | *smṛtyupasthāna* |
|---|---|
| rūpa | kāya |
| vedanā | vedanā |
| vijñāna | citta |
| saṃjñā | dharma |
| saṃskāra | dharma |

An explanation of the *sāmānyalakṣaṇas* is promised for later.

There follows an objection: Surely there is nothing sacred

about the number four. Many other numbers are conceivable, for example:

1. One might subsume these under the rubric of *mahābhūmi*, in which case the number would be only one.[22]

2. A twofold distinction could be made, viz., between what has outflows *(sāsrava)* and what has not *(nirāsrava)*.

3. A threefold distinction might be made, viz., of the soft *(juan*, i.e., the dull, *mṛdu)*, the medium *(chung, madhya)*, and the superior *(shang*, i.e., the sharp, *tīkṣṇa)*.

6. These three may be further subdivided into those having outflows and those having none.

8. The Four Stations of Mindfulness, each with and without outflows, total eight.

9. The threefold distinction given in (3) may itself be further divided so that each is of three kinds, thus giving a total of nine.

12. Each station of mindfulness may be viewed internally, externally, or both, totaling twelve.

18. The nine mentioned in (9) may be distinguished as to presence or absence obsence of outflows, thus totaling eighteen.

24. Each of the Four Stations of Mindfulness may be viewed as in (12), and each of those views may, in turn, be distinguished as to presence or absence of outflows, thus totaling twenty-four.

36. The process indicated in (12) may be multiplied by three, viz., disgust *(yen li, virati?)*, lack of pleasure *(pu lo, arati)*, and examination *(kuan ch'a, vyavacāraṇa, parīkṣā, pratirūpaṇa?)*, thus totaling thirty-six.

72. The Four Stations of Mindfulness may be multiplied by the nine categories mentioned in (9), and this product, in turn, by the distinction of the presence or absence of outflows, thus totaling seventy-two.

X. If discrimination is made on the basis of individual moments *(jo nien nien fen pieh, yadi kṣaṇakṣaṇato vikalpyate?)*, the resulting categories can be infinite. Why, in the view of the above, does one limit oneself to four?[23]

The answer follows: As a matter of convenience, since errors tend to come in fours, to group their counteragents also in fours. For example, there are the four misconstructions *(ssu tao, catvāro viparyayāḥ* or *viparyāsāḥ)*, the four aliments *(ssu shih, catvāra āhārāḥ)*, the four stations of cognition *(ssu shih chu, catvāri vijñānasthānāni)*, the skandhas, and the like. In the case at issue, the station of mindfulness of the body is preached in order to counteract false notions *(tien tao, viparyaya, viparyāsa)* of purity *(śuci, śubha)* and impurity *(aśuci, aśubha)*; that of sensation in order to counteract those of pleasure *(sukha)* and pain *(duḥkha)*; that of thought in order to counteract those of permanence *(nitya)* and impermanence *(anitya)*; that of dharma in order to counteract those of self *(ātman)* and notself *(anātman)*.

Question: How are these stations of mindfulness fulfilled?

Answer: In two ways, viz., by demolishing the fields of cognition *(huai ching chieh, viṣayasaṃvartana? dhātusaṃvartana?)* and by fostering one's wholesome roots *(shan ken tseng, kuśalamūlavardhana?)*. By the former is meant analyzing matter into atoms *(chi wei, paramāṇu)* and time into moments *(kṣaṇa)*, while by the latter is meant building up one's wholesome roots from the dull through the middle to the sharp.[24] This is what is meant by "fulfilled."

Question: Why does one speak first of the station of mindfulness of the body and so on, and only then speak of the station of mindfulness of the dharmas?

Answer: This is done in order to be in keeping with the order of their origin *(ch'i sui shun ku, utpādānuvṛttivaśāt?)*. For the Buddha preached three kinds of accordance, viz., accordance with order of origin, that with order of preachment *(shuo sui shun, pravacanānuvṛtti?)* and that with the uninterrupted *(? wu chien teng sui shun, nirantarānuvṛtti?)*. "Accordance with order of origin" means that the practitioner of the stations of mindfulness, of the *dhyānas* (*scilicet* of the

Sphere of Form), and of the Formless (Trances) first produces the station of mindfulness of the body and so on, and only then produces the station of mindfulness of the dharmas. This is the reason that the Buddha preached them in this order. The *dhyānas* and the Formless (Trances) are also to be understood in the same way.[25]

"Accordance with the order of preachment" means the following: The Right Severances, the Powers to Do as One Pleases, the Bases, the Strengths, the Limbs of Enlightened Intuition, and the Vehicles are produced in a single *kṣaṇa*. Since, (however,) it is easier to speak of perfecting the Four Right Severances through vigorous advance, as a matter of practical device one has (the practitioner) sever the unwholesome dharmas already produced and so on, and similarly, as a matter of device, one has him preserve the wholesome dharmas already produced, and so on. This is the manner of right severance. One preaches them in the order in which they are done, not as a matter of substantial entity.

"Accordance with the uninterrupted" means that a person who puts the Four Noble Truths into practice deals first of all with the first of them, the Truth of Suffering, which is boundless.[26]

Question: Why does the practitioner first produce the station of mindfulness of the body and so on, and only then produce the state of mindfulness of the dharams?

Answer: By reason of grossness. Of the five skandhas, which is the grossest? The four elements *(catvāri mahābhūtāni)* and the things made up of them *(bhautikāni)*. This is why one considers them first. While sensation is not material, still its operation is relatively gross, which is why it is mentioned next. This means that, when, for example, the hands or the feet are in pain, sensation follows *(wei shou tsu teng t'ung shou tse sui chuan, yadā hastapādādi duḥkhyate tadā vedanānuvartata ity arthaḥ/?)*. Notions and constituents, while still relatively gross, are connected with nirvāṇa. The station of mindfulness of the dharmas comes last because it is the subtlest. It is for this reason that one views thought, then dharmas. Now it is true that the notion of dharma comprises everything, but the use of the term in this context does not fly in the face of this concept. This is why there is only one station of the mindfulness of dharmas, not more.

Saṃghavarman's version has a passage missing from the other two. It begins with a question about how many stations of mindfulness there are. The question is answered with a śloka followed by a prose commentary. The śloka is as follows:

> In three kinds are preached the Stations of Mindfulness:
> [Those of] own nature and the mixed [ones],
> As well as another, preached under the name of "object."
> The wisdoms derived from hearing and the like are also thus.

Next comes a prose commentary, the content of which will now be paraphrased. The verse is telling us that the stations of mindfulness are of three kinds, viz., mindfulness in terms of their own nature *(tzu hsing, svabhāva)*, of mixture with other things *(kung, saṃsarga)*, and of their character as objects *(yüan, ālambana)*. By the first is mentioned wisdom free of distortions *(pu tien tao hui, aviparyastā prajñā?)*. That is to say that one views the respective objects in the order preached. The body is the first object of mindfulness on the part of the wise person, who does not pick his objects at random.[27]

Mindfulness in terms of own-nature having been dealt with, one now proceeds to the other two. By "mixture" are meant dharmas joined to the fruit of right gnosis. For the Buddha did say, "O *bhikṣus*, by the 'accumulation of wholesome dharmas' are meant the Four Stations of Mindfulness." Thus is concluded the principal exposition.

There remain to be treated the stations of mindfulness in terms of their character as objects. This includes all dharmas, for the Buddha has also said that the expression "all dharmas" refers to the Four Stations of Mindfulness.

By "principal exposition" is meant that this treatment is inclusive of everything but objects (?). Mindfulness of mixture with other things severs the defilements and leaves no residue. As for mindfulness in terms of own-nature, though it does take some account of fields of perception *(ching chieh, dhātu? viṣaya?)*, it is not complete, and something more inclusive is needed, if the defilements are to be severed completely (?). As for the third type of mindfulness, though it is all-inclusive, its fields of perception tend to get out of hand, and a certain restriction is needed, if the same object, severance of the defilements, is to be achieved.

Question: Are these stations of mindfulness the only things grouped in three, or are there others as well?

Answer: There are the three wisdoms, derived from hearing and the like, and other things besides. The three wisdoms are derived from hearing *(wen, śruti)*, thought *(ssu, cintā)*, and practice *(hsiu, bhāvanā)*. The first of these is focused on names and concrete objects, and is derived from a teacher's explanation of scripture *(ch'i ching, sūtra)*, monastic code *(lü, vinaya)*, and *abhidharma*. Thought may or may not be associated therewith. Practice, for its part, is not focused on words at all. This is like three men learning to swim, the first a beginner, the second a person at the halfway mark, the third an expert. The beginner stays close to shore; the second man moves now close in, now far out; the expert does not remain near shore at all. The first is analogous to wisdom gained from hearing, the second to that gained from thought, the third to that gained from practice. The first two kinds of wisdom are by no means useless, since both of them conduce to the third, which severs all defilements and dispenses with all verbalization, and which also achieves right concentration *(cheng ting, samyak-samādhi?)*. One who has achieved the wisdom gained from practice has perfected the Four Stations of Mindfulness and has severed all defilements, both individually and collectively. This is why the station of mindfulness of the dharmas is not useless. It is of two kinds, depending on whether or not it maintains or annihilates objects *(yüan, ālambana)*. If wisdom has visible matter as its object, this is the station of mindfulness of the body; if sensation, of sensation; if thought, then of thought; if notions or constituents, then it maintains objects (?). The station of mindfulness of dharmas shall now follow.[28]

On the next step in the sequence, the three versions are almost verbatim. Saṃghadeva's śloka reads as follows:

> Having entered into the dharmas, he takes a general look,
> Beholding identically the marks of the dharmas:
> "These four [objects of mindfulness] are impermanent,
> Empty, selfless, unpleasant."

For Saṃghadeva's seco d foot *(t'ung kuan chu fa hsiang)*, the other two have "gaining the reality-marks of the dharmas" *(te fa chen shih hsiang*, representing something like *dharmāṇāṃ tattvalakṣaṇaṃ prāpnoti?)*. Each is followed by a prose commentary, of which Saṃghadeva's alone is interrupted by a repetition of the fourth foot just quoted. Saṃghadeva's prose commentary says the following:

> Having entered into *dharmasmṛtyupasthāna*, the adept takes an overall view of the *ākāras*.[29] Once having done this, he nurtures his thought and engenders the pure eye of wisdom.[30] He then takes the following overall view of the Four Stations of Mindfulness: "Since they depend on one another for their production, therefore they are impermanent. Since they do not control themselves, therefore they are empty. Since they are not their own masters, therefore they have no self. Since they are evil and calamitous, therefore they are woeful."[31]

Narendrayaśas's commentary, which is the longest of the three, says the following:

> The practitioner, knowing what is appropriate [if that is the meaning of *fen ch'i*] treats the stations of mindfulness as objects, but only as an expedient device *[hsiu fang pien*, for *upāyaṃ bhāvayati?]*. Then, by viewing the common marks *[sāmānyalakṣaṇāni]* of all dharmas, he demolishes *[huai*, for *prahanti?]*[32] the stations of mindfulness as objects. That is to say, he first conducts this exercise repeatedly with respect to body, sensations, and dharmas, then with respect to body and thought,[33] then, finally, with respect to all four at once.

Question: What does this mean?

Answer: The four stations of mindfulness are impermanent, empty, selfless, and unpleasant. If it comes to that, the same is true of all constituted dharmas. They are "impermanent" in the sense that they are constantly shifting and decaying; "empty" in the sense that they are devoid of any substantial entity; "selfless" in the sense that they do not control themselves; "unpleasant" in the sense that they are constantly being chased about by the triple woe.[34] If a person, in his wish to annihilate the *kleśas*, seeks their source, he must learn to distinguish cause from effect. This means two things: Things with outflows have the origin of suffering as their cause and suffering itself as their effect. Those without outflows have the road to the extinction of suffering as their cause and the extinction itself as their effect. Hence he proceeds to the wisdom derived from hearing and thought. In the process of abandoning the Four Stations of Mindfulness as objects, the practitioner sees the Four Noble Truths in a total of sixteen aspects (already described).

Saṃghavarman's version does not differ from these, except to say that the practitioner views two skandhas at a time as objects: first *rūpa* and *vedanā*, then *rūpa* and *saṃjñā*, next *rūpa* and saṃskāra, finally *rūpa* and *vijñāna*.[35]

## NOTES

1. Leon Hurvitz, "The Road to Buddhist Salvation as Described by Vasubhadra," *Journal of the American Oriental Society* (874), pp. 434–486.

2. Étienne Lamotte, *Le Traité de la Grande Vertu de Sagesse de Nāgārjuna*, Mahāprajñāpāramitāśāstra, *avec une nouvelle Introduction*, vol. III (Louvain: Université de Louvain, Institut Orientaliste, 1970), pp. 1329–1430.

3. Mr. Burton Watson, who once said to me, "A fellow working on this stuff is entitled to all the help he can get."

4. Cf. V. V. Gokhale, ed., "The *Abhidharmakośakārikā* of Vasubandhu," *Journal of the Asiatic Society of Bombay* 22 (1946):73–102; hereinafter referred to in text as "Gokhale."

5. Cf. Louis de la Vallée-Poussin, *L'Abhidharmakośa de Vasubandhu* (Paris: Geuthner, 1923–31); hereinafter referred to in text as "LVP."

6. Chinese *yi tz'u shang yi sheng tao ku*, representing a possible *tadut-taraikāyanatvāt?* If I am right, it means that everything beginning with the *niyatabhāgakuśalamūlas* can lead to only one thing, viz., Buddhahood, and is in that sense *ekāyana*. This question does not, of course, concern the present study, whose focus is on (b).

7. Gunabhadra, trans., *Tsa a-han ching*, Taisho vol. II, 90.

8. Translator unknown, *Pieh yi tsa a-han ching*, Taisho vol. II, 100.

9. Translator unknown, *Tsa a-han ching*.

10. This identity is tenuous enough, but that proposed by Mr. Akanuma, viz., 47.41, is more tenuous yet.

11. The original reads *fu hsieh*, of which the former may represent either *fu* (to help) or *pu* (to supplement), the latter meaning "to pour." I presume the former to be a copyist's error, but I am not prepared to say what the original might have been.

12. To the foregoing the corresponding Pāli is the *Akusalarāsisutta*. As to the remainder of this entry, the corresponding Pāli is 47.47.

13. Cf. U. Wogihara, ed., *The Sphuṭārthā Abhidharmakośavyākhyā by Yaśomitra* (Tokyo: The Publishing Association of *Abhidharmakośa vyākhyā*, 1932, 1936), p. 397.

14. The expression, which has no analogue in the two other versions, reads, *pu t'ing hsin che pu neng ch'i cheng chien*, possibly standing for something on the order of *yaś cittaṃ na niṣṭhāpayati na śaknoti sa samyagjñānam utpādayitum*.

15. This last sentence must surely be a veiled reference to some of the other schools. The Theravāda, for instance, posits only three, viz., *anat-talakkhaṇa*, *aniccalakkhaṇa*, and *dukkhalakkhaṇa*. Cf. *Visuddhimagga Buddhaghosa*, by Henry Clarke Warren, trans., (Cambridge: Harvard University Press, 1950), xx. 103.

16. It will have been noted that in the *Vyākhyā* (see note 13), at least, each of the *smṛtyupasthānas* is applied to one particular *viparyāsa*, not each to all four.

17. If that indeed is the meaning of *chüeh kuan*, usually the equivalent of *vitarkavicāra*.

18. *Chien hsing che yi chieh fang pien kuan tu* may stand for something on the order of *yo dṛṣṭibhiś cāryate sa dhātuparīkṣaṇayā tāryate*. At any rate, it is clear from what follows that *mithyādṛṣṭi* is counteracted by analyzing the body into *dhātus* (i.e., *mahābhūtas*).

19. If this is the meaning of *shih chieh ho ku yu so tsao tso*, which I take to signify that the body would be so much dead weight but for *vijñāna*.

20. "Mind" renders *hsin*, which in turn stands for *citta*, elsewhere rendered consistently with "thought." I have departed from that here because of the exigencies of English. Actually, no single English word will do justice to *citta*.

21. If this is the meaning of *chüeh ting i chieh*, for which Saṃghavarman has no analogue.

22. For this, as well as the other categories, cf. note 23 below.

23. (1) For *mahābhūmi*, cf. la Vallée-Poussin, *L'Abhidharmakośa*, ii.152, note 2, where it is indicated that Kyokuga 4.3ab cites the *Vibhāṣā*. The text of the latter will be found in T27.80b. La Vallée-Poussin paraphrases the pertinent passage as follows:

> b. Quelques-uns disent: La pensée est grande, à cause de la supériorité de sa nature et de son activité; elle est grande et elle est *bhūmi*, on l'appelle donc *mahābhūmi*, parce qu'elle est le lieu qui sert de point d'appui aux *caittas*. Les dix *dharmas*, *vedanā*, etc., parce qu'on les rencontre partout dans la *mahābhūmi*, sont nommés *mahābhūmika-dharmas*.

The "ten dharmas" are given (*ibid*., p. 153) as "sensation *(vedanā)*, volition *(cetanā)*, notion *(saṃjñā)*, désir d'action *(chanda)*, contact *(sparśa)*, discernement *(mati)*, mémoire *(smṛti)*, acte d'attention *(manaskāra)*, approbation *(adhimukti)*, recueillement ou concentration *(samādhi)*." Thought *(citta)*, being the basis of them all, is called *mahābhūmi*.

(2) There is no need to repeat what others have said so well about the "outflows." To oversimplify, a thing is *sāsrava* if it conduces to further worldly existence, *anāsrava* or *nirāsrava* if it does not. For extensive treatment, as well as for detailed secondary references, cf. LVP v. *passim (Les anuśayas)*. One passage (v.79) merits citation here:

> Les *anuśayas* . . . coulent *[asravanti, gacchanti]* du ciel suprême *[bhavāgra = naivasaṃjñānāsaṃjñāyatana . . . ]* à l'Avīci . . . ; ils découlent *[kṣar]* par les six organes qui sont autant de blessures. Ils sont donc nommés *āsravas*.

(3) The number three is ubiquitous in Buddhism. Among other things, it is used to classify categories both wholesome and unwholesome into three, viz., acute *(tīkṣṇa)*, middle *(madhya)*, and dull *(mṛdu)*. Here, I suspect, the reference is to congenital faculties, i.e., *tīkṣṇendriya*, *madhyendriya*, and *mṛdvindriya*.

(9) Each of the above categories may, in its own turn, be further subdivided into *tīkṣṇa*, *madhya*, and *mṛdu*.

(36) Of *arati* I am not certain, since in the *Kośa*, at least, it is listed as a vice, while the other two are given as virtues. In all likelihood, *pu lo* represents something other than *arati*.

24. This last, which reads *wei yi juan shan ken chung yi chung tseng*, is surely corrupt.

25. This seems to mean that the *smṛtyupasthānas*, the dhyānas, and the *ārūpyas* were preached by the Buddha in the order in which these respective states of mind are in fact achieved.

26. Certain Buddhist schools, but by not means all of them, held that all is suffering, that pleasure and joy do not exist at all. This certainly seems to be the view of our own author. Cf. LVP vi.129 ff.:

> iv. Certains maîtres nient la sensation agréable, affirment que tout est douloureux. Ils démontrent cette thèse par l'Écriture et le raisonnement Écriture. Le Sūtra dit: "La sensation, quelle qu'elle soit, la douleur s'y trouve," "La sensation agréable doit être regardée comme douloureuse," "C'est une méprise de regarder comme agréable ce qui est douloureux."
>
> Raisonnement. 1. Parce que les causes de plaisir ne sont pas tourjours causes de plaisir *(sukhahetvavyavasthānāt)*. Les choses qu'on prétend être causes de plaisir, aliment, boisson, froid, chaud, etc., lorsqu'elles sont prises ou éprouvées en excès ou à contre-temps, deviennent causes de souffrance. Or il est inadmissible qu'une cause de plaisir, parce qu'elle est accrue, ou parce que, tout en demurant la méme, elle se présente à un autre moment, (5b) produise la souffrance. Par conséquent ces prétendues causes de plaisir sont, dès l'origine, causes de souffrance et non pas causes de plaisir: plus tard la souffrance s'accorît et devient sensible. De même en va-t-il des quatre attitudes *(īryāpatha)*, attitudes couchée, assise, etc. . . .
>
> 2. Parce que la notion de plaisir a pour objet, non un réel plaisir, mais tantot un remède de la souffrance *(duḥkapratikāra)*, tantôt une modification de la souffrance *(duḥkhavikapa)*. (a) Aussi longtemps que l'homme n'est pas tourmenté par la douleur que causent la faim, la soif, le froid, la chaleur, la fatigue, le désir, aussi longtemps il n'a aucune sensation qu'il sente agréable *(sukham iti)*. Par (130) conséquent le ignorants ont l'idée de plaisir, non à l'égard du vrai plaisir, mais à l'égard de l'allègement d'une souffrance. (b) Les sots ont aussi l'idée de plaisir à l'égard de la modification de la souffrance: par exemple faire passer le fardeau d'une épaule sur l'autre.
>
> Par conséquent l'agréable n'existe pas.

27. In the phrase *pu wang shou yüan ku*, I presume both *wang* and *shou* to stand for their respective homophones. Otherwise I cannot construe the phrase.

28. For the position of the *Kośa* on this question, cf. kārikā vi.15–16:

*niṣpannaśamathaḥ kuryāt smṛtyupasthānabhāvanām / kāyaviccitta-dharmāṇāṃ dvilakṣaṇaparīkṣaṇāt //15// prajñā śrutādimayy anye saṃsargālambanāt kramaḥ / yathotpatti catuṣkaṃ tu viparyāsavipakṣataḥ //16//*

Cf. also LVP vi.158–62:

14 a-b. Ayant réalisé le calme, il cultivera les *smṛtyupasthānas.*
Comment cela? (1b)
14 c-d. Par la considération des caractères, doubles, du corps, de la sensation, de la penseé des *dharmas.*
En considérant le caractère propre *(svalakṣaṇa)* et les caractères généraux *(sāmānyalakṣaṇa)* du corps, de la sensation, de la pensée et des *dharmas.* (159) . . . Quelle est la nature des *smṛtyupasthānas?* Le *smṛtyupasthāna* est triple: *smṛtyupasthāna* en soi *(svabhāva),* par connexion *(saṃsarga),* en qualité d'objet *(ālambanasmṛtyupasthāna).* Le *smṛtyupasthāna* en soi est 15 a. *Prajñā.*
Quelle est la *prajñā?*
15 a. Provenant d'audition, etc. Provenant d'audition, de réflexion, de recueillement *(śrutamayī, cintāmayī, bhāvanāmayī).* Le *smṛyupasthāna* est également triple, provenant d'audition, de réflexion, de contemplation.
15 b. Les autres, par connexion et comme objet. (160)
Les autres *dharmas,* les *dharmas* qui ne sont pas *prajñā,* quand ils sont des *dharmas* coexistant à la *prajñā,* sont *smṛtyupasthāna* par connexion *(saṃsarga);* quand ils sont l'objet de la *prajñā* et des *dharmas* coexistant à la *prajñā* (en d'autres termes, quand ils sont l'objet du *svabhāva* et du *saṃsargasmṛtuypasthāna),* ils sont *smṛtyupasthāna* comme objet *(ālambanasmṛtyupasthāna)* . . . (162)
15 b-c. L'ordre est celui de leur production. Pourquoi sont-ils produits dans cet ordre?—D'après les Vaibhāṣikas, parce qu'on voit d'abord ce qui est le plus grossier . . .
15 c-d. Quatre, contecarrants des méprises. Les *smṛtyupasthānas* sont enseignés dans l'ordre comme contrecarrants de la quadruple méprise *(viparyāsa),* croire à la pureté, au bonheur, à la permanence, au soi . . . Ils sont donc quatre, ni plus, ni moins.

29. That is, the four aspects under which each of the Four Noble Truths may be viewed. See LVP vii.30–39.

30. This renders *tseng chang yang hsin sheng wu kou chih yen,* accepting the variant *hsin* is preference to the Taisho's *chih.* This may represent something on the order of *cittaṃ vardhayitvāmalaṃ prajñācakṣur janayati.*

31. There are the four *ākāras* of the First Noble Truth. With due allowance made for muddy wording (a not uncommon fault in the early translations), this seems to be a Vaibhāṣika view, at least as described previously in the *Kośa.*

32. Kārikā v.61 (cf. Gokhale 92) reads as follows:

> *ālambanaparijñānāt tadālambansaṃkṣayāt /*
> *ālambanaprahāṇāc ca pratipakṣodayāt kṣayaḥ //61//*

LVP v. 102 ff. renders it as follows:

> 60 a-c. Destruction par la connaissance de l'objet, par la destruction des *kleśas* dont ils sont l'objet, par l'abandon de l'objet . . . (103) . . .
> 60 d. Destruction par la naissance du contrecarrant.

The *prahāṇa* of the original, accurately rendered by la Vallée-Poussin with "abandon," is rendered by Hsüan-tsang (Kyokuga 21.20b) with *tuan*, literally, "sever," and by Paramārtha (29.264b) with *mieh*, literally, "extinguish, annihilate," both rather free. In view of the *huai* of our own text, it is possible that all three translators were taking *prahāṇa* not as a *-na-* derivative of *prahiṇoti* but as a *vṛddhi-* derivative of *prahanti*.

33. The text as it stands is strange, but this, I believe, is what it says.

34. The triple woe refers to *duḥkhaduḥkhatā* (the quality inherent in things that are painful in and of themselves), *saṃskāraduḥkhatā* ( . . . in constituted things, since in their very nature they are impermanent, hence the pleasure derived from them is doomed to extinction), *pariṇāmaduḥkhatā* ( . . . in things that turn from pleasant to unpleasant).

35. Kārikā vi.17 (cf. Gokhale 93) reads as follows:

> *sa dharmasmṛtyupasthāne samastālambane sthitaḥ /*
> *anityaduḥkhataḥ śūnyānātmatas tān vipaśyati //17//*

LVP vi.162 renders it thus:

> 16. Placé dans le *dharmasmṛtyupasthāna* d'objet mêlé, mettant ensemble le corps, la sensation, etc., il les voit sous le quadruple aspect d'impermanent, de douloureux, de vide, de non-moi.

It is not beside the point that in Hsüan-tsang's version the śloka is rendered with a quatrain whose last two feet read, *hsiu fei ch'ang chi k'u k'ung fei wo hsing hsiang:* "he cultivates the characteristics *(hsing hsiang, ākāra)* of impermanence and of woe, of emptiness and of not-I." As indicated already, these are the *ākāras* of the First Noble Truth. It is possible that Hsüan-tsang was glossing. On the other hand, he may have had a somewhat different text, for Paramārtha has *hsiang*, while the Sanskrit, as we have it, has nothing to correspond to either Chinese equivalent.

# Buddhist Devotional Meditation: A Study of the *Sukhāvatīvyūhôpadeśa*

*Minoru Kiyota*

The *Sukhāvatīvyūhôpadeśa* is a composition traditionally attributed to Vasubandhu[1] (fifth century A.D.), a native of the city of Puruṣapura in Gandhāra. It was translated into Chinese by Bodhiruci[2] in about 529 and is known as *Wu-liang shou-ching yu-p'o-t'i-she yang-sheng chieh,*[3] "The Verses on the Vow to be Born in Pure Land Paradise and the Instruction on the Sutra of Eternal Life" or, more commonly, *Ching-t'u lun*, the Chinese rendition of the Sanskrit *Sukhāvatīvyūhôpadeśa.*

The term *Sukhāvatī* is derived from *sukha* and literally means "possessing ease or comfort, full of joy or pleasure."[4] In Chinese it is rendered *ching-t'u* or *chi-lo*, meaning Pure Land or extreme bliss (i.e., paradise).[5] In Japanese it is called *jōdo* or *gokuraku. Vyūha* means "orderly arrangement of the parts of a whole."[6] In compound, *Sukhāvatī* refers to the Pure Land Paradise of Buddha Amitāyus. *Sukhāvatī-vyūha*, meaning "glorifying Pure Land," is a Mahāyāna work which praises and glorifies Buddha Amitāyus's career and his world. *Upadeśa* means "pointing out, instruction, prescription."[7] Herein the *Sukhāvatīvyūhôpadeśa* will be referred to simply as the *Upadeśa.*

*The Upadeśa* consists of instructions to enable all sentient beings (sattvas) to be born in the Pure Land Paradise of Buddha Amitāyus. Though the term "rebirth" is frequently employed to designate the realization of Pure Land Paradise, this study avoids the use of that term. In Buddhism, rebirth is a term technically associated with the notion of saṃsāra, the cyclic process of life and death of the beings in the six destinies (*gatis*): hellish beings, hungry spirits, beasts, fighting spirits, men, and gods. The term "birth," as employed in the Chinese Pure Land tradition, is *wang-sheng* (*ōjō* in Japanese). It is usually preceded by the prefix *ching-t'u* or *chi-lo*. *Chi-lo wang-sheng* (*gokuraku ōjō* in Japanese) means birth in Pure Land Paradise (or simply Pure Land), which transcends the realm of rebirth in the six destinies.

Buddhist literature describes many kinds of paradises: e.g., the Eastern Paradise of Buddha Akṣobhya, the Bhaiṣajyagūru-vaiḍūrya-prabhāsa of Tathāgata Bhaiṣajyagūru, the Tuṣita Heaven of Bodhisattva Maitreya and Mount Potalaka of Bodhisattva Avalokiteśvara. These forms of paradise are visual representations conceived by the writers of sūtras and śāstras for meditational purposes. Buddha Amitāyus (or Amitābha) reigns in the Western Paradise.

*Amita* is the negative form of *mita*, meaning to measure. It is cognate with the French word *meter*. Amita therefore means "unmeasured, boundless, infinite."[8] Amitāyus *(Amita + āyus)* means Immeasurable Life (sometimes translated as Eternal Life), that is, he who enlightens all beings at all times; Amitābha *(Amita + ābha)* means Immeasurable Light (sometimes translated as Eternal Light), that is, he who enlightens all beings of all quarters. Eternal Life signifies compassion (karuṇā); Eternal Light signifies wisdom (prajñā). The former represents the essential nature of Buddha Amitāyus; the latter, the essential nature of Buddha Amitābha. Both are one and the same Buddha. The names reveal the two attributes of the same Buddha expressed in his vow to enlighten all beings of all quarters at all times.

Because the title of the *Upadeśa* in the Chinese translation is Eternal Life, the term "Amitāyus," rather than "Amitābha," is employed in this study. The *Upadeśa* deals with the description of *Sukhāvatī*, the Pure Land of Buddha Amitāyus (also cited as Buddha-land) and the bodhisattva practices, which are designed to purify *(vyavadāna)* the world of defilements *(saṃkleśa)*.

The Japanese Jōdo Shin (True Pure Land) school enumerates seven patriarchs[9] representing the traditional lineage of the Pure Land school: (1) Nāgārjuna (ca. 150–250 A.D.), (2) Vasubandhu (fifth century), (3) T'an-luan (476–542), (4) Tao-ch'o (562–645), (5) Shan-tao (613–681), (6) Genshin (942–1017), and (7) Hōnen (1133–1212).[10] The first two are Indians, followed by three Chinese and two Japanese. Japanese Pure Land consists of two major schools: Jōdo (Pure Land) and Jōdo Shin (True Pure Land). Hōnen is the founder of Jōdo. Shinran (1173–1262),[11] not enumerated as a Pure Land patriarch, is the disciple of Hōnen and the founder of Jōdo Shin.

Hōnen selected three canonical sources as the doctrinal basis of his Jōdo school: (1) the *Larger Sukhāvatī-vyūha-sūtra*,[12] (2) the *Smaller Sukhāvatī-vyūha-sūtra*,[13] and (3) the *Amitāyur-dhyāna-sūtra*.[14] The central personality in the *Larger Sukhāvatī-vyūha-sūtra* is Dharmākara, a fictitious personality, who in his long journey in quest for enlightenment makes forty-eight vows to enlighten men and later becomes Buddha Amitāyus. The *Smaller Sukhāvatī-vyūha-sūtra* glorifies Amitāyus's Paradise and emphasizes the merits one derives from chanting the name of Buddha Amitāyus. The central personality in the *Amitāyur-dhyāna-sūtra* is Queen Vaidehī (Vehidī). One day a soothsayer informs her that the child she is about to deliver is destined to kill her husband, King Bimbisāra. Hence, when the child is born, Vaidehī, with the consent of her husband, drops the infant from the window of her palace. The child survives. He is called Ajātaśatru. Ajātaśatru becomes a young man and is told by Devadatta of the events surrounding his birth. Thereupon Ajātaśatru imprisons his parents. His father subsequently dies and his mother remains in prison. Śākyamuni hears of the tragedy that has taken place at the palace. This sūtra is his sermon delivered to Queen Vaidehī. It teaches that even a wicked woman, such as Vaidehī, who had suffered one of the greatest tragedies of life—the witnessing of her own child killing her husband and imprisoning her—can realize salvation through faith.

The two *Sukhāvatī-vyūha-sūtras* glorify Pure Land. The *Amitāyur-dhyāna-sūtra* depicts Amitāyus as the object of worship.

The first three patriarchs placed emphasis on the two *Sukhāvatī-vyūha-sūtras*; the last four on the *Amitāyur-dhyāna-sūtra*. Shinran placed emphasis on the *Larger Sukhāvatī-vyūha-sūtra*. He followed T'an-luan's *Wang-sheng lun-chu*,[15] commonly referred to as the *Lun-chu*, line of thought. The *Lun-chu* is a commentary on the *Upadeśa*. Shinran's major work, the *Kyō-gyō-shin-shō (Teaching, Practice, Faith, and Realization)*,[16] makes frequent reference to the *Lun-chu*. The *Upadeśa* therefore is one of the important Pure Land texts in the Sino-Japanese Pure Land tradition. It neatly organizes ideas which are described in a less structured manner in the *Larger Sukhāvatī-vyūha-sūtra*.

Professor Susumu Yamaguchi claims that Pure Land thought is a part of the Mahāyāna tradition based on Nāgārjuna's Mādhyamika and Vasubandhu's Yogācāra thoughts.[17] His interpretation of the *Upadeśa* is based on Yogācāra. He entertains no doubts whatsoever that Vasubandhu is the author of the *Upadeśa*. This is not saying that Yogācāra preceded Pure Land devotionalism. Pure Land devotionalism preceded Yogācāra: Kasugai and Ishida,[18] among others, speculate that Pure Land literature originated in Western Gandhāra about the middle of the second century A.D. As noted before, Vasubandhu lived in the fifth century. Professor Yamaguchi, an eminent Buddhologist, Indologist, Tibetologist, and Sinologist, is fully knowledgeable of the history of the development of Buddhist literature and thought. His contention, like that of many other Japanese Buddhologists, is based on the presupposition that Vasubandhu in his later life embraced the Pure Land faith. This presupposition will have to be maintained until positive evidence can be produced that is sufficient to negate the notion that Vasubandhu is the author of the *Upadeśa*, as recorded by Bodhiruci in the Chinese translation of the *Upadeśa*. A brief comment on Vasubandhu and on the historicity of the *Upadeśa* suffices at this time.

Vasubandhu was initially trained in the Sarvāstivāda and Sautrāntika schools, composed the *Abhidharma-kośa-śāstra*, and later became a Yogācāra-vijñānavādin. Tradition has it that he was converted to Mahāyāna by his brother Asaṅga. At the time of conversion, it is said that he attempted to cut off his tongue for having committed blasphemy against Mahāyāna, but that Asaṅga advised him to vindicate himself by devoting the rest of his life to promoting the causes of Mahāyāna. Following the footsteps of his brother, Vasubandhu became a Yogācāra master and produced many Mahāyāna texts: the *Madhyānta-vibhāga-bhāṣya*, *Vimśatika-* and *Triṁśika-vijñapti-kārikā*, *Daśabhūmi-vyākhyāna*, *Mahāyāna-samgṛaha-bhāṣya*, as well as commentaries on such popular Mahāyāna sūtras as the *Saddharmapuṇḍarīka*, *Tathāgata-garbha*, *Nirvāṇa*, and others.

Judging from the amount of work Vasubandhu produced, it is not difficult to imagine the tremendous intellectual vitality that this great Indian philosopher possessed. More important, the fact that his interest shifted from one school to another is an indication not only of his intellectual vitality but of the range of spiritual pilgrimage that this philosopher experienced. Vasubandhu probably took a liking to Yogācāra philosophy but most likely embraced the Pure Land faith in his later career.

The central theme of Yogācāra is that the external world is but a mental construction. According to this school, the mind that conceptually fragments the world is *vijñāna*, the discriminating consciousness; the mind that cognizes the world just as it is—without arbitrary fragmentation—is jñāna, more specifically, *ādarśa-jñāna*, literally, the "mirror-mind." *Ādarśa-jñāna* refers to a mind that is "pure as a mirror" and hence capable of reflecting the world just as it is. The Yogacarins attempt to transform *(prāvṛtti) vijñāna* to jñāna through meditation (yoga). Transformation here is the act of turning things upside down, a mental revolution. Professor Yamaguchi claims that the Yogācāra concept of pure mind is what the *Upadeśa* describes as Pure Land.[19]

The *Upadeśa* is extant only in the Chinese translation; it is not extant in Sanskrit nor in a Tibetan translation. Though this may or may not bear significance, the theory that the *Upadeśa* (like many other sūtras and śāstras, such as the *Prajñāpāramitā Sūtra on the Benevolent King*, the *Vajrasamādhi-sūtra*, and the *Awakening of Mahāyāna Faith*) is a Chinese pseudepigraphon cannot be entirely ignored. Nevertheless, there is neither conclusive nor even circumstantial evidence of the kind to refute the authorship of, say, the *Awakening of Mahāyāna Faith*, which would warrant the wholesale rejection of the traditional notion that Vasubandhu is the composer of the *Upadeśa*. Granting the fact that Paramārtha (one of the early translators of Vasubandhu's works into Chinese) arrived in South China in 546 A.D., that T'an-luan (the author of the *Lun-chu*) died in 542 (four years before Paramārtha arrived in China), and that T'an-luan therefore was not exposed to Vasubandhu's Yogācāra thought, it is nevertheless reasonable to assume that Bodhiruci (the translator of the *Upadeśa*) was exposed to this thought. In fact, the *Upadeśa* displays strong traces of Yogācāra thought, though the *Lun-chu* does not.

Be that as it may, what is important to note here is that the practice of purification, a theme strongly articulated in the *Upadeśa*, is not uniquely of the *Upadeśa* nor of the Yogācāra tradition. It appears, for example, in the *Prajñāpāramitā* literature as well as the *Vimalakīrti-nirdeśa-sūtra*. It is therefore more reasonable to say that the Pure Land model of salvation is found in the larger context of the Mahāyāna tradition *per se*, the tradition which emphasizes universal salvation and the improvising of skillful means to enable all beings to realize it. This is the theme that Professor

Yamaguchi articulates.[20] He examines Pure Land as a school of devotionalism based on Yogācāra philosophy (just as many other Mahāyāna schools, such as Hua-yen and Zen) and indicates that such a thesis does not contradict the Pure Land devotional thought as conceived by T'an-luan, which tradition was eventually transmitted to Shinran. His conclusion is that Shinran transmits the Yogācāra philosophy of Vasubandhu and the Pure Land devotional tradition of T'an-luan.

The purpose of this essay is neither to investigate the authenticity of the author nor to argue whether the text is a Chinese pseudepigraphon or not, but to investigate the text itself. For regardless of what future research may uncover, the fact remains that the *Upadeśa* exists as a Chinese Buddhist text and has played an important role in shaping Pure Land devotionalism in China and Japan. As previously mentioned, the *Upadeśa* is the basis of T'an-luan's *Lun-chu*, which in turn forms one of the basic sources of Shinran's *Kyō-gyō-shin-shō*. Both are important Pure Land texts in the Sino-Japanese tradition.

The *Upadeśa* consists of two parts, the verses and the prose. The former summarizes the central theme of the text; the latter analyzes and interprets that theme. However, following the *Lun-chu* format, this paper establishes ten arbitrary topic headings. Each topic is an elaboration of the preceding one, an organizational pattern frequently observed in Sanskrit texts, for which reason repetition may somewhat obscure the continuity of thought. This pattern must be considered throughout the examination of the *Upadeśa* in order to understand the central theme of that text. A summation of each topic is presented in the following sections.

## VOW

An understanding of the central theme of the *Larger Sukhāvatī-vyūha-sūtra* is a prerequisite for understanding the intent of the vow: After years of spiritual practice, accumulating insight at each stage of practice, Bodhisattva Dharmākara, a fictitious Pure Land pilgrim, finally becomes Buddha Amitāyus. At each stage he makes a vow. The eighteenth stipulates as follows:

> Even when I am able to attain Buddhahood, if sentient beings of the ten quarters, with sincerity and faith, desire to be born in my land by practicing up to ten thoughts [i.e., chanting the name of Buddha Amitāyus] and are not born there, I will not accept supreme enlightenment.[21]

Etymologically, Dharmākara breaks down into *Dharma*, which, in the *Upadeśa*, means "merits," and *ākara*, meaning "a mine."[22] Thus Dharmākara literally means "a mine or a repository of many merits." The eighteenth vow constitutes the intent of Bodhisattva Dharmākara to enable all sentient beings to realize birth in Pure Land. It is the most significant vow, according to Shan-tao, Hōnen, and Shinran. They claim that this vow is intended to demonstrate the Buddha's infinite compassion, that it provides the possibility of birth in Pure Land by all beings, and that what it assures is in accord with the teaching of the Buddha. Hence the *Upadeśa* says,

> I shall explain the vow [to be born in Pure Land] in verses, the essence of which is in accord with the teachings of the Buddha.[23]

The *Upadeśa*, however, does not identify the eighteenth vow as the primary one. That, as said, is a view entertained by Shan-tao, Hōnen, and Shinran, and endorsed by Japanese Pure Land believers.

## FAITH

Birth in Pure Land is realized through faith. This section describes that faith in terms of the five items of mindfulness *(anusmṛti)*. They are:

1. Worship
2. Praise
3. Vow
4. Meditation
5. Transferring merits

Worship means to be mindful of the power of Buddha Amitāyus. Praise means the chanting of his name *(namo' mitābhāya buddhāya)*. Vow means the determination to realize birth in Buddha-land. Meditation means to visualize the merits of Buddha-land, Buddha Amitāyus, and the bodhisattvas. Transferring merits means practicing compassion, that is, the transferring of merits (accumulated by the four previous practices) to lead all beings to Buddha-land. The first four describe the process of enlightening oneself, the fifth describes the process of enlightening others.

The textual source on which the five items are based is uncertain. They do, however, parallel the general practice-prescription of the *Ta chih tu lun* (Nāgārjuna's commentary on the *Prajñāpāramitā-sūtra*), the *Bodhicitta-śāstra (The Awakening of Enlightenment)*, and many other Mahāyāna texts: i.e., the purification of body *(kāya)*, speech *(vāc)*, and mind *(manas)* as preparatory items to perfect the bodhisattva practices. Worship and praise (which the *Upadeśa* identifies as *śamatha*, i.e., mental calm) parallel the practices of body and speech, respectively; vow and meditation (which the *Upadeśa* identifies as *vipaśyanā*,[24] i.e., insight derived from *śamatha*) parallel the practice of mind-perfection. The four (worship, praise, vow, and meditation) are prerequisites to the final practice, the transferring of merits. But the *Upadeśa* does not presuppose a system of graded stages of practice of the *Abhidharma-kośa* type nor of the type described in the Chinese *Moho chih-kuan*. Faith encompasses all practices. An outline comparing the practice-prescription of the *Bodhicitta-śāstra* and the *Upadeśa* is presented below.

Within the context of faith, communion—i.e., the response of the Buddha to the sum total of men's worship, praise, vow, and meditation—is realized. In the *Bodhicitta-śāstra*, communion is identified as *adhiṣṭhāna*, meaning integration. In the *Upadeśa*, it is identified as *hsiang-ying*, co-responding. Communion in the *Bodhicitta-śāstra* is the instrument to realize integration with dharmakāya (truth *per se*). Faith in the *Upadeśa* is the instrument to realize birth in Pure Land. Pure

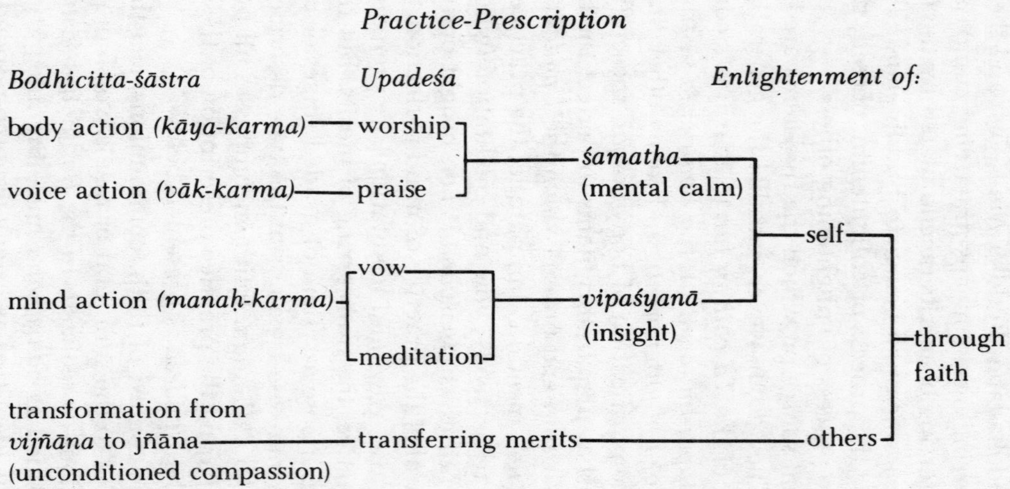
Practice-Prescription
Bodhicitta-śāstra
Upadeśa
Enlightenment of:
body action (kāya-karma)
worship
voice action (vāk-karma)
praise
śamatha
(mental calm)
self
mind action (manaḥ-karma)
vow
meditation
vipaśyanā
(insight)
through
faith
transformation from
vijñāna to jñāna
(unconditioned compassion)
transferring merits
others

Land is the *Upadeśa*'s version of dharmakāya. But the realization of birth in Pure Land by the individual practitioner is not the ultimate objective of the *Upadeśa*. It is the practice dedicated to enabling all beings to realize birth in Pure Land. For that reason, the practice of transferring merits is strongly articulated, as it is in all Mahāyāna texts.

Transferring merits is as important as the four previous practices. But the practice of transferring merits is guided by insight *(vipaśyanā)* and insight by meditation *(śamatha)*. In the *Upadeśa*, worship and praise are the instruments to purify the mind; vow and meditation refer to the state which has realized pure mind. The two are not distinct and apart. The *Upadeśa* therefore says,

> . . . with singleness of thought, we should be mindful that we would ultimately be born in his land of bliss because we seek to practice *śamatha* [meditation] as it really should be.[25]

It further says,

> We meditate by means of wisdom: we meditate on him with right mindfulness because we seek to cultivate *vipaśyanā* [insight] as it really should be.[26]

The insight derived from meditation, however, must be directed to the object "placed in front" *(praṇidhāna)*, that is, sentient beings, because the *Upadeśa* presupposes that insight is perfected when it maintains an object to which it can be applied. Insight means wisdom. The *Upadeśa* stipulates that wisdom must be related to the needs and problems of all beings. Sentient beings therefore are bound *(niṣyanda)* to be enlightened. *Niṣyanda* literally means the "inevitable flow or necessary consequence"[27] of perfect wisdom. In the *Upadeśa*, *niṣyanda* specifically means transferring merits, which is conceived as the "necessary consequence" of those who have realized the Pure Land Dharma. Therefore, it says,

> Without abandoning all suffering beings, we constantly make vows—the transferring of merits being the primary one—to perfect the state of great compassion.[28]

In sum, faith (which is spelled out in terms of the five items of mindfulness) is the instrument to realize birth in Pure Land. Birth in Pure Land, however, involves the enlightening of oneself and others. The former requires *śamatha* and *vipaśyanā* practices. The *Upadeśa* considers that insight derived from these practices requires an object to which it can be applied. Sentient beings are the objects of that insight. Transferring merits means the application of that insight to all sentient beings. It means the purification of all beings. Enlightenment in the *Upadeśa* requires the constant feedback between the practices of self-enlightenment and enlightenment of others. The act of transferring merits is given primary concern because it activates this feedback process. Faith, then, in the *Upadeśa* involves a firm conviction that all beings will realize birth in Pure Land (because of the compassion of Amitāyus) and the practice toward its realization.

## OBJECTS OF FAITH

Whereas the previous section described the content of faith, this section describes the objects of that faith. They are described in terms of twenty-nine merits: seventeen merits of Buddha-land, eight merits of Buddha Amitāyus, and four merits of the bodhisattvas. The *Upadeśa* glorifies the merits of Buddha-land, Buddha Amitāyus, and the bodhisattvas.

The seventeen merits are a representation of Pure Land. The first represents the essential nature of Pure Land. The sixteen merits which follow are features of Pure Land which consist of the merits of the substance, marks, and functions of Pure Land and the beings of that land. They are described below.

*Seventeen Merits of Buddha-land*

- essence
  - (1) Pure Land
- features
  - Pure Land
    - substance
      - (2) its size
      - (3) its quality
    - mark
      - (4) its form
      - (5) the many things it contains
      - (6) its color
      - (7) the touch sensation one derives from it
      - (8) the three elements
      - (9) its rain
    - function
      - (10) its light
      - (11) its sound
  - beings of Pure Land
    - substance
      - (12) the King
      - (13) his dependents
    - mark
      - (14) the reward they receive
      - (15) the state of nonanxiety provided them
    - function
      - (16) Great Teaching (the vow to spread the Pure Land Dharma)
      - (17) all-complete (i.e., the fulfillment of all things desired)

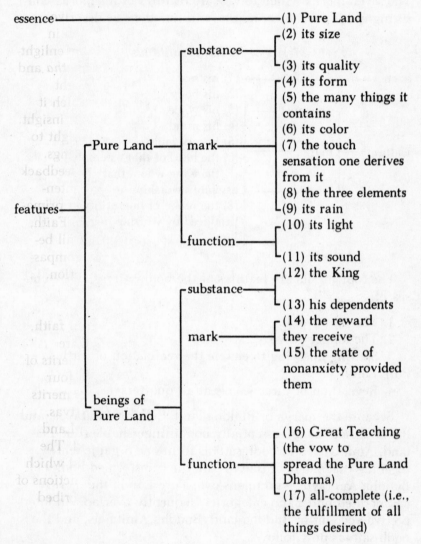

The eight merits are a representation of Buddha Amitāyus. The first represents the essential nature of Buddha Amitāyus. The seven merits which follow are features of his merits consisting of his substance, marks, and functions as described:

*Eight Merits of Buddha Amitāyus*

- essence — (1) his seat
- features
  - substance — (2) his body; (3) his voice; (4) his mind
  - marks — (5) his assembly; (6) the head of that assembly
  - function — (7) the King whom that assembly worships; (8) the realm of nonfutility produced by worshipping him

The four merits are features of the bodhisattvas. They consist of:

1. The immovable
2. The all-pervasive
3. Sparing no being to enable the realization of birth in Pure Land
4. Revelation of three jewels at all quarters

Because the merits of Buddha-land, Buddha Amitāyus, and the bodhisattvas are essentially nondistinguishable (Buddha-land, Amitāyus, and bodhisattvas form one organic .entity, meaning that the bodhisattvas are the transformed bodies of Buddha Amitāyus who reigns over Pure Land), the merits enumerated under the categories frequently overlap. An interpretive account of Buddha-land, Buddha Amitāyus, and the bodhisattvas now follows.

## BUDDHA-LAND

The *Upadeśa* describes the merits of Buddha-land as follows:

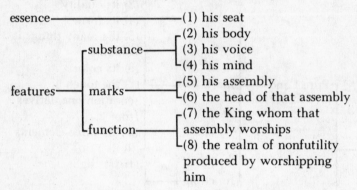

> We speak of the merits which glorify Buddha-land because they refer to the perfecting of the power *[bala]* beyond conceptual thought *[acintya]* which is like a wish-fulfilling jewel *[cintāmaṇi]*.[29]

*Cintāmaṇi*, traditionally conceived as a rare jewel which responds to and satisfies all that a man wills, is symbolic of the quality of Buddha-land, the repository of the variety of merits which a man can extract at will. Buddha-land is the *Upadeśa*'s version of supreme truth, the dharmakāya, which is "beyond conceptual thought." Because it is "beyond conceptual thought," the *Upadeśa* describes it by means of seventeen merits. Hence the *Upadeśa* says,

> They [the seventeen merits] reveal the perfection of the power of the great merits which benefit the tathāgata and the perfection of the merits which benefit others.[30]

Buddha-land is revealed as a means *(prajñapti)* to communicate the essential nature of dharmakāya to men. It is the representation of dharmakāya. In other words, the seventeen merits are features of dharmakāya and the means by which supreme truth is revealed as conventional truth and by which men are to realize supreme truth. Supreme truth refers to the transcendental, i.e., dharmakāya; conventional, to the worldly. All sentient beings realize birth (salvation or enlightenment) in Buddha-land (dharmakāya) through faith in Buddha Amitāyus. Buddha Amitāyus, in the Pure Land tradition, is the link between dharmakāya and all sentient beings.

The seventeenth merit sums up the essence of all previous merits.

## BUDDHA

The seat, described as the pure lotus platform, is the *Upadeśa*'s version of dharmakāya. Buddha Amitāyus is not the pure lotus platform. He sits on it. The lotus represents supreme truth. The Buddha, sitting on the lotus platform, is a symbolic expression of the tathāgata revealing himself in the phenomenal world in order to purify it. The scene represents the revelation of supreme truth in terms of conventional truth. It also represents the revelation of Buddha's wisdom, compassion, and skillful means. Because the enlightened one reveals himself in the world to purify it, we can identify Buddha Amitāyus as saṃbhogakāya, literally, the "rewarded-body," that is, one embodied with dharmakāya. Saṃbhogakāya is the corporeal instrument through which the historical man realizes dharmakāya. It is through saṃbhogakāya that the dharma is "bound to flow" *(dharmatāniṣyanda)* to all quarters without discrimination. Because the intent of the Buddha is to purify the world by employing all possible means, the *Upadeśa* says,

> In meditating on the power of the primary vow of the Buddha, [one comes to realize that] there is no one, who, on meeting him [i.e., having faith in him], passes him in vain. He enables the speedy realization of the merits of the great jewel-sea [i.e., he instantly responds to those who chant his name].[31]

This is the only passage in the *Upadeśa* where the term primary vow *(pūrvapraṇidhāna)* appears. The primary vow is the basis for all other vows. The *Upadeśa* comments on it as follows:

> . . . when the bodhisattvas, who have not realized pure mind [i.e., the bodhisattvas in the first to the seventh *bhūmis*], see the Buddha, they would inevitably realize the dharma-body [i.e., the realization of the bodhisattvas above the seventh *bhūmi*], because the bodhisattvas possessed of pure mind [i.e., the bodhisattvas in the eighth *bhūmi*] and the bodhisattvas in the upper [ninth and tenth] *bhūmis* ultimately realize the same nirvāṇa.[32]

Nirvāṇa here means the unconditioned; however, here it is endowed with the great compassion, which constitutes the nature of the primary vow. Being unconditioned, it is devoid of discrimination. It is therefore equal to *prajñāpāramitā*, the wisdom perfected through the infinite processes of transcending the subject-object dichotomy, and so on; conversely, the processes of transcending the dichotomy are the practices to perfect wisdom. For this reason, the *Upadeśa* distinguishes "the bodhisattvas who have not yet realized pure mind" (i.e., the bodhisattvas in the first to the seventh *bhūmis*), "the pure mind bodhisattvas" (i.e., the bodhisattvas in the eighth *bhūmi*), and "the bodhisattvas in the higher *bhūmis*" (ninth and tenth). (For the meaning of *bhūmi*, see note 32.) The bodhisattvas in the eighth and above are equipped with nondiscriminative wisdom *(nirvikalpa-jñāna)* and the knowledge to exercise compassion which is guided by that wisdom.

The Buddha-land, then, is the realm of the transformation of the sum total of the bodhisattva merits: it is the product of meditation and insight; it is derived from nondiscriminative wisdom. From this premise develops the central theme of the *Upadeśa*, that all beings are bound to be saved. Faith *(śraddhā)* in the *Upadeśa* therefore means absolute confidence in the primary vow of the Buddha, which is perfect compassion. Implicit in that term is wisdom. It is for this reason that Shan-tao, Hōnen, and Shinran identified the eighteenth vow as the primary.

## BODHISATTVAS

The bodhisattvas are nirmāṇakāya, the historical men who are enlightened and equipped with the knowledge to perfect all things *(kṛtyānuṣṭhāna-jñāna)*, that is, to enlighten all beings. It is the quality of this knowledge that is described as merits. Among them, the last is of foremost importance. It reveals the intent of the *Upadeśa:* the perfection of Buddha-deeds *(Buddha-kriyā)*, the purification of men and their world. The process of perfecting Buddha-deeds means the inevitable flow of Pure Land dharma (dharmakāya) to all quarters of the universe through the instruments of the bodhisattvas, the transformed bodies of the Buddha.

In sum, the Buddha-land represents dharmakāya; Buddha Amitāyus, saṃbhogakāya; and the bodhisattvas, nirmāṇakāya. Dharmakāya is truth *per se*; saṃbhogakāya, the rewarded body, represents one who has realized dharmakāya; and nirmāṇakāya is the historically manifested enlightened body, according to the Sino-Japanese tradition. The rationale underlying the theory of the three bodies is that truth *per se* is realized by the historical man only through the means of saṃbhogakāya, who is Buddha Amitāyus. Saṃbhogakāya is most important: it is through Buddha Amitāyus that sentient beings can be born in Buddha-land. But dharmakāya, saṃbhogakāya, and nirmāṇakāya (like Buddha-land, Amitāyus, and the bodhisattvas) form one organic entity. The three categories (whether dharmakāya, saṃbhogakāya, and nirmāṇakāya, or Buddha-land, Amitāyus, and the bodhisattvas) are means to describe the interrelationship of this one organic entity, a subject which will be taken up in the next section.

## ONE DHARMA

The three categories of merits (of Buddha-land, Buddha Amitāyus, and the bodhisattvas) represent the vows of Buddha Amitāyus which the *Upadeśa* glorifies. The *Upadeśa* describes the vows as follows:

> These three [modes] to perfect [merits] are accomplished by glorifying the vows [of the Buddha]. They ought to be known. In sum, they [i.e., the three modes of perfection described in twenty-nine verses] are distilled into the One Dharma verse, the verse on purification [i.e., the first of the seventeen merits of Pure Land]. This purification verse [represents] the true wisdom [of the Buddha], the unconditioned dharma-body *[asamskṛta-dharma-kāya]*. There are two kinds of purification. They ought to be known. What are the two? The first is to purify the physical world *[bhājana-loka]*; the second is to purify the beings of that world *[sattva-loka]*.[33]

One Dharma means Pure Land: One means universal, Dharma refers to the twenty-nine merits. One Dharma is the realm which embraces all twenty-nine merits and hence embraces dharmakāya (Pure Land), saṃbhogakāya (Buddha Amitāyus), and nirmāṇakāya (the bodhisattvas), as described below:

| | | |
|---|---|---|
| Buddha-land (seventeen merits) | dharmakāya | One-Dharma faith |
| Buddha Amitāyus (eight merits) | saṃbhogakāya | One-Dharma faith |
| bodhisattvas (four merits) | nirmāṇakāya | One-Dharma faith |

One-Dharma faith—the all-embracing faith—enables all beings of the world to be transformed into the beings of Pure Land, the representation of the unconditioned realm *(asaṃskṛta-dharma-kāya)*. Transformation, however, requires skillful means.

## SKILLFUL MEANS

This section emphasizes the need for one who has realized One Dharma to turn to the world of saṃsāra and share the dharma-reward with all beings of that world.

It will be recalled that Dharmākara vowed that he would "not accept supreme enlightenment" if other beings had not yet realized it. He therefore involves himself in the practices of purifying all sentient beings and the world they live in. These practices are referred to as transferring merits.

The practices of Dharmākara represent the *Sukhāvatīvyūha-sūtra*'s version of transforming prajñā (perfect wisdom) to jñāna (nondiscriminative wisdom). In the *Upadeśa*, the prajñā-jñāna transformation is described as skillful means *(upāyakauśalya)*. The terms "transformation" (from prajñā to jñāna) and "skillful" means are synonymous.

With reference to the prajñā-jñāna transformation, we ought to note that prajñā and jñāna are contingent on one another. The "long" and the "short" forms of practices, terms which the *Upadeśa* employs, refer to the prajñā-jñāna feedback: prajñā is insight into One Dharma, the "short" (twenty-nine merits distilled into an essence) version; jñāna is insight into the ways and means to deal with the world of sentient beings, the "long" (the distilled expanded into twenty-nine merits) version (see note 75). Hence, prajñā and jñāna are not two distinct entities, nor is Pure Land a distinct realm existing outside the world of sentient beings. The world of sentient beings is the field of "prajñā performing through jñāna," which the *Upadeśa* spells out as "the practice of purification." But because practice is perfected through the instrument of jñāna, jñāna is the instrument of skillful means. This is described in outline form, employing a Yogācāra model, for clarification:

*Instruments of Skillful Means*

<table>
<tr><th>Yogācāra</th><th>Definition of the four jñānas</th><th>Upadeśa (birth in Pure Land by glorifying twenty-nine merits)</th><th></th></tr>
<tr><td>ādarśa</td><td>mirror (pure) mind</td><td>seventeen merits of Buddha-land</td><td rowspan="4">One Dharma</td></tr>
<tr><td>samatā</td><td>nondiscriminating mind</td><td>eight merits of Buddha Amitāyus</td></tr>
<tr><td>pratyavekṣaṇā</td><td>insight to deal with the beings of the world</td><td rowspan="2">four merits of the bodhisattvas</td></tr>
<tr><td>kṛtyānuṣṭhāna</td><td>knowledge of carrying out the practices of purifying the beings of the world</td></tr>
</table>

## THE THREE TEACHINGS TO ELIMINATE THE THREE ERRORS

Improvising skillful means—the transferring of merits—is a means of eliminating obstacles which hinder the realization of enlightenment *(bodhi)*. The rationale underlying this theory is that action (karma) produces latent or habit seeds *(avijñapti-bīja)* and habit seeds in turn shape future action. This simply means that wholesome actions produce wholesome habits and wholesome habits produce wholesome actions. Conversely, unwholesome actions produce unwholesome habits and unwholesome habits produce unwholesome actions. The unwholesome habits are greed, idleness, and self-conceit. They are referred to as the three errors. Of the three. greed is eliminated by cultivating wisdom (prajñā), idleness by cultivating compassion (karuṇā), and self-conceit by cultivating skillful means *(upāya)*. Wisdom, compassion, and skillful means are the three teachings to eliminate the three errors.

## THREE PURE STATES OF MIND

The bodhisattvas who have eliminated the three errors realize the three pure states of mind. They are:

1. Pure mind which seeks the undefiled (i.e., the absence of greed)
2. Pure mind which brings peace to all beings
3. Pure mind which enables universal salvation

The first enlightens oneself, the last two, others. Of the last two, the first eliminates the errors of men, the second spreads the Pure Land Dharma by skillful means.

## THE CONVENTIONAL AND THE SUPREME

Means is the external expression of compassion ("karuṇā" means empathy with men's tragic condition) which is guided by wisdom. But means (action) is shaped by a feeling of compassion (a state of mind), and compassion (which is action when externally expressed) is shaped by wisdom (a state of mind). This is saying that thought shapes action and action, in turn, shapes thought. Wisdom in this context, then, is acquired, not inherent.

Here we must note that Buddhism conceives two levels of truth: the supreme *(paramārtha)* and the conventional *(saṃvṛti)*. The understanding of conventional truth needs insight into supreme truth in order to deal effectively and unpervertedly with the problems of sentient beings. In this context, then, the conventional and the supreme are not unrelated. They are contingent on one another. Skillful means, the external expression of compassion, is dependent on the feedback between the conventional and the supreme: Pure Land is the representation of inherent wisdom; the means, which is inclusive of compassion and acquired wisdom, is the conventional instrument to lead sentient beings to Pure Land. Means derives its insight to deal with the problems of sentient beings from Pure Land. It is the sole link between the two levels of wisdom.

## PERFECTION OF ALL THINGS VOWED

The vow of Bodhisattva Dharmākara is to save all beings, a matter that is realized by the Pure Land practitioner by observing the five items of mindfulness. A reexamination of the five items now follows.

The object of faith is One Dharma, which encompasses the seventeen merits of Buddha-land, the eight merits of Buddha Amitāyus, and the four merits of the bodhisattvas. But enlightenment in the *Upadeśa* consists of the enlightenment of oneself and others. Self-enlightenment is realized through the practices of worship, praise, vow, and meditation; that of others is realized through transferring merits. The prescription for the enlightenment of self and others follows the Mahāyāna model of universal enlightenment, as previously described.

Buddha Amitāyus, then, is the one who is enlightened and has the insight and the means to enlighten others. "Tathāgata" is another name assigned to a Buddha. Conze analyzes tathāgata as *tathā-gata* or *tathā-āgata*, "thus gone" or "thus come."[34] Yamaguchi analyzes and interprets it as follows: *tathā-gata*, one who leaves the realm of saṃsāra for the realm of enlightenment, and *tathā-āgata*, one who comes to the realm of saṃsāra from the realm of enlightenment.[35]

In the Sino-Japanese tradition, the term "tathāgata" has this twofold meaning, "leaving" and "coming." The Vajradhātu Maṇḍala of the Shingon school describes the path of self-enlightenment and the path of enlightening others through its nine assemblies, the iconographic representation of this twofold meaning.[36] The *Upadeśa*'s description of enlightening oneself and others, employing the *tathā-gata*⟷*tathā-āgata* model, is outlined below.

The perfection of all things vowed means the enlightenment of self and others through faith in One Dharma.

## THE PRACTICES TO BENEFIT OTHERS

Practices here refer to the practices of perfection, of which there are five. They are the products of the practices of the five items of mindfulness. The five are:

1. Nearing Pure Land by worshipping Amitāyus (product of worship)
2. Joining the congregation which praises Amitāyus (product of praise)
3. Entering Amitāyus's domain by vowing to be born in his Pure Land (product of vow)
4. Entering his palace (product of meditation)
5. Entering the garden of saṃsāra and enjoying the work of enlightening others (product of transferring merits)

The first four are preparatory stages for the bodhisattvas to lead others to Pure Land, a matter which the fifth deals with. The bodhisattvas, as mentioned previously, are the transformed bodies of Buddha Amitāyus. This means that all beings who live in Pure Land are entities of Saṃbhogakāya Amitāyus, the representation of dharmakāya. Men's realization of birth in Pure Land essentially means the reintegration of men with dharmakāya through faith in Buddha Amitāyus. But this is not the traditional Pure Land interpretation. As mentioned previously, that tradition does not employ the term integration *(adhiṣṭhāna)*. Instead, the Pure Land tradition articulates absolute faith in the other power which is designed to effect the realization of universal salvation.

## CONCLUSION

The central theme of the *Upadeśa* is universal salvation. Pure Land and Buddha Amitāyus are the means (visual representa-

*The Upadeśa's Prescription for Enlightening Oneself and Others*

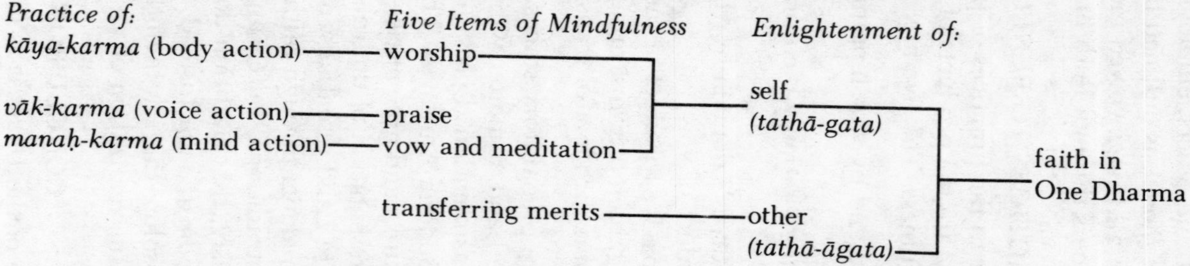

tions) to enable men to realize salvation. Whether the Pure Land model is found outside the doctrinal content of Buddhism, a matter which Iwamoto strongly suggests,[37] or not, is not pertinent. Many models of Buddhist thought are found in the Brahmanic tradition (e.g., karma, rebirth, tathāgata, buddha, yoga, and so on) as well as in the non-Indian tradition (bodhisattvas with wings are found in the wall paintings of Miran in Central Asia; Taoist models are employed in Hua-yen world description in China; Buddhist-Shinto, Buddhist-Nat, Buddhist-Phi, and other forms of religious syncretism are observed in Japan, Burma, Thailand, and other countries). Nor is the issue of whether the *Upadeśa* is a composition by Vasubandhu or a Chinese pseudepigraphon a crucial issue: there are many pseudepigrapha in the Buddhist canons, and in this connection it might be pointed out that it is extremely doubtful whether the Mahāyāna literature as a whole, or for that matter even the Pāli canon, represent the actual sayings of the Buddha.[38] The pertinent and the crucial issue is that, regardless of who the author may be, where it may have been composed, and what its model may be, the *Upadeśa* is a Mahāyāna text: it emphasizes the central Mahāyāna tenets, the transferring of merits to benefit others, and so on. It is this tenet, the transferring of merit for instance, articulating the virtue of self-sacrifice, that has inspired and has contributed to the establishment of the basis of social ethics among the Pure Land practitioners in East Asia for centuries. It is this tenet that motivated acts of self-immolation among Vietnamese monks in recent years. The note left by Thich Quang Duc, the first monk to burn himself to death in the political crisis of the early 1960s, says,

> I vow to sacrifice myself on the altar of the Buddha and by its merits to realize the perpetuation of the Dharma, the peace of Vietnam and of the world, and the well being of all mankind. Homage to Amitāyus.[39]

The fact that Pure Land is a visual representation, that Buddha Amitāyus is saṃbhogakāya, and that Dharmākara is a fictitious personality do not invalidate the religious significance of this tradition. They are a means to lead sentient beings to enlightenment. Buddha Amitāyus is the source of the religious experience of a Pure Land devotee from whom he derives the insight to relate himself to the problems of mankind.

Finally, we must reexamine the eighteenth vow, which ends with a rather disturbing line concerning birth in Pure Land. It says, "only excluding those who commit the five atrocities and abuse the True Dharma." In the popular Pure Land tradition, this line is omitted. However, T'an-luan in his *Lun-chu* and Tao-ch'o in his *An-yao-chi* claim that even "those who had committed the five atrocities and had abused the True Dharma" can realize birth in Pure Land by chanting the name of Buddha Amitāyus, because of the infinite grace of that Buddha.[40] Iwamoto is quite right that Pure Land is a doctrine of infinite grace. But the Pure Land doctrine of infinite grace falls within the confines of the Buddhist tradition, not outside of it. As such, Pure Land faith is not "blind" faith. It requires a complete understanding of the nature of Buddha Amitāyus, who is the tathāgata. Implicit in that term is the bodhisattva doctrine of universal salvation, a matter which requires improvising skillful means cultivated within the realm of meditation. There is, however, one annoying idea in this text: there is no woman in Pure Land.

---

## SUKHĀVATĪVYŪHÔPADEŚA

**[The Verses]**

[Invocation]

O Bhagavān,[41] with one mindedness,[42] I seek refuge in the tathāgata [Amitāyus], whose light [illuminates] all quarters and is unobstructed, and vow to be born in [his] Pure Land. Based upon the [twenty-nine] marks of the true merits of the *[Sukhāvatīvyūha-] sūtra*, I shall explain the vow [to be born in Pure Land] in verses, the essence of which is in accord with the teachings of the Buddha.

[The Dharma to Realize Birth in Pure Land]
*[The Seventeen Merits of Pure Land]*

1. In meditating on the marks of that world [i.e., Pure Land], [we realize that] it surpasses the ways [*gatis*][43] of the three[44] worlds.

2. Ultimately, it is broad and limitless, just like space.

3. The great compassion *[mahā-karuṇā]* of the right path [i.e., the Pure Land Dharma] arises from wholesome roots[45] *[kuśala-mūla]* which transcend the world [of saṃsāra].[46]

4. It is filled with pure light, just as the disc of a mirror or that of the sun and moon [are full of light].

5. It is furnished with qualities of precious jewels and is all-complete with sublime glories.

6. Its undefiled[47] *[āmala* or *vimala]* lights are vigorous and bright, illuminating and purifying the world [of saṃsāra].

7. The grasses [which possess] the merits of jewel-like quality softly [spread] around us; when touched, they give rise to ecstasy beyond that of touching soft cloth *[kācilindika]*.

8. The jewel-flowers are of ten million kinds, covering ponds, streams, and springs: when a breeze moves the flowers and leaves, their light interlacing each other dances about. From the towers of the palace [i.e., Pure Land], we can observe all quarters without obstruction: trees emit different lights [e.g., from a yellow flower-tree emits a red light] and jewel-railings surround [these trees]. [The light of] innumerable jewels blends. Indra's net [made up of innumerable jewels] covers the entire sky; bells [hanging from every knot] ring, proclaiming the sound of the True Dharma.

9. It rains flower-robes, [making Pure Land] glorious; [their] innumerable incenses perfume all things.

10. The wisdom of the Buddha—the illuminating and purifying sun—eliminates the world's delusion, darkness, and ignorance.

11. The sacred words [of this land] enlighten [men] for they are profound; they are heard at all quarters, though faint and subtle they may be.

12. The supremely enlightened Amitāyus abides [in Pure Land] and [governs] it as the King of the Dharma.

13. The bodhisattvas, the purifying flowers of the tathāgata, are born from the [tathāgata's] flower of supreme enlightenment.

14. They[48] enjoy the flavor of the Buddha-Dharma and nourish themselves with dhyāna[49] and samādhi.[50]

15. Having eternally severed their body and mind from defilements, they enjoy the pleasure [of Pure Land] without intermittence.

16. In the world [made up of] the wholesome roots of Mahāyāna [i.e., Pure Land], all are equal. [Here,] objectionable designations do not exist: women and those with defective senses and those belonging to the lineage *[gotra]* of the two vehicles [of the śrāvakas and pratyekabuddhas][51] are not caused.

17. What is wished by men is all fulfilled. I therefore seek to be born in the land of Amitāyus.

*[Eight Merits of the Buddha]*

1. The King [adorned with] immeasurable jewels [sits on] the marvelous pure-lotus-platform.

2. His marks [i.e., the thirty-two major and eighty minor marks] radiate for one arm's length [of the Buddha].[52] [The brilliance of his] form surpasses that of all living beings.

3. The marvelous voice of the tathāgata [i.e., the chanting of the name of the tathāgata Amitāyus], the sound of purification, is heard at all quarters.

4. Like [the five elements of][53] earth, water, fire, wind, and space, he is without discrimination.

5. The celestial beings, the immovable ones [i.e., the bodhisattvas in Pure Land], are born from the sea of the pure-wisdom[54] [of the Buddha].

6. Like the King of Mount Sumeru[55] [which is surrounded by smaller mountains], he [i.e., Buddha Amitāyus] stands exalted and unsurpassed, [surrounded by the bodhisattvas].

7. The male celestial beings [i.e., the bodhisattvas] pay homage, surround, and adore [Buddha Amitāyus].

8. In meditating on the power of the primary vow of the Buddha, [one comes to realize that] there is no one who, upon meeting [i.e., having faith in] him, passes him in vain. He enables the speedy realization of the merits of the great jewel-sea[56] [i.e., he instantly responds to those who chant his name].

### *[Four Merits of the Bodhisattvas]*

1. The land of bliss is pure. In it the immaculate Wheel of the Dharma[57] is always revolved by the bodhisattvas, the transformed bodies [i.e., nirmāṇakāyas] of the Buddha, who, like the sun, are self-abiding as Mount Sumeru [i.e., they remain in their original positions[58] but shine on the earth beneath them without discrimination].

2. The undefiled and the glorious light [of Pure Land] illuminates all assemblies of the buddhas, instantly and simultaneously, benefiting all beings.

3. In raining heavenly music, flower robes, exotic incenses, and other things as offerings, and praising the merits of the buddhas, they do not discriminate.

4. If there are any worlds where the merits of the Buddha-, dharma-, [and saṃgha-] jewels are lacking, I [i.e., a bodhisattva] seek to be born in all of them to reveal the Buddha-dharma just as the Buddha.

### [Conclusion]

I have composed this treatise, explaining it in verses [first of all]. I sincerely desire to see [i.e., have faith in] Buddha Amitāyus,[59] and, together with all beings to be born in [his] Pure Land.

I have completed in verses a summary of the passages of the *Sukhāvatī-vyūha-sūtra*.

**[The Prose]**

[I. Vow]

Discourse [on the verses] follows:

Question: What do the verses [on the vow to be born in Pure Land] attempt to reveal?

Answer: [I have composed the verses] because [I wish] to reveal [the way] to meditate on Pure Land, to see Buddha Amitāyus, and to be born in his land.

[II. Faith]

Q: How should we meditate and awaken Faith?

A: If good sons and daughters[60] observe the five items of mindfulness [leading to birth in Pure Land] and perfect them, they shall ultimately realize birth in Pure Land and see Buddha Amitāyus.

Q: What are the five items?

A: They are:

1. To worship [Buddha Amitāyus]
2. To praise [i.e., to invoke the name of Buddha Amitāyus]
3. To vow [to be born in Pure Land]
4. To meditate [on the glories of Pure Land]
5. To transfer one's merits [for the benefit of others]

Q: How do we worship?

A: We worship Amitāyus [who is] the tathāgata,[61] the arhat,[62] and the samyaksaṃbuddha[63] through bodily action *[kāya-karma]* with the desire to be born in his land.

Q: How do we praise [his name]?

A: We praise [his name] through vocal action *[vāk-karma]:* we chant the name of the tathāgata because, by observing these practices as truly as they should be, we seek to bring about the unity [between those practices] and what his name-essence[64] and illumination-wisdom[65] [stand for].[66]

Q: How do we make a vow?

A: We should constantly be mindful of making a vow: with singleness of thought, we should be mindful that we would ultimately be born in his land of bliss because we seek to practice *śamatha* [meditation] as it really should be.

Q: How do we meditate?

A: We meditate by means of wisdom: we meditate on him with right-mindfulness[67] because we seek to cultivate *vipaśyanā* [insight] as it really should be. There are three ways to meditate.

Q: What are the three?

A: They are:

1. The meditation on the merits which glorify Buddha-land
2. The meditation on the merits which glorify Buddha Amitāyus
3. The meditation on the merits which glorify the bodhisattvas

Q: How do we transfer merits?

A: Without abandoning all suffering beings, we constantly make vows—the transferring of merits being the primary one—to perfect the state of great compassion.

## [III. Objects of Faith]

### *[Seventeen Merits of Pure Land]*

Q: How should we meditate on the merits which glorify Buddha-land?

A: [We speak of] the merits which glorify Buddha-land because they refer to the perfecting of the power [bala] beyond conceptual thought *[acintya]*,[68] which is like a wish-fulfilling jewel *[cintāmaṇi]*.[69] There are seventeen ways to meditate to perfect the merits which glorify Buddha-land. They ought to be known.

Q: What are the seventeen?

A: They are [the meditations] to perfect the merits which glorify:

1. [The essence of] purification [of his land]
2. Its immeasurable [size]
3. Its [wholesome] qualities
4. Its form
5. The many things [it contains]
6. Its color
7. The touch [sensation one derives from it]
8. Its three elements

9. Its rain
10. Its light
11. Its sound
12. Its King
13. His dependents
14. The reward [they receive]
15. The [state of] nonanxiety [provided them]
16. The Great Teaching
17. The fulfillment of all things desired [as described above]

1. It is the perfection of the merits which glorify [its essence of] purification because the verse says, "In meditating on the marks of that world [i.e., Pure Land], [we realize that] it surpasses the ways [*gatis*] of the three worlds."

2. It is the perfection of the merits which glorify its immeasurable [size] because the verse says, "It is broad and limitless, just like space."

3. It is the perfection of the merits which glorify its [wholesome] qualities because the verse says, "The great compassion *[mahākaruṇā]* of the right path [i.e., Pure Land Dharma] arises from wholesome roots *[kuśalamūla]* which transcend the world [of saṃsāra]."

4. It is the perfection of the merits which glorify its form because the verse says, "It is filled with pure light, just as the disc of a mirror or that of the sun and moon [are full of light]."

5. It is the perfection of the merits which glorify the many things [it contains] because the verse says, "It is furnished with qualities of precious jewels and is all-complete with sublime glories."

6. It is the perfection of the merits which glorify its color because the verse says, "Its undefiled *[āmala* or *vimala]* lights are vigorous and bright, illuminating and purifying the world [of saṃsāra]."

7. It is the perfection of the merits which glorify the touch [sensation one derives from it] because the verse says, "The grasses [which possess] the merits of jewel-like quality softly [spread] around us; when touched, they give rise to ecstasy beyond that of touching a soft cloth *[kācilindika]*."

8. It is the perfection of the merits which glorify its three

elements which consist of three [substantial] matters. They ought to be known. What are the three? Water, earth, and space. The perfection of the merits which glorify water refers to the verse which says, "The jewel-flowers are of ten million kinds, covering ponds, streams, and springs: when a breeze moves the flowers and leaves, their light interlacing each other dances about." The perfection of the merits which glorify earth refers to the verse which says, "From the towers of the palace [i.e., Pure Land], we can observe all quarters without obstruction: trees emit different lights [e.g., from a yellow flower-tree emits a red light] and jewel-railings surround these trees." The perfection of the merits which glorify space refers to the verse which says, "[The light of] innumerable jewels blends. Indra's net [made of innumerable jewels] covers the entire sky; bells [hanging from every knot] ring, proclaiming the sound of the True Dharma."

9. It is the perfection of the merits which glorify its rain, because the verse says, "It rains flower-robes, [making Pure Land] glorious; [their] innumerable incenses perfume all things."

10. It is the perfection the merits which glorify its light because the verse says, "The wisdom of the Buddha—the illuminating and purifying sun—eliminates the world's delusion, darkness and ignorance."

11. It is the perfection of the merits which glorify its sound because the verse says, "The sacred words [of this Land] enlighten [men], for they are profound; they are heard at all quarters, though faint and subtle they may be."

12. It is the perfection of the merits which glorify its King because the verse says, "The supremely enlightened Amitāyus abides [in Pure Land] and [governs] it as the King of the Dharma."

13. It is the perfection of the merits which glorify his dependents because the verse says, "The bodhisattvas, the purifying flowers of the tathāgata, are born from the [tathāgata's] flower of supreme enlightenment."

14. It is the perfection of the merits which glorify the reward [they receive] because the verse says, "They enjoy the flavor of the Buddha-dharma and nourish themselves with *dhyāna* and samādhi."

15. It is the perfection of the merits which glorify the [state of] nonanxiety [provided them] because the verse says, "Having eternally severed their body and mind from defilements, they enjoy the pleasure [of Pure Land] without intermittence."

16. It is the perfection of the merits which glorify the Great Teaching because the verse says, "In the world [made of] the wholesome roots of Mahāyāna [i.e., Pure Land], all is equal. [Here,] objectionable designations do not exist: women and those with defective senses and those belonging to the lineage *[gotra]* of the two vehicles [of the śrāvakas and pratyekabuddhas] are not caused." [One who has received] the Pure Land reward parts from the two types of errors which [men] abhor. They ought to be known: body and designation. Body is of three kinds: [the body of] the people of the two vehicles; [the body of] women; and [the body of] those whose sense organs are not complete. [In Pure Land] these three errors do not exist. Therefore, those [in Pure Land] are called those who have parted from the bodies [men] abhor. Designation is of three kinds: [Pure Land is a realm] devoid of the three bodies; it is devoid even of the names of women, two vehicles, and those with defective senses. It is therefore called [the realm that has] parted from the names we abhor; it is oneness, meaning the one [universal] mark of equality.

17. The perfection of the merits which glorify the fulfillment of all things desired [as described above] refers to the verse which says, "What is wished by men is all fulfilled."

In sum, the perfection of merits which glorify the Land of Buddha Amitāyus has been described: They [the seventeen merits] reveal the perfection of the power of the great merits which benefits the tathāgata himself and the perfection of the merits which benefits others. The glory of the Buddha-land of eternal life is the wondrous realm *[saṃvṛti]* [which is found in the midst] of supreme truth *[paramārtha]*.[70] The sixteen verses [which described the features of Pure Land in detail] are distilled into the one verse [i.e., the seventeenth verse which sums up the essence of all previous merits of Pure Land]. They [i.e., the seventeen verses] have been explained in due order. They ought to be known.

*[Eight Merits of the Buddha]*

Q: How should we meditate to perfect the merits which glorify the Buddha?

A: There are eight kinds of meditation to perfect the merits which glorify the Buddha. They ought to be known.

Q: What are the eight?

A: They are the perfection of the merits which glorify:

1. His seat
2. His body
3. His voice
4. His mind
5. His assembly [i.e., the assembly of the bodhisattvas who reside in the eight *bhūmis*]
6. The head [i.e., Buddha Amitāyus who reigns over the bodhisattvas]
7. The King [whom the bodhisattvas in the ninth and tenth *bhūmi* worship]
8. [The Buddha Amitāyus] who abides in the realm of nonfutility

1. What is the perfection of the merits which glorify his seat? The verse says, "The King [adorned with] immeasurable jewels [sits on] the marvelous pure-lotus-platform."

2. What is the perfection of the merits which glorify his body? The verse says, "His marks [i.e., the thirty-two major and eighty minor marks] radiates for one arm's length [of the Buddha]. [The brilliance of his] form surpasses that of all living beings."

3. What is the perfection of the merits which glorify his voice? The verse says, "The marvelous voice of the tathāgata [i.e., the chanting of the name of the Tathāgata Amitāyus], the sound of purification is heard at all quarters."

4. What is the perfection of merits which glorify the mind? The verse says, "Like [the five elements of] earth, water, fire, wind, and space, he is without discrimination." Without discrimination means without discriminative thought.

5. What is the perfection of merits which glorify his assembly [i.e., the assembly of the bodhisattvas who reside in the eight *bhūmis*]? The verse says, "The celestial beings, the immovable ones [i.e., the bodhisattvas in Pure Land], are born from the sea of the pure wisdom [of the Buddha]."

6. What is the perfection of the merits which glorify the head [i.e., Buddha Amitāyus who reigns over the bodhisattvas]? The verse says, "Like the King of Mount Sumeru [which is surrounded by smaller mountains] he [i.e., Buddha Amitāyus] stands exalted and unsurpassed, [surrounded by the bodhisattvas]."

7. What is the perfection of the merits which glorify the King [whom the bodhisattvas in the eighth and ninth *bhūmis* worship]? The verse says, "The male celestial beings [i.e., the bodhisattvas] pay homage, surround, and adore [Buddha Amitāyus]."

8. What is the perfection of the merits which glorify [the Buddha's power that enables men] to abide in the realm of nonfutility? The verse says, "In meditating on the power of the primary vow of the Buddha, [one comes to realize that] there is no one who, upon meeting [i.e., having faith in] him, passes him in vain. He enables the speedy realization of the merits of the great jewel-sea [i.e., he instantly responds to those who chant his name]."

In other words, when the bodhisattvas, who have not yet realized pure-mind [i.e., the bodhisattvas in the first to the seventh *bhūmis*], see the Buddha, they will inevitably realize the dharma-body, because the bodhisattvas possessed of pure-mind [i.e., the bodhisattvas in the eighth *bhūmi*] and the bodhisattvas in the upper *bhūmis* [i.e., the bodhisattvas in the ninth and tenth *bhūmis*] ultimately realize the same nirvāṇa. In sum, the eight passages reveal the process of perfecting the merits which glorify the tathāgata who brings benefits to oneself and others. They ought to be known.

### *[Four Merits of the Bodhisattvas]*

Q: What is the meditation on perfecting the merits which glorify the bodhisattvas?

A: In meditating on those bodhisattvas [in Pure Land], [one comes to realize that] there are four kinds of [marks leading to perfecting] the merits of right practices. They ought to be known.

Q: What are the four?

A: As follows:

1. [A bodhisattva] is able to pervade all quarters while remaining unmoved in Buddha-land, and by means of his transformed body [nirmanakaya], he cultivates the practices [of benefiting others] as they really should be, and constantly performs Buddha-deeds. The verse says, "The land of bliss is pure. In it the immaculate Wheel of the Dharma is always revolved by the bodhisattvas, the transformed bodies [i.e., nirmanakayas] of the Buddha, who, like the sun, are self-abiding as Mount Sumeru [i.e., they remain in their original position but shine on the earth beneath them without discrimination]." [The Pure Land Sun] opens the flower [i.e., pure mind] of all beings [nurtured in the environs of] muck [i.e., defilements].

2. The transformed bodies are at all times, without [the thought of] before or after [i.e., at proper moments], with one-mindedness, and at one instant thought [i.e., with faith] radiate the great light throughout all quarters of the world to convert all beings. Improvising skillful means, they remove and extinguish all pains of sentient beings. The verse says, "The undefiled and glorious light [of Pure Land] illuminates all assemblies of the buddhas, instantly and simultaneously, benefiting all sentient beings."

3. In illuminating the beings of the great assemblies *[mahāsaṃgha]* of all worlds, the bodhisattvas leave no one unattended: they make vast and innumerable offerings with unsparing efforts, and pay homage and praise the merits of the buddhas and tathāgatas. The verse says, "In raining heavenly music, flower robes, and exotic incenses, and things as offerings, and praising the merits of the buddhas, they do not discriminate."

4. In all quarters of all worlds, wherever the three jewels [buddha, dharma, saṃgha] are lacking, [the bodhisattvas] abide in the great sea-merits of the buddha-, dharma-, saṃgha-jewels, glorify them, reveal them all over, and enable all beings to understand the true practices. The verse says, "If there are any worlds where the merits of the buddha-, dharma-, [and saṃgha-] jewels are lacking, I [i.e., the bodhisattva] seek to be born in all of them to reveal the buddha-dharma just as the Buddha."

### [IV. One Dharma]

The meditations to perfect the merits which glorify the Buddha-land, the Buddha, and the bodhisattvas have been explained. These three [modes] to perfect [merits] are accomplished by glorifying the vows [of the Buddha].[71] They ought to be known. In sum, they [i.e., the three modes of perfection described in twenty-nine verses] are distilled into the One-Dharma[72] verse, the verse on purification [i.e., the first of the seventeen merits of Pure Land]. This purification verse [represents] the true wisdom [of the Buddha], the unconditioned dharma-body *[asaṃskṛta-dharma-kāya]*.[73] There are two kinds of purification. They ought to be known. What are the two? The first is to purify the physical world *[bhājanaloka]*;[74] the second is to purify the beings of that world *[sattva-loka]*.

1. [The practices to] purify the physical world consist of perfecting the seventeen merits which glorify the Buddha-land, as described previously. They are called [the practices] to purify the physical world.

2. [The practices to] purify the beings of that world include perfecting the eight merits which glorify the Buddha and the four merits which glorify the bodhisattvas, as described previously. They are called [the practices] to purify the worlds of beings.

Thus, One Dharma contains two meanings of purification. They ought to be known.

[V. Skillful Means]

The bodhisattvas practice [the meditation to realize] mental calm *[śamatha]* and insight *[vipaśyanā]*—the "short" and "long" forms of practice[75]—practice the state of flexibility,[76] and truly understand the principle [of the flexibility of practices].[77] In this manner, [the bodhisattvas] perfect skillful means to transfer their merits. What do we mean by the bodhisattvas's skillful means to transfer merits? The means consists of their describing all merits of wholesome qualities, which they have accumulated by the five practices—worship and others—because it is their desire [to engage in the work] of plucking out the pain [i.e., karmic seeds] [of all beings] without seeking to abide in their own bliss, to embrace all beings, and to vow that [all beings] may be born in the Pure Land of the Buddha. These are the practices to perfect the bodhisattvas's skillful means to transfer merits.

### [VI. The Three Teachings to Eliminate the Three Errors]

If the bodhisattvas are thoroughly knowledgeable of the skillful means to transfer merits, they will part from the three kinds of errors. What are the three? They are:

1. [Eliminating greed by cultivating wisdom]: Severing themselves from clinging [to the notion of] greed, [the bodhisattvas] do not seek [to realize] their own bliss because of wisdom [prajñā].
2. [Eliminating idleness by cultivating compassion]: Severing themselves from idleness, [the bodhisattvas] pluck out the pains of all sentient beings to bring about peace to all because of compassion [karunā].
3. [Eliminating self-conceit by cultivating skillful means]: Severing themselves from conceit—the giving of offerings and paying homage to themselves being the foremost—[the bodhisattvas] exercise compassion to all sentient beings and improvise skillful means.

These are called [the three teachings which enable the bodhisattvas to] part from the three kinds of error that are detrimental to realizing enlightenment.

### [VII. The Three Pure States of the Mind]

Having parted from the three errors, the bodhisattvas realize the fulfillment of the three states of the mind which are in accord with [the teaching to realize] enlightenment. What are the three?

1. The pure mind [that seeks for] the undefiled: it does not seek bliss for one's own sake.
2. The pure mind [that seeks for] peace: it plucks out pains from all sentient beings.

3. The pure mind [that seeks for] bliss: it enables all beings to realize the great enlightenment *[mahā-karuṇā]*.

[Because the three pure states of the mind embrace all sentient beings], they are called the fulfillment of the three states which are in accord to realizing enlightenment. They ought to be known.

### [VIII. The Conventional and the Supreme Truths]

The previously explained [Section VI] three teachings—wisdom, compassion, and means [which are conceived as conventional truth in that they are directed to enlightening sentient beings]—are embodied in [supreme] truth, [the theory being that conventional truth is rooted in supreme truth].[78] But it ought to be known that supreme truth is [conversely] embodied in conventional truth [inasmuch as supreme truth is expressed only through the media of conventional truth]. As previously stated, the three teachings sever the notions of self which causes greed and idleness and which obstructs the bringing about of peace to all sentient beings; and conceit which makes one give offerings and pay homage to oneself. These are [the ways] to sever the obstacles which prevent [the realization of] the enlightened mind *[bodhi]*. They ought to be known.

The previously explained [Section VII] three pure states of the mind—the undefiled, peace, and bliss—are abridged as one [all-encompassing] mind, which is the perfection of the state of supreme bliss and the highest truth.[79] It ought to be known.

### [IX. Perfection of All Things Vowed]

Thus [the mind of] the bodhisattvas [embodying] wisdom, means, nonobstacles, and supreme truth, arises to purify the Buddha-land. It ought to be known that this [state of mind] is called the bodhisattva-mahāsattvas's self-abiding perfection, which accomplishes all things according to will by following the five teachings [i.e., the five items of mindfulness], because, as mentioned previously, the works of body [worship], speech [praise], mind [vow], wisdom [meditation], and means [transferring of merits] are in accord with the teachings [of the Buddha].

[X. The Practices to Benefit Others]

There are also the five teachings which gradually [enable the bodhisattvas to] perfect merits [as the result of having practiced the five items of mindfulness]. They ought to be known. What are the five?

1. Nearing [Pure Land by worshipping Amitāyus]
2. Joining the congregation [which praises Amitāyus]
3. [Entering Amitāyus's] domain [by vowing to be born in his Pure Land]
4. [Entering his] palace
5. [Entering] the garden of saṃsāra and enjoying [the work to save others]

Among these five, the first four [deal with] the perfection of entering [the realm of] merits [i.e., leaving the realm of saṃsāra and entering Pure Land by accumulating merits]; the fifth, the perfection of coming out from [the realm of] merits [i.e., coming out from Pure Land and entering saṃsāra to transfer merits for the benefit of others].

The first of [the four] entrances enables one to realize birth in Pure Land by worshipping Amitāyus and desiring to be born in his Land. This is called the first entrance gate.

The second is to join the congregation [in Pure Land] by praising Amitāyus, by chanting the name of Tathāgata [Amitāyus] with the understanding of what his name means, and by cultivating practices which are illuminated by the tathāgata's light of wisdom. This is called the second entrance gate.

The third is to realize entrance to the world of the lotus-store by vowing with whole-heartedness to be born in Pure Land and by practicing *śamatha-samādhi* of tranquility. This is called the third entrance gate.

The fourth is the enjoyment of the dharma-flavored blisses, after reaching Pure Land, by observing the glory [of Pure Land] and by cultivating *vipaśyanā*.

The fifth is to observe the sufferings of all sentient beings with great compassion: revealing oneself in transformed bodies, entering the garden of saṃsāra, the grove of delusions, and reaching the realm of converting others by delightfully exercising superknowledge, because [the purpose of] the primary vow [of the Buddha] is to transfer merits. This is called the fifth gate, the gate of exit [from nirvāṇa].

The bodhisattvas perfect the practices of benefiting self at the four entrance gates. These [practices] ought to be known. The bodhisattvas perfect the practices of transferring merits [accumulated at the previous four gates] to enlighten others at the fifth, the gate of exit. The bodhisattvas thus cultivate the practices of the five items of mindfulness, enlighten themselves and others, and thereby perfect supreme enlightenment *[anuttara-samyak-saṃbodhi]* immediately.[80]

[Conclusion]

The essence of "The Verses on the Vow to be Born in Pure Land Paradise and the Instructions on the Sūtra on Eternal Life" has been interpreted.

## NOTES

I wish to express my very deep gratitude to Dr. Gadgin Nagao, Professor Emeritus of Kyōto University, for his instructions in the composition of this essay and in the translation of the text; and to Dr. Susumu Yamaguchi, Professor Emeritus of Ōtani University, with whom I consulted many years ago. Without their help, this paper could not have been prepared. Any misrepresentation, however, is my sole responsibility.

1. For a biographical account of Vasubandhu, see Taishō vol. 50, no. 2049, pp. 188 ff.

2. For a biographical account of Bodhiruci, see Taishō vol. 49, no. 2043, pp. 48, 88.

3. See Taishō vol. 26, no. 1524, pp. 230–233.

4. Sir M. Monier-Williams, *Sanskrit-English Dictionary*, new ed. (Lon-

don: Oxford University Press, 1951), p. 1221b–c.

5. See the *Larger Sukhāvatī-vyūha-sūtra*, translated by K'ang seng K'ai as *Fo-shuo wu-liang-shou ching*, Taishō vol. 12, no. 360, p. 271b.

6. Monier-Williams, *Sanskrit-English Dictionary*, p. 1041a.

7. *Ibid.*, p. 199a.

8. *Ibid.*, p. 81c. In Tantrism, Aṃrta, which Monier-Williams defines as "immortal" (p. 82b), is a Brahmanic deity which Buddhism may have incorporated into its pantheon. But there is no evidence to suggest a correlationship between Aṃrta and Amita, historically or doctrinally, in the Sino-Japanese Pure Land tradition.

9. For a study on the seven patriarchs, see Tatsurō Fujishima and Shunjō Nogami, *Dentō no seija [The Sages of the Transmission of the Lamp]* (Kyoto: Heiraku-ji shoten, 1961).

10. For a biographical account of Hōnen, see Harper H. Coates and R. Ishizuka, *Hōnen the Buddhist Saint* (Kyoto: Society for the Publication of Sacred Books of the World, 1949).

11. Biographical accounts of Shinran in Japanese are numerous. One of the most exhaustive studies is Junkō Matsuno, *Shinran* (Tokyo: Sanshō-dō, 1968).

12. Taishō vol. 12, no. 360.

13. Translated as *Fo-shuo kuan-wu-liang-shou-fo ching*, Taishō vol. 12, no. 365.

14. Translated as *Fo-shuo a-mi-t'o ching*, Taishō vol. 12, no. 366.

15. T'an-luan, *Wang-sheng lun-chu*, Taishō vol. 40, no. 1819.

16. Shinran, *Kyō-gyō-shin-shō*, Taishō vol. 83, no. 2646. The title of the text is taken from the chapter headings of the text. The text essentially is an analysis of the eighteenth vow, considered the primary vow in the Japanese Jōdo and Jōdo Shin traditions, related in the *Larger Sukhāvatī-vyūha-sūtra*. According to Shinran, the primary vow embraces vows eleven, twelve, thirteen, and seventeen. The eleventh vow enables all beings to realize through birth in Pure Land through the merits of Buddha Amitāyus. The twelfth is to enlighten all beings of all quarters (Eternal Light Vow). The thirteenth is to enlighten all beings at all times (Eternal Life Vow). The seventeenth assures the penetration of compassion to all quarters of the universe. "Teaching" and "Practice" refer to the seventeenth vow. "Realization" refers to the eleventh. Though not indicated in the title, the *Kyō-gyō-shin-shō* has two more chapters: "The True Realm of the Buddha" and "The Realm of the Transformed Buddha." The former refers to the twelfth vow, the latter to the thirteenth. Finally, "Faith" refers to the eighteenth vow, which as previously noted is inclusive of the eleventh, twelfth, thirteenth, and seventeenth vows. "Faith" means faith in the primary vow.

17. Susumu Yamaguchi, "Ryūju-seshin ni okeru jōdo shisō" [Pure Land

Thought of Nāgārjuna and Vasubandhu], in Shōshon Miyamoto, ed. and comp., *Bukkyō no konpon shinri [Fundamental Truth of Buddhism]* (Tokyo: Sanyōsha, 1956), p. 593; see also pp. 608–609.

18. Shinya Kasugai, "Jōdo kyōten no keisei" [The Development of Pure Land Literature], in Miyamoto, *Bukkyō no konpon shinri*, p. 517. See also Mitsuyuki Ishida, *Jōdo-kyō kyōri-shi [History of Pure Land Doctrine]* (Kyoto: Heiraku-ji shoten, 1962), pp. 14–27.

19. Susumu Yamaguchi, *Daijō to shite no jōdo [Pure Land as a Mahāyāna School]* (Tokyo: Riso-sha, 1963), pp. 76 ff.

20. *Ibid.*

21. Taishō vol. 12, no. 360, p. 268a (ii.26–28).

22. Monier-Williams, *Sanskrit-English Dictionary*, p. 127c.

23. *Sukhāvatīvyūhopadeśa*, p. 230c (1.4).

24. *Ibid.*, p. 231b (11.18–20).

25. *Ibid.*, p. 231b (11.17–18).

26. *Ibid.*, p. 231b (11.19–20).

27. Monier-Williams, *Sanskrit-English Dictionary*, p. 564b.

28. *Sukhāvatīvyūhopadeśa*, p. 231 (11.23–24).

29. *Ibid.*, p. 231b (11.25–26).

30. *Ibid.*, p. 232a (11.12–13).

31. *Ibid.*, p. 232b (11.28–29).

32. *Ibid.*, p. 232b (11.1–3). Mahāyāna texts generally conceive fifty-two stages of bodhisattva practices, as follows: (1) ten stages of faith, (2) ten stages of understanding, (3) ten stages of practice, (4) ten stages of transferring merits, (5) ten final bodhisattva stages, and (6) *samyak-sambuddha* and *annutara-samyak-sambuddha*. The final bodhisattva stages are referred to as *bhūmis*. Following them are the two buddha-stages. The *Sukhāvatīvyūhopadeśa* articulates the ten *bhūmis (daśabhūmi)* as: (1) joyous stage *(pramuditā)*, (2) immaculate stage *(vimala)*, (3) light-giving stage *(prabhākarī)*, (4) brilliant stage *(arciṣmatī)*, (5) difficult-to-conquer stage *(sudurjaya)*, (6) coming face to face with wisdom *(abhimukhī)*, (7) far-reaching stage *(dūraṁgamā)*, (8) immovable stage *(acala)*, (9) power-perfection stage *(sādhumatī)*, and (10) dharma stage *(dharmameghā)*.

The ten *bhūmis* can be divided into three categories: (1) knowledge, corresponding to the first stage, *pramuditā*; (2) practice, consisting of the five pāramitās (*vimala*, *prabhākarī*, *arciṣmatī*, *sudurjaya*, and *abhimukhī*, corresponding to *śīla*, *kṣānti*, *vīrya*, samādhi and prajñā, respectively), and *dāna* (*dūraṁgamā*, *acala*, and *sādhumatī*, corresponding to *upāya*, vow, and caused without recognition, respectively); and (3) realization, corresponding to the last stage, *dharmameghā*. The rationale underlying these three categories is that knowledge has its validity only when it is translated into practice, only through which realization is possible. Practice therefore is of paramount importance. It consists of the five pāramitās, which are self-disciplinary practices, and *dāna*, which, in the context of the *Sukhāvatīvyūhopadeśa*, is transferring merits.

33. *Sukhāvatīvyūhopadeśa*, p. 232b (11.23–27).

34. Edward Conze, *Buddhist Thought in India* (London: George Allen and Unwin, 1962), p. 172, note.

35. Susumu Yamaguchi, Enichi Ōchō, Toshio Andō, and Issai Funabashi, *Bukkyō-gaku josetsu [Introduction to Buddhism]* (Kyoto: Heiraku-ji shoten, 1961), pp. 616–617.

36. Minoru Kiyota, "Shingon Mikkyō Maṇḍala," *History of Religion* VIII (August, 1968): 39–49.

37. Yutaka Iwamoto, *Gokuraku to Jigoku [Hell and Paradise]* (Tokyo: San'ichi shobō, 1965), pp. 88–92.

38. Tominaga Nakamoto (1715–1746) probably was the first historian to claim that Mahāyāna literature does not represent the actual sayings of the Buddha, and that it is extremely doubtful whether the Āgamas of Theravāda tradition constitute an actual record of the Buddha. See his *Shutsujō gogo* in Hajime Nakamura, Bunyū Masutani, and Joseph M. Kitagawa, eds., *Gendai bukkyō meicho zenshū [Collection of Modern Works on Buddhism]*, vol. I (Tokyo: Ryubunkan, 1971). See "Shutsu-jō gogo," p. 7 ff. Richard Robinson states: "Modern philologists in the West, India, and Japan have done sufficient work on the Pāli Canon to discredit the orthodox Theravāda view as to its authorship and literal reporting of Śākyamuni's words." See his "Implications of Human Sciences for Buddhism," unpublished manuscript, p. 9.

39. The note was observed by this writer at Vien Hoa Dao, Saigon, in July 1965.

40. See *Shinshu seikyō zenshū [Collected Works on the Sacred Teachings of the True Pure Land School]*, vol. 1, (Kyoto: Kōkyo shoin, 1940), p. 330 *(Lun-chu)*; and p. 410 *(An yao-chi)*.

41. Bhagavāt = Bhagavān, meaning the glorious, divine, adorable, venerable. It refers to the Buddha.

42. One mindedness = the mind which embraces three kinds of faith: in Buddha Amitāyus, in the Pure Land Dharma, and in realizing birth in Pure Land.

43. The "ways" refer to the paths of the beings of the six destinies: hellish beings, hungry ghosts, beasts, fighting spirits, men, and gods.

44. Three worlds = (1) world of desire *(kāma-dhātu)*, (2) world of form *(rūpa-dhātu)*, and (3) formless world *(arūpya-dhātu)*.

45. "Wholesome roots" refer to sense organs which produce wholesome actions. Here the term refers to absence of greed, hate, and delusion.

46. Saṃsāra = transmigration of beings in the six destinies.

47. Undefiled (absence of *kleśa*) lights = pure-mind-wisdom, i.e., wisdom absent of such mental defilements as greed, hate, and delusion.

48. "They" refer to the beings of Pure Land, i.e., the bodhisattvas who are the transformed bodies of Buddha Amitāyus.

49. Dhyāna is a form of meditation to calm the mind and to realize pure mind by eliminating mental defilements.

50. Samādhi is another form of meditation. It enables one to realize the state of cessation of conceptual discrimination. Samādhi is realized through dhyāna.

51. A śrāvaka, literally a "hearer," is a direct disciple of Śākyamuni. A pratyekabuddha, literally a "lone-buddha," is one who realizes enlightenment without the aid of a master. Both attempt to realize self-enlightenment. As such, Mahāyāna gives them a lower rating than a bodhisattva, one destined for self-enlightenment who yet renounces it to work for the enlightenment of all beings.

52. The description of the buddhas and bodhisattvas by a variety of marks is a tradition which probably developed in Gandhāra, possibly under the influence of Greek art. The tradition of depicting the buddhas and bodhisattvas with thirty-two major marks and eighty minor ones was presumably established then. It was an attempt to depict the buddhas and bodhisattvas as superhuman. For details of these marks see Har Dayl, *The Bodhisattva Doctrine in Buddhist Sanskrit Literature* (London: Kegan Paul, Trench, Trubner and Co., 1932), pp. 299–305. With reference to the term "one arm's length," the Chinese reads *i-hsin*, a term understood to be "two arms' length" (not one), roughly six feet. But even this length is quite unreasonable, for the Buddha is alleged to have possessed "unobstructed and immeasurable light" which shines on the whole universe. The term *i-hsin* is the artist's concept of immeasurable light, which is actually depicted as two arms' length of the Buddha.

53. The five elements represent a metaphoric description of the qualities of the tathāgata.

54. "Pure-wisdom" is the *Sukhāvatīvyūhopadeśa*'s version of *ādarśa-jñāna* of the Yogācāra school.

55. Indian cosmology conceives of Mount Sumeru as the center of the universe.

56. "Jewel-sea" = the realm of the Buddha, which contains many jewels.

57. "Immaculate Wheel of the Dharma" refers to the spreading of the Pure Land Dharma.

58. "Original position" refers to Pure Land.

59. "To see the Buddha" means to have faith in the Buddha. The *Nirvāṇa Sūtra* (Ch. 27) also speaks of "seeing the Buddha," the implication being that without faith one cannot "see" or "hear" the Buddha. Taishō vol. 12, nos. 374, 375.

60. The terms "good sons and daughters" *(kulaputra* and *kuladuhitṛ)*, employed in the *Sukhāvatīvyūhopadeśa*, specifically refer to those who chant the name of Buddha Amitāyus to realize birth in Pure Land.

61. See notes 34 and 35.

62. "Arhat" means one who has attained the stage of "no further learning" *(aśaikṣa)* and therefore is worthy of receiving the offerings of others.

63. *Samyak-saṃbuddha* literally means the correctly and completely enlightened buddha; omniscience.

64. The term "name" refers to the name of the Tathāgata; "essence" refers to his wisdom. "Name-essence" therefore means the knowing of what the name "tathāgata" stands for.

65. "Illumination" means the (external) marks of wisdom. The term is employed to indicate that the Buddha's wisdom is capable of illuminating all quarters. Illumination and wisdom are distinguished here to indicate that wisdom (prajñā) is the source of the tathāgata's illumination.

66. This sentence means that the practice of chanting the name of Buddha Amitāyus, referred to as *nien-fu* in Chinese and *nembutsu* in Japanese, brings about the response of Buddha Amitāyus.

67. "Right-mindfulness" means not doubting that one will be born in Pure Land.

68. "Power beyond conceptual thought" *(acintya)* means Buddha-wisdom or superknowledge *(abhijñā)*: psychic power, heavenly eyes, cognition of the extinction of the outflows of mental impurities. These are attributes assigned to the Buddha.

69. "*Cintāmaṇi*" = a legendary wishing-jewel believed to have been extracted from the head of Nāga-rāja which produces all things one wills.

70. In Buddhism, the term "supreme truth" *(paramārtha-satya)* is employed in contradistinction to conventional truth *(loka-saṃvṛti-satya)*. "Supreme truth" refers to dharmakāya (or tathatā), which is described in terms of the seventeen marks of Pure Land. Conventional truth, which is here described as "the wondrous realm," is the manifestation of supreme truth.

71. "Vows of the Buddha" refer to the forty-eight vows that Buddha Amitāyus made while he was Bodhisattva Dharmākara, as explained in the *Sukhāvatī-vyūha-sūtra*.

72. "One-Dharma" refers to tathatā. "Tathatā" in the *Sukhāvatīvyūhopadeśa* means Pure Land.

73. *Asaṃskṛta* means unconditioned. "Dharmakāya" refers to tathatā. *Asaṃskṛta-dharmakāya* therefore means that which is cognized by pure mind.

74. "Physical world" *(bhājana-loka)* here means Pure Land. Yamaguchi's contention that Pure Land is the *Sukhāvatīvyūhopadeśa*'s version of *ādarśa-jñāna* is, perhaps, derived from the notion that the purified physical world of saṃsāra is Pure Land.

75. The vow (to be born in Pure Land) is equated with *śamatha*; meditation (on the glories of Pure Land) is equated with *vipaśyanā*. The twenty-nine merits are divided into the "short" and the "long" forms of practice.

"Short" refers to the realization of One Dharma into which the essence of the twenty-nine merits are distilled. "Long" refers to the twenty-nine merits, not the distilled essence. But whether distilled into an essence or not, the twenty-nine merits are the "objects" of *vipaśyanā*, meaning, therefore, that the "objects" of *vipaśyanā* can be described either in terms of the "short" One-Dharma version or the "long" twenty-nine merit version. But as *śamatha* is prerequisite to *vipaśyanā* (that is, *vipaśyanā* is realized with *śamatha* practice), *śamatha* includes both the "short" and the "long" forms of practice as well. The correlation between *śamatha-vipaśyanā* and the "short" and the "long" forms of practice is:

| | | |
|---|---|---|
| śamatha | short | (One Dharma) |
| vipaśyanā | long | (twenty-nine merits) |

76. The Chinese reads *jou-uan*, soft or tender. The term refers to the functions of *śamatha-vipaśyanā*, i.e., one can realize Pure Land either in the "short" One-Dharma version or in the "long" twenty-nine merit version.

77. That is, the "principle" that Pure Land can be realized in either its "short" or its "long" version.

78. The Chinese reads *chih-hui*, a translation of "prajñā." Because the same line also employs the term *pan-yao*, a transliteration of "prajñā," the terms must be distinguished. *Pan-yao* means inherent wisdom; *chih-hui* is acquired wisdom. The former cognizes tathatā. The latter is the wisdom manifested as *upāya*. Inherent wisdom gives rise to acquired wisdom by confronting the problems of saṃsāra. Hence, acquired wisdom (karuṇā) and *upāya* are synonymous.

79. Highest truth. It means *paramārtha-satya*. See note 70.

80. See note 63.

# Bibliography

WESTERN WORKS AND TRANSLATIONS

The following abbreviations are used in the Bibliography.

| | |
|---|---|
| WZKSO | Wiener Zeitschrift für die Kunde Sud-und Ostastiens und Archiv für Indische Philosophie |
| PQ | Philosophical Quarterly |
| JBBRAS | The Journal of the Bombay Branch of the Royal Asiatic Society |
| JOAS | The Journal of Asian Studies |
| PEW | Philosophy East and West |
| JBORS | Journal of the Bihar and Orissa Research Society |
| BSOAS | (London University) School of Oriental and African Studies Bulletin |


Bettoni, E. *Duns Scotus*. Washington: Catholic University of America Press, 1961.

Bury, R. G. *Timaeus* of Plato. Cambridge: Harvard University Press, 1961.

Chang, Garma C. C. *The Buddhist Teaching of Totality*. University Park: Pennsylvania State University Press, 1971.

Coates, Harper H. and R. Ishizuka, *Hōnan the Buddhist Saint*. Kyoto: Society for the Publication of Sacred Books of the World, 1949.

Conze, Edward. *Aṣṭasāhasrikā Prajñāpāramitā*. Calcutta: Asiatic Society, 1958.

———. "Buddhist Saviors" in *The Savior God*. Manchester, England, 1963.

———. *Buddhist Thought in India.* London: Allen and Unwin, 1962.
———. *Buddhist Wisdom Books.* London: Allen and Unwin, 1958.
———. *The Large Sutra on Perfect Wisdom.* London: Luzac, 1961.
———. *Thirty Years of Buddhist Studies.* Columbia: University of South Carolina Press, 1968.

Cook, Frank. "The Meaning of Vairocana in Hua-yen Buddhism," PEW, vol. 22, 1972.

Dayl, Har. *The Bodhisattva Doctrine in Buddhist Sanscrit.* London: Kegan Paul, Trench, Trubner and Co., 1932.

Demieville, Paul. *Le Concile de Lhasa.* Paris: Bibliotheque de l'Institut des Hautes Études Chinoises, vol. VII, 1952.

Eggeling, Julius. *Śatapatha-Brāhmaṇa.* Delhi: The Sacred Books of the East, 1963.

Eliade, Mircea. "Time and Eternity in Indian Thought." Reprinted in *Man and Time,* 1958 (papers from the Eranos Yearbooks. vol. 20, 1951, pp. 219–252).

———. *Yoga: Immortality and Freedom.* Princeton: Princeton University Press, 1969.

Feinberg, I. "Hallucinations, Dreaming, and REM Sleep." in *Origins and Mechanisms of Hallucinations.* New York: Plenum Press, 1970.

Fowler, Harold N. Sophist *of Plato.* Cambridge: Harvard University Press, 1961.

Frauwallner, E. "Dignaga, sein Werk und seine Entwicklung." WZKSO, Bd. III, 1959.

Gokhale, V. V. "The *Abhidharmakośakārikā* of Vasubandhu." *Journal of Asiatic Society of Bombay,* New Series 22 (1946): 73–102.

———. "Fragments from the *Abhidharmasamuccaya.*" JBBRAS, vol. 23, 1957.

Govier, T. "Variations on Force and Vivacity in Hume." PQ, vol. 22, 1972.

Gregory the Great, St. *Morals on Job.* Oxford Library of Fathers, 1851.

Hattori, M. *Dignāga on Perception.* Cambridge: Harvard University Press, 1968.

Horner, I. B. *Majjhima Nikāya, The Collection of Middle Length Sayings.* London: Luzac (for the Pāli Text Society), 1954.

Hume, David. *A Treatise on Human Nature.* Cambridge: Oxford University Press, 1975.

Hurvitz, Leon. "The Road to Buddhist Salvation as Described by Vasubhadra." JOAS 87:4.

I-tsing. *Records of the Buddhist Religion.* Translated by J. Takakusu. Oxford: Clarendon Press, 1896.

Johnston, E. H., ed. *The Ratnagotravibhāga Mahāyānottaratantraśāstra.* Patna: Bihar Research Society, 1950.

Kajiyama, Yuichi. *An Introduction to Buddhist Philosophy*. Translation of the *Tarkabhāṣā* of Mokṣākaragupta. Kyoto: Memoirs of the Faculty of Kyoto University, 1966.

Kern, K., trans. *Saddharmapuṇḍarīka Sūtra*. New York: Dover Publications, 1963.

Kirchberger, C. *Richard of St. Victor: Selected Writings on Contemplation*. London: Faber and Faber, 1957.

Kirk and Raven. *The Presocratic Philosophers*. New York and London: Cambridge Press, 1969.

Kiyota, Minoru. "Singon Mikkyō Mandala." *History of Religion* 8 (1968): 31–59.

Lamotte, Etienne. *L'Enseignement de Vimalakīrti*. Louvain: Bibliothèque du Muséon, 1962.

______. *Histoire de Bouddhisme Indien*. Louvain: Bibliothèque de Muséon, 1958.

______. *La somme du grand vehicule d'Asanga* (Mahāyāṇasaṃgraha). Louvain: Bureaux du Muséon, 1938.

______. *Le Traité de la grande vertu de sagesse de Nāgārjuna*. Louvain: Université de Louvain, Institut Orientaliste, vol. I, 1944; vol. II, 1949; vol. III, 1970.

La Vallée-Poussin, Louis de, ed. and trans. *L'Abhidharmakośa*. Paris: P. Geuthner, 1923–31.

______. *Bouddhisme: Opinions sur l'histoire de la dogmatique*. Paris: G. Beauchesne, 1925.

______, ed. Madyamakāvatāra *of Candrakīrti*. St. Petersbourg, 1912.

______. *Vijñaptimātratā-siddhi (La siddhi de Hiuan-Tsang)*. Paris: Geuthner, 1928–48.

Levi, Sylvain, ed. *Mahāyānasutralāṃkāra*. Paris: H. Champion, 1907.

______, ed. *Viṃśatika*. Paris: H. Champion, 1925.

Matilal, B. K. *Epistemology, Logic, and Grammar in Indian Philosophical Analysis*. The Hague: Mouton, 1971.

May, Jacques, trans. Prasannapadā Madhyamakavṛtti *of Candrakirti*. Paris: Adrien Maisonneuve, 1959.

McDermott, Charlene. "Direct Sensory Awareness." PEW (July 1973): 343–60.

______. *An Eleventh Century Buddhist Logic of "Exists."* Dordrecht, Holland: D. Reidel Publishing Co., 1969.

Monier-Williams, Sir M. *Sanskrit-English Dictionary*. London: Oxford University Press, 1951.

Nagao, Gadjin M., ed. Madyāntavibhāgabhāṣya *of Vasubandhu*. Tokyo: Suzuki Research Foundation, 1964.

Nishida, Kitaro. *A Study of Good*. Tokyo: Print Bureau, Japanese Government, 1960.

Obermiller, Y. Y. *Analysis of the* Abhisamayālaṃkāra. London: E. J. Brill, 1933.

Rahula, Walpola. *What the Buddha Taught*. Rev. ed. Bedford, England: G. Fraser, 1967.

Robinson, Richard. *The Buddhist Religion*. California: Dickenson Publishing Co., 1970.

———. *Early Madyāmika in India and China*. Madison: University of Wisconsin Press, 1968.

———. "Implications of Human Sciences for Buddhism." Unpublished manuscript.

Ruegg, David Seyfort. *La théorie du Tathagatagarbha et du gotra*. Paris Ecole François d'Extrême Orient, 1969.

Sankṛtyayana, Rahula, ed. "Commentary on Dharmakirti's *Pramāṇavārttika*." JBORS Appendix to vols. XXIV, XXV, XXVI, 1938–40.

Shackleton Bailley, D. R. *The* Satapañcaśatka *of Māṭrceṭa*. Cambridge: University Press, 1951.

Shah, J. *Akalanka's Criticism of Dharmakirti's Philosophy*. Ahmedabad, 1967.

Shastri, Swami Dwarikadas, ed. *Śāntarakṣita's* Tattvasaṃgraha, with Pañjika of Kamalasila. Varanasi: Buddha Bharati, 1968.

Sopa, Geshe and Jones, E. "A Light to Yogācāra Svātantrika: the Three Bhāvanākramas of Kamalaśila." Unpublished manuscript.

Staal, J. F. "Negation and the Law of Contradiction in Indian Thought: a Comparative Study." BSOAS 25 (1962): 52–71.

Stcherbatsky, F. T. *Buddhist Logic*. New York: Dover Publications, 1962.

———, trans. *Madhyāntavibhāgasūtra*. Bibliotheca Buddhica XXX, 1936.

Suzuki, D. T., trans. *Laṇkāvatara Sūtra*. London: Routledge and Kegan Paul, 1925.

Takakusu, J. M., trans. *Records of the Buddhist Religion by I-tsing*. Oxford: Clarendon Press, 1896.

Takasaki, Jikido. *A Study on the Ratnagotravibhāga*. Roma: Instituto Italiano per il Medro ed Estremo Oriente, 1966.

Tart, C. *Altered States of Consciousness*. New York: John Wiley & Sons, 1969.

Taylor, T. "*De Anthro Nympharum* of Porphory." In *Select Works of Porphory*. London: T. Rodd, 1823.

Thomas, E. J. *The Life of Buddha as Legend and History*. London: Routledge and Kegan Paul, 1960.

Tucci, G. *Minor Buddhist Texts*. Roma: Instituto Italiano per il Medro ed Estremo Oriente, Part I, 1956; Part II, 1958.

Vajirañaṇa, Mahathera. *Buddhist Meditation*. Columbo, Ceylon: M.D. Gunasena, 1962.

Vanhoye, Albert. *Situation du Christ*. Paris, 1969.

Warren, Henry Clarke, trans. Buddhaghosa's *Visuddhimagga*. Cambridge: Harvard University Press, 1950.
Wayman, A. "The Buddhist Theory of Vision." In *Añjāli*. Peradeniya, 1970.

## SANSKRIT AND PĀLI WORKS

### *Sūtras*

*Aṅgutarra-nikāya*. Bihar: Pāli Publication Board, 1960. Also London: Oxford University Press, 1951–55, for the Pāli Text Society.
*Kathāvatthu*. Bihar: Pāli Publication Board, 1961. Also London: M. Milford, 1915, for the Pāli Text Society.
*Laṅkāvatāra-sūtra*. B. Nanjio, ed., Kyoto: Otani University Press, 1956. P. L. Vaidya, ed., Patna: K. P. Jayaswal Research Institute.
*Saddharmapuṇḍarika-sūtra*. B. Nanjio, ed., St. Petersbourg: Bibliotheca Buddhica X, 1912. (See also: Kern, H.)
*Samādhirāja-sūtra*. P. L. Vaidya, ed., Darbhanga: Mithila Institute, 1961.
*Sukhāvatīvyūha-sūtra*. Translated in *Buddhist Mahāyāna Texts*. Delhi: Motilal Banarsidass, 1965.
*Vimalakīrtinirdeśa*.See Lamotte, E.

### *Śāstras*

Asaṅga. *Abhidharmasamuccaya*. P. Pradhan, ed., Santiniketan: Visva-Bharati, 1950.
*Bodhisattvabhūmi*. U. Wogihara, ed., Tokyo: 1930–36.
*Mahāyānasaṃgraha*. See Lamotte, E.
Candrakīrti. *Madhyamakāvatāra*. See La Vallée-Poussin, L. de.
*Prasannapadā*. See May, J.
Dharmakīrti. *Nyāyabindu*. F. Stcherbatsky, ed., St. Petersbourg: Bibliotheca Buddhica VII, 1918.
*Pramāṇavārttika*. Sandrtyayana, ed., Varanasi: Bauddha Bharati, 1968.
Dharmottara. *Nyāyabinduṭīkā*. F. Stcherbatsky, ed., St. Petersbourg: Bibliotheca Buddhica VII, 1918.
Jñānaśrīmitra. *Yogiṇirnayaprakārana*. A. Thakur, ed., Patna: Kashi-Prasad Jayaswal Research Institute, 1959.
Kamalaśila. See Tucci, G.; also Shastri, S. D.
Maitreya [-natha]. *Madhyāntavibhāga*. Battacharya, V. S., and Tucci, G., eds., London: Luzac, 1932 (Calcutta Oriental Series no. 24). Pandeya, R. C., Delhi, 1971. See also Stcherbatsky, F. T.
*Mahāyānasutralāṃkāra*. See Levi, C.
*Ratnagotravibhāga (Uttaratantra)*. See Johnston, E. H.; also Takasaki, J.

Māṭrceṭa. *Satapañcaśatka*. See Shackleton Bailey, D. R.
Mokṣākaragupta. *Tarkabhāṣā*. See Kajiyama, Y.
Nāgārjuna. *Vigrahavyāvartanī*. Patna: edited for K. P. Jayaswal Research Institute, 1960.
Ratnakīrti. *Nibandhāvalī*. A. Thakur, ed., Patna: K. P. Jayaswal Research Institute, 1957. (Tibetan Sanscrit Works Series vol. III).
See also McDermott, C., *An Eleventh Century Logic of "Exists."*
Śāntarakṣita. See Sastri, D. S.
Vasubandhu. *Abhidharmakośa* See La Vallée-Poussin, L. de.
*Madhyāntavibhāgabhāṣya*. See Nagao, G. M.
*Viṃśatika*. See Levi, S.
Yasomitra. *Abhidharmakośa vyākhya*. Wogihara, U., ed., Tokyo, 1932–36.

## PĀLI CANON

Bihar: Pāli Publication Board, 1960–62.

## TIBETAN WORKS

### *Sūtras*

*Prajñāpāramitā-sūtra* (Pañcavimśati). T. T. (see Tibetan Canons) vol. 88, no. 5188.
*Sandhinirmocana-sūtra*. T. T. vol. 29, no. 744.

### *Śāstras and Classical Works, Including Translations*

Asaṅga. *Bodhisattvabhūmi [Rnal 'byor spyod pa'i sa las byang chub sems dpa'i sa]*. T. T. vol. 110, no. 5538.
*Śrāvaka bhūmi [Rnal 'byor spyod pa'i sa las nyan thos khi sa]*. T. T. vol. 110, no. 5537.
'Jams dbyangs bzhad pa. *Sgrub mtha' chen mo*. Tibetan block print.
Je btsun pa. *Dbus ma'i sphyi don*. Tibetan block print.
Jig med dbang bo. *Rin po che'i phreng ba*.
Kamalasila. *Madyamakālaṃkārapañjika* [Tibetan translation]. T. T. vol. 101, no. 5286.
Maitreya [-natha]. *Abhisamayālaṃkāra kārikā* [Tibetan translation]. T. T. vol. 88, no. 5184.
*Madhyānta-vibhāga kārikā* [Tibetan translation]. T. T. vol. 108, no. 5522.
*Mahāyāna sutrālaṃkāra kārikā* [Tibetan translation]. T. T. vol. 108, no. 5521.
Mchims 'jam dbyangs. *'Grel pa mngon pa'i rgyan*. Tibetan block print.
Nāgārjuna. *Prajña nama mulamadhyāmaka kārikā* [Tibetan translation]. T. T. vol. 95, no. 5224.

*Śunyatāsaptati-kārikā* [Tibetan translation]. T. T. vol. 95, no. 5227.
*Vigraha-vyavartinī-kārikā* [Tibetan translation]. T. T. vol. 95, no. 5228.
*Yuktisaṣṭika* [Tibetan translation]. T. T. vol 95, no. 5225.
Ratnākaraśānti. *Prajñāparamitopadeśa* [Tibetan translation]. T. T. vol. 114, no. 5579.
Rgyal tshab. *Rig thigs 'grel pa.* Tibetan block print.
*Rnam bshad snying po'i rgyan.* Tibetan block print.
*Thar lam bsal byed.*Tibetan block print.
Śāntarakṣita. *Madhyamakālaṃkāra-kārikā* [Tibetan translation]. T. T. vol. 101, no. 5284.
*Madhyamakālaṃkāravṛtti* [Tibetan translation]. T. T. vol. 101, no. 5285.
Tsong kha pa. *Lam rim chen mo [Skyes bu gsum gyi nyams su blang ba'i rim pa thams cad tshang bar ston ba'i byang chub lam gyi rim pa].* T.T. vol. 152, no. 6001.
*Legs bshad snying po [Drang ba dang nges pa'i don rnam par phye ba'i bstan bcos legs bshad snying po shes bya ba].* T. T. vol. 153, no. 6142.
*Rigs pa'i rgya mtsho [Dbu ma rtsa ba'i tshig le'ur byas pa shes rab ces bya ba'i rnam bzhad rigs pa'i rgya mtsho shes bya ba].* T. T. vol. 156, no. 6153.
Vasubandhu. *Abhidharmakośakārikā* [Tibetan translation]. T. T. vol. 115, no. 5590.
*Trimśika kārikā* [Tibetan translation]. T. T. vol. 113, no. 556.

*Tibetan Canons*

[T. T.] *The Tibetan Tripitaka.* Peking reprint edition. Daisetz T. Suzuki, ed. Tokyo: Suzuki Research Foundation, 1962.

## CHINESE AND JAPANESE WORKS

*Sūtras*

*Amitāyur-dhyāna-sūtra.* Taishō vol. 12, no. 336.
*Avataṃsaka-sūtra.* Taishō vol. 9, no. 278, and Taishō vol. 10, no. 279.
*Ch'ang a-han ching.* Taishō vol. 1, no. 1.
*Chung a-han ching.* Taishō vol. 1, no. 26.
*Keyūra-sūtra.* Taishō vol. 16, no. 656, and Taishō vol. 24, no. 1485.
*Larger Sukhāvatīvyūha-sūtra.* Taishō vol. 12, no. 360.
*Mahāyāna-parinirvāṇa-sūtra.* Taishō vol. 12, nos. 374, 375.
*Pieh yi tsa a-han ching.* Taishō vol. 2, no. 100.
*Prajñāpāramitā-hrdaya-sūtra.* Taishō vol. 8, nos. 251–56.
*Smaller Sukhāvatīvyūha-sūtra.* Taishō vol. 12, no. 365.

*Tsa a-han ching.* Taishō vol. 2, nos. 99, 101.
*Tseng-i a-han ching.* Taishō vol. 2, no. 125.
*Vajracchedikā prajñāpāramitā-sūtra.* Taishō vol. 8, nos. 235–37.

*Śāstras and Classical Works, Including Translations*

Chien Ch'ien-i. *Pan-jo hsin ching lueh shu hsiao ch'ao.* Zokuzōkyō I.41 (pp. 357–90).
Chung-hsi. *Pan-jo hsin ching lueh shu hsien cheng chi.* Zokuzōkyō I.41 (pp. 340–56).
Fa-tsang. *Hua-yen i ch'eng chiao i fen-ch'i chang.* Taishō vol. 45, no. 1866.
*Pan-jo po-lo-mi-to hsin ching lueh shu.* Taishō vol. 33, no. 1712.
Nāgārjuna. *Bodhicitta-śāstra.* Taishō vol. 32, no. 1665.
Sāramati. *Ta-ch'eng fa-chieh wu ch'a-pieh lun.* Taishō vol. 31, nos. 1626–27.
Shih-hui. *Pan-jo hsin-ching lueh shu-lien-cha-chi.* Taishō vol. 34, no. 1713.
Shinran. *Kyō-gyō-shin-shō.* Taishō vol. 83, no. 2646.
T'an-lüan. *Wang-shen lun-chu.* Taishō vol. 40, no. 1819.
Tu-shun. *Hua-yen wu chiao shih-küan.* Taishō vol. 45, no. 1867.
Vasubandhu. *Fo-hsing lun.* Taishō vol. 31, no. 1610.
______. *Sukhāvatīvyūhôpadeśa.* Taishō vol. 26, no. 1514.

*Contemporary Works and Studies, Including Translations*

Fujishima, Tatsurō and Nogami, Shunjō. *Dentō no seija.* Kyoto: Heiraku-ji Shoten, 1961.
Ishida, Mitsuyuki. *Jōdo-kyōri-shi.* Kyoto: Heiraku-ji Shoten, 1962.
Iwamoto, Yutaka. *Gokuraku to jigoku.* Tokyo: San'ichi Shobō, 1965.
Kamata, Shigeo. *Chūgoku Bukkyō* Shirō Kenkyū. Tokyo: Shunjusha, 1968.
*Chūgoku Kegon Shisō-shi no Kenkyū.* Tokyo: Zaidan Hōjin Tokyo Daigaku Shuppankai, 1965.
Kamekawa, Kyōshin. *Kegon-gaku.* Kyoto: Hyakka-en, 1949.
Kasugai, Shinya. "Jōdo Kyōten no Keisei." In *Bukkyō no Kompon Shinri,* Shōson Miyamoto, ed. Tokyo: Sanyōsha, 1956.
Matsuno Junko. *Shinran.* Tokyo: Sanshō-dō, 1968.
Nakamura, H., Masutani, B. and Kitagawa, J. M. *Gendai Bukkyō Meicho Zenshū.* Vol. I. Tokyo: Ryūbunkan, 1971.
Tsong kha pa. *Lam rim chen mo.* Nagao, Gadjin, trans. Tokyo: Iwanami, 1954.
Yamaguchi, Susumu. *Daijō to shite no Jōdo.* Tokyo: Risō-sha, 1963.
"Ryūju-seshin ni okeru Jōdo Shisō." In *Bukkyō no Kompon Shinri.*
*Sthiramati: Madhyāntavibhāgaṭīkā.* Nagoya: Librairie Hajinkaku, 1934.
Yamaguchi, S., Ōchō, E., Andō, T. and Funabashi, I. *Bukkyō-gaku Josetsu.* Kyoto: Heiraku-ji, 1961.

Yusugi, Ryōei. *Kegon-gaku Gairon*. Kyoto: Ryūkoku University Press, 1941.

*Buddhist Canons*

*Shin-shū Seikyō Zenshu [The Collected Works on the Sacred Teachings of the Pure Land School]*. Kyoto: Kōkyō Shōin, 1940.

*Taishō Shinshu Daizōkyō [The Taishō edition of the Tripiṭaka in Chinese]*. Tokyo: Society for the Publication of the Taishō Edition of the Tripiṭaka, 1924–34.

*Zokuzōkyō* [The Addition to the Manji Tripiṭaka in Chinese]. Kyoto: Kyoto Zokuzō-shōin, 1905–12.

# Glossary

## Chinese and Japanese Words, Phrases, Names, and Titles

*A*
An-yao-chi 安樂集
*A-p'i-t'an hsin lun* [title] 阿毘曇心論

*C*
chao-chien 照見
chen shih hsiang [phrase] 眞實相
cheng 正
cheng chih 正智
cheng ting 正定
chi 集
chi wei 極微
chieh 戒
chieh fang pien kuan [phrase] 界方便觀
chien 見
chien hsing che yi chieh fang pien kuan tu [phrase] 見行者以界方便觀度
chih 止
chih-hui 智慧
chih-kuan 止觀
chih-te-kuo-fo-hsing [phrase] 至得果佛性
chi-lo [place name] 極樂
chi-lo wang-sheng [phrase] 極樂往生
ching 境
ching chieh 境界
ching chieh yi chieh ssu wei fen [phrase] 淨潔已解思性分
Ching-t'u [place name] 淨土
*Ching-t'u lun* [title] 淨土論
chung 中

Chung-shi [proper name] 仲希
chüeh kuan 覺觀
chüeh ting i chieh [phrase] 決定意解

*CH'*

ch'i ching 契經
ch'i sui shun ku [phrase] 起隨順故
Ch'ien Ch'ien-i [proper name] 錢謙益
ch'üan-t'i [phrase] 筌蹄

*F*

fa-chieh yüan-ch'i [phrase] 法界緣起
Fa-chiu [Dharmatrāta?; proper name] 法救
Fa-sheng [proper name] 法勝
fa-t'i 法體
fen-ch'i 分齊
fen-tuan 分段
*Fo-hsing lun* [title] 佛性論
*Fo-shuo kuan-wu-liang-shou-fo ching* [title] 佛說觀無量寿佛經
*Fo-shuo a-mi-t'o ching* [title] 佛說阿彌陀經
*Fo-shuo wu-liang-shou ching* [title] 佛說無量寿經
fu hsieh 扶瀉

*G*

gokuraku [Japanese place name] 極楽
gokuraku ōjō [Japanese phrase] 極楽往生

*H*

hai-yin san-mei 海印三昧
hsiang 想
hsiang 相
hsiang hsü fan lao [phrase] 相續煩勞
hsiang-tso 相作
hsiao 小
hsin 心
*hsien sheng p'in* [chapter title] 賢聖品
hsiu 修
hsiu fang pien 修方便
hsiu fei ch'ang chi k'u k'ung fei wo hsing hsiang [phrase] 修非常及苦空非我性相
hu-wang 互亡
hu-ts'un 互存
*Hua-yen i ch'eng chiao i fen-ch'i chang* [title] 華嚴一乘教義分齊章
*Hua-yen wu chiao shih-kuan* [title] 華嚴五教止觀
huai 壞
huai ching chieh [phrase] 壞境界
huan 幻
hui 慧

*J*

je nao 熱惱
jo nien nien fen pieh [phrase] 若念念分別
juan 軟
Jōdo [Japanese place name] 浄土

*K*

ken 根
ku 故
kuan 觀
kuan ch'a 觀察
Kuan tzu-tsai [proper name] 觀自在
Kuan-yin [proper name] 觀音
kung 共
kung hsiang 共相
*Kyō-gyō-shin-shō* [Japanese title] 教行信証

*K'*

k'ung 苦
k'ung 空

*L*

lao 勞
li 理
li-shih 理事
*Li-tai san-pao-chi* [title] 歷代三寶紀
liang 量
Liu Sung [proper name] 劉宋
liu-t'ung 流通
Lu-shan Hui-yüan [proper name] 廬山慧遠
lü 律

*M*

mi-mi-pan-jo [phrase] 祕密般若
mi-yü 祕語
mieh 滅
min 泯
ming chü wei shen [phrase] 名句味身
*Moho chih-kuan* [title] 摩訶止觀

*N*

neng-so 能所

*O*

ōjō [Japanese phrase] 往生

*P*

*Pan-jo hsin-ching lüeh-shu-hsiao-ch'ao* [title] 般若心經略疏小鈔
*Pan-jo hsin-ching lüeh-shu-hsien-cheng-chi* [title] 般若心經略疏顯正記
*Pan-jo hsin-ching lüeh-shu-lien-chu-chi* [title] 般若心經略疏連珠記
*Pan-jo po-lo-mi-to hsin-ching lüeh-shu* [title] 般若波羅密多心經略疏
pan-yao 般若
Pei-Ch'i [proper name] 北齊
*Pieh yi tsa a-han ching* [title] 別譯雜阿含經
pien-yi 變易
*P'o-sou-p'an-tou fa-shih-ch'uan* [title] 婆藪槃豆法師傳
pu 補
pu ching [phrase] 不淨
pu lo 不樂
pu tien tao [phrase] 不顛倒
pu tien tao hui [phrase] 不顛倒慧
pu t'ing hsin che pu neng ch'i cheng chien [phrase] 不停心者不能起正見
pu wang shou yüan ku [phrase] 不忘[妄]授[受]緣故

*P'*

p'ing-teng 平等
p'u [see *sa (p'u-sâ)*] 菩
p'u 溥

*S*

sa [see *p'u (p'u-sa)*] 薩
san 三
se 色
shan chih shih 善知識
shan ken tseng 善根增
shang 上
shen shen kuan nien ch'u [phrase] 身身觀念處
shen shih hsiang che wei pu tien tao hsiang ju yi yeh [phrase]
身實相者謂不顛相如義也
shih 事
shih 施
shih chieh ho ku yu so tsao tso [phrase] 識界合故有所造作
shih-hsiang 實相
Shih-hui [proper name] 師會
shih-shih wu-ai 事事無礙
shih tsu 識足
shih yeh 始業
shou 授
shou sui shun [phrase] 說隨順
ssu 思
ssu-chih 四執
ssu shih 四食
ssu shih chu 四識住

ssu tao 四倒
ssu wei yi tu [phrase] 思性已度
su-chi 速疾

*T*

*Ta-ch'eng fa-chieh-wu-ch'a-pieh lun* [title] 大乘法界無差別論
*Ta-chih-tu lun* [title] 大智度論
Tao-an [proper name] 道安
te fa chen shih hsiang [phrase] 得法眞實相
teng 等
*Tsa a-han ching* [title] 雜阿含經
tseng chang yang hsin sheng wu kou chih yen [phrase] 增長養心生無垢智眼
tsung 總
tuan 斷
tzu hsiang 自相
tzu hsiang nien ch'u [phrase] 自相念處
tzu hsin [phrase] 自心
tzu-hsing-chu-fo-hsing [phrase] 自性住佛性

*T'*

t'an yu 貪欲
t'ung kuan chu fa hsiang [phrase] 通貫諸法相

*TZ'*

tz'u hsin 此心

*W*

wang 亡
wang 忘
wang-sheng [phrase] 往生
*Wang-sheng lun-chu* [phrase] 往生論註
wei-ch'ang-pu-chin [phrase] 未嘗不盡
wei-ch'ang-pu-li [phrase] 未嘗不立
wei shou tsu teng t'ung shou tse sui chuan [phrase] 謂手足等痛受則隨轉
wei ts'eng te chüeh ting fen shan ken [phrase] 未曾得決定分善根
wei yi juan shan ken chung yi chung tseng [phrase] 謂依軟善根中依中增
wen 聞
wu 物
wu ch'ang 無常
wu chien teng sui [phrase] 無間等隨順
wu chu ch'u hsing [phrase] 無住處行
wu erh 無二
wu erh yu tz'u wu shih erh ming k'ung hsiang ku fei yu fei pu yi yi pu yi [phrase]
無二有此無是二名空相故非有非不異亦不一
wu hsiang 無上
*Wu-liang-shou ching yu-p'o-t'i-she yuan-chieh-chu* [title]
無量寿經優婆提舍願生偈註

*Wu-liang shou-ching yu-p'o-t'i-she yang-sheng chieh* [title]
無量寿經優婆提舍願生偈
**wu-shang** 無上
**wu-teng** 無等
**wu-teng-teng** [phrase] 無等等
**wu wo** 無我
**wu yüan** 無願

**Y**

**yen li** 厭離
**yi** 恚
**yi** 以
**yi—ku** [phrase] 以……故
**yi hsi hsing** [phrase] 已習行
**yi shuo hsi ch'eng hsing** [phrase] 已數習成行
**yi tz'u shang yi sheng tao ku** [phrase] 以此上一乘
**yin** 因
**yin ch'u fo-hsing** [phrase] 引出佛性
**yu** 由
**yu-tz'u-wu** [phrase] 有此無
**yüan** 緣

# The Contributors

STEFAN ANACKER received his Ph.D. in Buddhist Studies from the University of Wisconsin-Madison.

FRANCIS H. COOK is an associate professor in the Program of Religious Studies at the University of California, Riverside.

LEON HURVITZ is a professor in the Department of Religion at the University of British Columbia.

ELVIN W. JONES is a graduate student in Buddhist Studies at the University of Wisconsin-Madison.

YUICHI KAJIYAMA is a professor in and chairman of the Department of Buddhist Studies at Kyoto University.

MINORU KIYOTA is a professor in Buddhist Studies at the University of Wisconsin-Madison.

CHARLENE McDERMOTT is an associate professor in the Department of Philosophy, University of New Mexico.

GADJIN M. NAGAO is professor emeritus of the Department of Buddhist Studies at Kyoto University.

GESHE SOPA is an associate professor in Buddhist Studies at the University of Wisconsin-Madison.